SHAKESPEARE
STUDIES

SHAKESPEARE STUDIES
Volume XLVII

EDITED BY

JAMES R. SIEMON
Boston University

and

DIANA E. HENDERSON
Massachusetts Institute of Technology

ASSISTANT TO THE EDITORS
LIAM CRUZ KELLY
Boston University

Madison • Teaneck
Fairleigh Dickinson University Press

Associated University Presses
10 Schalks Crossing Road
Suite 501–330
Plainsboro, NJ 08536

The paper used in this publication meets the requirements of the American National Standard for Permanence of Paper for Printed Library Materials Z39.48-1984.

International Standard Book Number 978-0-8386-4493-5
International Standard Serial Number: 0-0582-9399

Essays may be submitted for consideration at the journal web site: http://sites.bu.edu/shakespearestudies/. All other editorial correspondence concerning *Shakespeare Studies* should be addressed to the Editorial Office, *Shakespeare Studies*, English Department, Boston University, Boston, MA 02215 or by email to sstudies@bu.edu.

Orders and subscription inquiries should be sent to Associated University Presses at the address shown above.

Shakespeare Studies disclaims responsibility for statements, either of fact or opinion, made by contributors.

Dedicated to Harry Keyishian

THE EDITORS OF *Shakespeare Studies* and *Medieval and Renaissance Drama in England* join members of the editorial board of Fairleigh Dickinson University Press and a multitude of scholars, authors, students, and others in dedicating this volume to Harry Keyishian, who recently retired as Director of Fairleigh Dickinson University Press.

During his 40-year tenure, Harry oversaw the production of well over 1,000 books, many on Shakespeare and his contemporaries. Though he was known for his guidance and support, he did his own share of publishing as well, notably *Revenge: Victimization, Vengeance, and Vindictiveness in Shakespeare* (1995), *Michael Arlen* (1975), *Critical Essays on William Saroyan* (1995), and *Screening Politics: The Politician in American Movies, 1931–2001* (2003). Harry, whose NYU dissertation was on "Thomas Dekker and the Rival Traditions," taught Shakespeare and early modern drama at FDU-Madison for 45 years (1965 to 2010). He was one of the early associates of the Columbia University Shakespeare Seminar, a long-time member of the Shakespeare Association of America, and a frequent contributor to scholarly journals.

Harry's productive career as teacher/scholar and distinguished years as Director of the Press are enough to warrant applause. But the jewel in his academic crown remains an early act of courage: in 1964, as an assistant professor at a state university, he refused to sign a loyalty oath. The case went to the U.S. Supreme Court, Judge William J. Brennan presiding, and Harry prevailed. He lost his job, but after the landmark Keyishian v. Board of Regents 385 U.S. 589 (1967), academics no longer had to forgo certain first amendment rights. This country's academics owe much of their academic freedom to Harry.

FDU—the University and the Press—were the beneficiaries of Harry's honorable youth, as was poet-professor Marjorie Deiter, whom he met at FDU and who became his wife of more than 50 years. As our dedicatee approaches middle age (which begins at 87?), he continues to be an inspiration to many. It is with gratitude and affection that we celebrate his life and career.

Contents

8 CONTENTS

CONTRIBUTORS

ALICIA P. ANDRZEJEWSKI is an Assistant Professor of English at the College of William & Mary. She is currently completing a book on queer pregnancies in Shakespeare's plays—pregnancies that resist how reproduction is culturally organized and that allow homoerotic desires and bonds to flourish.

JILL MARIE BRADBURY is Professor of English at Gallaudet University. She is currently working on a book manuscript titled *Modalities of the Visual in Contemporary Shakespeare Performance.*

DEVIN BYKER is Assistant Professor of English at the College of Charleston. He is currently working on a book project on the drama of dying in late medieval and early modern England.

SHEILA T. CAVANAGH is Professor of English at Emory University and Director of the World Shakespeare Project. She is currently working on a book project focused on Shakespeare for specialized performers and audiences.

JOHN LEE CLARK is a writer, and Braille and Protactile instructor. He is the author of the essay collection *Where I Stand* (Handtype Press, 2014). His poems have been published in *Ecotone, McSweeney's, The Nation, Poetry, Rattle,* and many other venues.

KATHARINE A. CRAIK is Reader in Early Modern Literature at Oxford Brookes University. She is currently working on a book about Shakespearean vividness, and is editing a collection of essays entitled *Shakespeare and Emotion* for Cambridge University Press.

ESTHER R. ELLIOTT is a theater practitioner and writer, based in the UK. She is currently working with visually-impaired actors on a new stage version of *King Lear.*

11

LAUREN ERIKS CLINE is Assistant Professor of English at Hampden-Sydney College. Her current book project examines narratives of theatrical spectatorship in nineteenth-century Britain.

JEAN E. FEERICK, Associate Professor English at John Carroll University, is the author of *Strangers in Blood: Relocating Race in Renaissance Literature* (Toronto, 2010) and co-editor with Vin Nardizzi of *The Indistinct Human in Renaissance Literature* (Palgrave, 2012). She is currently at work on a project investigating the elemental underpinnings of human identity in early modern literature.

EDWARD GIESKES is Associate Professor of English at the University of South Carolina. He is completing a book about genre and generic change in early modern English drama.

RACHEL GROSSMAN is co-founder and the Ensemble Director of dog & pony dc. She is a member of HowlRound's National Advisory Committee and presents regularly with the National Arts Market Project.

JASON HERBERS teaches DeafBlind Interpreting at Cincinnati State Technical and Community College in Cincinnati, Ohio. He frequently gives workshops on ProTactile.

HEATHER HIRSCHFELD is Professor of English at the University of Tennessee. She recently edited *The Oxford Handbook of Shakespearean Comedy* (2018) and the New Cambridge Shakespeare *Hamlet* (2019). She is currently working on a book on the language of hell in Renaissance England.

LAURIE JOHNSON is Professor of English and Cultural Studies at the University of Southern Queensland. He is currently researching a book on the impact of climate shifts on the rise of early modern playhouses and company business models.

EMILY GRUBER KECK is an adjunct faculty member at Radford University. She is at work on a book exploring the roles food and hunger play in staging social protest in early modern drama.

SAWYER K. KEMP is a doctoral candidate in English at the University of California, Davis. Their research investigates the rhetoric and practices that construct "accessibility" in contemporary Shakespeare performance.

DANIEL KNAPPER is a PhD candidate in the English department at The Ohio State University. He is completing a dissertation on the reception and influence of Saint Paul's rhetorical style in Reformation literary culture.

ALEXANDER PAULSSON LASH recently completed his PhD in English and Comparative Literature at Columbia, with a dissertation on the uses of theatrical space across the seventeenth century.

TARA L. LYONS is an Associate Professor of English Studies at Illinois State University. She publishes on early modern drama and book history.

JOYCE GREEN MACDONALD is Associate Professor of English at the University of Kentucky. She is currently completing a book on black women and modern Shakespearean adaptation.

ROWAN MACKENZIE is a PhD researcher at the Shakespeare Institute and a prison Shakespeare practitioner, working on "Creating Space for Shakespeare: Non-traditional and Applied Theatre Settings."

VICTORIA MAGLIOCCHINO taught language arts at the Florida School for the Deaf for 35 years and has been retired since 2014. She is currently the president of Florida Deaf-Blind Association.

SUBHA MUKHERJI is Senior Lecturer in English at the University of Cambridge and Principal Investigator on the interdisciplinary ERC-funded project, "Crossroads of Knowledge in Early Modern England: the Place of Literature." She is writing a book on *Knowing Encounters: Questioning Knowledge in Early Modern Literature.*

JASPER NORMAN is DeafBlind Latinx. He is co-founder of Pro-Tactile Theatre and working on a touring production of the PT play *Gift of the Magi.* He also advocates ProTactile to the DeafBlind community.

SHANKAR RAMAN is Professor of English and MacVicar Teaching Fellow at the Massachusetts Institute of Technology. He is currently completing a book on literature and mathematics in early modern Europe, tentatively entitled, *Before the Two Cultures.*

YASHAIRA ROMILUS proudly identifies herself as DeafBlind Latinx. She currently works as the Deafblind Community Class/Retreat Team Staff at Seattle Lighthouse for the Blind.

ROBERT SHAUGHNESSY is Professor of Theatre at Guildford School of Acting, University of Surrey. He has published extensively on historical and contemporary performance; his most recent books are *Shakespeare in Performance: As You Like It* (2017) and *The National Theatre, 1963–1975: Olivier and Hall* (2018).

BAILEY SINCOX is a PhD Candidate at Harvard University. She is currently completing a dissertation about female revenge on the early modern stage.

ROBERT T. SIRVAGE is from Canada. He owns a consulting business called Emic Design Research. He currently teaches at Carleton University under the Linguistics and Languages Studies department.

NANCY SMITH-WATSON is the Project Director of Feast of Crispian Inc. She delivers and manages all the direct work with veterans in Milwaukee, WI and is currently coordinating new Feast of Crispian branches in Seattle/Tacoma and Madison, WI.

ELIZABETH E. TAVARES is Assistant Professor of English at Pacific University Oregon. She is currently completing a book on the evolution of the repertory system before Shakespeare.

EVELYN TRIBBLE is Professor of English at the University of Connecticut. Her most recent book is *Early Modern Actors and Shakespeare's Theatre: Thinking with the Body* (Bloomsbury, 2017).

STEPHEN UNWIN is an experienced British theater and opera director. He has written eight books, twelve translations and three original plays. He is Chairman of KIDS, a national charity for disabled children and their families.

LISA VAN DER MARK is from Rotterdam (the Netherlands) and works at the University of Leiden as research assistant on projects about African sign languages.

CORINNE ZEMAN is a doctoral candidate at Washington University in St. Louis. Her dissertation explores Anglo-Islamic cultural traffic on the early modern stage.

SHAKESPEARE STUDIES

FORUM:

Shakespeare for Specialized Performers and Audiences

Introduction: "All Our Abilities"

SHEILA T. CAVANAGH

THIS FORUM HIGHLIGHTS some of the many Shakespeare programs being presented internationally for specialized performers and/or audiences. Such activities are proliferating, and are attracting increasing scholarly attention. Several sessions devoted to related topics were featured at the 2018 British Shakespeare Association meeting in Belfast, for instance. The Hudson Strode Center at the University of Alabama hosted a 2018 conference entitled "Shakespeare Inside and Outside the Classroom." Robert Shaughnessy and Rowan Mackenzie (both featured here) organized an Applied Shakespeare Symposium at The Shakespeare Institute in Stratford-upon-Avon in March 2018. Later that month, the third Shakespeare and Prison Conference took place at San Diego's Old Globe Theatre under the guidance of Freedome Bradley-Ballentine, Shakespeare Behind Bars' (SBB) Curt Tofteland, and others working in areas concerned with corrections and the arts.

This Forum presents reflections by people involved in some of these multi-faceted endeavors, which include Shakespeare programs for audiences and performers from a wide range of circumstances. The authors provide their perspectives on such endeavors offered for the elderly; for veterans; for actors or audiences with visual, verbal, or hearing impairments; for those with autism and/or learning disabilities; and for people living with a variety of other, often challenging, circumstances. Having been fortunate enough to witness many of these impressive undertakings first-hand, I am delighted to bring some of them to the attention of the broader community of Shakespeareans. The initiatives vary widely, but those involved share a desire to integrate Shakespeare into work devoted to populations with specialized needs. The writers included here offer individual rationales and experiences in their undertakings, which frequently take place in contexts with limited

21

resources. Some of those invited to participate, such as Blue Apple Theatre in Winchester, U.K, are too busy and working with too few staff members to present their accomplishments in print at this time.[1] Such endeavors take enormous amounts of time, energy, and commitment. They also generate substantial enthusiasm—for the work in general and for Shakespeare in particular—on the part of those involved. The actors at Blue Apple, for instance, who are drawn from a population with Down Syndrome and other learning challenges, speak passionately about their love of Shakespeare. Although they have presented diverse performances in England and the United States, including devised pieces focused on their location in historic Winchester, several of the cast members proclaim their enthusiastic preference for Shakespeare.[2] While opinions vary about the specific significance of Shakespeare in programs focused on specialized populations, the programs described here demonstrate the frequent vibrancy and success of such Shakespeare-centered initiatives.[3]

Many of these Shakespeare-inspired groups work in isolation from one another, but occasionally individual institutional circumstances facilitate a range of activities that not only support their own projects, but which can help develop and nurture similar efforts elsewhere. Shakespeare at Notre Dame, for example, under the leadership of McMeel Family Professor of Shakespeare Studies Peter Holland, and Mary Irene Ryan Family Executive Director Scott Jackson, sponsors several programs involving Shakespeare with specialized populations. It also spearheaded the first two Shakespeare in Prison conferences, in collaboration with SBB's Curt Tofteland, and helped support a third conference at the Old Globe. Shakespeare at Notre Dame's successes in this area emanate from the energetic vision of Holland, Jackson, Board Chair, Dr. Daniel Ryan, and Christy Burgess, Shakespeare Outreach Director of the Robinson Community Center at Notre Dame. These undertakings are also facilitated by their intersection with the university's mission statement, which states, in part: "the University seeks to cultivate in its students not only an appreciation for the great achievements of human beings but also a disciplined sensibility to the poverty, injustice and oppression that burden the lives of so many. The aim is to create a sense of human solidarity and concern for the common good that will bear fruit as learning becomes service to justice." [4] Shakespeare at Notre Dame's accomplishments with specialized audiences, which coexist with a prestigious academic program and a successful Shakespearean Theater Festival, make it an important model for the multiple ways that Shakespeare can reach disparate constituencies in the twenty-first century.

Many of Notre Dame's programs flourish because of the significant intellectual support and tangible resources provided by Holland, Ryan, and others. They also thrive in response to Jackson's creativity, organizational ability, and commitment to social justice. The oversubscribed first Shakespeare in Prison Conference, for example, coincided with his initiation of a Shakespeare program at Indiana's Westville Correctional Center. This facility, a run-down building that first served as a mental hospital, provides a fairly dismal room, some chairs, and a large group of enthusiastic Shakespeareans. The guards have had to learn that performance exercises can be loud, so that they are less likely to worry when these Friday night sessions include yelling and other unexpected noises. Tofteland's SBB "circles" at the Earnest C. Brooks Correctional Facility in Michigan sometimes focus on discussion as well as scene work, but Jackson's class sessions emphasize acting. As those who work in the many Shakespeare in Prison programs around the world realize, each venue carries its own set of rules and expectations. At Westville, participants are not allowed to enroll more than once. Consequently, previous students regularly express the hope that they can rejoin these activities, but this is not currently possible. Tofteland's circles, in contrast, have members who have been involved for many years, which allows for significant long-term mentoring in addition to SBB theatrical presentations. Some prison programs perform full-length plays; others focus on scenes or self-generated works. While these distinct initiatives share many common facets, they also differ significantly.

Jackson's students are part of a special program at Westville, as a *South Bend Tribune* article highlighting this initiative describes: "The class takes place within the Purposeful Living Units Serve, known as the PLUS Unit, a voluntary 16-month program in which inmates work toward re-entry through faith-based and character-based initiatives. Consider it the best of the best of those in prison. The men go to classes, do volunteer work around the prison campus and even raise money for charity through Relay for Life." [5] Jackson goes on to note that Shakespeare provides one of the few non-religious options available at the prison: "Right now, there's a lot of religion in the prison; I respect that and those churches that go in week in and week out," Jackson says. "There also needs to be something that's an individual engagement, and I think Shakespeare and theater in general helps them engage and find purpose in the self." Jackson's talent as an actor and director and his commitment to his students encourages them to try these challenging new dramatic undertakings even though this constituency has typically never previously considered themselves connected to Shakespeare. Nevertheless, they eagerly help turn this dingy institutional setting into a vibrant rehearsal space. Since the program began, its actors have worked on *Hamlet, Macbeth, Tempest,* and *King Lear.* The incarcerated thespians at Westville also benefit from Shakespeare at Notre Dame's sponsorship of Actors from the London Stage, a troupe that begins an annual American residency with performances at this correctional facility. [6] From Jackson's perspective, the positive results of this endeavor emanate directly from the skills presented through engaging with Shakespearean texts in performance:

> The results are best seen in interpersonal engagement through ensemble-based learning, focusing on a reemergence of self. The guys find a safe space in which to be themselves and explore theatre's "magic" together in an atmosphere of trust and healthy risk-taking.
>
> What they gain are tools to identify (and release) tension and stress in positive ways. They also must embrace their own vulnerability in order to succeed as an ensemble. These tools are transferable to their lives in general post-release.[7]

Shakespeare at Notre Dame's creation and sponsorship of the Shakespeare in Prison conferences and the related electronic Shakespeare in Prison Network have brought together innumerable arts practitioners, educators, and justice system personnel from numerous countries, including several of the participants in this Forum. Unfortunately, the writer who was planning to write specifically on Shakespeare in Prison had to withdraw, but as the many articles, books, dissertations, and conference presentations focused on such programs attest, this is a lively and productive field.[8] The venue for the 2020 Shakespeare in Prison Conference has not yet been announced, but its previous incarnations suggest that it will also be an invigorating event, since the gathering invariably features a dedicated group of skillful and inspirational participants who discuss the challenges and successes associated with such efforts. [9] In San Diego, for example, former prison actors Dameion Brown and Sammie Byron spoke about the continuing significance of Shakespeare within their lives after incarceration.

Brown talked about playing Othello professionally in 2016 for the Marin Shakespeare Company, which oversees the program he previously joined during his incarceration.[10] Byron (who now works full-time and mentors other SBB alumni) presented his one-man show "Othello's Tribunal," which interweaves Shakespeare's play with details about Byron's crime and his evolution towards life outside of prison. Continuing to work closely with SBB's Tofteland, Byron also helps train aspiring prison practitioners, including a group of actors, directors, and lawyers from the Rome, Georgia Shakespeare Festival[11] who are about to inaugurate a new program in their region.

The Shakespeareans at Notre Dame do not only work with incarcerated populations, however. In collaboration with South Bend Civic Theater (whose Executive Director, Aaron Nichols, used to work for Shakespeare at Notre Dame), they created a 2018 production of *As You Like It,* designed for audience members on the autism spectrum. During the 2016 Shakespeare anniversary year, Jackson attended a Shakespeare and Accessibility Symposium at Emory (several of those participants or their colleagues are represented in this Forum) and became intrigued by the work presented about the Hunter Heartbeat Method, which was originated in the UK by former RSC and National Theatre actor Kelly Hunter. Genevieve Simon and Andrew Trimmer represented the Hunter program during Emory's Symposium and offered two workshops at the Tapestry School, an Atlanta-area charter school designed both for students on the autism spectrum and for those designated as neurotypical. After participating in these events, Jackson brought Hunter to Indiana, where she introduced her work and trained a group of actor/facilitators as they prepared to fashion their own Hunter Method production. As Robin Post, one of Hunter's collaborators at the Ohio State University, explains, "The Hunter Heartbeat Method transforms the complexities of Shakespeare's poetry and storytelling into a sequence of games that are specifically tailored to meet the needs of children with ASD [Autism Spectrum Disorder]. The work employs the rhythm of the iambic pentameter and the exploration of movement, emotional and vocal expression of Shakespeare's characters."[12] At the Ohio State University, the Theatre Department partnered with the university's Wexner Medical Center's Nisonger Center, to assess the program's outcomes. As a result of this detailed study, Post states confidently "Those children who participated in the workshops showed measured improvement in social functioning, overall adaptive functioning, and language skills and showed greater improvement than the children in the wait-control group."[13]

Robert Shaughnessy's contribution to this Forum discusses Hunter's productions in Europe, but this performance method has also grown significantly in the United States, as demonstrated here. This *As You Like It,* directed by Jackson and Burgess, incorporates exercises previously devised by Hunter, but also includes new segments developed by the American performers. Like earlier productions emerging from this methodology, *As You Like It* invites its disparate audience members to participate in various scenes with the actors. This production includes more text directly from Shakespeare than Hunter's ensemble generally presents, although it pares down some of complexities of the play in the narrative and games it employs to portray Shakespeare's pastoral story. This newly crafted production serves as a worthy successor to Hunter's versions of *A Midsummer Night's Dream* and *The Tempest* adapted for those on the autism spectrum, in part because *As You Like It*'s "Seven Ages of Man" speech, as well as its presentation of love stories, wrestling, and sheep, all translate well into an immersively interactive combination of music, storytelling, and physical activities. The families comprising this production's audiences were uniformly enthusiastic and discussions have already begun about the continuation of this work in South Bend.

Shakespeare also figures prominently at the Robinson Community Learning Center, which operates in conjunction with Notre Dame, serving a population with significant ethnic and socioeconomic diversity reflecting the often stark "town and gown" differences evident in this area. While the university clearly thrives, much of the surrounding non-academic community has never fully recovered economically from the closure of its once-prominent Studebaker factory in 1963. The Robinson Center draws its students from across the city's broad socioeconomic and racial expanse. Under Burgess's bold and energetic leadership, the Center's Shakespeare Program has developed a number of robust initiatives, which led to its teen ensemble being invited to perform *Cymbeline* in Stratford-upon-Avon during the summer of 2017. This opportunity, which included workshops and performances at Shakespeare's Globe Theatre and at the Royal Shakespeare Company, brought this intrepid group to the UK in recognition of their many previous accomplishments and their long-term participation in Shakespearean realms. Although many of the students self-identify as "shy," their sophisticated performances give no indication of this personality trait.[14]

Burgess works with students of many ages at the Robinson Center and in local schools. The production in Stratford materialized in response to the group's combination of talent and enthusiasm, which has been nurtured through years of ensemble building and performances and which was successfully showcased at one of the Shakespeare in Prison events at Notre Dame. A delegate from that conference issued the invitation to perform in Stratford after participating in a workshop run by the Robinson students. A number of fund-raising events allowed these students, some of whom were first-time fliers, to undertake the memorable and productive adventure. Many of the teenagers who journeyed to the UK have been involved in these dramatic activities since they were young children. Burgess's achievements as a talented educator and director reflect her expertise in developing the students' innate abilities, while providing overt and subtle incentives to encourage them to embrace Shakespeare with vigor, talent, and hard work. One response reflects common attitudes expressed by the students:

> Before I started acting in the Robinson Shakespeare company, I was a shy little girl, afraid of the world and embarrassing myself in front of my peers. Everybody in the company immediately made me feel welcome. Now 8 years later I am a confident young woman, ready to take on any obstacle in my path. The Robinson Shakespeare Company has made me a much more brave and adventurous person. I'm open to trying new things, and I've learned that failure helps you be better in the future, and mistakes are merely learning experiences.

The group engage in a range of dramatic activities. These Shakespeareans participate, for instance, in an annual 24-hour "reading Shakespeare" fundraiser, but only the older students are allowed to stay all night. The younger actors wait eagerly for their turn to take part in the entirety of this yearly adventure. The group earns financial support from donations pledged for their reading, but they also enjoy the excitement generated by goals shared with an ensemble working together closely and supportively.

As the choice of *Cymbeline* suggests, the Robinson Center Shakespeareans do not limit their endeavors to plays from the conventional canon. While Burgess has resisted their requests to perform *Titus Andronicus* due to potential parental opposition, she never

underestimates their ability to engage passionately and productively with any of Shakespeare's plays or poems. Thus far, they
have performed nearly twenty productions, including several history plays and a number of lesser-known Shakespearean dramas.
As each year progresses, the students perform scenes and full productions, present speeches at the local and national English-
Speaking Union Shakespeare competitions, and learn the valuable
lessons that come from growing up in an environment that fosters
mutual respect and an appreciation for the rewards of diligent
training and practice. The Robinson Center Shakespeareans are a
fortunate group of students, whose performance in Stratford and
presentations at the Shakespeare Theatre Association meetings in
Indiana and Ohio have given them noteworthy opportunities to
share their insights and abilities. Like the many other Shakespearean groups described in this Forum, they demonstrate the high
level of achievement that these diverse endeavors encourage, particularly since Burgess insists that they never change the language
or do anything else that might "dumb it down."[15]

The students involved recognize the significance of their accomplishments, as one high school participant explains:

> I started this program when I was in third grade, so roughly 8 years old.
> I'm 15 now, so I don't really remember who I was before starting in the
> company. This company has raised me, shaped me, made me who I am
> today. This program has been a second home in a lot of ways. I spend a
> lot of time here with people I've known for years and it's still surprising
> me. I'd be lying if I said I didn't discover something new about myself
> every day. And when you find a place or a program like that, you stick
> with it because it's so valuable to your maturity and to your self-growth.
> I've become such an intelligent and responsible individual because of
> the Robinson Shakespeare Company and I'd have it no other way.

Students nurtured through this program consistently report that
their lives have benefited from this experience.

Shakespeare at Notre Dame obviously has access to resources
that not everyone can match, although the social justice work done
there also relies heavily upon volunteer labor and donations. Nevertheless, this organization's many accomplishments demonstrate
the wide-ranging results that talent and commitment can produce
when confident of a strong institutional base. Some of the programs
featured in this Forum also benefit from the support of larger institutions, while others survive with more limited resources. The

authors represent a range of nationalities, ages, and professional situations. Some are affiliated with universities, as faculty, staff, or graduate students. Others are arts practitioners, who run organizations, work freelance, or partner with established or developing businesses. Some authors have personal experience of the situations facing the specialized populations on which they focus; others work with populations whose challenges do not correspond with those in their own lives.

Forum contributors bring different backgrounds to their Shakespearean engagements, but they invariably offer passionate energy, strong commitment, deep textual and artistic knowledge, and a desire to use Shakespeare for personal and communal development. Some of the programs have been in operation for many years. Other related efforts, such as Jeffrey Wilson's "Shakespeare for Cops" initiative, are not included here.[16] Wilson, an instructor in Harvard's Writing Program, has developed a well-conceived program that does not yet exist outside of his plans and vision. The rapid multiplication of such endeavors suggests, however, that Wilson and others are likely to diversify this field even further. While skeptics may question whether there is anything particular to Shakespeare's canon that undergirds these efforts, the diverse activities explored within this Forum demonstrate that there are many educators, arts practitioners, and participants who find Shakespeare compelling in such circumstances. The numerous Shakespearean opportunities represented in this Forum emphasize a common, though diffuse, conceptualization of Shakespeare's power to speak to a wide range of people in significant ways. The Shakespearean academic community typically shies away from claims of universality, and this Forum is not intended to suggest otherwise. Nevertheless, the voices included here demonstrate that Shakespeare is thriving in a range of unexpected venues, offering noteworthy benefits to increasing numbers of students, actors, and audience members who represent communities of diverse abilities in many countries.

Notes

1. http://blueappletheatre.com/
2. Their Shakespearean work can be seen in William Jessup's 2014 documentary "Growing up Downs" that details their creation of a touring production of *Hamlet* (https://www.imdb.com/title/tt3430362/).

3. Rob Pensalfini offers a chapter addressing this question: "What's So Special About Shakespeare?" (*Prison Shakespeare: For These Deep Shames and Great Indignities* [Houndmills, Basingstoke: Palgrave, 2016], 188–227).

4. www.nd.edu/about/mission-statement/

5. https://www.southbendtribune.com/entertainment/inthebend/arts/the -bard-behind-bars-shakespeare-acting-class-aims-to-show/article_3513f19e -9225–11e6–9a0a-e38e920254a9.html

6. https://shakespeare.nd.edu/actors-from-the-london-stage/

7. Scott Jackson, personal correspondence, November 11, 2018.

8. Among the noteworthy books focusing solely or partially on American and International Shakespeare in Prison programs are Rob Pensalfini (see note 3); Niels Herold, *Prison Shakespeare and the Purpose of Performance: Repentance Rituals and the Early Modern* (Houndmills, Basingstoke: Palgrave Pivot, 2014); Jonathan Shailor, ed., *Performing New Lives: Prison Theatre* (London: Jessica Kingsley Publishers, 2011); Laura Bates, *Shakespeare Saved My Life* (Naperville, Il: Sourcebooks, 2013); and Jean R. Trounstine, *Shakespeare Behind Bars: One Teacher's Story of The Power of Drama in a Women's Prison* (Ann Arbor: University of Michigan Press, 2004).

9. Rob Pensalfini discusses the various kinds of assessment models associated with such programs in his chapter entitled "The Claims of Prison Shakespeare" (130–87).

10. https://www.theatrebayarea.org/news/407667/A-Former-Inmate-Takes-on-a -New-Role.htm.

11. https://www.romeshakespearefestival.com/.

12. Robin Post, Foreword to Kelly Hunter, *Shakespeare's Heartbeat: Drama Games for Children with Autism* (London: Routledge, 2014), Kindle location 170.

13. Hunter, *Shakespeare's Heartbeat,* Kindle locations 226 and 241.

14. Student comments are drawn from surveys distributed by the Robinson Center.

15. "Fighting for Shakespeare for all." https://fightingfor.nd.edu/2017/fighting -for-shakespeare-for-all/

16. Wilson presented his work at the 2018 Strode Symposium referenced above. For more information, see his YouTube posting: https://www.youtube.com/ watch?v = SLr63evCxas

Joey's *Dream*

STEPHEN UNWIN

"The best in this kind are but shadows; and the worst are no
worse, if imagination amend them."
—*A Midsummer Night's Dream* (5.1.209–10)[1]

I DO NOT THINK I have ever understood Theseus's comments about
acting so clearly. Because in July of this year I saw something I have
never seen before: a group of profoundly disabled young people
staging a version of Shakespeare's great comedy and making the
audience see not just the play but the world afresh.

It was not the best-spoken production I have ever attended. In
fact, hardly a word of Shakespeare's text was spoken. This is
because many of the "learners" at St. Elizabeth's College (a much
acclaimed center for people with learning disabilities and epilepsy
in Hertfordshire, England) are non-verbal, and the ones who have
speech are very quiet and hesitant in using their voices. But, as
Theseus insists, we needed to use our imagination to "amend" their
disabilities. Certainly these extraordinary young people, helped by
their teachers and carers, had used theirs.

A small, desperately shy girl in a wheelchair, with bright red lipstick and a crown of flowers in her hair, played Titania. Puck was
acted by a non-verbal lad who dangled a bunch of lilacs into the
wrong eyes. Hermia and Helena showed that they despised each
other, if in the sweetest of tones: "I love Lysander, he's mine," said
the girl playing Hermia, so slowly and delicately that it was like
watching a butterfly emerge. The young men playing Lysander and
Demetrius were suitably cross with each other and stomped around
appropriately. Bottom was brilliantly raucous, a big cheerful bloke
who got very excited and tore his ass's ears off in frustration to a
huge cheer from the audience. The story of the play was narrated
by a girl who is a wheelchair user, with such finesse and care that
we were all on the edge of our seats listening to what happened

31

next. And a young man in the front room (with severe autism, I suspect) stood up abruptly and announced each scene number with
tremendous aplomb.

The *Dream* was performed in the college gym. On the back wall
hung a huge David Hockney-style painting of the woods that the
"learners" had spent several weeks making. And to one side, some
painted Greek columns represented Athens and a simple version of
Pyramus and Thisbe's stone wall. All the actors wore black jeans
and T-shirts, but each was decorated in their own individual way:
crowns of leaves on their heads, flowers round their waists, sparkling glitter on their cheeks, and little splashes of bright lipstick for
the girls. For the wedding at the end there was a beautiful arch
made of painted flowers through which all the actors emerged. And
then my Joey, in a golden crown and a golden toga, came on and
beamed his golden smile as Duke Theseus. And for his brother and
me, for a brief moment at least, all seemed well in the world.

As we clapped along to the music, this wonderful, eccentric and
oh so different cast took their curtain calls—though Joey (22), who
is non-verbal, has Severe Learning Disabilities (SLDs), intractable
epilepsy, and is on the Autistic spectrum (ASD), does not know
how to bow and so clapped and laughed at us gleefully instead. As
I went round congratulating the staff who had put this amazing
event together—and led the performers onto the stage and stood
next to them whispering gentle reminders in their ears—they all
said the same thing: the students had done everything, it was nothing to do with them and they resolutely refused to take any credit
for what had been achieved. I realized yet again the quality of the
people who work with the profoundly disabled. Their commitment
shows a remarkable combination of vocational passion and gritty
professionalism, deep humanity and sheer pragmatism. And I
know that St. Elizabeth's is not alone in this.

But what can we learn from this?

The first thing is the need to be absolutely honest when we are
considering arts for the profoundly disabled. Of course, we should
emphasize the positive and celebrate what can be done, not just
bewail the problems. But, despite Theseus's imprecations, I think
we need to work from reality, not fantasy. When I announced on
FaceBook that Joey had been cast as Theseus, friends who had no
idea about the extent of his disability congratulated me (and him)
for the casting: "You must be so proud, the poetry is wonderful and

it's such a brilliantly drawn character," I was told. So much of the discussion about disability is about physical disabilities, or mild neuro-disabilities, that the realities of SLD—and non-verbalism—are too often forgotten.

We should also question the cultural value of Shakespeare in such a context. And here, as a lifelong Shakespearean, I think we need to ask ourselves to what extent the success of such an event is dependent on the status and fame of the writer and how much is innate in the texts themselves. For good and understandable reasons there is a deep desire to share our cultural pleasures with the profoundly disabled, partly as a way of showing our affection and respect for people who do not have our own intellectual abilities. And, of course, the story of the *Dream* (taken from Ovid, among others) appeals to something deep in the human psyche, including, perhaps, people with SLDs. But I am sceptical when I hear that the rhythm of the iambic pentameter can help release the autist, and I think that the laudable attempts at "therapy" and "cure" through high art are questionable in such extreme cases. "Shakespeare has something for everybody, however excluded, however marginalised," it is argued, usually by people whose livelihoods are dependent on sustaining the notion of such universality. Playing and working together is invaluable, but I am not convinced that Elizabethan drama is essential to that.

The uncomfortable fact is that, like it or not, Shakespeare signally fails to return the compliment and does not include people with SLDs in his *dramatis personae.* The policeman, Dull, in *Love's Labour's Lost* is sometimes thought to have some kind of learning disability (he is patronized as "only an animal, only sensible in the duller parts" [4.2.26–27]), but in a play of vertiginous language and daunting scholarship, he speaks for many when he answers the concern that he has "spoken no word all this while" with the one-line quip, "nor understood none neither" (5.1.143–45). Dull may be dull, but he knows what he does not know, which is more than can be said for his betters, and the line inevitably brings the house down. This is hardly the stuff of learning disabilities.

It is sometimes presumed that Shakespeare's fools have learning disabilities and many of us have seen performances that suggest as such. But while recent research by the historian Suzannah Lipscomb has suggested that the "natural fools" of early modern England were people with cognitive disabilities, the "artificial fools" in the drama are highly intelligent men who satirize their "betters" and suggest, often obliquely, sometimes explicitly, a better way of organizing society.[2] As for characters like Bottom, Dogberry, and Elbow, however uneducated and unrefined they may be, they are ambitious, self-confident, and aspirational men, hardly the stuff of learning disabilities, let alone SLDs. Likewise, the young servant Peter in *Romeo and Juliet* may be illiterate, but is simply an example of Shakespeare's social realism (most Elizabethan working people could not read) rather than a comment on innate cognitive disabilities.

Shakespeareans will point to Macbeth's metaphor of life as "a tale told by an idiot," but until the late nineteenth century at least, the primary meaning of the word "idiot" was a person whose social and financial means were so limited that he played no public role. As Patrick McDonagh argues so convincingly in *Idiocy: A Cultural History,* the phrase was rich with class associations, but carried no sense of intellectual limitations.[3] Indeed, with the enduring conflation of low class and low IQ, the time has come for a reassessment of our views of Shakespeare's working people: are they the "simpletons" of theatrical tradition or robust representatives of an overlooked class offering fresh perspectives on the antics of their betters?

Many reasons can be deduced for the fact that Shakespeare did not feature characters with SLDs (apart from anything, it was not recognized as a category at the time), but the experience has also been pretty much ignored by mainstream dramatists ever since. None of the great nineteenth- and early twentieth-century playwrights included characters with SLDs, and even the mighty Arthur Miller disowned his son Daniel who has Down Syndrome, and, some have claimed, never visited him. Perhaps they were taking their lead from the disturbed Virginia Woolf who wrote in her diary in January 1915 that:

> On the towpath we met & had to pass a long line of imbeciles. The first was a very tall man, just queer enough to look twice at, but no more; the second shuffled, & looked aside; & then one realised that every one in that long line was a miserable ineffective shuffling idiotic creature, with no forehead, or no chin, & an imbecile grin, or a wild suspicious stare. It was perfectly horrible. They should certainly be killed.[4]

Evidently, impeccable progressives like Woolf and Miller found the sight of people with SLDs too distressing—or perhaps simply too embarrassing. In modern times, the quadriplegic, non-verbal, daughter in Peter Nichols' *A Day in the Death of Joe Egg* (1967) inspires similarly murderous fantasies in her father, and in the original production the name of the actress who played her did not even appear on the poster. People sometimes point to *The Curious Incident of the Dog in the Night-Time* (2003), but not only has Mark Haddon disavowed any intention of writing a disability story, but high-functioning autism is hardly relevant. But nothing has shocked me as much as Brad Fraser's *Kill Me Now* (2015), which seemed to suggest that no greater love could a father show his profoundly disabled son (also called Joe) than to give him sexual relief in the bath.

More common is the use of derogatory terms about SLDs in modern drama. Thus in the first few lines of Nina Raine's critically acclaimed *Consent* (2017) a new mother expresses relief that her baby is not "retarded" and the same vile word is used in Annie Baker's *The Flick* (2013) without raising an eyebrow. I am certainly not interested in censoring language in drama, but it is striking how equally offensive words about race, sexual orientation, or gender usually carry palpable dramatic jeopardy for a character who speaks them.

As an experienced director and occasional playwright I know just how difficult it is to do justice to severe disabilities. Indeed in *All Our Children* (2017, London; 2019, New York), my play about the appalling murder of thousands of profoundly disabled children by the Nazis, I made the decision not to feature any of the victims. Nothing, I thought, could be more grotesque than bringing on stage people whose abilities—very like my Joey's—were such that they would never have understood the subject of the play, or what their fictional characters were being subjected to. And I certainly was not going to write characters with SLDs and let them be played by the neurotypical. This stuff is genuinely difficult, and anyone who thinks it is not either has no experience of SLDs or knows nothing about the theater.

There are of course many playwrights and theater people actively engaged in offering us something better. But even there we need to be careful. Thus, last year I was asked for practical advice from the director and producer of Stephanie Martin's *Joy* (2017), a significant new play which features two young women with Down Syndrome and a lad with moderate cognitive difficulties. I think I rather shocked them by stating baldly that "people with learning disabilities have *learning* disabilities," and that, as a result, they needed to plan for more rehearsal time, a different approach to the working day, and a sea change in attitudes from everyone involved. Because most forms of diversity—race, gender, sexual orientation, even physical disabilities—require only minimal adjustments, the hard realities of SLDs are sometimes forgotten. And they must not be.

The fact is that creating theater with and for people with SLDs is a highly specialized activity. So much so that, even with 35 years working as a professional director and 10 years as a campaigner for the rights and privileges of disabled people, I have turned down offers of doing so because I know I do not have the appropriate skills or mind-set. Specialist British companies like Oily Cart, Mind the Gap, Blue Apple, and others know exactly what they are doing, and I would not dream of jumping in. The point is that inclusion is genuinely challenging, and when it comes to SLDs we cannot just rely on goodwill.

So the real lesson I take from the *Dream* at St Elizabeth's is little to do with what great drama can offer people with SLDs. Although what I saw took its inspiration from a masterpiece, its real achievement was a testimony to a professional culture of care and education that offers infinite patience, staggering levels of hard work, highly developed skills, and an unshakeable belief that nothing is too good for those who cannot help themselves.

All art is political, it is often said, and what I witnessed was an example of good politics in action. Providing appropriate housing and care for people with SLDs is expensive, and when they have additional medical needs the costs rocket. But attempting to offer a real quality of life is especially challenging. In Britain today the disabled child's right to play is no longer regarded as a statutory duty for local authorities and the kind of specialist playgrounds for disabled children that KIDS—the charity of which I am chairman—runs are under threat. All people of goodwill want the most vulnerable to have as enjoyable and meaningful a life as we can give them. What I saw at St. Elizabeth's was the most profound repudiation of so much that is wrong with our world. But only a new social contract between government and taxpayer will ensure that it is not a thing of the past.

What Joey's *Dream* also reminded me was that laughter and love, dressing up and pretending to be someone else, are fundamental to being a human being. What is more, it showed me that working together on a common pursuit, in which the strongest help the weakest while also learning from them, is central to our identity as social beings. "The wall is down that parted their fathers," says Bottom in act 5, and that afternoon at St. Elizabeth's I saw the walls between the disabled and the non-disabled, the specialist teacher and the learner, the parent and the child and, in my case, the professional and the amateur, come crashing down. It was an amazing event that I will never forget.

Shakespeare would not have recognized his play but he would, I hope, have approved of the human endeavor behind it. So should we all.

Notes

1. All Shakespeare citations from *The Arden Shakespeare Complete Works,* ed. Richard Proudfoot, Ann Thompson, and David Scott Kastan (Walton-on-Thames: Thomas Nelson and Sons, 1998).

2. https://www.historytoday.com/suzannah-lipscomb/all-king's-fools

3. Patrick McDonagh, *Idiocy: A Cultural History* (Liverpool: Liverpool University Press, 2008).

4. *The Diary of Virginia Woolf,* ed. Anne Olivier Bell, vol. 1 (1915–1919) (New York: Harcourt Brace, 1977), 13.

Shakespeare for Veterans: Feast of Crispian

NANCY SMITH-WATSON

What should such fellows as I do, crawling between earth and heaven?[1]

—*Hamlet* 3.1.128–29

AFTER THE MURDER OF HIS FATHER, Hamlet cannot respond with action. He lashes out at people he once loved, and stares into himself, unable to recognize whom he sees. As if before trauma and after trauma are two actual places, he wanders, stuck somewhere in between.

Leaving the landscape of war, dropped back into a place he once knew as home, our military veteran wanders in unrecognizable territory. Lost, he can neither pick up the threads of the past nor figure out where to begin again. An actor's nightmare; characters from a play he should know stare at him as he is set down on a stage without costume, without story, and without lines.

Shakespeare lived inside his characters, embodied their heartaches, losses, rages, and joys in order to find words that sent shivers of experience through the bodies of his audience. Through his exploration, he widened the passage from humanity to *understanding* humanity. Warfare, being curiously embedded in human development, became one of his touchstones in telling the human story. Maybe it is his most over-arching metaphor for the human condition.

Many of us lucky enough to stand on a stage and speak the beautiful poetry of William Shakespeare have a deeply rooted faith that it makes us better people. His words plunge us into our deepest emotional selves, make sense of pain, and float us on waves of ecstatic love. They enlighten us to the complexity of our humanness and forge deep connection with, and compassion for, our human family.

So strong is our faith that we are called to share this love (a word appearing 2,191 times in the canon) with others who might not yet have experienced it.[2] What has an English playwright who died in 1616 to offer the modern warrior? There are words that evoke the experience of PTSD, depression, the struggle with alcohol, the alienation of husband and wife, and the contemplation of suicide. His plays tell stories of families, battles, journeys, and honor. The metaphors describe the experiences of love, of loss, of hurt and anger in terms that teach the body to feel again. And provide a mask:

> Shakespeare is an opportunity to be open without exposure, or the vulnerability that comes with sharing a deep and hidden part of my past. Being able to connect with a character psychologically and act it out physically [. . .] is amazing.
> (Omar Kebir, Army Veteran)

Feast of Crispian (FoC), founded in 2012, grew out of our founder's needs to share Shakespeare and the urgent need to establish arts-based programs for the emotional reeducation of returning military service people. This use of the arts to back up traditional therapies is now so well accepted that in 2013 the VA put out White Papers on the subject.[3] Although Feast has no entrance criteria for participation, the foundation of our work is the three-day intensives for vets living in the domiciliary on the VA campus, receiving residential care and programming. In general, our participants are (mostly) men who have hit bottom and have checked into residential programming as a last-ditch effort to relearn living life as a civilian. (Let me offer this caveat: only about 10 percent of veterans access any level of healthcare from the VA system. The majority of veterans have neither seen combat, nor had any traumatizing event, and return to civilian life with minor transition challenges. Speaking of veterans' challenges throughout, I am referring to the population that makes up the majority of our participants: post-trauma survivors.)

The challenges our veteran participants face are many but we, the facilitators, make the experienced assumption that PTSD is at the core of it all. In "normal" life, human beings recognize a multi-level tier system of stress that enables us to successfully navigate small hurdles like hurrying to catch a bus, and bigger events like the loss of a job, and still return to functional internal equilibrium. Inside PTSD, all stress is experienced as life threatening and leads to autonomic life-saving responses, fight, flight, or freeze. Obviously, these responses would grossly complicate running late or a job search. One of the things necessary to returning to successful navigation of stress is the opportunity to repeatedly traverse manageable bits of stress in order to begin to re-associate non-traumatic stress as low risk to survival. Theater, defined for our purposes as ensemble storytelling, becomes a perfect medium for experiencing manageable bits of stress through the controlled use of the imagination.

Before introducing participants to acting scenes from Shakespeare, we give them small imaginary excursions through inescapable, day-to-day, unpredictable events: hurrying to an appointment they are late for, leaving an unpleasant place/event, leaving a place they do not desire to leave, going to a place/event they cannot wait to get to, going to a place/event they do not want to go to but must, etc. Physically walking through the imaginary realm allows for them to have control over the size of challenge they choose and the time they spend in the response, but the brain lights up all the areas of response as if it is actually happening. Occasionally, a veteran will not be able to tolerate even this much stimulation and will take himself or herself out of the room and back to the domiciliary. As practice at responding to stress cannot be successful if one is currently in the activation of fight or flight, we understand this response to be wholly appropriate and hope we will see them in the future when they are able to spend more time in the "Window of Tolerance."

More commonly, the feedback to this exercise is elation. This is true even if the veterans have sweated or cried through some of the places we asked them to imagine. What they tell us is that they are surprised that responses really do happen. When asked to "pay attention" they found themselves feeling different things in different situations; it feels magical. It feels alive. The fact that the brain recognizes imaginary scenarios just as well as real situations is a revelation to people who have not voluntarily used their imaginations since early childhood. The most basic tool of the actor, the magic "if," opens the door to safely exploring the internal landscape, and becomes a way of trying out different future outcomes. Small, imaginary scenarios (re)mind us of times we felt like this, or a place we have actually been, or a person that made/makes us happy, and small stories are invited into the room.

Two aspects of this first glimpse of the actor's skills are particularly important: the use of the imagination, and the active embodiment of the scenarios. Much of what we do has been honed by the constantly emerging science on brain function, both normal and within PTSD. The fact that the body participates in whatever is happening in the brain can be both limiting and liberating. In the case of PTSD, many parts of the brain that allow us to experience the sensations of anger, joy, love, fear, and so on, as well as the sensory experience of taste, smell, and touch, have been taken "off line." How do we recognize our self without feeling our feelings and sensations? Therefore, embodiment—regaining access to the feelings and sensations in our bodies—is necessary to (re)membering ourselves and to living a full and satisfying life.

Military service people enter service for many reasons: they want to serve their country, they need money for school, they are facing homelessness, they want the structure and discipline, it is a family tradition, and so forth. Many of them are devoted to the military, proud of their service, and prefer the structure and clear expectations of their service job. Some of them hated the tight structure, the boredom, the seemingly arbitrary orders, the busywork, or came out of service feeling betrayed by the institution or the government. No matter their active duty experience, every one of them deeply misses the close unit cohesion, camaraderie, and the sense that those around you understand what you have been through, have your back, and recognize you.

Back in their home communities, separated from their military "tribe," they encounter the expectation, from family and friends, that they should be the same person they were before military service. They quickly learn that their service stories are incomprehensible, or worse, horrifying to their civilian relations. Or worse still, they realize some of their stories are incomprehensible and horrifying to themselves. Just keeping those stories inside seems like the only option.

Shakespeare explores the purpose, meaning, motivation, needs, slights, honors, fears, and humor of people trying to figure out something they are going through. The characters ask the questions that our veterans ask: Why is this happening to me? What is the meaning of my life? Who understands me? What do I believe? How did I get here? What do I do now? Who am I now?

HAMLET
To be, or not to be, that is the question:
Whether 'tis nobler in the mind to suffer
The slings and arrows of outrageous fortune,
Or to take arms against a sea of troubles
And by opposing end them.

(*Hamlet* 3.1.56–60)

Telling story: From Philippi to Iraq.

BRUTUS
Remember March, the ides of March remember.
Did not great Julius bleed for justice' sake?
What villain touch'd his body, that did stab,
And not for justice?

(*Julius Caesar* 4.3.18–21)

When we stand at the shoulder of a combat vet and "feed" him Brutus's lines about honor and justice, he then speaks these words out loud. He says, "remember," and "justice," and "touch'd his body," and "bleed." For these veterans those are hot-button words.

As we sit and discuss Brutus—a man who believes that all actions, even fighting a war, must be honorably done—and Cassius—a man who believes that the purpose of fighting a war is to win, whatever it takes—a veteran "actor" tells us that this scene feels like his own internal struggle. Once, he was a man of integrity who acted out of a sense of "right," but alcohol has manipulated him into doing whatever it takes to get him what he wants. He speaks the words of Brutus—"You have done that you should be sorry for!"—and calls out his own dishonorable self. Standing firmly on his feet and yelling in righteous indignation, he rejects the idea of "winning at any cost." His scene partner (and metaphorical "bad" self) forcefully defends himself and clings to self-denial. Brutus chooses honor and the veteran feels the sensation of himself as a "good" man. He tells us he had forgotten that feeling, and wants to feel that way again.

In therapy, he has no doubt discussed this idea. He has talked about who he used to be and what he "should" be doing to get out of his self-destructive behavior. Ideas that are familiar, accepted, desirable, but ideas nonetheless; ideas that, in the therapeutic setting, carry a judgment of "good and bad" or "right and wrong." To have the opportunity to feel the muscles tense with strength, to feel the need for a full breath in order to shout the angry words, to be *encouraged* to shout out in anger, and to make the physical shapes of anger; clenched fists and furrowed brow, he experiences the power of his honorable self and gets a sensation of his "better self" inside his own skin. A scene between Brutus and Cassius becomes a visceral connection between a veteran and his own story. A room full of people saw him be his better self and heard him claim his agency in being that self again.

As actors, the bias is that all emotions are equally good, necessary, and effective at moving us from one place to another, whether that is literal or metaphorical. Actors usually find great pleasure in fully expressing the wilder ranges of emotions and feel accomplished when a role is freely expressed. Words alone are unreliable in communicating our internal truths. Emotions are the most elemental storytelling tool we have, and we relish the cathartic sensation of clearly and specifically communicating a character's emotional response to a plot point. Among some actors there is a debate about whether it is "real" emotion or technique that allows us to have our acting recognized as truthful. With the introduction of the MRI into the research on brain function, there is not much support for the idea that technique alone can communicate emotional reactions without *experiencing* real emotions. Acted emotions apparently light up the brain identically to the way real emotions light up the brain.[4] The complexity of language and its interconnectedness with emotions is part of the actor's basic homework when working on Shakespeare. Feast actors have become adept at using the rich metaphor and hyperbolic adjectives to gently elicit emotional responses in people who are not telling personal stories.

Language is a symbolic system that allows us to enter into a richer depth of relationship and interaction. As a symbolic system, it is also incapable of fully communicating the inner experience of an individual human being. This makes it both profoundly useful and a dangerous stumbling block to communication. One possible reason why Shakespeare is still around today is because his words elicit emotions and sensations. Is this the thing that makes us human: recognizing our emotions and sensations? The thing that connects us as social, pack animals, tribal, is recognizing and feeling the emotions of others.

A picture of the brain when the subject is using metaphor shows the sensory centers alight.[5] The comparison of two disparate things paired together—plum lips—needs the *experience* of these things as well as the understanding of the individual things themselves. Plums = juicy, sweet, smooth, delicious, reddish purple. Paired with lips, that sounds like something wonderfully kissable! If you have never had an experience with a plum, you cannot understand the lips-like-plums metaphor. Even if you do not like plums, the ability to extrapolate is there based on the understanding that, in general, other people find them delicious. If you have no knowledge of plums, or if the part of your brain that recognizes and catalogues experience is disconnected, you cannot make sense of this metaphor.

In the case of PTSD, the sensory centers are essentially on "sleep" mode rather than disconnected, so when encountering a metaphor, the sensory center will blink on and the person with PTSD is gently reminded of that sweet, little sensation. Shakespeare is loaded with metaphors. Shakespeare is full of rhyme and meter, which rhythmically ticks time off in the brain. Trauma freezes the brain in a moment of terror that keeps the survivor stuck in that moment. Rhythm, in poetry and music, gently help the brain move forward.

Our veterans enter the room with nothing better to do. They come in, in various states of disquiet. The event does not begin on time, as we are always waiting for the stragglers, remembering that in PTSD time is problematic. Our opening circle introductions, are set up to give all in attendance a sense of their weekend community but it also offers a revelation in how little our outsides reveal. This revelation is a good illustration of what we tell the group, and remind them of multiple times throughout the weekend, that we are constantly making up stories based on our past experiences. Facilitators are surprised, every time, by the people in the room when looks do not match expectations. We tell the veteran participants, although everything is welcome, we require no personal information. Together, we are just going to do some storytelling with Shakespeare. After the evening's walk through the imagination, the surprise and elation turn into a commitment for the weekend, and our "band of brothers" and sisters is formed.

Our techniques allow us to ensure success for our vet participants. After a brief synopsis of the story and an explanation of the scene, we stand at their shoulder and "feed" them a line or a half line or a phrase or word—as much as they can hold on to. We ask provocative, even personal questions about the emotional content of the lines. These questions are not meant to be answered, but any emotion they elicit is put on the line itself. Movement is encouraged and suggested. Full voice is encouraged. In the debrief that follows, the veterans tell us they feel a release. Many times they laugh and hug or fist-bump their scene partner. We can see by the body language and the bright eyes that this man is now alive in the room. That's enough. When, on our first day, we tell them everything about the weekend, we say that all we are looking to provide is one emotional experience, one pop that will allow them to feel and notice what that is like. For many of these men who have spent weeks at best and usually much longer in disassociation, it is enough to have one fully felt, fully expressed emotion. Sometimes they get more than that.

Shakespeare has offered up the very specifics of so many conflicts. Not just the stories but also the common and personal intricacies of relationships. The words are both foreign and strange, and also exactly and perfectly describe the experience of our inner confusion and turmoil:

> LEONTES
>   Is whispering nothing?
> Is leaning cheek to cheek? is meeting noses?
> Kissing with inside lip? stopping the career
> Of laughter with a sigh (a note infallible
> Of breaking honesty)? horsing foot on foot?
> Skulking in corners? wishing clocks more swift?
> Hours, minutes? noon, midnight? and all eyes
> Blind with the pin and web but theirs; theirs only.
> That would unseen be wicked? is this nothing?
> Why, then the world and all that's in't is nothing,
> The covering sky is nothing, Bohemia nothing,
> My wife is nothing, nor nothing have these nothings,
> If this be nothing.
>
> (*Winter's Tale* 1.2.284–96)

The Viet Nam-era Marine, pointing his finger at his scene partner, spits out the words of jealousy and heartbreak. The FoC facilitator feeds him, "My wife is nothing . . ." He stands frozen, his face flushing with emotion. The facilitator urges him, "Put it on the line. Just say the words." As he chokes out, "My wife is nothing!" tears spill down his cheeks, and he cries out, "But my wife is EVERYTHING!" His story spills out with the tears, and he tells the room of the courage of his wife who understood that as long as they remained together, he would keep drinking. She loved him enough to leave him. The next day, his wife sits in the room with us and holds his hand as our final day wraps up. This vet has come back to us many times. Sometimes just popping into the room to dole out hugs and original poems. He still tells us that this was the moment that got him "un-stuck." He returned, for the first time in years, to his vocation and works full-time.

It is a great luxury to have the amount of time we have. Relationships are forged and depths can be reached, explored, and emerged from in a way that is not possible in a class or a one-off block of time. We can take an hour per scene. Still, it works even in shorter amounts of time. A colleague working with only one hour a week sees the same spine-straightening, eye-brightening results.

Nearly seven years into the direct delivery of working with veterans, we still sit around at our rare social gatherings, beer in hand, and analyze what it is that is pulling our participants back from the brink. Is it giving them a new tight-knit unit to be a part of, getting to be seen and heard telling story, letting them practice with high-stress/low-risk activities, giving them a safe place to express rage, giving them a place to talk about things with no one present who will adjust their medication or change their therapy target, or is it the magical properties of Shakespeare? All of these things are powerful and likely a part of the beneficial results. There also seems to be something about getting the thoughts and memories that devastate the inner life, outside the body. A veteran songwriter friend of ours told us the story of the CD he composed and recorded after returning from Iraq. Before that artifact, when he had conversations about his PTSD, the conversation was about him, his body and his mind. After he could pull out the CD of his songs, the conversation became about this thing outside of him; the same conversation, but it no longer felt like people were peering into his head.

For these men and women who may have been through experiences of violence that we civilians cannot imagine, holding the stories in or telling them to people who shrink away in horror are a means to a horrible end. Straight-up talk therapy works for many but for some, telling the stories of the things they did and saw is impossible. Art in general, and theater in particular offers an oblique way of putting personal stories outside of their heads and can "*gentle their condition.*" Speaking someone else's words and saying those words with the emotions of a character can allow for what we at FoC think of as the "Barrel Full of Monkeys" effect: one story hooks onto another, then pulling out one more and then one more.

Those rare times when we sit with a beer and talk, we inevitably wonder, silently or aloud who we are, as the actor facilitators, in this picture. Currently, to the best of our understanding, we tell our future staff that we work consciously and explicitly to be actors sharing our skill set. We tell our trainees, do your own work. This work is not about being a savior or the leaders or fixing what is broken, nor is it being less important than people who served or "just an actor" but one of the unit, part of the community. Judgment has no place in this room. Any one of us can quickly smell judgment in any interaction and know how that will shut down the free sharing of our inner thoughts. We work and work at sitting in the circle of compassion as witnesses to what is there.

We at FoC are particularly interested in sharing our work in order to broaden the perspective on inclusion of the arts, and in particular, the expressive arts in any conversation about healing trauma. Trauma is at the core of nearly every public health crisis and sustains misery in individuals in every community in our nation. Meeting this need with allopathic medicine and CBT (Cognitive Behavior Therapy) alone has proven ineffective in significantly reducing the suffering of millions. Science has been increasingly supportive of the neurological benefit of expressing emotional experience and the long-term benefits of the act of *making art*. The qualitative evidence is powerful. The acting skills and understanding of Shakespearean text that FoC shares are eminently teachable and translatable into a wide range of professional targets, from reducing symptoms of PTSD, to supporting substance abuse recovery, to energizing educational settings. Emotional re-education is becoming more and more important as our technological society finds it more and more difficult to connect with one another.

Actors hone skills and practice the techniques that allow us to journey into and map and express the inner landscape of human interaction and experience. Feast actors believe that this has made us more compassionate and empathetic people. As guides into the inner human realm for people who have lost the path we have found great purpose. We walk beside our veteran brothers and sisters into their darkest memories and feelings, and Shakespeare provides the lifeline back out into the light.

Notes

1. All Shakespeare quotations from *The Arden Shakespeare Complete Works,* ed. Richard Proudfoot, Ann Thompson, and David Scott Kastan (London: Thomas Nelson, 1998).

2. Marvin Spevack, *A Complete and Systematic Concordance to the Works of Shakespeare* (Cambridge, MA: Harvard University Press, 1973).

3. www.americansforthearts.org

4. https://bigthink.com/how-to-think-like-shakespeare/this-is-your-brain-on -shakespeare

5. http://news.emory.edu/stories/2012/02/metaphor_brain_imaging/

Disturbing Shakespeare and Challenging the Preconceptions

Rowan Mackenzie

OUT OF CHARACTER Theatre Company is a York-based charity that produces theater to challenge audience's preconceptions that those with mental health issues are somehow different from other people. [1] In their production *Disturbing Shakespeare,* they used a pastiche of Shakespearean characters reimagined in a mental health unit to create a theatrical heterotopia.[2] While many of the characters included have been interpreted as mad it is unexpected to see such iconic figures from the canon within an asylum setting. The intention behind this production, as is the case with much of their work, was to challenge beliefs about mental health issues, and this was done through the creation of a specific, alternative reality space in which the characters interacted differently than Shakespeare's originals. Heterotopias[3] are "worlds within worlds, mirroring and yet distinguishing themselves from that which is outside."[4] As this paper shows, Out of Character uses this different world, populated by Shakespearean characters, to demonstrate that those with mental health issues can be just like the audience themselves as, in this production, as in life, "the line between madness and sanity is blurred."[5] By considering the heterotopia created in this production we are able to consider how the company used Shakespeare's characters to challenge the stigma of mental illness that currently widely exists.[6]

Foucault described theater as a heterotopia because "it is capable of juxtaposing in a single real place several spaces, several sites that are in themselves incompatible."[7] This concept has been developed by Kevin Hetherington, Louis Marin and, recently, Joanne Tompkins in *Theatre's Heterotopias* outlines her process for isolating the heterotopia within a production.[8] Tompkins describes her

49

heterotopic methodology in detail by summarizing Hetherington's description of heterotopias having the "effect of making things appear out of place," and she details Marin's contribution to this critical thinking before outlining the three elements she defines when isolating the heterotopia (reminiscent of Henri Lefebvre's spatial triad): constructed space, abstracted space, and, between these, the heterotopia.[9] She defines constructed space as that in which the production is set while abstracted space is a "contrasting spatial environment that may be located in a geographically determined place." [10] She then describes how heterotopia can be created from the way in which the constructed space and the abstracted space are juxtaposed. This method of analyzing theatrical performances is helpful in the context of *Disturbing Shakespeare,* in which the play uses the well-known characters and speeches of Shakespeare in the disturbing context of the asylum with the explicit intention of making people realize that mental illness comes in many guises. I concur with Tompkins' assertion that heterotopias can prompt a rethinking or reassessment of the world that is incremental to prompting social change.

I am using the asylum as the constructed space, and the characters replace the abstracted space with an abstracted concept; the cultural capital of these recognized figures becomes the other element which creates the disturbing juxtaposition. My definition of heterotopia is the glimpse of something unexpected that challenges what the anticipated norm would be through combining these two. Whereas Tompkins describes heterotopia as existing between two spaces, for me in this context it is something created by the proximity of them. By overlaying the expected and the unexpected Paul Birch (Artistic Director, Out of Character) provided a glimpse into an alternative reality where audience members have their perceptions of mental illness unsettled. The character of Jacques is central to this; his commentary to the audience highlighted the issues causing madness that so often befall us all in everyday life—noting Hamlet's bereavement and his encounter with his father's ghost; berating Orlando for "being out of [his] mind"; and observing, "As Shakespeare himself said, 'Love is a madness' and everyone ends up in love at some point. So everyone ends up a little bit nuts." [11]

To give some context to the heterotopia it is useful to consider the distinct disciplines of drama and dramatherapy; the first being art; the second using dramatic techniques to explore personal issues.[12] Dramatherapy is an increasingly popular and widespread field, the benefits of which are explored and articulated in multiple texts by Sue Jennings and others.[13] Jennings describes dramatherapy as "an art form [which] has the potential for healing. It has the potential for allowing people to view and experience the unhelpful stages of their lives and transform them. Drama, as rehearsal and performance, is intrinsic to human development."[14]

Dramatherapy uses the techniques of theater but does not culminate in a performance—the benefits come from the process of the techniques, not in a final output. However, Out of Character crosses the boundaries between drama and dramatherapy to some degree as it is formed entirely of mental health service users who perform public productions.[15] Their work uses theater to bring psychological issues to public attention through both public and NHS performances. Within the field of drama there are many who attest to the psychoanalytic importance of the works of Shakespeare and the way in which he captures the true essence of issues that trouble the human mind.[16] Dorothy T. Grunes and Jerome M. Grunes claim that "in Shakespeare's dramas, characters develop—rather than simply unfold—as a result of reconceiving themselves. How this reconception takes place is of great significance, since it is close to [the psychoanalyst's] own clinical work." [17]

Birch is a theater director, not a mental health specialist; his primary objective is to produce high-quality theater with a group of community actors. *Disturbing Shakespeare* was his first production with the company. The play was performed in 2014 and then reprised in 2015 with a conflated text and additional scenes, most markedly making Macbeth Lady Macbeth's alter ego.[18] Only two of the cast had previous experience performing Shakespeare, and there was some initial nervousness about the challenge of his work, but plays were selected through group discussion and included "the obvious plays that explicitly explore madness and those which were less obvious, allowing the cast to deconstruct the stereotype of madness."[19] Birch created a draft of the script to suit the strengths of his actors with the intention of "reflect[ing] the richness of Shakespeare's work in blurring the lines between madness and sanity" through presenting a range of psychological conditions.[20] By demonstrating personality disorders, depression, and even the emotional experience of falling in love he showed how we can all experience such changes in mental state during our lifetimes.[21]

The opening stage directions made clear the intended con-

structed space was "transformed to Bedlam, the notorious psychiatric 'hospital' of Shakespeare's day" along with multiple
characters milling around the stage paying no attention to anyone
else. [22] This initial sense of dislocated beings trapped in their own
worlds gave the audience an immediate sense of disorder and
chaos, until Jacques intervened and demanded they "give it a
bloody rest."[23] This constructed space was one that audiences were
likely to recognize from many theatrical and fictional portrayals of
psychiatric hospitals.[24] Instead of a physical/geographic abstracted
space there was an abstracted concept using the cultural capital of
Shakespeare's characters. [25] Shakespeare is so embedded in our
society that the characters have a cachet of their own and it is this
intrinsic familiarity that imbues them with power in creating the
heterotopic potential. The audience would have recognized the
characters and many of their speeches, but these newly juxtaposed
interactions required that they be considered in different contexts.

The plays used as source material were *As You Like It, Macbeth,
Hamlet, A Midsummer Night's Dream, King Lear, Richard III,* and
Henry VI, Part III. Each was selected to draw out a different perspective on madness: from the more obvious characters such as
Macbeth, Hamlet, Ophelia, and Lear to the temporary delusions of
Titania and Bottom and a psychopathic Richard III.[26] Some characters were portrayed sympathetically to "provoke the audience into
realizing that all human beings can get a bit crazy from time to
time" through experiences such as suffering bereavement or being
subjected to excessive pressure.[27] The abstracted space of the world
of Shakespeare's cultural capital combined with the constructed
space of the psychiatric institute worked to generate the heterotopia within which audience members were encouraged to have
their perceptions challenged. The psychiatric unit would be unfamiliar, personally, to the majority but instead known from popular
films and dramas; while the characters they saw populating it
would also be recognizable but as belonging to the higher cultural
echelons of dramatic art; the tension arising from encountering the
familiar in an unfamiliar and unexpected context was intended to
engage the audience with the possibility that we can all have mental health issues.[28]

Shakespeare used choric figures in plays such as *Henry V* to great
effect, allowing them to highlight the difference between words
and action. Birch employed Jacques in a similar role; he engaged
with the audience and acted as their conduit to other characters,

providing background explanations throughout the play. He remained onstage throughout, challenging and mocking the other characters, to highlight aspects of their mental conditions. As Juliet Dusinberre observes, "Jaques is a dissident in Shakespeare's play. . . . an observer not a participator, the odd man out at a party."[29] And it was precisely this role he fulfilled as he guided the audience through meetings with a number of characters who wander on and off the stage. There was no attempt to link the stories of the plays together, and the result was a disjointed yet surprisingly cohesive text that gave a feeling of madness and disorientation to evoke in the audience a sense of disassociation to emulate an element of the disturbing nature of mental illness. Jacques' lines were written by Birch in a modern idiom, highlighting the clinical setting through references to "Flurazepam" and through lines that asserted such claims as "like most of us in here. We're not in our 'right mind.' "[30]

In this adaptation, as in Shakespeare's play, Jacques was a comedic yet reflective figure, but he mounted a vehement defense of Richard III, challenging the unfair and inaccurate stereotyping of him as a maniac when in reality he was "actually quite a nice fella."[31] When defending Richard he comments on Richard's physical hunch that "didn't make him a psychopath," accentuating that sometimes people are judged on their physical differences when in reality his psychopathic tendencies are revealed through the pleasure he takes in killing.[32] Jacques' humor and jibes at the other characters diminished over the course of the play, suggesting that he became worn down by the stark reality of the mental hospital. His final solo line in response to Orlando's attempt to make him laugh about parking charges in York was filled with pathos—"It's hard to laugh when some people are so very, very sad"—and highlighted the more reflective elements of his personality.[33] The repetition of "very" was reminiscent of Lear's repeated "never" in the final scene of *King Lear* and added an air of poignancy. [34]

The opening scene was adapted from *Hamlet* 4.5 with Ophelia arbitrarily giving flowers to the audience and talking of a dead father the other patients in the unit know nothing about; thus emphasizing an overtly mad element in her behavior. A number of lines have been allocated to different characters.[35] For example, Gertrude's "Alas, sweet lady, what imports this song" (4.5.27) is now voiced by the physician, subtly nuancing the meaning of this line to register a clinical relationship rather than an expression of human compassion. He also orated Claudius's line "conceit upon her father" (4.5.45) suggesting the death of her father as the cause of her illness. Jacques' comment "that's love for you" may have referred to her love for her father or for Hamlet.[36]

The next scene portrayed Titania and Bottom with fairies behaving like rude mechanicals. Peaseblossom challenged the language of the play as incomprehensible, stating "because it's Shakespeare I don't really understand it." [37] This served, in my view, both to mark the fairies as potentially less educated and articulate but also to make anyone in the audience struggling with the language feel that they were not alone in this. There was a sense of these characters siding with the audience if they felt the play to be difficult; however, this was somewhat ironic given that the interweaving of threads from multiple plays made the plot far harder to follow than in any of Shakespeare's plays, and the context for the language was often lost in the editing. Therefore, there was little wonder that the audience may have felt somewhat out of their depth, unless they had a deep knowledge of Shakespeare prior to the production. Bottom does not end the scene as Titania's beloved with the line "tie up my love's tongue, bring him silently" being taken literally and Bottom gagged and carried off. [38] This infused the scene with a darker undertone, reminding the audience that those with mental health issues are at times restrained, a topic discussed at length in the Mind Report *Mental Health Crisis Care: Physical Restraint in Crisis*.[39] The physical restraint of Bottom provided a stark reminder of the setting for the play; he was not in a moonlit wood, but rather a secure hospital, and his freedom was illusory.

After a scene from *As You Like It* where Orlando and Rosalind discussed love before Jacques ridiculed Orlando that "the worst bloody fault you have is to be in love," the subsequent entrance of Richard III and Macbeth was a jarring change of mood. [40] Richard's speech about "dead midnight" presented him, within the heterotopia, as a psychopath.[41] However, this view is disputed by Jacques later in the play when he challenged "that Southern propaganda" which made Richard "a villain."[42] Benson (who played Jacques) had a keen interest in Richard III and "passionately created a monologue about the historical Richard III" that led to the inclusion of the character when he would not have been otherwise. [43] Birch describes in his online blog how Benson "wrote from the heart about. . . . Richard III." [44] And Benson's text was included along with some topical local jokes regarding his heritage and that he should be returned to York, where the play was set. The contrast between the behavior the audience saw from Richard and Jacques' defense of him was a powerful reminder that everyone is perceived differently by different people and we all have multiple elements to our personalities a theme which Georgia Slowe articulates when describing her experiences in *Shakespeare Comes to Broadmoor*.[45]

An on-stage storm ensued in which Richard's knife was dropped and picked up by Macbeth, who then ruminated on the moral issues of regicide using lines from Shakespeare.[46] However, the actor morphed onstage between Macbeth and Lady Macbeth, giving the audience a sense of multiple personality disorder. The debate between the Macbeths took on a new meaning when spoken by one person with two visages as an internal debate about whether the intended plot would succeed or fail. The final element of this scene was taken from act one, scene five, with Lady Macbeth's soliloquy about the "fatal entrance of Duncan" (1.5.38) edited to remove reference to her maternal experience, which gave a more androgynous feel to the role.[47] A further storm then marked the end of this scene and moved the action from *Macbeth* to *King Lear*. As in Shakespeare's plays, the storms signified a sense of turmoil and struggle, such are played out in the character's speeches. The constructed storm scenes heightened the heterotopian nature of the space that encompassed the audience; they were encouraged to experience the raging elements of the weather and the accompanying expression of mental turmoil by the characters. Lear's lines "blow, winds, and crack your cheeks! rage!" argue with the weather as if it is another angry person, emulating the earlier argument between the two personalities of Macbeth/Lady Macbeth and the rant of the psychotic Richard as he kills the Fool. [48]

While Lear retained the famous "blow winds" speech (3.2.1), the Fool offered a modern prose response and prophesied a time when "no-one will tell the mad from the sane" with the inference being that that time has been reached based on the description he gives of contemporary life. [49] This modernization of the lines was designed to make the role accessible to "one of the actors who struggles with literacy but is a very funny performer."[50] The actor who played Lear is a Shakespeare enthusiast, an attraction he ascribes to the Bard's "amazing humanity and attention to detail, he notices the small things about people."[51] Kent's feigned madness in *Disturbing Shakespeare* added a further layer to the constructed space of Bedlam. Shakespeare's Kent enters "disguised" (3.2.36 SD), but Birch's Kent enters "pretending to be mad," which was

conveyed entirely through gesture and behavior as the text provided no evidence of madness when Kent encouraged Lear to seek
shelter from the storm in a hovel. [52] There was no Edgar/Poor Tom
in this production, but instead Kent pretended to be mad, allowing
the audience to contrast the acted insanity with that which was real
within Lear. Kent's madness was signified through his actions emulating the stereotypes of madness and thus enabled the heterotopia
to show the audience that what they may witness can differ from
reality.

The disappearance of the Fool from *King Lear* after 3.6 has
widely been acknowledged as problematic by directors and actors,
and in Adrian Noble's 1982 RSC production he was stabbed to
death by a mad Lear, while Sam Mendes' 2014 production had him
bludgeoned to death in a bathtub.[53] Birch substituted a deranged
Lear with a psychotic Richard III. The majority of speeches in the
play were Shakespearean monologues but frequently interrupted or
repurposed to be addressed to other characters. For example, Richard of Gloucester's famous speech—"What, will the aspiring blood
of Lancaster/ Sink in the ground?"[54]—was spoken, not to the dying
Henry VI, but instead to Lear's Fool who he murdered onstage
despite their only having had a four-line interaction prior to the
stabbing. This attack on a stranger adds to the image of Richard as a
psychopath, and it brought to life Birch's stage direction: "Richard,
Duke of Gloucester enters with a knife. He is the cliché of Richard
the 3rd and is very scary indeed." [55] This random murder for no
apparent personal gain brought with it a different tone than that
conveyed through Shakespeare's presentation of a power-hungry
Gloucester who would stop at nothing to advance his own position.
Here, Birch portrayed a man who murdered another patient in the
hospital for no discernible reason, but Jacques rebutted this stereotyping of Richard with Benson's monologue asserting a more positive side to Richard although his evil remains clear. The effect was
to highlight the complexity of human nature as no one is all good
or all bad. This was also the turning point for Jacques when he
seemed to cease his sarcastic commentary on the characters and
instead admitted to being affected by their melancholy, as though
no one could resist the effects of another's suffering indefinitely.
The audience is encouraged to glimpse that they themselves are
touched by mental illness, just as Jacques is, and that it is not something "other" but something intrinsic to human nature.

This adaptation constructed Bedlam as a quasi-Shakespearean/

quasi-modern psychiatric hospital in which the patients were restrained; a place where the audience was bombarded with noise and movement. Some of Birch's adaptation decisions were likely to have been unconscious, given that Shakespeare has so permeated our culture. As David Edgar states, "Shakespeare's scenes reflect human behaviour—his techniques are hard-wired into us not just because they are human but because of the gradual sedimentation of his work within us."[56] This sedimentation is precisely what makes it difficult to fully analyze each decision about this production: Birch was not coming to Shakespeare for the first time when he edited the works into Out of Character's adaptation, and therefore the "ghosting" of that history will have influenced decisions at a subconscious level.[57] However, such subconscious knowledge enabled the creation of an innovative and dynamic text that encouraged audiences to realize that people with mental illness come in many guises and that there is a fine line between mental health and mental illness.

Notes

1. Out of Character was formed in 2009 in York from a project called Converge that aims to provide educational opportunities for mental health service users (over 18s) in the York area in collaboration with York St Johns University. Converge continues to operate and includes drama, music, and dance. Out of Character is now a registered charity (1161399). Out of Character are widely known for their openness about the challenges of mental health issues including treatment and stigmatization. The company has flourished with bi-annual productions of all kinds from classic texts (including Kafka) to devised works of their own. All of their members are addressing mental health issues or have done so in the past but they are also required to demonstrate an acceptable level of acting as entry to the company is now strictly by audition.

2. *Disturbing Shakespeare* was performed March–May 2015 at Friargate Theatre, York by Out of Character using the 2014 script. It also toured a number of UK university venues in 2015, performing the 2015 script.

3. Michel Foucault, *Critique of Everyday Life: Three Volume Text* (translated by John Moore and Gregory Elliott), (London: Verso, 2014).

4. Dr. Peter Johnson describing Foucault's work on heterotopias which was the basis for Johnson's PhD thesis "On Heterotopia," http://www.heterotopiastudies.com/.

5. Personal interview with Paul Birch, Artistic Director of Out of Character Theatre Company since 2014, and dramaturg for the script for *Disturbing Shakespeare* (18 April 2016).

6. Norman Sartorious, "Stigma and Mental Health," *The Lancet* 370: 9590

(2007): 810–11 https://www.thelancet.com/article/S0140–6736(07)61245–8/ abstract.

7. Michel Foucault, "Of Other Spaces," *Diacritics* 16, no. 1 (1986): 22–27; 25.

8. Joanne Tompkins, *Theatre's Heterotopias: Performance and the Cultural Politics of Space* (New York: Palgrave Macmillan, 2014).

9. Kevin Hetherington, *The Badlands of Modernity: Heterotopia and Social Ordering* (London: Routledge, 1997), 50.

10. Tompkins, *Theatre's Heterotopias,* 32.

11. Paul Birch, *Disturbing Shakespeare: Version 2015* play script, 2, 12, 5.

12. The British Association of Dramatherapists which was founded in 1977 and is the professional body for UK dramatherapists. The Association states that "Dramatherapy has as its main focus the intentional use of healing aspects of drama and theatre as the therapeutic process. It is a method of working and playing that uses action methods to facilitate creativity, imagination, learning, insight and growth." <http://badth.org.uk/>.

13. Sue Jennings is a consultant Dramatherapist and Senior Research Fellow at the University of London and Honorary Lecturer at the University of Derby as well as the Director of Dramatherapy Consultants. She has written multiple books, including *Dramatherapy with Families, Groups and Individuals: Waiting in the Wings* (London: Jessica Kingsley Publishers, 1992); *Art Therapy and Dramatherapy: Masks of the Soul* (co-written with Ase Minde) (London: Jessica Kingsley Publishers, 1995); and *Introduction to Dramatherapy: Theatre and Healing* (London: Jessica Kingsley Publishers, 1997).

14. Jennings, *Dramatherapy with Families, Groups and Individuals,* 12.

15. Interview with Paul Birch, York, 18 April 2016 in which he described how the entire ensemble have been or are current service users, with the exception of himself. He was appointed Artistic Director in 2014 but had no previous background in mental health work.

16. Publications such as Inge Wise and Maggie Mills, eds., *Psychoanalytic Ideas and Shakespeare* (London: Karnac Books, 2006) and B. J. Sokol, *The Undiscovered Country: New Essays on Psychoanalysis and Shakespeare* (London: Free Association Books, 1993) describe close links between Shakespeare and psychoanalysis.

17. Dorothy T. Grunes and Jerome M. Grunes, *What Shakespeare Teaches us about Psychoanalysis* (London: Karnac Books, 2014), xiii. Although some neuroscientists are dismissive of psychoanalytical models, the field of neuropsychoanalysis aims to combine the objective, exterior analysis of neuroscientists with the subjective, interior analysis of psychoanalysts and the Neuropsychoanalysis Association (NPSA) leads international work in this area https://npsa-association.org/.

18. The 2014 version of the play included Queen Gertrude who is omitted from the 2015 version. Only Lady Macbeth appears in the 2014 version, but both Lady Macbeth and Macbeth appear in the 2015 version. The majority of the cast was unaltered, but a few roles were reallocated between the two productions. Many of Out of Character's plays are amended and revised during performance as the ensemble suggest ideas to further develop the themes. The unpublished 2015 script is referred to throughout this paper as it contains scenes that are omitted from the original version.

19. Personal email communication received from Paul Birch 6 July 2016.

20. Ibid.

21. Paul Birch's *Disturbing Shakespeare: Version 2015* play script portrayed personality disorders through the characterization of Macbeth and Lady Macbeth as a single person with differing personas; Jacques openly mentioned his depression, and Rosalind, Orlando, and Titania all demonstrated temporary distortions of vision and the changes to temperament caused by falling in love.

22. Ibid., 2. Bedlam is explored and documented in Catharine Arnold, *Bedlam: London and Its Mad* (London: Simon and Schuster, 2008).

23. Birch spells the character's name "Jacques." Paul Birch, *Disturbing Shakespeare: Version 2015* play script, 2.

24. Famous plays such as *Marat/Sade* (written Peter Weiss, dir. Peter Brook, 1965), films such as *One Flew over the Cuckoo's Nest* (dir. Milos Forman, 1975), *A Clockwork Orange,* (dir. Stanley Kubrick, 1971) and *Girl, Interrupted* (dir. James Mangold, 1999), as well as more recent novels such as Paulo Coelho's *Veronika Decides to Die* (trans. Margaret Jull Costa), (London: HarperCollins, 1999) portray psychiatric hospitals as places filled with people who cannot interact appropriately with others and often feature excessive noise and chaotic behavior, playing into and reinforcing negative stereotypes about mental illness.

25. For cultural capital, see Pierre Bourdieu, "The forms of capital" (1986) in *Cultural Theory: An Anthology,* ed. Imre Szeman and Timothy Kaposy (Chichester: Wiley-Blackwell, 2011), 81–93.

26. Interview with Paul Birch, York, 18 April 2016.

27. Personal email, Paul Birch 6 July 2016.

28. Interview with Paul Birch, York, 18 April 2016.

29. *As You Like It,* ed. Juliet Dusinberre (London: Bloomsbury/ Arden, 2006), 107. All citations from this edition.

30. Paul Birch *Disturbing Shakespeare: Version 2015* play script, 2.

31. Ibid, 19.

32. Ibid.

33. Ibid.

34. *King Lear,* ed R. A. Foakes (London: Bloomsbury/Arden, 1997), 5.3.307. All citations from this edition.

35. *Hamlet,* ed. Harold Jenkins (London: Methuen, 1982), all citations from this edition. "A document in madness, thoughts and remembrance fitted" (4.5.176–77) spoken by Laertes is now allocated to Gertrude. "I will not speak with her" (4.5.1) was Gertrude's opening line, but is spoken by Claudius, as is the amended response of "what's wrong with her" in place of "what would she have?" (4.5.3). "How now Ophelia" spoken by Gertrude (4.5.22) is replaced by Claudius's "Alright Ophelia? How are you? Doing well are we?"

36. Paul Birch, *Disturbing Shakespeare: Version 2015* play script, 5.

37. Ibid., 8.

38. *A Midsummer Night's Dream,* ed. Harold F. Brooks (London: Methuen, 1979), 3.1. 194.

39. *Mental Health Crisis Care: Physical Restraint in Crisis – A Report on Physical Restraint in Hospitals in England,* (foreword Dr. S.P. Sashidharan), June 2013, https://www.mind.org.uk/media/197120/physical_restraint_final_web_version.pdf [accessed 24 July 2016]; the report notes almost 1000 incidents of physical injury following restraint in England during 2012.

40. Birch, *Disturbing Shakespeare: Version 2015,* 12. Jacques' line echoes Rosa-

lind in *As You Like It*—"Men have died from time to time, and worms have eaten them, but not for love" (4.1.97–99).

41. This Richard III is based on Richard of Gloucester in *Henry VI, Part III* rather than *Richard III*.

42. Birch, *Disturbing Shakespeare: Version 2015,* 19.

43. Paul Birch, *Disturbing Shakespeare is put to rest* Out of Character blog.

44. Ibid.

45. Murray Cox, ed., *Shakespeare Comes to Broadmoor: "The Actors are Come Hither"* (London: Jessica Kingsley Publishing, 1992), which features an interview with Georgia Slowe, who played Juliet, describing her realization that these were "normal every day people, who . . . weren't born with a label saying 'I want to grow up and kill someone for no reason whatever', did very much close the gap between the 'us and them.'" Slowe notes that this insight came "with the realisation that it is possible suddenly to lose the three-quarters of your mind that tells you that you can't do something; and that loss of control need only last for a moment" (47).

46. *Macbeth,* ed. Sandra Clark and Pamela Mason (London: Bloomsbury/ Arden, 2015), 1.7.1–2, 1.7.7, 1.7.12–16. All citations from this edition.

47. Birch, *Disturbing Shakespeare: Version 2015,* 1. Macbeth/Lady Macbeth's speech is "And fill me from the crown to the toe top-full / Of direst cruelty! Come, thick night"—omitting 1.5.42–49 from Shakespeare's *Macbeth*.

48. Birch, *Disturbing Shakespeare: Version 2015,* 15.

49. Ibid., 17.

50. Personal email communication received from Paul Birch 6 July 2016.

51. Interview with Laurie Furnell, 16 June 2016.

52. Birch, *Disturbing Shakespeare: Version 2015,*16.

53. Adrian Noble (dir.), *King Lear,* Royal Shakespeare Company, Stratford-upon-Avon, 1982; Sam Mendes (dir.), *King Lear,* National Theatre, London, January—July 2014.

54. William Shakespeare, *King Henry VI, Part 3,* ed. John D Cox and Eric Rasmussen (London: Arden/Bloomsbury, 2001), 5.6.61–62.

55. Birch, *Disturbing Shakespeare: Version 2014,* 17.

56. David Edgar, "Shakespeare's Structures," talk, The Swan Theatre, Stratford-upon-Avon, 23 July 2016.

57. Marvin Carlson, *The Haunted Stage: The Theatre as Memory Machine* (Ann Arbor: University of Michigan Press, 2001), 104.

Reflections on "Social Dreaming" with Shakespeare

ESTHER R. ELLIOTT

| DOCTOR | You see, her eyes are open. |
| GENTLEWOMAN | Ay, but their sense are shut. |

(*Macbeth* 5.1 25–26)[1]

FOR MANY YEARS I was a working professional actor, training at Bristol Old Vic Theatre School before joining several Shakespeare-based theater companies, including the Royal Shakespeare Company and Shakespeare at the Tobacco Factory. I left this profession due to debilitating issues with visual impairment (VI). Wanting to remain involved in this area while reaching underrepresented sections of society, I now develop inclusive Shakespeare-based projects for visually impaired actors, through Extant Theatre, London and with elderly Shakespeareans at the Mary Fielding Guild House. This piece includes some of my thoughts about the practical and philosophical aspects of grappling with *Macbeth* and *King Lear* in these contexts.

My practice with these groups incorporates work I did as an actor with Cicely Berry, teaching methods from my work at the Shakespeare's Globe as an Education Practitioner; and methodologies derived from my extensive experience in rehearsal rooms. Throughout these endeavors, I keep returning to Peter Brook's reflections on the semiotics of space, particularly when looking at what constitutes "inclusive" rehearsal spaces for VI actors and asking what their most *essential* elements may be. In addition, I have spent many years as an actor with VI, who now works with others who face challenges when they attempt to access Shakespeare as printed text. This population includes blind/VI actors and international visitors as well as more traditional actors-in-training. I also

61

work with a group of elderly Shakespeareans, who generally do not fear the text, but face other difficulties.

In my training and practice, I typically consider our "senses" as a kind of first-response unit: that space-field that restrains one before experiencing an immediate response. The space that exists before a sense is made 'sense' of as *Macbeth* suggests: "Art thou not, fatal vision, sensible / To feeling, as to sight?" (2.1.36–37).

With actors, senses frequently lead to activity and connectivity. Typically therefore, our starting point for "sensory prompts" in exercises and rehearsals are the literal clues about the senses found within speeches. We then build out from there. If one can identify these places in a Shakespearean speech and unlock their potential, such moments provide useful starting points for textual exploration. *Macbeth* for instance, has proved to be a particularly pliable text for this purpose. For Extant's blind/VI actors, the rehearsal process begins with the actors participating in a series of "Sensing Shakespeare" exercises devised to strengthen their contact with the space and each other—largely through the use of rhythm-based techniques. Drumming, for example, proves useful in engaging the actors not only with the linguistically percussive nature of *Macbeth* but with how those percussive variants might indicate character differentiation.

Sensory–sensitive performance exercises facilitate our exploration of what each of us brings to Shakespeare's texts and what we individually and collectively find there. Denise Albanese suggests that Shakespeare is a "repository for social dreaming," where Shakespeare, as a resource, should be put back in to the public arena.[2] Believing that to be true, I reflect on such possibilities with Shakespeare's *King Lear* from my position as a theater-maker interested in Inclusive Shakespeare. When we try to put social dreaming into practice with Inclusive Shakespeare, we might ask: "What is already there for us?" "What is absent?" and "Where are there any empty spaces for us to experiment in?" "Is it best to create and inhabit new, empty spaces?" As part of this exploration, I note that the VI actors I work with generally prefer the term "inclusivity" over "accessibility." Accessibility implies to them that there is a journey that they must make, while inclusivity suggests that they have already arrived (along with everyone else) and that they can therefore *begin* their work from this starting point rather than always playing catch-up. Currently, practice with blind/VI actors tends to emphasize inclusivity, but the next progressive stage of that journey lies in integrated practice. In my remarks below, I will describe what this path entails.

As an artist, however, I resist much "official" terminology for such undertakings. Nevertheless, applications for Arts Council funding in the UK stress the "Creative Case for Diversity," a phrase that contains a moveable feast of words professing to emphasize social mobility. From this perspective, "Diversity" becomes an umbrella term for "Accessibility," "Inclusivity," and "Creative Inclusion." Theater-makers must often embrace these kinds of parameters to gain support for their work, even while recognizing that governmental influences can threaten the artistic process. This Extant project for example, was funded by the Arts Council, which exerted pressure to restrict the casting to VI actors. Their rationale targeted Extant's status as a National Portfolio Organisation which identifies it as a single-issue organization focused solely on the support and development of Visually Impaired Artists. This narrow remit means that individual practitioners can only present projects situated within restricted models of "inclusivity." As a result, the apparently positive goal of creating *inclusion* for this specific population may actually result in an unintended appearance of *exclusivity*. "Single-issue" companies, therefore, risk becoming disconnected from the broader diversity dialogues that are cracking open theater. Fortunately for my current desire to bring sighted and VI actors together, my new Arts Council-funded Shakespeare project will be run independently, giving me the opportunity to bring together actors representing a wide spectrum of visual abilities.

My work in these realms, which led to the production of *King Lear* described below, emerged from my own experiences as a practitioner. During the many years I worked as a professional theater actor, I was secretly negotiating with sight issues that eventually became too difficult to navigate on a mainstream stage. As a result, I took myself out of the "traditional" theater, returning through a different route, with a keener-felt sense about *inclusion* and *exclusion*. This sense of being *in* and *out* is explored in *King Lear,* of course, and reflects the nature of sight and sight loss, both what it is and what it is not, for myself and the actors I have been working with. Since many of us spend long afternoons in the Moorfield's Eye Hospital's overcrowded NHS clinic, nursing over-interrogated eyes, it is perhaps no surprise that this particular play resonates. The performance considered here was produced through Extant

Theatre and directed by Artistic Director Maria Oshodi, who is blind.

Shakespeare, to my mind, is one of the most "inclusive" writers we have at our disposal if we read him closely from this perspective. His ability to make things "land" with his diffuse audiences, from groundlings to lords, and the consistent "paint-ability" of his descriptions for the mind's eye become particularly striking during work for a sight-impaired audience. Poor Tom's line to Lear, for instance—"Let not the creaking of shoes, nor the rustling of silks, betray thy poor heart to woman" (3.4. 93–95)—has a full soundscape within it. Such specific sound descriptions speak volumes for sight-impaired audiences. Focusing on these instances of highly descriptive text enables sight-impaired audiences to experience an expanded "hearing journey." These elements are especially poignant in *King Lear,* which emphasizes sight and seeing repeatedly in the midst of its considerations of existence around society's margins. Such issues actually provide the play's framework. Accordingly, I am interested too in what resonance there might be in those scenes when played by blind actors. Do we, for example, portray Lear as blind, or expose the actor's blindness, or both?

In the version of *King Lear* I wrote while working with Extant, Cordelia was "sighted" and Lear blinded throughout, as he staggers between ancient landscapes and the ruggedness of City Road near Moorfield's Eye Hospital. Cordelia in this rendition, is brought back from exile to serve as a "sighted" narrator throughout, observing and steering her unaware father between Shakespeare's Ancient Britain and Moorfield's modern facility, until the pair are reunited at the end. The performers' desire to be identified as actors first, rather than being categorized primarily by their personal sight issues, focused my attention upon showing the blindness of Shakespeare's characters. Not surprisingly, these themes also resonated personally for the actors. As a result, numerous "character-to-self" tensions occurred when they encountered some of these scenes from *King Lear,* something I perceived as a fluctuating power play between acceptance and resistance.

The development week of *King Lear,* prior to the full-rehearsal, involved four VI actors: Steve, Karina, Margo, and Giles. Maria directed scenes from the play, and I served as writer-in-residence. There were also three access workers involved. All of the contributing artists face significant vision issues. Margot and Maria, for example, are registered blind. Diverse visual difficulties immediately became significant factors as we crafted rehearsal room strategies. I know only too well that it is painfully hard to process Shakespeare Folio lines through accessible computer software such as Dragon, since I wrestled with this technology throughout my M.A. in Global Shakespeare. Additional challenges quickly emerged as we began rehearsals. A standard, "inclusive" version of the text was impossible, for instance, since the broad range of visual issues requiring attention could not be accommodated so narrowly. A printed script would not suit everyone involved. Each performer needed a script tailored to individual needs, so the group never experienced a common, shared text. Not surprisingly, we realized immediately that the written Shakespeare version I sent to the director ahead of rehearsal would not work for many of the actors. I consequently audio-recorded all of the chosen scenes. This became a lengthy process whereby I created an edited version of Shakespeare on the hoof, since Maria asked me to introduce the character's name before I repeated each line. On the first day of rehearsals, moreover, each actor had a different mode of accessing the text. Giles read Shakespeare two lines at a time on a continually swishing iPhone, for example, while Steve confronted highlighted text in large magnification on his iPad. Rehearsal time became curtailed, as we often had to wait for screens to unfreeze. These constraints also restricted interactivity between actors. It quickly became apparent that if we wanted to cut text as we worked or decided to cross-link ideas via text analysis, we needed the actors to know the whole scene by heart, something that could not be accomplished expeditiously. In more conventionally designed productions, texts are distributed in standardized formats that individual actors can personalize during rehearsal. But in this kind of setting the text needs to be individualized much earlier. In the case of Steve and Giles, they were always working in the moment during rehearsal, two lines at a time, facing what Douglas Lanier might call their Deleuzean "lines of flight" and altogether new directions of thought.[3]

Access workers became line feeders for two blind actors: Karina playing Cordelia (as a "sighted" character) and Margot portraying Goneril and the Fool. This process resembled procedures undertaken elsewhere, but with key differences. As part of Michelle Terry's inaugural season, for example, the 2018 *Hamlet* production at Shakespeare's Globe was rehearsed for the first four weeks with the whole cast in a circle, line feeding each other. This approach, adopted throughout the season's rehearsal period, aimed to decrease advance planning of the production. Creating characters in the rehearsal room allowed actors such as Betrys Jones (who played Laertes) to facilitate "an authentic emotional reaction to come through. Allowing everything that happens, in front of you."[4] For Extant's blind actors, however, grappling with such large amounts of text, and being able to *hear* it in this way becomes a necessity rather than an interesting directorial choice. At the same time, blind/VI actors are not necessarily able to experience a fully "authentic emotional reaction" through the process of line feeding. Their level of dependence on the line feeder, moreover, is particularly strong in the early days of rehearsal, as they orient themselves to the space. Unlike the Globe rehearsals, where all actors continually shared the work of line feeding, each of our actors had one dedicated line feeder working with them consistently. In our process, in fact, the line feeding became part of the action. Joining the actors throughout the rehearsal process, access workers were key players. Paid through the government program "Access to Work," they assisted in a variety of ways. Notably in this process, an artistic symbiosis developed between actor and line feeder that significantly influenced our performance choices. The line feeders, for instance, determine how many words of a line to provide the actor in each segment. Accordingly, they interpret dialogue as they simultaneously edit a new text. Line fundamentalists like myself find this procedure quite challenging. Consequently, I suspect that for a future production, I will probably mark up line feeders' texts with them prior to rehearsal.

Audio description is fast becoming a theatrical conceit in the Blind/VI theater community as performers consider how these technologies might be brought directly into the action in order to more broadly explore inclusive story-telling potential. Accordingly, while Cordelia is not present at the meeting between Poor Tom and Lear, I use her as the audio describer, allowing her to serve as a conduit between the audience and Shakespeare's characters and to help draw a non-sighted audience further into the action. In this dramatic realm, there appears to be potential to *add* to Shakespeare's written language. Throughout this process, I watched the action and wrote relevant "script" for Karina, since it is challenging for a blind actor to improvise during these activities. An audio-describer's role, therefore, evolves into watching the action and turning it into vivid, aural pictures for the audience. Moreover, it is difficult for blind actors to have the same initial free play with written text as sighted actors experience. Since the need for line feeders and interpreters of visual action for the purposes of audio description demands the inclusion of sighted artists in the room, a level playing field for non-sighted actors is hard to accomplish. Nevertheless, we encourage participants not to use theater's privileged sense of sight unthinkingly, and urge them rather to "see it feelingly" (*Lear* 4.6.145).

Technology often assisted us in overcoming these various obstacles. Use of Foley Sound, for instance, helped us focus on less visual aspects of the text, a task which is made easier since Shakespeare tends to write inclusively in terms of sounds and their effects upon us. The impact of sounded landscapes and terrains, for example, heightens our emotional response to self and space at any given moment. During this rehearsal process, BBC Foley artist Alison Wray (paid for as part of their Outreach program) brought with her a selection of bells and door knockers since we were hoping to create the storm in *Lear* by using objects found in the home and in the rehearsal space. Actor Margot was originally trained as a musician, but she had given up playing instruments when she became blind. Over the course of the week, however, she brought and played an increasing number of instruments, such as the double recorder, which she introduced at the start of the Shakespeare's "map scene" (1.1). Alison also suggested that Margot—as the Fool—might wear bells on her feet. Such decisions, when introduced thoughtfully, become extremely useful in transporting a non-sighted audience directly inside the action. This *King Lear* greatly benefited from the array of talents the ensemble brought into the process.

Coincidentally, while I was developing this production of *King Lear* with the blind, I was also working on the same play with a group of elderly women whose reflections and ideas gave me much "insight" into how to approach Lear. Due to these women's particular sight issues, we provide very large-font passages of text when they come together in a leaderless learning circle. The Shakespeare Group at Mary Fielding Guild House has been running under the aegis of ex-teacher Keith Richards (age 86) for over two years. I joined at the end of 2017. It is an all-female group with ages ranging from 86 to 98 years old. Casting is determined by one of the ladies in the group, and Richards selects specific passages two weeks prior to the session. The scenes are typed up by members of staff at

Guild House and distributed to all the women, in font 16 or 18. The group experiences significant hearing difficulties in addition to sight problems, so a few of the women can read their parts but then are unable to participate in the ensuing conversation. After the scenes are read, however, there is a discussion about the language and the meaning of the text with those able to join in.

Richards is interested primarily in the "linguistic journey not the psychological."[5] But the discussions open out to lively conversations about psychology, particularly around Freud, since one of the participants is a psychoanalyst. For Richards, "Everything is the group." When he began the gathering, he used to shift the desks to make a circle. He did not want to be at the head of the table giving a lecture, so he moves around, as do I. Often, the women lean forward, clearly wanting a lecture, but they are beginning to take a more active role. I recently brought in sound recordings of Olivier doing *Hamlet* and copies of early-modern sheet music for an original *King Lear* production. I also bring in films of the productions we are encountering, such as Peter Brook's *King Lear* starring Paul Scofield, which some of those gathered saw during its original production. I also reflect on Global Shakespeare, and it has been a revelation to the women that Shakespeare's stretch is so wide. Fortnightly sessions run between 11:00–12:00, and start with coffee.

It is probably worth noting that most of these women are financially comfortable. It is not inexpensive to be there; it is not a nursing home. Many of the women have been privately educated and have experienced Shakespeare as part of their English Literature classes at school. In the Guild, they each have their own rooms, which are scaled-down versions of their former residences. Of the eight women generally participating, there is a Doctor of Literature who at 93, still rises at 6:00 a.m. to translate Pushkin from Russian into English. There is also a Donald Wolfit dancer, who was Mustardseed in one of his productions, as well as a 94-year-old woman who still attends the Dartington Literary Festival. They are mentally agile, but physically less so. The Guild House was set up for such women. They are passionate about Shakespeare and remember *Macbeth* and *King Lear* from their youth.

The texts speak clearly to these participants. As Richards suggests, when reflecting on the "outsider" in *King Lear:* "There's always that kind of figure—with Jaques for example, in *As You Like It*—so I suppose it can be somebody that's older or wiser." In regards even more specifically to *Lear,* he adds: "The play is really about change. We look at change. Lear goes through everything— goes to being a child again- suggested by all the inhabitations, of woods, heaths, castles, this constant process of change. The under- going change of people is memorably examined." For this group, "age" is the "who's in and who's out" that cries out for inclusivity. This becomes apparent through *Lear.* If, as Beckett's HAMM in *Endgame* says, "the end is in the beginning and yet you go on"; so too, to my mind, can there be beginnings in the end. When I sug- gested to the women, for instance, that I struggled with how, as a director, you choose to play the later mad scenes with Lear turned child, facing dementia, the women suggested that I felt challenged because I have not gotten to that point yet. These scenes could not be entirely understood, they indicated, until one has reached old age. Once again, such perspectives remind me of Lanier's reflection about the nature of the Shakespearean Rhizome, being "never a sta- ble object but an aggregated field in a perpetual state of becoming."[6] It has reminded and encouraged me to consider the end as a start- ing point when looking at Shakespeare's play and to think about the idea of "becoming." This group's line of flight and its direction might be different than those of other readers/viewers of the play, but their interpretation of *King Lear* reflects where they are in their lives and expresses elements of their status as people contending with reduced social recognition. There is also an opportunity for these elderly women to re-connect to Shakespeare, re-experiencing a play they last encountered as a younger person and to observe it in a different way. This has proved to be an enriching experience. Discussions of the play, and characters' trajectories are often spo- ken about in correspondence with their own lives. *King Lear* became a particularly poignant choice, for example, when the women revisited their thoughts on familial relationships. Their experience with the text also offers something that is by its nature inclusive and ahead of its time. All these actors are old—and they choose to play their characters with their aged voices. They do not put on young voices to play younger characters like Cordelia, and Lear is read by a very elderly woman, a process that allows this aged old man-king to resonate more forcefully. These women remind us that when we are considering diverse voices, we must not overlook the aged. Just as we increasingly embrace concepts suggesting that Shakespeare's characters can be played by anyone, elderly players should remain part of that. If there are directors wanting a real insight into how this play can be cracked open to "see it, feelingly" then look to these kinds of voices for how we might really socially dream *King Lear.*

These disparate groups of VI and elderly actors bring out aspects of *Lear* that we can all appreciate. Their efforts illustrate the value of incorporating a wide range of players into this work. There are still many performative and textual lessons to be learned through such endeavors, and the Shakespeare world has only begun to understand and appreciate this richness.

Notes

1. Shakespeare citations from *The Arden Shakespeare Complete Works,* ed. Richard Proudfoot, Anne Thompson, and David Scott Kastan (Walton on Thames: Thomas Nelson, 1998).

2. Denise Albanese, *Extramural Shakespeare* (New York: Palgrave Macmillan, 2010), 114.

3. Douglas Lanier, "Shakespearean Rhizomatics: Adaptation, Ethics, Value," http://www.academia.edu/12170317/Shakespearean_Rhizomatics_Adaptation_Ethics_Value

4. Personal Conversation, October 2018.

5. Private conversation, 2018.

6. Lanier, "Shakespearean Rhizomatics."

"Give me your hands"

Robert Shaughnessy

"Give me your hands, if we be friends . . ."[1]

"**D**OYOYOYOYING!" There are two players in this game, facing each other at the center of a circle, one with thumbs and forefingers making an O-shape, miming eyeballs, the kind that in classic-era cartoons leap out on stalks on the cue of love at first sight. One plays Titania, the other Bottom, and the exchange distils the first encounter between the weaver and the fairy queen in three lines ("Doyoyoyoying! / I love thee"; "Nay!") and matching gestures; Bottom's task is to prowl the circle, evading Titania's hungry gaze, hers is to catch his eye. At this instant, Titania is played by an actor, Bottom by a young male teenager, an audience member turned active participant in Flute Theatre's version of *A Midsummer Night's Dream,* a show devised, as the company publicity states, specifically for autistic young people and their families, as part of the broader mission of creating Shakespeare for inclusive audiences. They play through the sequence three or four times, then swap roles, and they are joined in the circle by more of the ensemble's six actors, and by more of the dozen or so audience participants. The game lasts for some six or seven minutes, until a gentle ping of a hand-held cymbal, performed by the show's director, Kelly Hunter, signals that it is time to move on to the next episode, and the next game: "I'll give thee fairies to attend on thee . . ." (3.1.292).

I shall return to this moment below; first, some context. Flute's *Dream,* directed by Hunter, designed by Daisy Blower with music composed by Tom Chapman, premiered at the Orange Tree Theatre, Richmond, in October 2017, and has subsequently been performed at the Heart of America Shakespeare Festival in Kansas City (January 2018), at the Bridge Theatre, London (February 2018), again at the Orange Tree (October 2018), at the Chichester Festival Theatre

(March 2019) and, in a Catalan version with Spanish actors, at the Teatre Lliure, Barcelona (March 2018).[2] It is the second of the company's full-scale autism-centered Shakespeare productions; the first was *The Tempest,* which was the product of a three-year collaborative partnership between Hunter and The Ohio State University, and which was staged at the RSC's The Other Place in 2014.[3] This in turn grew out of Hunter's workshop practice, developed with autistic young people from the early 1990s onwards; which stemmed, firstly, from what the American late-modernist poet Louis Zukofsky identified as an interwoven thematic preoccupation in Shakespeare's work with love and reason, the eyes and the mind, and, secondly, from what she terms "Shakespeare's heartbeat," the steady (and steadying) pulse of iambic pentameter.[4] Arriving, via Zukofsky, at "Shakespeare's definitions of seeing, thinking and loving," Hunter "stumbled upon the processes that those on the [autism] spectrum find so difficult to achieve," and the mechanism of the heartbeat offered a means of anchoring these sensations within the individual and collective bodies of performers and participants, thereby addressing the "dissociation of body and mind" that is endemic to autism.[5] To briefly summarize: a condition affecting around one per cent of the population in the United Kingdom (two per cent in the United States), autism is a spectrum of abilities, behaviors, and challenges that range from the highest functioning to the lowest; and that are characterized, to varying degrees, by difficulties with (in the terms of the classic "triad of impairments" model) communication, imagination, and social interaction. Its manifestations are as various and diverse as the individuals who inhabit it, and may include, on the one hand, stereotypical, repetitive and socially inappropriate behaviors, limited verbal expression, obsessive special interests, restlessness and physical impulsiveness, and the apparent inability to read the emotions and intentions of others; and, on the other, an extraordinary aptitude for detailed intellectual work, memorization, and creative and artistic (especially musical) expression. Such labels only get us so far; the "dissociation" that Hunter identifies is perhaps better articulated from within the experience of autism itself, as in this account by the (at the time of writing) thirteen-year-old autistic writer Naoki Higashida:

Now your mind is a room where twenty radios, all tuned to different stations, are blaring out voices and music. The radios have no off-switches or volume controls, the room you're in has no door or window, and relief will come only when you're too exhausted to stay awake. To make matters worse, another hitherto unrecognized editor has just quit without notice—your editor of the senses. Suddenly sensory input from your environment is flooding in too, unfiltered in quality and over-whelming in quantity. Colors and patterns swim and clamour for your attention. The fabric conditioner in your sweater smells as strong as air-freshener fired up your nostrils. Your comfy jeans are now as scratchy as steel wool. Your vestibular and proprioceptive senses are also out of kilter, so the floor keeps tilting like a ferry in heavy seas, and you're no longer sure where your hands and feet are in relation to the rest of you. You can feel the plates of your skull, plus your facial muscles and your jaw: your head feels trapped inside a motorcycle helmet three sizes too small which may or may not explain why the air-conditioner is as deaf-ening as an electric drill, but your father—who's right here in front of you—sounds as if he's speaking to you from a cell phone, on a train going through lots of short tunnels, in fluent Cantonese.[6]

Higashida's evocation of the cacophonous sensorium of autism, a world of stimuli that can be neither filtered nor disentangled, and of rhythms that are fractured and dyssynchronous, offers a clue to the appeal of the steady, grounded pulse of the iambic heartbeat.

Whether in workshop or performance, this beat is both start and endpoint of action, as well as its latent, implicit pulse throughout. The *Dream* begins with performers and children forming a circle on the edges of a large cloth, daubed with swirls of various shades of forest green flecked with russet brown; they may take time to set-tle (and some prefer to hover beyond the circle, engaged or disen-gaged after their own fashion). They are watched by a further outer circle of parents, carers, and friends. Hunter initiates the "Heart-beat Hello": right hand, palm flat, beats softly against chest, a per-cussive accompaniment to the half-said, half-sung "Hel-*lo* . . . Hel-*lo* . . . " that spreads and swells around the inner, then outer, cir-cles, and that is sustained, sometimes, for many minutes, "to give space and time," as Hunter puts it, "for 'internal panics' to soothe."[7] The sequence is mirrored at the close of the play, which ends with Puck joining hands first with Titania ("take hands with me"), and then with each child in the circle, and spinning; the resettling that follows is a leave taking "Good-*bye* . . . Good-*bye*," again semi-sung, with a descending cadence. Following the "Heart-beat Hello," the game shifts to "Throwing the Face," wherein the play's dramatic personae (the lovers, Titania, Puck, and Bottom), as well as its emotional palate, are introduced by Hunter and the actors as a series of set facial expressions, caricature masks (Happy, Angry, Sad, Fearful, Disgusted, Surprised), collectively mimicked and "thrown" with a flick of the head from one player to the next. Finlay Cormack, as Puck, leaps into the center:

> I'll follow you, I'll lead you a round,
> Sometime a horse I'll be, sometime a hound,
> A hog, a headless bear, sometime a storm;
> And neigh, and bark, and grunt, and roar, and stir,
> Like horse, hound, hog, bear, storm at every turn.[8]

Turning on a dime multiple times in every line, Puck models each of his transformations in extravagant gesture and sound: a snout fashioned from twisting fists, accompanied by snorting; barks and yelps; the roar of a headless (and so, surely, mouthless?) bear; jazz-hands flashes of lightning; the children play along after their own fashion and with varying levels of engagement and skill. There are three rounds of this, then the performance moves into the first of the adaptation's two worlds, Fairyland (The Lovers follow; of the Mechanicals' plot, Bottom's adventure in Fairyland alone remains). Loosely preserving the outlines of two of Shakespeare's three narrative strands, Flute's *Dream* stages a series of episodes, with each redacted scene first demonstrated by the actors, and then replayed, in the abbreviated form of a game, with the participants. The Fairyland section thus begins with Bottom's metamorphosis, rendered in the terms of the Shadow Game. Two lines set the scene: Oberon's "I am invisible" (2.1.186, here assigned to Puck), and Bottom's defiant declaration that he will "walk up and down" (3.1.261–62). Mimicking and exaggerating his movements, Puck shadows Bottom as he paces the circle, all the while singing a jaunty little air ("Sneaky Pete"):

At intervals, Bottom stops, as if sensing the presence of his stage-invisible stalker, and swivels on his axis while Puck (to the accompaniment of a comedy slide whistle) ducks to his knees; slightly baffled, Bottom resumes the pacing. Once the pattern of pace-turn-duck-pace is established, the player-participants are encouraged into the space to form a ragged crocodile of Pucks and Bottoms, all singing, bobbing, ducking; and then Puck engineers Bottom's ass-transformation by "throwing" the donkey face (a pair of pointing-finger ears) first to the whole group, and then to the Bottom actor: "Eeh Aw!"

Allegro

Fig. 1. "Sneaky Pete"

As the action unfolds, the sequencing of games at once sustains a sense of narrative momentum, reiterates the thematic coherence of the love-reason-eyes-mind framework, and ensures an incremental and accumulative approach to addressing the challenges of the autistic condition, which can be charted in terms of a movement from low- to (relatively) higher-risk, higher-stakes activities. A key component of the Shadow Game, Hunter stresses, is not just that it allows autistic participants to explore the often hard-to-handle sensation of experiencing someone behind and out of sight, but also the space it affords to play with the classically difficult matter of eye contact ("What we're actually looking at," writes Higashida in a formulation uncannily reminiscent of Bottom's dream, "is the other person's voice . . . we're trying to listen to the other person with all of our sense organs").[9] "With some of these children," Hunter observes, "the fact that Puck is invisible seems to eliminate their fear of eye contact, as if being unseen renders the eyes unseeing, allowing the child to explore looking into another's eyes and to experience being looked at without fear."[10] In the Shadow Game, the impetus is with the feet; in the scene that follows ("Puck's Petals"), Puck's enchantment of the kneeling Titania (a tinkle of finger-cymbals as he mime-sprinkles into her sleeping eyes) is conducted *en pointe.* For the actors, such footwork is a way of entering the imaginative and sensorial world of autism; the tendency of autists to tip-toe, and to jump, is well-known—as Higas-

hida puts it, "it's as if my feelings are going upward to the sky . . .
the motion makes me want to change into a bird and fly off to some
faraway place."[11]

It is in this light that we may return to the moment with which
we began this account: the "Doyoyoyoying" game played by love-
struck Titania and reluctant Bottom. Again, the challenge of eye
contact is centrally at issue, tackling "what for many children is a
crippling problem"; the imperative, Hunter insists, is to ensure that
"the game is as playful and funny as possible, countering the
child's intense struggle with an equal measure of play and enjoy-
ment."[12] In a sense, the game is pivotal, and its resonances are neither confined to this scene nor, indeed, to this play. In Flute's *The
Tempest,* the moment plays out at the first meeting of Ferdinand
and Miranda, where it is lent a particular poignancy and force by
Prospero's observation that "At the first sight / They have changed
eyes" (1.2.440–41): "O you wonder!" (1.2.426), they cry together,
"Doyoyoyoying!" In *Dream,* it is the desperate mating-call of the
mismatched lovers' quartet when they are first introduced:

> HELEN
> We should be wooed, and were not made to woo
> I love Demetrius						(jealous doyoyoyoying)
> DEMETRIUS
> I love you not therefore pursue me not
> I love Hermia						(frustrated doyoyoyoying)
> HERMIA
> Lysander and myself shall fly this place
> I love Lysander						(lovesick doyoyoyoying)
> LYSANDER
> The course of true love never did run smooth
> I love Hermia						(amorous doyoyoyoying)

The exchange escalates while language degenerates ("woo / doyoyoyoying"; "not / doyoyoyoying"; "fly / doyoyoyoying"; "love / doyoyoyoying"), and the catchphrase becomes the performance's
leitmotif: "Doyoyoyoying/ And run through fire for thy sweet
sake"; "Doyoyoyoying/ O Helen goddess nymph perfect divine";
finally, and satisfyingly, the resolution of the lovers' conflicts is
articulated as a musical joke. Released by Puck from the spell, the
lovers rise to their feet, caper and prance, and, with a sly nod to
Mendelssohn's "Wedding March, "dong" out the marriage bells as
a four-part round:

Fig. 2. **"Wedding Doyoyoyoyings"**

Following this, Puck's lifting of the spell ("Be as thou wast wont to be/ See as thou wast wont to see" [4.1.527–8]), Titania's "What visions have I seen" (4.1.532), and Bottom's "I have had a dream. . . . The eye of man hath not heard, the ear of man hath not seen . . ." (4.1.658–63) are extraordinarily resonant.

There is no question that Flute's work in Shakespeare and autism is profoundly engaging for those who involve themselves in it, whether as performers, players or observers, and that, at least for the duration of performance time, it can be liberating, even transformational. Reports from parents, carers, practitioners and others testify to the work's unique beauty and power. Writing about the 2017 Orange Tree performance of *Dream,* a parent noticed how the actors "entered into Tim's world, rather than demanding that he enter theirs":

> At one point, an actor tapped a repeated single chime on a bell, and in the ensuing silence each participant in turn closed their eyes and turned to follow the direction of the sound. This was a spellbinding, beautiful moment with everyone in the room intensely focussed on each child. The silence and calm was magical. It felt almost religious, as though a sacred space had been created, within which something transformative was happening.

Another parent reports a moment of rougher magic: "When we got home, we had to do the bean [*sic*]/ maypole skit for 15 minutes and then she wanted to sword fight. I love that she wanted to interact with me; even though she was chopping me with a sword—I'll take it" (the skit referred to is the 'Maypole & Bead' game, which renders Hermia and Helena's exchange of insults—"thou painted maypole"; "You bead, you acorn" (3.2.297, 331)—as a danced duel of leaps and rolls). Theater artist Michael Whistler, participating in a Kansas City performance, describes the physical and verbal reactions of a young man, "perhaps 17 years old": "Sometimes he laughs or shrieks wildly at a moment in the play or the games, or rolls full on his back, grabbing his cross-legged ankles," at other times, he "continues to create rejoinders from non-sequiturs, referencing 'Rocket J. Squirrel' and 'Bagheera' from *The Jungle Book.*" His response to Hermia's "I love thee'": "ICEBERG AHEAD!" For Whistler, the realization comes that "these are not non-sequiturs: they are the landmarks within his landscape."[13]

The harder question to answer is what it is about the work that makes it so affecting. I have indicated some of the elements that make it so amenable to accommodating the autistic condition (and the flexibility, openness and accepting responsiveness of the actors is not the least of these): the strongly patterned and iterative nature of the games align with autistic preference for repetition and predictability; the emphasis on rhythmically coordinated imitation and synchronized action addresses some of autism's key areas of difficulty, fostering the mutual empathy, interaction, communication (both verbal and non-verbal) and prosociality that the condition is understood to inhibit. To conclude, however, I want to foreground an aspect that has already been noted in the foregoing pages, one that is heard not only in the airs and theme tunes, and in Tom Chapman's delicately haunting, near-continuous guitar score, but also in the "Helloes" and "Goodbyes" that hover between speech and song, and the "Doyoyoyoyings" that literally turn into a musical phrase: its musicality. The relationship between music and autism has received increasing attention in recent years, both in the sense that (as mentioned at the start of this essay) the condition has been associated with high, sometimes exceptional, levels of musical ability, and in the growing recognition that music making offers many autists a unique and unparalleled means of interaction, communication and self-expression. The reasons why this is so are much-discussed and complex, but are generally agreed to be rooted in the distinctive mental architecture of autism itself. Higashida, again, provides a way in: differentiating the ways in which autists and non-autists (or, if you prefer neurodivergent and neurotypical persons) perceive the world, he writes:

When you see an object, it seems that you see it as an entire thing first, and only afterwards do its details follow on. But for people with autism, the details jump straight out at us first of all, and then only gradually, detail by detail, does the whole image sort of float up into focus. When part of the whole image captures our eyes first depends on a number of things. When a colour is vivid or a shape is eye-catching, then that's the detail that claims our attention, and then our hearts kind of drown in it . . .[14]

Transposed from the field of vision to that of audition, this richly perceived acoustic and sensory environment is the positive corollary of the overwhelmingly hyperstimulatory soundscape evoked earlier; it is an account of what is variously referred to as (negatively) the "weak central coherence" or (positively) "detail-focused" processing style that is characteristic of autism. For music and autism expert Adam Ockelford, this capacity to prioritize the detail over the Gestalt, at least initially, is one of the traits that enables an autistic person to instantly apprehend the individual notes and pitches within complex musical structures, and also to perceive order in apparent chaos. The result, Ockelford conjectures, is that the autist's experience of music is "likely to be very different from that of the majority: more vivid, more intense, more exciting, more exhausting. . . . Each pitch may be like a familiar friend in an otherwise confusing world."[15]

For Ockelford and others, collaborative music-making creates the potential to address at least two of the three components of the classic triad of impairments, fostering as it does both social interaction and mutually empathic communication; moreover, the emphasis on autistic musicianship as an *ability* rather than a symptom of *dis*ability is in tune with the broader turn from a deficit model of autism to one of diversity and difference. In the music of Flute's Shakespeare, there is yet a further dimension; one that reaches into the third corner of the autism triad, and one that music making, perhaps, cannot engage on its own. Activating the "as if" within a musical framework it invites its players to interact, to communicate, and also to *imagine* differently, sometimes with startling results ("I love thee"; "ICEBERG AHEAD!"). On these terms, Shakespeare's world is a "third space" co-inhabited by the neurodivergent and the neurotypical, owned by neither. It is a space in which to meet, a space to play, and, most of all, a space to dream.

Notes

My thanks to Kelly Hunter and the members of Flute Theatre for their help with this essay.

1. *A Midsummer Night's Dream,* 5.2.76. References to Shakespeare's plays come from Gary Taylor et. al., eds, *The New Oxford Shakespeare: The Complete Works* (Oxford: Oxford University Press, 2016), and, where specified, to the unpublished working script of Flute Theatre's *A Midsummer Night's Dream,* 2017.

2. The original cast was Tom Chapman, Finlay Cormack, Tas Emiabata, Oliver Grant, Paula Rodriguez, and Katy Stephens.

3. The original cast was Greg Hicks, Chris McDonald, Kevin McClatchy, Mahmoud Osman, Robin Post, and Eva Lily.

4. See Louis Zukofsky, *Bottom: On Shakespeare* (Berkeley, CA: University of California Press, 1987).

5. Kelly Hunter, *Shakespeare's Heartbeat: Drama games for children with autism* (London: Routledge, 2015), 4–5. I am aware that Hunter's identification of iambic pentameter with the human heartbeat (which also has been proposed by practitioners such as Patsy Rodenburg) is open to challenge, as what W. B. Worthen would term a "naturalizing metaphor" which (in his view misleadingly) "appears to enable the body to recapture itself" (*Shakespeare and the Authority of Performance* [Cambridge: Cambridge University Press, 1997], 99): more technically, as Derek Mong puts it, "the iamb *resembles* the heartbeat, but it is no more innate or biologically justified than free verse *or* another of the world's many meters" ("Iambic Pentameter has Nothing to do with your Heart," *The Kenyon Review,* 16 April 2016, https://www.kenyonreview.org/2016/04/iambic-pentameter-nothing-heart/). For current purposes, as I have argued elsewhere, the value of the heartbeat equation, as with any acting tool, lies less in its theoretical or biomedical rigor than in what, in workshop, rehearsal or performance, it manages to get done. See Robert Shaughnessy, "'All eyes': Experience, Spectacle and the Inclusive Audience in Flute Theatre's *The Tempest,*" in *Shakespeare: Actors & Audiences,* ed. Fiona Banks (London: Bloomsbury Arden Shakespeare, 2018), 119–38.

6. Naoki Higashida, *The Reason I Jump: one boy's voice from the silence of autism,* trans. K. A. Yoshida and David Mitchell (New York: Random House, 2016), 2–3.

7. Hunter, *Shakespeare's Heartbeat,* 5.

8. Flute *Dream,* n.p., cf. 3.1.249–54; "storm" emends "fire" at 252 and 254.

9. Higashida, *The Reason I Jump,* 43.

10. Hunter, *Shakespeare's Heartbeat,* 26.

11. Higashida, *The Reason I Jump,* 76–77.

12. Hunter, *Shakespeare's Heartbeat,* 36.

13. All comments taken from the Flute Theatre website, http://www.flutetheatre.co.uk/

14. Higashida, *The Reason I Jump,* 91–92.

15. Adam Ockelford, *Music, Language and Autism: Exceptional Strategies for Exceptional Minds* (London: Jessica Kinsgsley, 2013), 226.

ProTactile Shakespeare: Inclusive Theater by/for the DeafBlind

JILL MARIE BRADBURY, JOHN LEE CLARK, RACHEL
GROSSMAN, JASON HERBERS, VICTORIA MAGLIOCCHINO,
JASPER NORMAN, YASHAIRA ROMILUS, ROBERT T. SIRVAGE,
LISA VAN DER MARK

> All changes in space which we see, hear, smell or taste are liter-
> ally tactile impressions. All our senses are variations of our
> unique sense of touch.
>
> *Rudolf von Laban*[1]

Introduction

IN 2016, the National Endowment for the Arts awarded Gallaudet
University a $25,000 grant to develop and document models of the-
ater for DeafBlind people by DeafBlind people. Using *Romeo and
Juliet* as the starting point, the project proposed to explore how
immersive theater techniques could be leveraged to create a dramatic experience rooted in the emerging DeafBlind language
known as ProTactile (PT) and the perceptual experiences of Deaf-
Blind people.[2] The grant project had two main goals. First, to generate models and practices that could be shared with the national and
international DeafBlind community. Second, to challenge conventional paradigms of dramatic performance. How do artistic processes and practices lead to exclusionary theater? How does access
for, rather than inclusion of people with disabilities reinforce these
exclusions? What would inclusive, rather than accessible, theater
processes and practices look like for DeafBlind actors and audiences?

In July/August 2018, six DeafBlind participants, a sighted Deaf project director, and a sighted hearing theater artist advisor gathered for a week of intense playing with Shakespeare, PT, and tactile/olfactorial/gustatorial props. At the end of the ProTactile Theater Institute (PTTI), participants workshopped scenes from *Romeo and Juliet* for a small audience composed of DeafBlind, Deaf, and sighted individuals. Unlike the hierarchical and director-led framework of much traditional theater, our process was intensely group oriented. Every element of the theatrical experience, from performance model, script, set design, costume elements, props, tactile cues, came out of collaborative discussion and decision making. To respect the nature of this work, this article is also structured as a collaborative piece in which participants reflect on their experience and share insights from a week spent living, breathing, and dreaming PT Shakespeare.[3]

Overview

ProTactile began to emerge in 2007. As aj granda and Jelica Nuccio explain, their work at the DeafBlind Service Center in Seattle, Washington led them to develop efficient ways to communicate with each other without interpreters. They also began formulating the PT philosophy of autonomy and respect for DeafBlind space.[4] As Nuccio explains in a video interview, "Touch becomes a means for DeafBlind to be more autonomous. This means, for example, that we set up a ProTactile zone that is open to DeafBlind with no barriers. We DeafBlind don't have to wait for someone sighted to come and lead us around."[5] While PT practices are still developing, granda and Nuccio have documented its central principles. One of the most important is the idea of contact space. While ASL uses the space around the body, PT uses the body instead. Arms, chest area, and legs are used to express linguistic information conveyed by pointing, role shifting, and air space in ASL. Bodily touch is also used for backchannelling, communicating visual information such as head nodding or shaking, and intensity of emotional response (4–7). Another important PT principle is using signs that are easy to feel and are grounded in tactile, rather than visual experience (13). Spatial mapping, in addition to being expressed on the body, also uses tactile markers rather than visual ones. As granda and Nuccio write in their statement of principles:

Suppose you are giving directions to someone in the same place where you are communicating, for example, they are a visitor in your home and they want to know where the kitchen is. You start by finding a physical thing nearby that will not move, such as a table, a railing, or a door. That will function as a landmark for the starting place. Once the listener has touched the starting place, explain where to go by describing additional landmarks on the body of the listener in relation to the starting place (10).

Finally, granda and Nuccio emphasize that PT is not just "a way of explaining things to DeafBlind people that they can't see" but a way of connecting people through shared experiences (14).

ProTactile Theatre Institute participants spent the week devising a theatrical model and practices grounded in how they experience the world through touch. Their adaptation was similar in approach to immersive theater productions such as Punchdrunk's *Sleep No More,* in which audiences move through a series of rooms and view performance tableaux portraying *Macbeth.* Unlike *Sleep No More,* however, interaction between actors and audience members was central to the experience. PT requires contact—hands touching hands—in two-way or three-way communication. Each patron, as the audience members were called, could engage with only one or two actors.[6] This shaped how the workshop production of *Romeo and Juliet* was structured, as discussed by John Lee Clark and Robert Sirvage below. Actors needed to maintain physical connection with patrons throughout the entire performance. Dialogue between characters had to be devised to be easily understood by the patron, using PT principles. Given the limited time frame and enormous task of developing new conventions for everything from set design to taking final bows, participants did not devote much time to translation of Shakespeare's language into PT dialogue. Rather, they focused on identifying the key emotions in the various scenes and how to express those through touch. As Lisa van der Mark explains, though, the actors did create a DeafBlind-centered translation of Juliet's famous line, "You kiss by the book."

The production contained five parts; the prologue, the Capulet party, the balcony rendezvous, Tybalt's murder, and an epilogue. Because the PTTI lasted only one week, the scenes were condensed considerably. The Capulet party, for example, focused on Romeo meeting Juliet and then finding out about her identity from the Nurse. Mercutio was cut from the fight scene. Instead, a drunk Tybalt accosts Romeo, who ends up killing him. The total performance time for each patron was about twenty minutes. The cast included two Romeos and two Juliets, so that patrons could be staggered about ten minutes apart. As Victoria Magliocchino explains, patrons began their theatrical experience in a lobby. They met each actor and felt the costumes to help them recognize the character when encountered during the performance. One actor played a Townsperson who delivered the prologue to each participant, gave them a bead necklace, and then led them into the Capulet party. Patrons ate, drank, and socialized with each other while waiting for their individualized performance to begin. At the end of the performance, each patron met the Townsperson again, who provided narrative closure through the epilogue. Once a patron finished the performance, the actors returned to the party scene to pick up a new patron and begin again. Patrons also returned to the party after removing their bead necklaces. This allowed the actors to identify which patrons had already experienced the performance and which had not.

The individualized performance began when an actor playing Romeo approached a patron looking for a beautiful woman he had just met. Romeo took the patron in search of Juliet and found her, leading to the pilgrim hands scene. The Nurse then interrupted and sent Juliet off to her mother (allowing the actress to get in position for the next scene). The Nurse also informed Romeo who Juliet's family is. Romeo left in despair (allowing the actor to get into position for the next scene as well). The Nurse and patron then went to Juliet, transitioning the patron to the balcony scene. While Juliet was bewailing her fate, Romeo found her and vowed to give up his family name for her. They made plans to marry the next day. The Nurse interrupted several times during this and finally pulled Juliet away (the actress then went back to the party to wait for the next performance round). Romeo and the patron then snuck back through the Capulet hall where they encountered Tybalt. A fight ensued and spilled out onto the street (i.e., hallway); Romeo killed Tybalt, then told the patron they must split up and pushed him/her through a door (then the actor returned to the party to start another performance with a new patron). The patron was met outside the door by the Townsperson, who performed the epilogue and then led the patron back into the party. Having them return helped maintain the feeling of a crowded party, as well as lengthening the overall experience for the patrons.

As Robert Sirvage discusses below, the set reflected DeafBlind space principles. It was small, encompassing a lobby, a narrow room, a patio, and part of a hall. The dimensions facilitated Deaf-Blind orientation and interactions, as well as tactile cues for the actors, by keeping everyone in close proximity. Scents were also integrated to identify characters. Because the audience included DeafBlind with varying degrees of vision loss, the set did include visual, as well as tactile and olfactory elements. All patrons were also offered masks to help focus on the tactile experience, if desired.

Reflections

Jill Bradbury, Project Director

My inspiration for this grant project came from conversations with John Lee Clark, a DeafBlind writer. Clark made me aware that theater for DeafBlind people does not exist. What little access Deaf-Blind people have to theater comes through tactile interpretations of productions designed for hearing patrons. Even the world's only DeafBlind theater troupe, the Israeli Nalaga'at, performs for sighted audiences. As Clark explains in "My Dream Play," "A one-person show might be OK; poetry and storytelling are nice. But there's nothing more alien to DeafBlind culture than a play on a stage . . . For DeafBlind people, there is no direct connection. It all comes through an interpreter, secondhand, in a jumble, and you're lost."[7] I wanted to help make Clark's dream play a reality.

From the beginning, I thought of this project as inclusive, rather than applied, theater. As Mojisola Adebayo writes, the diverse practices covered under the applied label are similar in focusing on access or power dynamics for certain social groups and the potential of theater to challenge these hierarchies. But, as she also points out, applied "suggests that someone is doing something to someone else by implementing theatre."[8] This account matches the approach that seems common in groups that work on theater with autistic and developmentally disabled individuals without involving them in the process of creating the theatrical practices themselves. In contrast, our project brought together DeafBlind people to explore together how immersive theater techniques could be leveraged to create a dramatic experience rooted in the DeafBlind community's unique ways of being in the world and the emerging language known as PT. As the two sighted people involved, theater artist Rachel Grossman and I aimed to support DeafBlind autonomy and avoid being "intervenors."[9] While we gave advice when asked, our primary role during the PTTI was to organize the resources needed to enable DeafBlind decision making and artistic experimentation. As when anyone from a privileged group works with a socially marginalized group, we experienced moments of tension. At times, we behaved in ways that were insensitive to the social conventions of interacting with DeafBlind people. But, through willingness to own our mistakes and the commitment of the group to making the project a success, we were able to resolve these difficulties. The result was creative and beautiful theater that challenges conventional theatrical practice and aesthetics.

John Lee Clark, DeafBlind Writer

"My Dream Play" described PT theater as designed for a Deaf-Blind audience. No stage, no rows of chairs. A theater where Deaf-Blind people can take all the roles—director, actor, translator, set designer, choreographer, costume designer. I also explained a basic model that I called "the mingle" where attendees and actors interact. It does not matter what order attendees take in the overall story. Each actor has a goal to accomplish while meeting each attendee. For *Romeo and Juliet,* we could have two fake corpses, in their death shrouds, and the event is the funeral. Attendees would meet all the key characters of the play, except for Romeo and Juliet. They get different characters' reactions and attitudes. They may even meet a young couple who were inspired by Romeo and Juliet's love.

For the PTTI, I developed several versions of this model to structure the interaction between audience members and actors. The first is a series of scenes with different characters. This approach involves setting things up and placing actors in a series of rooms or areas. Attendees would go through these in order and interact with the actors that belong to these rooms. If a play is broken into two distinct acts, it would then be possible to meet some or all the characters again, played by the same actors.

The second model I call the "conveyer belt." This is similar to the first model in that it involves a series of scenes—different rooms or areas. But attendees are being propelled by tagging along with a character. It is possible for an attendee to tag along with a character then get passed over to another character. With PT, we can have two-way or three-way interactions for dialogue. Each scene would basically either have one or two characters. This may call for having multiple actors play Romeo or Juliet. If there are, for example, three Romeos, Romeo A can go first, and when Romeo A is done with the first scene, Romeo B goes into the first scene with the second attendee, and Romeo C follows afterwards. If this play is split into two acts, this means two shorter conveyor belts rather than a longer conveyor belt. The three Romeos, for example, might go through three scenes twice for the first act. This means processing six attendees, before everyone moves on to the second act.

What do the attendees do after they go through first act and before they can proceed into the second act? This brings up a concept I am calling the Flood. It is crafted into the production and is a flexible, elastic intermission. Minor characters or extras could be involved with that, to help attendees stay engaged in the story. Such characters could "gossip" with attendees and flesh out their understanding of the story. Attendees could eat or inspect objects during this time. The second act could begin immediately after the last attendee is done with the first act, or the Flood may have something that will happen with everyone involved. This is one way to incorporate a fight scene. Have everyone crowded together and the actors push and shove, like a mosh pit, before the second conveyor belt starts moving. Parallel conveyor belts would help process more attendees. A simple conveyor belt could mean having three Romeos but only one Juliet—that is to say, Juliet is tied to a scene or scenes, while the three Romeos move through in turn—while a parallel conveyor belt may mean needing three sets of actors playing Romeos and Juliet.

The final model was inspired by the annual Seabeck DeafBlind Retreat. In this model, all the players become directors of, as well as an actor in, a short one-scene performance. Each player takes two attendees, helps them don a costume, discusses the scene with them, gives them each a role, walks them through the scene, shows them the props, etc., then the three perform the scene. For *Romeo and Juliet,* the double suicide situation is great. The actor could take the role of a Friend, while two attendees adopt the roles of Romeo and Juliet. There can be a bed or a mat, maybe some flowers to give a whiff of a funeral. This approach makes attendees at once both actors and audience. Juliet can feel Romeo shaking her, expressing tactile gestures of shock and grief, she can feel that Romeo and the Friend are arguing about something via their tactile signing on her body, and she feels Romeo "die" over her or next to her. When she "wakes up," Romeo, now playing dead, can feel her waking up and shaking him, expressing herself tactilely, arguing with the Friend, and so on. This is a fusion of acting and being an audience, of performance and enactment—it is all about experience and not at all about being on display.

Jasper Norman and Yashaira Romilus, Institute Facilitators

In the fall of 2017, we created the first ever theater production for DeafBlind by DeafBlind. We used *Gift of the Magi* as our script and performed it again in May 2018. From these two productions, we learned how to convey the major points of the story into PT language, key components of room-mapping technique as in feeling tactile markers in our environments, PT cues and tricks to identify a person's turn or how to comfortably perform a kiss without actually kissing the person, tips from PT Theatre team, and about maintaining a PT Zone throughout the play in a space designed for and by DB people.

We applied these lessons throughout the *Romeo and Juliet* group experience. The PTTI taught us the value of PT communication. As facilitators, we knew communication would be a crucial key in working as a team. It was a challenge working with sighted non-PT users in a strong PT Zone. We learned how to work with DeafBlind people with various communication styles and background experiences. We also learned about foot movements from Rachel Grossman. Foot movements specify how to move while acting in coordination with each other in a room. For example, Juliet's balcony scene in a dreamy expression changing to fear while being mindful of where and how feet are being moved. We also kept full PT language inclusion with mindful foot movements as well.

Fortunately for our PTTI group, we had two of four DeafBlind participants who could explain Shakespeare to everyone. It was interesting to learn about *Romeo and Juliet*'s characters and the metaphors in the storyline. The most cherished moment was the enthusiastic responses shared by the patrons who experienced a full tactile historical story through PT. The full tactile coordination of *Romeo and Juliet* was built upon the PTTI group's creativity. A part of the PT philosophy emphasizes teamwork, and the PT philosophy was reflected in the whole PTTI story development which incorporated the PT language naturally into the creativity of the group. In the future, PT Theatre will visit different DeafBlind communities to share PT language and philosophy through a full tactile production experience.

Victoria Magliocchino, Institute Participant

Mingling with five other DeafBlind participants who are brilliant and proficient at PT was a mind-blowing experience for me. The *Gift of the Magi* performance by Jasper and Yash helped give us ideas about how we could present *Romeo and Juliet.* John Lee Clark's models also helped! As I learned PT principles, I realized we do not need to use the exact lines from Shakespeare but can express the story line and emotions in PT. We can easily modify Shakespeare's language into PT while keeping the themes/symbols. Since the project was experimental, we did not mount a full production. We chose scenes to convey the most important ideas. We included the party, balcony, and fight scenes with Tybalt.

For the performance, we chose John Lee Clark's model of the conveyor belt. We had two Romeos, two Juliets, one Nurse, one Tybalt and one Townsman/narrator. At the start of the performance, we stood in line and introduced our characters to the patrons. The patrons felt our costumes and learned our family affiliation. The Townsperson/narrator then took each patron and began the prologue. After that, the patrons entered the party scene. Patrons, characters, and some "extras" mingled together in a small space with food and drinks, giving the feel of a large party. The first Romeo then began the action with the first patron. When that patron moved to the balcony scene, the second Romeo found the second patron and began the action. After the fight, the Townsperson met each patron and provided an epilogue. At the same time, the Romeos went back to the party scene and began with the next patron.

During our week together, we developed tactile cues to orient us in the set and to time our scenes. Our set was small, which allowed us to navigate the space easily. For example, Nurse stood next to Romeo during the "pilgrim hands" part. This allowed her to get the cue from him to take over with the patron when he needed to leave to get in place for the next scene. The balcony scene was just out the door of the room on a patio with metal railings. We added plants to give the feeling of being outdoors and to suggest that the balcony belonged to a rich family. We also used the railings to find our places. During the balcony scene, Romeo banged on the railing to give Nurse, who was waiting in the corner, the cues to interrupt his exchange with Juliet. For future plays, it should be possible to use furniture and props to find our way around and identify our places. It is important that they be placed properly. I remember that with the second patron, Romeo could not find the lavender bouquet to give to Juliet. Nurse had to feel around the buffet table and find the flowers for Romeo. In the future, someone needs to be responsible for making sure the props go back to the proper places for the subsequent performances.

We also experimented with scents. We chose peony for Juliet (a fruity and youthful scent), lavender for Nurse (a scent for older ladies), and men's cologne for Romeo. We also had Tybalt drink beer between scenes, to help the patrons understand his hot tempered and violent actions. In post-performance interviews, patrons said they noticed the scents.

Lisa van der Mark, Institute Participant

We had a dynamic group, and each person added a personal touch to the play, providing valuable input from their own characters and experiences. We had an English teacher who would tell us how the scenes actually went in Shakespeare; a Deaf Space architect to design our space and invent cues to make the play run more smoothly and naturally; and two actors who taught and practiced with us how to better perform our roles. One participant was an expert in PT and would provide feedback if our lines were unclear. He loved deep discussions about details. It was an honor to work, discuss, and learn with them.

Working with *Romeo and Juliet* was fun. We kept saying, "Remember, these were kids of 13 and 16 years old! So young . . . so full of hormones, impulsive actions, and so absorbed in each other." Discussing and acting it out provided a deeper insight into their world. I found that the choosing of the scenes came almost naturally. Of course, there was reason behind it. No *Romeo and Juliet* could exclude the balcony scene. But it was in our hands how long it would take and how important it should be. And by not following the plot too closely (not aiming to replicate exactly how Shakespeare wrote it), we were better able to translate it into our DeafBlind experience, through setting, scene design, etc. For example, the fight scene happened to develop "by accident" when we

were just playing around with body language. We had put a mattress on the floor. For fun, we started fighting each other off the mattress by pushing or pulling the other person. After this, the activity
leader put a cup in a corner, and one of us had to defend it, while
the other was to try to get the cup. These were helpful exercises to
be comfortable physically and 'read' other people's body movement. Then we decided to see how these activities might apply to
the fight scene in the play. At first, we set it up so that Romeo was
with the patron and Tybalt stood back to back with the patron. This
let the Tybalt actor secretly give a clue to the Romeo actor that he/
she was there. Then Tybalt would move around to the front and
attack Romeo while the patron was between them. The fists were
going relatively slow and soft, hitting Romeo and Tybalt's body, but
also the patron's body, so the patron was part of the fight. The final
fight scene ended up differently: Romeo and the patron run into
Tybalt on the way out of the Capulet party, and the fight was much
rougher and more realistic. It ended with Tybalt being stabbed and
crushed to death on the ground. When we were rehearsing, there
was less space used, with no sandwiching and Tybalt practically
half-thrown on the mattress; the patron would sometimes fall down
with Tybalt. This was not very productive, of course, as we all
would be unable to continue, because laughing so hard at the
resulting clumsiness. So the fight scene was different from the body
language experiment, but I think it might not have been part of the
production if we had not first played around like that. With the
fight scene, I believe the actors genuinely enjoyed themselves and
the reactions of the patrons varied the most. A hearing sighted
woman with lots of experience in the theater world got the opportunity to experience this play with her eyes covered. She thought
the fight scene was scary, which was a surprise to me; I realized
how much our personal experiences had influenced the way we
each felt the play.

The scenes presented interesting challenges in how to convey
their messages and emotions to the audience. During the party, two
different actors would be with the patron, and the challenge was to
balance this and not to leave someone waiting alone. We had discussions about how to express Romeo's passion, which manners
and which wordings would work, and how to convey the fact that
it was a REAL kiss, not just two hands, bodies, and heads moving
together. How could we convince the patron that the lips touched,
or at least the kiss was near the lips? In the end, Romeo would hold

Juliet's face with both hands, one of which also held the patron's hand, and suggest a passionate kiss by strong movements towards Juliet's head and actually kissing near the lips. We left the rest to the patron's imagination.

Speaking of kissing, we did not spend much time on translation but we did come up with a version of the line "You kiss by the book" that incorporated DeafBlind culture. When I first read the line, I thought that it was a compliment, that it was a perfect kiss as if Romeo had studied how to do it. But in discussion it became clear that this was not a compliment at all, but that the kiss was dry and boring, passionless. First, we translated the line literally in visual ASL, then we signed the line partially on the visitor's body using the V classifier (which is how you sign read in ASL). Then we came up with a DeafBlind version of kissing by the book. I signed 'book' on the patron's body, making the chest one page and my hand the other part of the book. Then I would use the flat O classifier to represent lips 'kissing' the 'book's page'—the part of the book on the patron's chest—and moved my fingers across the chest as if kissing again and again. This process reminded us of Braille, because the fingertips touching the 'page' resembled reading by touching each dot of a Braille cell.

Jason Herbers, Institute Participant

Growing up, I never liked theater and could not keep myself engaged when I went to performances. That changed on October 20, 2017, when I attended Jasper Norman and Yash Romilus's *Gift of the Magi.* I was truly blown away by how I was immersed into the world of the play through PT. I was impressed with how everything worked and wanted to learn all of it. So, I applied to participate in PTTI even though—ahem—I was not familiar with *Romeo and Juliet.* I ended up learning a lot about the play, thanks to a couple of castmates who had extensive knowledge and were able to convey the story in PT. It was fun trying to translate the dialogue between Romeo and Juliet, including emotions that had to be conveyed by touch, not through visuals. The best part was that the team worked hard to figure out cues for when it was time to go in and out of scenes and to let other castmates know to begin their lines—all without having the DeafBlind patron be aware, in order to ensure that the patron was fully engrossed in the play without reality interrupting. We designed the set in a way that made it possible for DeafBlind to be independent and move around. For example, we used rugs and the placement of tables to give tactile cues for the actors to know where they were in the set. Some people who identify as DeafBlind have residual vision, so we did have to think about how to set up cues that did not look out of place. We also had some interesting discussions about what weapons would be used in a DeafBlind, tactile world. Swords would not work because one would have to be at a distance from an opponent and be able to see. Robert suggested brass knuckles, since these are used in fighting up close. These could also have tactile designs that show family affiliation. When I first read the word "sword," I immediately said, "No, why not dagger instead?" A dagger is small and can easily be fit on the arm or hip, and its use does not require much movement. We looked for one that was retractable, so that it would go into its hilt when stabbed into the chest. Unfortunately, we were not able to get one that felt realistic, so we just mimed stabbing.

Robert Sirvage, Institute Participant[10]

One thing I learned from PTTI was that when it came to creating a DeafBlind theater production, the focus needed to be on process itself, not the product. Sighted hearing people might spend as much time on implementation of a project design as on the design itself. Instead of rushing into practice using a trial and error approach and being concerned with getting everyone on the same page, DeafBlind people treat the conceptualization stage as a consensus-building process (conceptualization and consensus entwine with each other more deeply). Proportion-wise, more time and resources need to be placed on early stage planning, even if it comes at the expense of other stages of the production. The end result will be better. To an outsider, the DeafBlind process might seem very slow. The first stage might actually be slow, but then when we start implementation, everything moves very quickly—even at lightning speed. During the PTTI, we invested more in discussion and analysis, going over things together again and again and again. An outside observer might feel like, "C'mon, let's go ahead and rehearse now!" But this extended discussion permitted us to go deep into how to structure the production and how to make connections between its different parts. When we were finally ready to rehearse, the process went very fast. This rhythm was different from my experience with sighted theater, where the initial discussion about design and concept with the cast was typically very brief, while the rehearsal time was long and drawn out.

An important element of this different process is the nature of PT communication. A PT conversation can involve no more than three people. So, during our week together, one facilitator shared information with two other people at a time. Then the facilitator would move to the next two people, and so on. Sighted people can stand up in front of a large group and simultaneously announce information to everyone. DeafBlind groups use the three-way communication process, which demands more extended time. It involves discussing, but also making sure we are all on the same page in our understanding of what is happening. We DeafBlind really value this consensus-building process. During PTTI, we had really good conversations about the set design, what tactile cues to use, how to move around the space, and more. We spent a lot of time on this. Then when everyone felt ready, we went ahead and started rehearsing. We spent much less time rehearsing because we took the time to build this consensus.

How we adapted the play, how the stage space evolved, how we developed the set design constituted a very fluid process that resulted in several important insights. We started discussing the story, then we played with some moments from the scenes. We experimented with translating the language into PT. Then we started thinking about how to connect the different scenes together. The first thing we noticed was that the room we were using as a "stage" was too big. So, we made it smaller by using tables to narrow the space. We actually set that up early in the week just to make the room easier for us to navigate and find each other. The smaller space increased the chances that we would bump into each other and be able to quickly discuss things. We did not think about that being part of the final set design. But this process of adapting the physical space to our needs ended up being a natural part of the production. For the performance, we narrowed the stage space even more. We set it up to be three body-lengths wide, so there would be a good chance that patrons and actors would come in contact with each other.

Something else I realized from PTTI is the need for a "thread," a way to connect different scenes and move actors and patrons between them. We set up tactile cues at different points in the set, but we also needed a path to connect them. As part of this process, I developed a tactile model made out of clay and flat marbles. It was not a floor plan as much as an aid for discussing how the scenes would unfold and how they would be connected. It showed the sequence of events in relation to physical layout of the space. It really helped us understand and discuss how to set up the path between the various action points. Some things we did to establish the thread were to arrange the tables with one sticking out a bit from the others; to set up rugs on the floor, to use existing features of the space such as the railing, and to stick clay nodes on the wall. It is important that the actors not need to take more than one or two steps to locate the thread, so they do not become disoriented in the stage space. The tactile cues for when to deliver lines and when to make contact with a patron were important, but without the thread, we would not be able to move from place to place following the storyline. All of these ideas for the production emerged naturally out of our own discussion and navigation of the space in the process of working in it. For this reason, it is important that DeafBlind actors work in the performance space from the beginning, rather than using one space for workshopping and then moving to the "stage" space for rehearsals after the set has been designed and built. It would be more natural if process space is something that "oozes into" stage space.

Rachel Grossman, Theater Artist Advisor

I joined the PTTI team a few days into the initial week, knowing that I possessed no comprehensive cultural knowledge or communication skills for entering a DeafBlind environment. I was the outsider coming into the space of a highly marginalized community. This was an experience for the participants, not for me. I was there to support their process on their terms, not mine. There was some social-political resistance to my involvement, which I fully understood even though it was hard to experience. Should I, as a hearing and sighted person, have been in their space? Was that even appropriate? But since DeafBlind and PT theater had not yet even emerged when I was asked to serve as an advisor, an alternate question could be "Why not me?"

The theater company that I co-founded, dog & pony dc, creates "audience integrated" theater, a holistic approach to generating and producing new plays that centers on the audience experience. In the early 2010s, we were developing increasingly more hands-on, audience responsive, small-group performances when I came across John Lee Clark's "My Dream Play." We were already pushing against mainstream and traditional ideas of what constituted a play; Clark's "dream" seemed to encourage us even further. What would it mean for us to make the dream play Clark described? We wanted to create more inclusive, rather than accessible, performances. What did this even mean to people of different social identities and backgrounds? How was theater exclusive? How were our artistic processes leading us, unintentionally or unconsciously, to make exclusionary performances?

One of the "unspoken" assumptions, rules, and rituals for makers and consumers of traditional theater is that stories are to be portrayed primarily through visual and auditory elements. And yet, humans have other senses—touch, smell, and taste—that inspire, just as vividly and perhaps more intimately. I started dog & pony dc's Sense-Able initiative to explore artists' and audience's biases about how theater is made and experienced, and through it we launched the "Shakespeare without Sight or Sound" project. Food is particularly effective at eliciting strong memories and triggering emotional responses, creating immediate performative touchstones that can be linked into a narrative journey. As dog & pony dc co-founder Lorraine Ressegger-Slone explains, "This is ultimately a performance-for-one, with the artist only suggesting a story and the audience member empowered as meaning maker, positioned to construct the story using sensory reaction, memory, emotional response, and imagination."[11]

Although our work was not oriented as theater for the DeafBlind, we were fortunate to have Deafblind individuals attend our various adaptations of Shakespeare's plays and provide feedback about their experience. We looked forward to sharing our sensorial discoveries and practices with DeafBlind theater artists during PTTI. This was not entirely successful for several reasons. The most important was that it came at the wrong point in the participants' artistic process and relationship to artistic collaborators. Both were in nascent stages during PTTI, and therefore needed room to develop. The facilitators were tasked with being translators, playwrights, directors, designers, and actors. They were also responsible for tending to the overall vision of the institute. From personal experience at dog & pony dc, this is impossible to do. At the start of "Shakespeare Without" I was intentionally not a part of the artistic ensemble but served as the artistic director—a mentor and guide—to project director Ressegger-Slone. In this way I was the ensemble's "facilitator" and also an artistic gadfly, encouraging the group to explore their choices more deeply, to artistically struggle more.

It is hard to break with western theater's prescribed set of "unspoken" assumptions, rules, and rituals for makers and consumers about what constitutes a play and how stories should be portrayed. This is true no matter how much you want to part with them, nor how much those traditions do not include you. There was not sufficient time or space provided, nor experience within the artist group, for that breaking with assumptions to occur. The PT *Romeo and Juliet* was equivalent to our 10-minute *Sense-Able: A Play:* a "cut and lift" of the original Shakespeare into a non-English immersive performance for an audience-of-one. The two shows were literal in their approach. Some examples: while there was early discussion over email around weaponry in an exclusively DeafBlind world, with brass knuckles proposed as more appropriate to the DeafBlind experience, in the end Romeo stabbed Tybalt with a dagger. Time-period specific full-body costumes, environmental props, and set décor were requested, yet only cursorily interacted with in the production. I make no value judgment in saying this. It was a limitation of the one-week timeframe, the participants' lack of exposure to alternative theater forms (theater of the oppressed techniques, immersive theater, audience integration theory), and the absence of a designated person to care for the long-term process.

I believe the multi-sensory theater techniques involving taste, touch, smell, movement that dog & pony dc developed during "Shakespeare Without" could be immediately and directly incorporated in PT theater. There would have to be, at minimum, exploration and testing with DeafBlind artists and audience, and experimentation in how to incorporate those techniques into PT theater design elements. It would be an honor to be a part of developing this further. It would be thrilling to be an audience, as it is my dream play too.

Conclusion

The PT adaptation of *Romeo and Juliet* yielded significant insights into how to stage theater by DeafBlind people for Deaf-Blind people. The participants developed and refined techniques for navigating the stage space, creating a storyline path, and establishing unobtrusive cues for the actors. They explored how to incorporate the principles of PT communication in dramatic performance, creating stage action and dialogue that were fully accessible to patrons. They learned which tactile elements of costumes and props would make meaningful contributions to the patrons' understanding of the story, characters, and themes. They also experimented with character development through scent and taste. They wrestled with translation issues as well, such as the challenge of finding tactile equivalents to visual language and imagery. While they chose to focus on expression of emotion and the basic plot in creating the dialogue, future productions can build on their preliminary work on translation and incorporation of sensory elements such as taste and smell. The PTTI also developed a new model for applied theater work with disability communities and individuals with disabilities, one that prioritizes inclusion of the target audience at all levels of planning, artistic conceptualization, and production. Finally, both the production and the institute raised important questions that go beyond the DeafBlind context, challenging our fundamental understanding of theater as an art form. PT theater questions the sighted bias inherent in even radical definitions such as Jerzy Grotowski's "what takes place between spectator and actor" or Peter Brooks' "A man walks across this empty space whilst someone else is watching him and this is all that is needed for an act of theatre to be engaged."[12] It raises aesthetic issues in general and with respect to theater as art. What is beauty to a DeafBlind person? On what aesthetic principles can we evaluate a performance grounded in tactile and sensorial experience? We look forward to future productions that will explore and offer answer to these questions.

Notes

1. Rudolf von Laban, *The Language of Movement,* ed. Lisa Ullmann (New York: Plays, Inc., 1974), 29.

2. While American Sign Language (ASL) is a visual-spatial language, ProTactile is haptic-spatial. It incorporates vibration and touch to communicate visual and auditory information. DeafBlind PT users have developed unique linguistic features to convey environmental information, nonverbal cues, and noises/facial expressions (see Terra Edwards, "Language Emergence in the Seattle DeafBlind Community," Doctoral Dissertation, University of California, Berkeley, 2014; and "Sign-Creation in the Seattle Deafblind Community: A Triumphant Story about

the Regeneration of Obviousness," *Gesture* 16: 2 [2017], 307–32). The PT philosophy also emphasizes autonomy and direct interaction between DeafBlind individuals, rather than mediated via sighted interpreters. See https://protactile connects.weebly.com/ and https://www.tactilecommunications.org/about-1.html

3. Jill Bradbury wrote the introduction, overview, and conclusion, and edited participants' contributions together. Participants reviewed and approved their sections prior to publication.

4. aj granda & Jelica Nuccio (2018). *Protactile Principles* (Seattle, WA: Tactile Communications, 2018).

5. Unpublished interview with Jelica Nuccio. August 29, 2018. Seattle, WA

6. We chose to call the audience members "patrons" because the sign for audience comes from a visual image. It represents people seated and viewing a performance, which was conceptually the opposite of what we were creating.

7. John Lee Clark, "My Dream Play," *Scene4 Magazine,* April 2015.

8. Mojisola Adebayo, "Revolutionary Beauty out of Homophobic Hate" in *Applied Theatre Aesthetics,* ed. Gareth White (London: Bloomsbury, 2015): 123–55, 125.

9. "Despite the many barriers we encounter in society, we can gain much awareness about the world around us. But when we go exploring or when we just exist, sighted and hearing people rush in to intervene. Can they help us? Please don't touch. They will be happy to describe it to us. They will guide us. No, they will get it for us. It's much easier that way. Hello! My name is Katie and I'm your Intervenor!" "Distantism." *John Lee Clark: Notes from a DeafBlind Writer.* 3 August 2017. https://johnleeclark.tumblr.com/post/163762970913/distantism

10. Transcribed from ASL videos by Jill Bradbury.

11. Lorraine Ressegger-Slone, "Sense-Able: Placing Audience at the Heart of Experience," Unpublished conference paper. ASTR (Atlanta 2017), 2.

12. Jerzy Grotowski, *Towards a Poor Theatre* (London: Methuen, 1991), 32. Peter Brooks, *The Empty Space* (New York: Atheneum, 1969), 9.

NEXT GENERATION PLENARY

Next Generation Plenary

Introduction

W<small>E ARE DELIGHTED</small> to include in this volume five papers by distinguished young scholars that were chosen for the Shakespeare Association of America's Next Generation Plenary, which took place at the SAA's March 2018 annual meeting in Los Angeles. It is a pleasure and a privilege to share with our readers the work of these young Shakespeareans, and we hope to continue to publish essays from the *Next Gen Plen* in *Shakespeare Studies* in the years to come.

The Editors

"For her sake": Queer Pregnancy in *A Midsummer Night's Dream*

ALICIA ANDRZEJEWSKI

IN JULIE TAYMOR'S 2013–14 STAGING OF *A Midsummer Night's Dream,* the Indian votaress appears as a luminescent, yellow light when Titania speaks the words: "His mother was a votaress of my order" (2.1.124).[1] This light illuminates Titania's face against the "progeny of evils" born from her marital strife, softening the sounds of thunder that accompany Oberon onstage (2.1.115). As the Indian votaress warms the affective atmosphere of Fairyland, Titania conjures an exquisite vision of pregnancy—the Indian votaress grows "big-bellied" by "the wanton wind" and "gossips" by Titania's side, laughing with her at the "conceiv[ing]" sails she imitates with ease and the "embarkèd traders" who steer ships "on the flood" (122–37). This gossip and laughter, the trifles passed between Titania and the Indian votaress, characterize pregnancy as a time of female-female eroticism, intimacy, and pleasure. Though the Indian votaress "of that boy did die," Titania protects the boy to whom she gives birth "for her sake" (125–36). The repetition of the phrase "for her sake" twice emphasizes the importance of the Indian votaress as distinct from her child, the Indian boy, who Oberon, scholars, and audience members alike continue to emphasize.[2]

In this paper, I join the scholarly conversation on Titania's monologue and the larger themes in *A Midsummer Night's Dream* by centering the Indian votaress's pregnancy as an object of study— she is the alternative "rose distilled" upon which a queer futurity, a better world for reproductive bodies, is conjured (1.1.76). The female-female intimacies Titania and the Indian votaress share fall outside of the early modern homosocial imaginary and its transactional relationship to sex and reproduction. As part of a compelling representation of love and world-making between women, the

Indian votaress's pregnancy is queer as it fails "to reproduce the
family in a recognizable form," to use Tim Dean's definition of
reproductive futurism;[3] and it is queer in how it resists a masculine
vision of the pregnant body—the authoritarian policing by Oberon,
his attempts to steal female labor for his own use, to fashion the
pregnant body as a vessel for masculine profit. The Indian votaress's presence in *A Midsummer Night's Dream,* thus, allows for an
anticipatory illumination of a queer world, warming Titania
against the "mazéd world" born of her marriage, the frosts that fall
"in the fresh lap of the crimson rose" (2.1.113, 111).

The Indian votaress is a ghost, "pure sound effect, like the vivid
report of the death of Ophelia" according to Patricia Parker, but the
question Shankar Raman asks of the Indian boy—what is the significance of the "absent presence" of these figures?—is a question
that also applies to the Indian votaress.[4] This space, the edge of
India, and the female intimacies that Titania fights to protect in *A
Midsummer Night's Dream* resist what José Esteban Muñoz might
call a "poisonous and insolvent" present; in *Cruising Utopia: The
Then and There of Queer Futurity,* Muñoz calls readers to "see otherwise, beyond the limited vista of the here and now," and to
approach a "then and there" that he argues "certain performances
of queer citizenship contain."[5] Despite being written centuries earlier than the modern era that is the focus of Muñoz's study, Shakespeare's plays often contain such "then and there" spaces. Titania's
vision of the Indian votaress is one of them.

My reading of the Indian votaress is part of a larger project in
which I argue early modern drama is a particularly generative
space to reimagine pregnancy as a queer experience. In queer
theory, the pregnant body is often subsumed into definitions of
heteronormativity, lives scripted "by the conventions of family,
inheritance, and child rearing."[6] The antisocial thesis in queer theory, most notably articulated in Lee Edelman's *No Future,* positions
queerness as antithetical to reproduction and futurity and therefore
in opposition to the pregnant body.[7] Queer theorists who apply
Edelman's antisocial theory to early modern literature have
inspired my approach to pregnancy, in that they deliberately turn
away from the child and the redemptive future it symbolizes; however, pregnancy is often seen as antithetical to queer studies in
Shakespearean scholarship, and this contributes to the erasure of
lesbian and bisexual women's and trans and nonbinary people's
respective experiences as pregnant people.[8] The assumptions that

only women get pregnant; that every pregnancy ends in the birth of a child; and that pregnancy always reproduces the family in a recognizable form are inherent in definitions of heternormativity, and these assumptions erase many people's lived experiences of pregnancy.

At first glance, the Indian votaress *is* a nameless mother, eclipsed by the presence of the child, her son, in scholarship and most productions.[9] *A Midsummer Night's Dream* begins with the trope of the sacrificing, invisible mother through the figure of "the rose distill'd": Theseus promises Hermia that undergoing this process, legitimizing her desire through marriage and making this desire matter through reproduction, will make her "earthlier happy" than "barren sisters" (1.1.67–76). This metaphor conflates the rose with the sexualized, female body and the distillation process—the freeing of the rose's prized essence, its perfume—with marriage and reproduction. The plucking, pruning, and policing of pregnant bodies lurks behind the floral imagery knitted to the experience of pregnancy in Shakespeare's sonnets, the carpe diem poetic tradition, contemporary gynecological texts, and *A Midsummer Night's Dream,* reflecting how pregnant bodies were, and continue to be, imagined: as disposable vessels, required to make violent sacrifices to body forth the child—the future.[10] Theseus's promise that the distilled rose is "earthlier happy" is challenged throughout *A Midsummer Night's Dream,* from the "hoary-headed frosts" that Titania and Oberon's marriage bodies forth, which fall "in the fresh lap of the crimson rose" (2.2.107–8), to the monstrous births Oberon meditates on in his marital blessing at the play's end (5.1.395). Shakespeare's use of the process of distillation in scene one does enough, however, to foreshadow the false promise of earthly happiness for the rose plucked from the bush or tree, showcased in bloom for but a few days, distilled, after which it is then discarded and ignored.

The Indian votaress, however, is a rose "of another sort" (3.2.388). As Holly Dugan notes of the damask rose, "its domestication in England was a profound agricultural achievement"; they were valued for their "outlandishness . . . an early modern term that emphasized foreign specimens."[11] Unlike Hippolyta and the Indian boy, the Indian votaress is never "forcibly removed from her culture," never plucked from the female community—the rose bush or tree—that Titania's monologue conjures.[12] The Indian votaress's death works against Theseus's oversimplified promise of happiness, illuminating the "dead ends and darkness" that Halberstam

finds crucial to a queer aesthetic, that characterize the lived experience of pregnancy in the period.[13] The Indian votaress's death
reminds audiences that she is mortal, human—she is not simply a
symbol or a trope.

In addition, the Indian votaress's pregnant body threatens the
reproduction of the illusory white, English child and the symbolic
future this child represents. Racial difference was central to troubling the Aristotelian model of generation that Theseus alludes to
when he tells Hermia that her father is the one who "composed
[her] beauties," that she is but "a form in wax / By him imprinted"
(1.1.49–50). The power and mystery of the pregnant body is inextri-
cably tied to racial difference in the period, as the competing generation narratives in *Titus Andronicus* demonstrate (4.2.154–61), in
which Moors and Goths give birth to children of various hues.[14]
The black child that gazes directly at male physicians from the
frontispiece of *Aristotle's Masterpiece, or the secrets of generation
displayed in all the parts thereof* (1684), the "most popular medical
book about sex and babies" from its publication through the nineteenth century, stands bold and defiant, like the Indian boy who
lives on at the end of *A Midsummer Night's Dream* to disrupt the
order of things.[15] Behind all of these queer children is the powerful,
pregnant body—the monstrous, female imagination.[16]

For all of these reasons, the Indian votaress's pregnancy exemplifies the queer nature of the pregnant body—a body that incorporates then shuts out the father necessary to create a child, claiming
dominion over itself in this refusal. While Titania's monologue
does not undo the violence women experience throughout *A Midsummer Night's Dream,* or the Indian votaress's death, this memory
of the past is "a being in, toward, and for futurity."[17] Titania's memory of the Indian votaress offers a blueprint for queer, feminist
world-making, conjuring a queer, pregnant woman of color who
seeks refuge in the shadows and borderlands of night, of female
community, of laughter. Taymor's staging of the Indian votaress as
a soft, yellow light reflects the intimacy between Titania and the
Indian votaress, as well as Madhavi Menon's definition of "queer":
the Indian votaress cannot be "fully or finally grasped," unlike the
Indian boy, who is eventually taken by Oberon and incorporated
into his train.[18]

In Taymor's production, the Indian votaress's ghost remains
onstage even after Titania speaks the devastating line, "But she,
being mortal, of that boy did die," cast into shadow only when
Oberon responds, "How long within this wood intend you stay?"

(2.1.138). This question ignores the Indian votaress's presence in the present, demonstrating that, during Titania's monologue, Oberon is only concerned with his own internal monologue, one in which he is planning to drug Titania to ensure she "fit [her] fancies" to his will (1.1.119). But part of the magic of both Shakespeare's and Muñoz's respective work is their ability to conjure queer intimacies that inspire audiences, then and now, to fight for queer utopias despite a "poisonous and insolvent" present for pregnant and potentially pregnant bodies.[19] Through the Indian votaress and her experience of pregnancy, *A Midsummer Night's Dream* reveals how badly the present can fail queer ways of being and knowing, while also providing a brief glimpse of a different kind of promise than the one Theseus makes Hermia—a "then and there" space outside of the dichotomy of barren sister and rose distilled—a vision that makes the labor of remapping a poisonous present seem possible.

Notes

1. Unless otherwise noted, quotations of *A Midsummer Night's Dream* follow Mario DiGangi's edition of the play (New York: Barnes and Noble, Inc., 2007).

2. As Ania Loomba observes, critics agree that the play's colonial investments "are best amplified by unraveling the significance of the 'lovely' Indian boy," but even Loomba's own instructive reading of *A Midsummer Night's Dream* centers on the boy instead of the Indian votaress ("The Great Indian Vanishing Trick—Colonialism, Property, and the Family in *A Midsummer Night's Dream*" in *A Feminist Companion to Shakespeare,* ed. Dympna Callaghan [London: Blackwell Publishing, 2000], 165). Mary Beth Rose goes as far to argue that "no mothers appear at all" in *A Midsummer Night's Dream* ("Where Are the Mothers in Shakespeare? Options for Gender Representation in the English Renaissance," *Shakespeare Quarterly* 42, no. 3 [1991]: 291–314; 292). Scholars interested in queer lives, in female-female love, desire, and eroticism, have attended to the erotic charge in Titania's monologue. Valerie Traub has argued that the child "is the manifest link of a prior affection between women that is associated with their shared fecundity and maternal largess," but moves swiftly on to "the fair vestal throned by the west" who exists *behind the seen* (*The Renaissance of Lesbianism in Early Modern England* [Cambridge: Cambridge University Press, 2002], 68, 69). Although Mario DiGangi argues that Titania's monologue also advocates for a more "harmonious model of mutual desire centered on female-female loyalty," he describes the Indian votaress "as a domestic servant the product of whose labors is to remain in her mistress's ownership"—"a woman who variously fulfills the roles of fertile wife, religious devotee, exotic pet, and domestic servant" (82–84). In other words, pregnancy is a bodily state that allows female communities and bonds to flourish, but the Indian votaress is perhaps too visible, too much a part

of the culturally predetermined orientalism built into Shakespeare's geographical allusion to India. Shankar Raman argues that "Shakespeare's (non)representation of the Indian Boy depends upon the historically specific practices and discourses of colonialism, through which England finally comes into actual contact with 'India'" (*Framing "India": The Colonial Imaginary in Early Modern Culture* [Stanford: Stanford University Press, 2001], 293); and Margo Hendricks describes the Indian votaress as "the fantasy of a silent, accepting native who neither speaks nor resists" ("'Obscured by Dreams': Race, Empire, and Shakespeare's *A Midsummer Night's Dream,*" *Shakespeare Quarterly* 47, no. 1 [1996]: 37–60; 60). Bindu Malieckal's study is a notable exception to these arguments, however, arguing that Titania's integration of the Indian boy into her household "might be a legitimate measure, since the bond between the Fairy Queen and the Indian 'vot'ress' seems more significant than the one between the Indian mother and the Indian king. The 'order' to which Titania and the changeling's biological mother belong is similar to the likes of a 'tharavad' or household that in early modern Malabar was owned and inhabited by related women and their offspring" ("Muslims, Matriliny, and *A Midsummer Night's Dream:* European Encounters with the Mappilas of Malabar, India," *The Muslim World* 95, no. 2 [2005]: 297–316; 309).

3. Robert L. Caserio, Lee Edelman, Judith Halberstam, José Esteban Muñoz, and Tim Dean, "The Antisocial Thesis in Queer Theory," *PMLA* 121, no. 3 (2006): 819–28; 826.

4. Patricia Parker, "Shakespeare's Sound Government: Sound Defects, Polyglot Sounds, and Sounding Out," *Oral Tradition* 24, no 2 (2009): 359–72; 361; Raman, *Framing "India,"* 242.

5. José E. Muñoz, *Cruising Utopia: The Then and There of Queer Futurity* (New York: New York University Press, 2009), 30, 22.

6. Jack Halberstam [Judith Halberstam], *In a Queer Time and Place: Transgender Bodies, Subcultural Lives* (New York: New York University Press, 2005), 2.

7. Lee Edelman, *No Future: Queer Theory and the Death Drive* (Durham: Duke University Press, 2004).

8. For the notable exception, see Melissa E. Sanchez's recent essay, "Antisocial Procreation in *Measure for Measure*" in *Queer Shakespeare: Desire and Sexuality,* ed. Goran Stanivukovic (New York: Bloomsbury Publishing, 2017), 263–77.

9. As Trevor Griffiths observes, nineteenth-century producers of *A Midsummer Night's Dream* were offended not by any intimation of lesbian desire in this passage but by the lines describing the votaress's pregnant body, which they typically cut (qtd. in DiGangi, 127–35n.). Apart from Taymor's staging of the Indian votaress's ghost, I have seen just one recent production of *A Midsummer Night's Dream* that actually bodied her forth. In this production, an Asian American actress played Titania, while the white actress playing Hermia quickly donned a prosthetic belly to glide across the stage past Titania as she spoke, kneeling on the floor, lightly touching her face before she moved once again to the margins of the stage.

10. The numerous images of "flowering women" in gynecological texts demonstrate the violence inherent in this pervasive metaphor. See, for example, Thomas Chamberlayne, *The Compleat Midwifes Practice* (London, 1656: Wing C1817C); The British Library Board, shelfmark E.1588[3]. The "flowering" woman (following p. 2) looks to the side, not directly at viewers. Plants grow up and around her legs, covering her genitalia; her stomach is cut open, blooming outwards to reveal

the child, and her skin appears to be petals marked with veins. Her left hand holds a flower while her right hand is open, facing upwards. It is not a coincidence that the anatomized pregnant body is characterized by floral imagery here—a reminder that physicians must cut a living body open in order to gain knowledge of and access to the child. Indeed, the distillation process, like gynecological surgery, is a scientific process that preserves and controls "rich merchandise" as opposed to generating these riches (2.1.134).

11. Holly Dugan, *The Ephemeral History of Perfume: Scent and Sense in Early Modern England* (Baltimore: Johns Hopkins University Press, 2011), 46–47.

12. Margo Hendricks, "Obscured by Dreams," 57.

13. Halberstam, *The Queer Art of Failure,* 96.

14. William Shakespeare, *Titus Andronicus.* ed. Barbara A. Mowat and Paul Werstine, (New York: Washington Square Press, 2005).

15. Mary Fissell, "Remaking the Maternal Body in England, 1680–1730," *Journal of the History of Sexuality* 26, no. 1 (2017): 114–39; 114.

16. Queer pregnancies, like the Indian votaress's, do not always end in the birth of a child, but some end in the birth of a queer child: a child who disrupts the heteronormative order, the coercive and normalizing "pride, optimism, and respectability" that accompanies visions of the future (Sanchez, 496). Even if the Indian boy is incorporated into Oberon's order by the play's end, in an attempt to straighten him out, his very presence queers the order of things in the Fairy Kingdom. As DK Dongkyun Lee argues, Lee Edelman's "Child" is always a white Child, a fantasy that "facilitates political discourse racially as anti-black as it does anti-Queer" ("The 'Child' Which is Never Black," https://medium.com/@dkdongkyunlee/the-child-which-is-never-black-65a56362428f).

17. Muñoz, *Cruising Utopia,* 91.

18. Madhavi Menon, ed., *Shakesqueer: A Queer Companion to the Complete Works of Shakespeare* (Durham: Duke University Press, 2011), 9.

19. Muñoz, *Cruising Utopia,* 30.

Audiences Writing Race in Shakespeare Performance

Lauren Eriks Cline

Hᴏᴡ ᴅᴏ ᴡᴇ ᴋɴᴏᴡ if an audience sees color? Sometimes, of course, the written record makes race-conscious reception explicit. When African American Ira Aldridge played Othello on the London stage, for example, his most critical reviews reflected nineteenth-century Britain's anti-black ideologies in largely the way that contemporary critics might expect.[1] Yet documented reactions are not always so clear. In 1833, the same year that Aldridge performed Othello at Covent Garden, actor-manager Charles Macready became one of the first to "brown up" the actress playing Cleopatra in his production of *Antony and Cleopatra;* but this racialized choice, Celia Daileader notes, did not provoke a strong reaction from reviewers. Nor did it change theatrical custom for representing the role, despite the fact that Edmund Kean's similarly "tawny face" had set a new trend for Othellos in 1814.[2] Similarly, when Roger Livesey became the first known actor to "black up" to play Caliban at the Old Vic in 1934, Trevor Griffiths notes that his choice of makeup excited "virtually no critical comment," even though representations of Caliban as black or indigenous were by this time widely available in cartoons and critical essays.[3]

Such curious moments, when spectators seem incurious about the meaning of race on stage, can pose problems for one of the dominant approaches to Shakespeare reception studies, which I think of as the "remaking Shakespeare in our own image" narrative. According to this theory, each age restages a Shakespeare play to represent its own particular preoccupations, so that there is a reflective relationship between cultural surroundings and theatrical performance. What happens offstage should register onstage, and the prevailing performance tradition of the moment should mirror its historical milieu.[4] This theory has helped produce many important studies of Shakespeare performance, because it is good at making certain things visible: namely, resemblances (places where stage signifiers seem similar to the signifiers used in other cultural contexts), parallel trajectories (places where shifts in performance practice seem to happen in tandem with other historical or aesthetic developments), and confirmation of predicted measurements (places where spectator response seems to provide corroborating evidence for existing historical narratives).

Yet this reflective approach to performance history can also make other things harder to see: especially those places where a Shakespeare production does not seem to have prompted the critical response that its social context would suggest.[5] If scholars begin by looking for a correspondence between a theater event and its time period, the performances that receive the most analysis will tend to be those that either comfortably fit or clearly contradict the historical narratives we expect to see mirrored on stage. If the reflection looks incoherent or opaque, that production may go unnoticed. Or, it may end up having its strangeness flattened by analytical filters aimed at enhancing visibility and symmetry.

In this essay, I gather some ongoing conceptual shifts in Shakespeare performance studies that I believe can help make sense of these opaque performances without trying to clear them up. While difficult to assimilate into traditional theater histories, productions that provoke unexpected audience responses can offer fruitful sites for analyzing a feature of stage Shakespeare that is itself inconsistent: the significance of race on stage. Indeed, "[t]he exact significance of an actor's race is perpetually in flux," Ayanna Thompson argues, "because we as a society have not been able to pinpoint a stable signification for race."[6] Given this fluctuation, I suggest that a reflective approach may not always be the best tool for understanding the role of race in Shakespeare performance. Taking up Thompson's call to develop methodologies that address the intersection between reception studies and critical race studies, I track three current shifts in these fields that have the potential to turn spots of imperfect visibility from an obstacle into an opportunity.

First, a shift from thinking about audience reception to thinking about spectator production. In urging scholars to develop tools for analyzing reception, Shakespeare performance critics like Barbara Hodgdon have helped call attention to audience "reading strategies."[7] Following Hodgdon's analogy—and honoring her attentiveness to theater reviews—I would add that *readers* of performance processes are also the *writers* of those performance meanings that survive in theater archives. By analyzing not only the semiotic codes through which audiences read theatrical signs but also the discursive strategies with which they write narratives of theater-going, scholars can approach audiences not as failing to see race, but as *using* techniques of incoherence, opacity, and indirection to construct racial meanings.[8]

Second, a shift from approaching stage productions and the audience responses they provoke as a reflection of historical changes to analyzing spectator narratives as refractions of those changes. While some racial meanings circulate close enough to the surface of visibility to cast a clear discursive reflection, others—especially those racial ideologies that depend for their effectiveness on going unseen or unspoken—may not create an impression that is directly representable.[9] More oblique than reflection, refraction enables critics to see how meaning passes from the medium of performance to the medium of narrative in indirect as well as symmetrical ways, so that spectator narratives can produce not only descriptions of objects but also changes in the direction, speed, and density of meaning.

Third, a shift from looking for race as a system of visible signs to seeing racial signifiers as produced through tensions between visibility and opacity. Critics like Thompson, Daphne Brooks, and Kyle Grady, for example, have pointed out how the historical significance of blackness has often depended on complex interactions between hyper-visibility, colorblindness, and passing.[10] Vivian Huang and Carla Della Gatta similarly explore how Asian-American and Latinx performances become meaningful not only through visibility but also through inscrutability and orality.[11] Reading reception alongside critical race theories, we learn that what looks at first like a spectator's failure to see race might turn out instead to be a strategy for making race invisible.

I want briefly to play out some implications of these shifts by examining the case study provided by a contemporary tale of two *Caesar*s: the Guthrie's Obama-inspired production in 2012 and the Trump-like tyrant at the Public Theater in 2017. Critical reactions to these *Caesar*s raise fascinating questions about the changing conditions for producing political Shakespeare. I focus on one: how can reading for spectator production, refraction, and opacity enhance our understanding of the way audiences write race in

Shakespeare performance? The responses I analyze are chosen not necessarily because they are representative of a general audience reaction, but because of how they represent, shape, and focalize partial reactions. I am interested in them not as a record of what audiences thought race meant but as a medium for making racial meanings.

In terms of their approach to blackness, the stories told about Bjorn DuPaty's *Caesar* at the Guthrie in 2012 were a mixed bag. While some writers explicitly mark the actor as black,[12] others paint a more opaque picture of the performance.[13] In many reviews, the race of the actor is not mentioned directly but instead constructed obliquely, through references to basketball, hip-hop music, and what one reviewer describes as "one of those shake-it/grasp-it/pound-it handshakes typically encountered in made-for-TV movies about urban youth."[14] Many narratives also obscure the full visibility of DuPaty's blackness by refracting it through a range of other contemporary signifiers, especially of class. Headlines in *The New York Times* and the *Star Tribune*—"Beware the Suited Men Wielding Letter Openers" and "Caesar Wears a Business Suit"—both suggest that DuPaty's performance is more prominently marked by costuming decisions that signal class status than it is by somatic markers of race.

But race takes on a different significance in the context of the Public Theater's *Caesar* in 2017. On June 11, Fox News Insider ran the headline "NYC Play Appears to Depict Assassination of Trump."[15] This story provoked a wave of new narratives competing to tell the story of what this "NYC Play" and its staged assassination mean. One thing they agree on: Gregg Henry's Caesar is meant to suggest Trump. Indeed, Fox News goes so far as to claim that the actor's body references Trump more clearly than it references Julius Caesar.[16] But the signifiers that spectators read as "Trump-like" are only inconsistently or indirectly linked to whiteness. Blondeness bears a recognizable racial association, but the signature red tie is a more characterological construction.[17] A reference to "Slavic wives" explicitly marks categories of ethnicity, but "petulance" points toward whiteness in less direct ways.[18]

By contrast, blackness becomes more visible in the 2017 spectator narratives. Not only does Bjorn DuPaty's race retrospectively take on added meaning but a number of spectators also cast the racial and gendered identities of Caesar's *assassins* as newly significant. Though the Guthrie production featured not only a black

Caesar but also a black Brutus (indeed, in a striking substitution, several of the 2017 articles looking back on the Guthrie's production ran with a picture of actor Will Sturdivant as Brutus, rather than a picture of DuPaty as Caesar),[19] in 2012, the blackness of one of Caesar's assassins went largely unremarked in spectators' responses. The most virulent criticisms of the Public's production, on the other hand, frame the attack on Caesar as explicitly or implicitly racialized. Not only did Fox News report that the performance "appears to depict President Trump being brutally stabbed to death by women and minorities," Fox writers repeatedly refer to the play itself as an "NYC Play": a phrase that, when compared with "a Shakespeare play," is loaded with non-white racial and ethnic meaning. Whereas narratives of the Guthrie's production stay selectively colorblind, many responses to the Public's *Caesar* either craft or contest the narrative of whiteness under threat, with conditions of hyper-visibility imposed on non-white actors.

While one might feel tempted to dismiss the outraged responses to the Public's performance as incoherent, ahistorical, and inconsistent, I linger with them, because incoherence, ahistoricism, and inconsistency are often precisely the discursive tools with which racial meanings are made. If we want to understand how audiences see Shakespeare in color, we will need analytical tools designed to register a full range of tactics—from spectacular visibility to strategic colorblindness—that function not only as casting techniques but also as spectator strategies.

Notes

1. Ira Aldridge's complex, transnational career has been the object of a range of historical and theatrical studies. For analyses of Aldridge's reception as a mainstage, London Othello, as well as the imbrication of his debut in broader changes in blackface performance, see Joyce Green MacDonald, "Acting Black: *Othello, Othello* Burlesques, and the Performance of Blackness," *Theatre Journal* 46 (1994): 231–49; Jennifer DeVere Brody, *Impossible Purities: Blackness, Femininity, and Victorian Culture* (Durham: Duke University Press, 1998); Diana E. Henderson, "Othello Redux? Scott's *Kenilworth* and the Trickiness of 'Race' on the Nineteenth-Century Stage," in *Victorian Shakespeares*, vol. 2 (New York: Palgrave Macmillan, 2003); Bernth Lindfors, "Ira Aldridge at Covent Garden, April 1833," *Theatre Notebook* 61.3 (2007): 144–69; and Hazel Waters, *Racism on the Victorian Stage: Representations of Slavery and the Black Character* (Cambridge: Cambridge University Press, 2009).

2. Celia R. Daileader, "The Cleopatra Complex: White Actresses on the Inter-racial 'Classic' Stage," in *Colorblind Shakespeare: New Perspectives on Race and Performance,* ed. Ayanna Thompson (London: Routledge, 2006). The history of "tawny-face" productions and spectacular orientalism during the nineteenth century represents a strand of racial performance both separate from and related to the emerging popularity of blackface minstrelsy. For more on the production and reception of "tawny" performances of Shakespeare, see Henderson, "Othello Redux?" and Edward Ziter, *The Orient on the Victorian Stage* (Cambridge: Cambridge University Press, 2003).

3. Trevor Griffiths, " 'This Island's Mine': Caliban and Colonialism," *The Yearbook of English Studies* 13 (1983): 159–80; citation 175. Griffiths situates performances of *The Tempest* within colonial discourses that involve imperial attitudes toward Ireland and the Caribbean as well as anti-blackness and commentary on the Civil War in the United States. See also J. S. Bratton, et al., eds., *Acts of Supremacy: The British Empire and the Stage, 1790–1930* (Manchester: Manchester University Press, 1991) for histories of theater and empire during the period.

4. Anthony Dawson's thorough study of *Hamlet* in performance provides some examples of the insights that this reflective approach can generate. Dawson analyzes how Restoration actor David Garrick's "acting became both a *reflection* of, and a contribution to, his culture's construction of Shakespeare"; how Victorian actor-manager Henry Irving "*mirror[s]* the time's interest in 'intensity' "; and thus how "the shifts from Garrick to Kean to Irving can . . . be used to trace the fitful trajectory of the human subject, at least in its European manifestations, over almost two centuries," *Hamlet: Shakespeare in Performance* (Manchester: Manchester University Press, 1995), 34, 59, and 62–63, emphases added. See also Virginia Mason Vaughan and Alden T. Vaughan's *Shakespeare's Caliban: A Cultural History* (Cambridge: Cambridge University Press, 1993), which aims "show how and, whenever possible, why each age has appropriated and reshaped [Caliban] to suit its needs and assumptions," and approaches performances of the role as a "sensitive barometer of intellectual and social change," ix, x, and xiv.

5. Griffiths, for example, finding no audience response to Frank Benson's ape-like Caliban that matches the explicitness and exhaustiveness of late-nineteenth-century racial ideologies, concludes that "critics were content to describe rather than analyse" the racial and ethnic implications of the performance, " 'This Island's Mine': Caliban and Colonialism," 168.

6. Ayanna Thompson, "Introduction," in *Colorblind Shakespeare: New Perspectives on Race and Performance,* ed. Ayanna Thompson (London: Routledge, 2006), 8.

7. See Barbara Hodgdon, *The Shakespeare Trade: Performances and Appropriations* (Philadelphia: University of Pennsylvania Press, 1998), 171. Marvin Carlson similarly takes up processes of reading as a mode of reception in "Theater Audiences and the Reading of Performance," in *Interpreting the Theatrical Past: Essays in the Historiography of Performance,* eds. Thomas Postlewait and Bruce A. McConachie (Iowa City: Iowa University Press, 1989).

8. For examples of studies that center specific modes and strategies of spectator writing, see Paul Prescott on reviews in *Reviewing Shakespeare: Journalism and Performance from the Eighteenth Century to the Present* (Cambridge: Cambridge University Press, 2013), Charlotte Canning on actress memoirs in "Constructing Experience: Theorizing a Feminist Theatre History," *Theatre Journal* 45,

no. 4 (1993): 529–40, and my own work on theatrical letters in "Epistolary Liveness: Narrative Presence and the Victorian Actress in Letters," *Theatre Survey*, forthcoming in 2019.

9. Miriam Gilbert, for example, has argued that the intensity of racial meaning in post-Holocaust productions of *The Merchant of Venice* led some directors and actors to deflect attention from the play's anti-semitism. See "Performance as Deflection," in *A Companion to Shakespeare and Performance*, ed. Barbara Hodgdon and W. B. Worthen (Malden, MA: Blackwell Publishing, 2005).

10. As a list of important and paradigm-shifting work on race in performance would be too long to compile here, I cite a small selection of scholars whose conceptions of opacity, passing, and inscrutability have been particularly influential to my own thinking. See Daphne Brooks, *Bodies in Dissent: Spectacular Performances of Race and Freedom, 1850–1910* (Durham, NC: Duke University Press, 2006) and Kyle Grady, "Othello, Colin Powell, and Post-Racial Anachronisms," *Shakespeare Quarterly* 67, no. 1 (2016): 68–83. In addition to Ayanna Thompson's introduction to *Colorblind Shakespeare*, see also Ayanna Thompson, *Passing Strange: Shakespeare, Race, and Contemporary America* (Oxford: Oxford University Press, 2011).

11. See Vivian L. Huang, "Some Island Unknown to the Rest of the World Inscrutability, Asian Americanness, Performance" (Dissertation, New York University, 2016) and Carla Della Gatta, "From *West Side Story* to *Hamlet, Prince of Cuba*: Shakespeare and Latinidad in the United States" *Shakespeare Studies* 44 (2016): 151–56.

12. "Review: Julius Caesar @ Guthrie," *Minneapolis-St.Paul Magazine*, December 19, 2013, http://mspmag.com/arts-and-culture/the-morning-after/review_julius_caesar_the_guthr/, Noah Millman, "Obama's Ides Of March: The Acting Company Production of *Julius Caesar*," *Millman's Shakesblog*, in *The American Conservative*, May 21, 2012, http://www.theamericanconservative.com/shakesblog/obamas-ides-of-march/

13. Eric Grode, "Beware the Suited Men Wielding Letter Openers: The Acting Company's Version of 'Julius Caesar,'" *The New York Times*, April 22, 2012, http://www.nytimes.com/2012/04/18/theater/reviews/the-acting-companys-version-of-julius-caesar.html, Graydon Royce, "Caesar Wears a Business Suit," *Star Tribune*, January 20, 2012, and Jay Gabler, "Acting Company and Guthrie Theater bring 'Julius Caesar' awkwardly into the 21st century," *Twin Cities Daily Planet*, January 21, 2012, https://www.tcdailyplanet.net/julius-caesar-guthrie-theater-acting-company-review/.

14. Gabler, "Acting Company and Guthrie Theater bring 'Julius Caesar' awkwardly into the 21st century."

15. "NYC Play Appears to Depict Assassination of Trump," *Fox News Insider*, June 11, 2017, http://insider.foxnews.com/2017/06/11/donald-trump-julius-caesar-stabbed-death-women-minorities-shakespeare-central-park

16. "'Assassination Porn': Activist Defends Disrupting NYC Trump Stabbing Play," *Fox News Insider*, June 19, 2017, http://insider.foxnews.com/2017/06/19/donald-trump-assassination-play-julius-caesar-shakespeare-new-york-laura-loomer-hannity

17. Blonde hair is almost universally described in critical narratives about the production. See, for example, Gordon Cox, "Controversial 'Julius Caesar' Play Opens to Standing Ovation in Central Park," *Variety*, June, 12, 2017, http://variety

.com/2017/legit/news/julius-caesar-opening-trump-like-play-1202463844/ and Travis Andrews, "Trump-like 'Julius Caesar' assassinated in New York play. Delta, Bank of America pull funding," *Washington Post,* June 12, 2017, https://www .washingtonpost.com/news/morning-mix/wp/2017/06/12/trump-like-julius -caesar-assassinated-in-new-york-play-delta-bank-of-america-pull-funding/?utm _term = .c273183c28f6

18. Sophie Gilbert marks the Trump resemblance through the presence of a Slavic wife in, "The Misplaced Outrage Over a Trumpian *Julius Caesar,*" *The Atlantic,* June 12, 2017, https://www.theatlantic.com/entertainment/archive/ 2017/06/the-misplaced-outrage-over-a-trumpian-julius-caesar/530037/, as does Jesse Green, "Review: Can Trump Survive in Caesar's Palace," *The New York Times,* June 9, 2017, https://www.nytimes.com/2017/06/09/theater/review-julius -caesar-delacorte-theater-donald-trump.html. Green also describes Gregg Henry as a "petulant, blondish Caesar in a blue suit."

19. See, for example, Michael Cooper, "Why 'Julius Caesar' Speaks to Politics Today. With or Without Trump," *The New York Times,* June 12, 2017, https:// www.nytimes.com/2017/06/12/theater/julius-caesar-shakespeare-donald-trump .html, and Jay Gabler, "Trump-like 'Caesar' causes freak-out, while Guthrie's '12 show had an Obama-esque Caesar and no one cared," *City Pages,* June 20, 2017, http://www.citypages.com/arts/trump-like-caesar-causes-freak-out-while-guthries -12-show-had-an-obama-esque-caesar-and-no-one-cared/427979593

"In That Dimension Grossly Clad": Transgender Rhetoric, Representation, and Shakespeare

Sawyer K. Kemp

I N MAY 2017, the Globe Theatre released a short blog post promoting its summer production of *Twelfth Night.* In the blog, scholar Will Tosh compares Viola's disguise as Cesario to the experience of contemporary trans and gender-nonconforming youth:

> Shakespeare's vision of a gender identity that can slip along the scale from female to male and back seems, in 2017, intriguingly familiar. [. . .] But if the number of transgender people seems greater today than in the past [. . .] it's worth remembering that gender fluidity is no 21st-century invention: Shakespeare's comedies show that when it comes to gender, it's all a matter of performance.[1]

Tosh suggests that one can use Shakespeare as historical documentation of gender fluidity in order to validate the legitimacy of transgender youth. In exchange, the implicit payoff for the Globe is that Shakespeare is rendered both sociopolitically relevant and (given that Tosh specifically cites the LGBT media monitoring organization GLAAD's statistic that "more than one in ten young people identified as gender non-conforming, compared to 3% of the over-50s") more accessible to younger audiences by the inclusion of gender-fluid characters. The Globe is not alone in this desire to model gender inclusivity as a feature of Shakespeare performance. California Shakespeare Theater's 2017 production of *As You Like It* specifically sought out a genderqueer actor to play Rosalind, and the program details cast engagement with local trans and gender-nonconforming community groups "to hear other's stories about gender journeys . . . inviting a deeper investigation of the character of Rosalind and her own journey."[2]

Obviously, attention to gender and cross-dressing have a long history in Shakespearean criticism, perhaps as long as the history of Shakespearean criticism itself, but as critics begin to annex older rhetorical maneuvers invoking the "transvestite" or "hermaphrodite" to the contemporary labels "genderqueer" and "transgender," it is worth pausing to try to sort out exactly what the connection is (or might potentially be) between Shakespeare and contemporary social justice movements.[3] The preponderance of scholarship on cross-dressed characters like Viola or Rosalind unraveling the gender binary would seem to suggest that trans identity—even avant-la-lettre—has indeed been integral to Shakespearean performance and criticism. However, because of both structural and social inequalities in casting practices, trans and gender nonconforming actors appear only rarely in these or any other roles in Shakespeare.[4] Living, non-fictional, self-identified trans people thus have both a privileged and completely disposable relationship to the bard.

Because we persist in reading androgyny or genderqueerness in the performance of a cis actor, we participate directly in constructing the image of androgyny and genderqueerness *from the performance of a cisgender body.*[5] The discussion of trans actors in theater is almost completely divorced from the discussion of genderqueer or androgynous characterization in Shakespeare performance. The desire to either inject sexualized androgyny into or de-gender a role—what Elizabeth Klett calls in her reading of Fiona Shaw's portrayal of Richard II "the sexless and the sexy" branches of androgyny—is almost always fulfilled by a cis actor through hair, makeup, and costume choices.[6] The willingness to see these as separate issues is both generative and problematic: it creates space within gender and gender performance, but edges trans people out of that conversation, as when Klett remarks "The body—both in real life and on the stage—cannot transcend or forget its gender," which seems momentarily to forget that trans people exist at all.[7] Dependence on the cis body for these readings then produces a fictional "trans" body continually defined by the same cisgender norms—a performative fiction of androgyny and genderqueerness that is uninterested in the varied branches of androgyny that medical and social transition have actualized.

While both Shakespearean performance and criticism rely fundamentally on the rhetoric of gendered bodies in transition, actual trans people and bodies are predominantly absent from discourse and performance. Even textually, the representation of cross-dressed characters varies importantly from the experience of contemporary trans people. So, are these cross-dressing characters "trans"? Or not? Are trans people important to Shakespeare? Or not?

I am not interested in rehashing the queer historicist debates which have had so much ink spilled on them already. Clearly, there is both a value in finding resonance across history for queer identities, as well as a cultural specificity and a separation of centuries that should give us pause. As Valerie Traub writes, "neither will we find in the past a mirror of ourselves nor that the past is so utterly alien that we will find nothing usable in its fragmentary traces."[8] Or, as Fran Dolan has put it, "Frankly, I don't feel all that at home in the present, either."[9] Yet, when we bring the language and lens of the present to the people and objects of the past, it is always in the service of the present. In this paper I argue that the current mode of "finding" trans people in Shakespeare's work not only loses the cultural specificity of early modern gender nonconformism, but also loses the cultural specificity of contemporary trans people and the narratives they have produced. Put simply, for a group of people who talk at length about genderqueer bodies and performance, some of us do not seem to listen very carefully to what trans people have said about their own experiences in self-fashioning.

This phenomenon is a result of a genealogy of scholarship that has long been a study of transvestism, which is to say that it was primarily concerned with clothing, not identity. It takes little more than a pair of pants to turn Rosalind into Ganymede, Viola to Cesario or Portia to Balthazar, which is inconsistent with the experience of anyone attempting to transition in 2018. This may be because, as Bridget Escolme writes, "Most disguises in the early modern theatres simply work."[10] Or it could be because protesting too much at the convention of cross-dressing might break the illusion in a theater which already relied on boys acting as women, but to read clothing and disguise as hallmarks of a proto-trans identity risks creating a binary between the body—which is "true" and essential—and the clothing that is "trans" but also deceptive. It also significantly elides the labor of constructing a habit (of clothes but also manners) that "passes." If you go to any internet forum for trans people, you will find people talking to each other about how to transition—practically, legally, socially—and pages and pages are devoted to passing. What this should suggest is not that passing is mandatory, but rather that it is *hard*. In Shakespeare, the magical transvestism of The Pants is instant and absolute. Although Orlando has been wandering the woods for days thinking of nothing but Rosalind, when presented with Ganymede—who presumably, still looks exactly like Rosalind, the person he has been thinking about continuously—he makes no connection, and addresses the stranger only as "pretty youth" (3.2.328).[11] Similarly, when Sebastian encounters Cesario at the end of *Twelfth Night,* he thinks Cesario looks, not like his lost sister, but like himself, as he marvels "Do I stand there? I never had a brother" (5.1.222). Even when Cesario explains that he had a father named Sebastian, and a brother also named Sebastian, and that he comes from their home of Messaline, Sebastian does not see his sibling in the person standing before him:

> Were you a woman, as the rest goes even,
> I should my tears let fall upon your cheek,
> And say "Thrice-welcome, drowned Viola!"
>
> (5.1.235–37)

Sebastian's inability to recognize Viola as Viola is rooted in his inability to believe she is not a man. He sublimates any doubt about gender to a doubt about identity. At the level of cognition, this cedes ontological and intimate knowledge of a person to the knowledge of their gender, seeming to suggest Sebastian knows his own sister less than he imagines he knows this stranger's genitals.

But for many trans people, their families are some of the most difficult people to convince of the legitimacy of their gender. Looking at online forums and digital communities, familial doubt is a common thread. One finds thousands of results for searches like "How can I get my parents to use my preferred name?," "How do I get my parents to use my pronouns?," and "My mom/dad/sibling doesn't believe I'm trans." Characters like Viola may present a *utopian* vision of transition: one of such ease and striking completeness that even your own brother would instinctively use the right pronouns. However, taking such instances as uncritical parallels for transness obscures much of the anxiety, ambivalence, and danger that this familiar scenario presents for many.

Indeed, Shakespeare gives what might now be considered very bad advice for passing. In *Cymbeline* when Pisanio instructs Imogen on how to pass for a man, he tells her to turn "fear and niceness . . . into a waggish courage, / Ready in gibes, quick-answer'd, saucy, and / As quarrelous as the weasel" (3.4.155–59). Equally pugnacious, *As You Like It*'s Rosalind promises Celia that they will "have a swashing and a martial outside" (1.3.117). Portia makes a similar brag in *Merchant of Venice* when she says she will "speak of frays / Like a fine bragging youth: and tell quaint lies" (3.4.68–69). Waggish, saucy, quarrelous, swashing, bragging—across the comedies, all parties agree that affecting the personality of a young, bravado-filled boy is the formula for passing. This spectacle of waggish masculinity seems out of step in the current cultural landscape where discovery is fatal and "stealth" is a virtue, where the common wisdom is that to pass you would do well to keep a low profile.[12] The popular FTM ("Female To Male") style blog The Art of Transliness suggests that "Dressing like a *generic* guy can often (though not always) increase your chances of being read as male" (emphasis mine).[13] Or, as Vice Chair of the Trans United Fund Allison Gill says in a 2016 NPR interview: "The last thing you as a trans person would want to do is draw attention to yourself."[14]

The point here is not that Shakespeare fails to prefigure the American transgender experience adequately, nor that we should never look for transgender resonances in the past, but rather to suggest that we need to challenge our scholarship to locate transgender identity in something other than clothing. Perhaps we need not a narrower criterion for identifying and applying trans theory to characterization and identity, but a *wider* one with the ability to draw on contemporary resonance in robust ways. What characters in Shakespeare might participate in discussions of body dysphoria, a major mental health issue for trans people? What characters experience harassment by law enforcement figures, as do over one third of trans people? What characters experience homelessness, a situation that affects one in five transgender people?[15] What characters experience sexual violence, something that over 50 percent of trans people report experiencing?[16] We can use these questions as a lens for our critique of cross-dressed characters—we might think about how Rosalind is kicked out of her home by her family, use dysphoria as a way of reading Joan la Pucelle's madness, or realize that in *Merry Wives*, it is while Falstaff is dressed as the Old Woman of Brentford that he is subject to Ford's harshest verbal and physical abuse. Or, we can de-center clothing entirely. Hamlet is disallowed from inheriting his military position, prevented from attending his school, deeply depressed, considering suicide, ejected from his home and filled with anxiety at the task that generations of scholars have insisted is the Ur-quest of masculinity and patrilineage and—I think I just outed Hamlet.[17]

If we as scholars are going to engage in a practice that believes trans people are integral to Shakespeare, it seems important to create scholarship that is rooted in experience, not abstraction. If we are going to visit the past to serve the present, it should actually and meaningfully serve those populations whose language, identities, and communities we are borrowing.

Notes

1. ShakespearesGlobeBlog. Tumblr. "What you will." 5/11/2017. http://blog.shakespearesglobe.com/post/160546033578/gender-in-twelfth-night.

2. Encore Arts Programs. "Cal Shakes: As You Like It." Program notes for Shakespeare's *As You Like It*. California Shakespeare Theatre. Dir. Desdemona Chiang. Orinda, California: Bruns Amphitheater, June 2017.

3. A complete bibliography of the transitional texts bridging "hermaphrodism," "transvestism," "genderqueer" and "transgender" would be its own project, but see: James C. Bulman, *Shakespeare Re-Dressed: Cross-gender Casting in Contemporary Performance* (Madison: Fairleigh Dickinson University Press, 2008); Simone Chess, *Male-to-Female Crossdressing in Early Modern English Literature: Gender Performance and Queer Relations* (New York: Routledge, 2016); Helen King, *The One-Sex Body on Trial: The Classical and Early Modern Evidence* (Burlington: Ashgate, 2013); Terri Power, *Shakespeare & Gender in Practice* (New York: Palgrave, 2016); Emily Rose, "Keeping the Trans in Translation: Queering Early Modern Transgender Memoirs," *TSQ: Transgender Studies Quarterly* (2016) 3(3–4): 485–505; and Alan Sinfield, *Shakespeare, Authority, Sexuality* (New York: Routledge, 2006).

4. No studies explicitly detailing the numbers of trans people in acting professions currently exist; however, I posit that given that the majority of MFAs in the United States are unfunded and/or costly *and* that the NCTE's large-scale survey of trans people in America in 2015 found trans people experience poverty and homelessness at rates above the national average, a de facto institutional barrier has been created. See "The Report of the 2015 National Transgender Survey" National Center for Transgender Equality, 2015, https://transequality.org/sites/default/files/docs/usts/USTS-Full-Report-Dec17.pdf

5. Although the stability of a legibly cisgendered body may be a fictional ontology, vis-à-vis Judith Butler, *Bodies That Matter: On the Discursive Limits of 'Sex'* (New York, NY: Routledge, 1993), an assumption of stability seems to underscore much of our scholarly fixation on Shakespeare's cross-dressing boy actors. Boy actors in female roles become a provocative site of gender investigation precisely (and to my mind, problematically) because the scholar already "knows" what they "really are."

6. Elizabeth Klett, "Many Bodies, Many Voices: Performing Androgyny in Fiona Shaw and Deborah Warner's *Richard II*," *Theatre Journal* 58, no. 2 (May 2006): 182.

7. Ibid.

8. Valerie Traub, *The Renaissance of Lesbianism in Early Modern England.* (Cambridge: Cambridge University Press, 2002), 32.

9. Frances Dolan, *Marriage And Violence: The Early Modern Legacy.* (Philadelphia: University of Pennsylvania Press, 2008), 17.

10. Bridget Escolme, "Costume, Disguise and Self-Display." *Shakespeare's Theatres and the Effects of Performance.* ed. Farah Karim-Kooper and Tiffany Stern (London: Bloomsbury, 2013) 118–140.

11. All Shakespeare citations from *The Arden Shakespeare Complete Works,* ed. Richard Proudfoot, Ann Thompson, and David Scott Kastan (Walton-on-Thames: Thomas Nelson, 1998).

12. The performance of masculine bravado actually combines two major passing hurdles: not only drawing attention to oneself, but also speaking. Voice is considered one of the biggest "tells," and a source of much community discussion—a YouTube search for "how to lower your voice pre-T[estosterone]" generates over twenty thousand results.

13. The Art of Transliness. Tumblr. "The Art of Transliness Guide to Being Read As Male." March 19, 2012. http://theartoftransliness.com/post/19575647114/the-art-of-transliness-guide-to-being-read-as-male. Emphasis mine. See also "The FTM's Complete Illustrated Guide to Looking Like a (Hot) Dude." September 29, 2014. http://ftmguide.rassaku.net/. Here, even a simple choice between boots or no boots is considered a make-or-break: "Boots are going to be eye-catching. Boots are not a 'safe' or fashion-neutral choice; on men, they make a statement, so if you are trying to sneak below the radar and pass for male without drawing attention to yourself, boots are not your best option." Similarly, see Man101. Tumblr. "Why You Don't Pass. Part 1." April 15, 2011. http://man101.tumblr.com/post/4634 418160/why-you-dont-pass-part-i which rules out buzzcuts, fauxhawks, and tank tops for similar reasons.

14. Jeff Brady, "When A Transgender Person Uses A Public Bathroom, Who Is At Risk?" Around the Nation. May 15, 2016. http://www.npr.org/2016/05/15/477954537/when-a-transgender-person-uses-a-public-bathroom-who-is-at-risk

15. "Issues: Housing and Homelessness" National Center for Transgender Equality, 2015, http://www.transequality.org/issues/housing-homelessness.

16. "Transgender Rates of Violence" FORGE, 2011, http://forge-forward.org/wp-content/docs/FAQ-10–2012-rates-of-violence.pdf.

17. I draw here on *Hamlet*'s performance history as a generative and gender-ambivalent space, especially Asta Nielson's female Hamlet (as distinct from female actors playing male Hamlets). See: Tony Howard, *Women as Hamlet: Performance and Interpretation in Theatre, Film and Fiction.* (Cambridge: Cambridge University Press, 2007).

Matisse in the Playhouse

Elizabeth E. Tavares

O<small>N MY WAY TO EAST LONDON</small> from a Shakespeare's Globe performance in August 2017, I noticed an advertisement in one of the Tube
stations. Accompanying the billing for the Royal Academy of Arts'
exhibition, *Matisse in the Studio,* was a quotation from Henri: "a
good actor can have a part in ten different plays; an object can play
a role in ten different pictures." It is from Museum Studies that we
borrow the word *curation:* the selection and arrangement of pre-
existing art objects for a particular experience. But this notion of
curation has now overleaped the bounds of the art world; "content
curation" is the stock-in-trade of every major marketing, consulting, and Big Data firm—from fashion to Facebook, from American
Girl to the American Dream. The concept of curation, which
exploded in the 1970s art world and again in the 2000s web-based
economy, is much older than Matisse's nineteenth century, however. In this essay, I argue that curation is a hermeneutic equipped
to account for repertory economics that structured the sixteenth-
century theater industry. Pre-Shakespearean cases will exemplify
how the field of Shakespeare Studies' approach to troupes could
evolve using this transdisciplinary paradigm.

Clicking for the Same Reasons

Repertory as a system for presenting theater is distinctive in that
it asks consumers to think about plays in sets—which is to say, rela-
tionally rather than as individual art objects. Repertory Studies and
several recently published company biographies have established
which plays were owned by which company at which point.[1] The
energy in these biographies is given to characterizing the venues
and neighborhoods in which the companies performed, the osten-

sible relationship between the companies and courtly patrons, and individual personnel. What about the ways in which the marketplace differed, not only from how mainstream US and UK audiences watch today (in seasons with a handful of plays running one at a time) but also from other contemporaneous performance economies? For example, while England was operating this professional repertory system—using the same stable of actors to perform a different play every night of the week—major Italian companies such as those in Venice were staging but two operas a summer, frontloading all of their investment in a single production until it grew stale for audiences. The sixteenth-century English repertory model is still in use not only in a minority of contemporary theaters in the UK, US, and Germany, but in the majority of regional US Shakespeare festival theaters. Consider the casting calendar in the annual program of the Utah Shakespeare Festival. Readers can locate actors on the y-axis to see what shows they will be in on the x-axis—a marketing feature aiming to cultivate returner audiences.

If you plan to visit the Getty—or many another major museum— sometime soon, you can test the effects of curation for yourself: the connections your brain makes when you move from one room to the next full of paintings and sculpture. Those pathways are not haphazard. The curators have something in mind for the visitor's experience by way of the selection and arrangement of the works encountered. Hans Ulrich Obrist, the leading voice on curation in the contemporary art world, argues that curation is "*the* medium through which most art becomes known."[2] Curation usefully produces a coherent set of investments from a selection of art without necessarily having to locate that coherence in an individual person—like a playhouse-landlord such as Philip Henslowe, say. That arrangement is not a product of a singular subject, however, but an accretion over time as a viewer moves through the exhibit. To extrapolate for the repertory system, a playgoer could now dictate the theatrical experience when adopting repeated habits of playgoing, or by selecting from repeatable factors, such as a favorite actor or a spectacular prop.

I would take Obrist's observations a step further to suggest that curation by audiences was one of the paradigm shifts that helped to define the English Renaissance—a mode of consuming cultural products that informed the theater's repertory system. Terry Smith locates the power of the curated exhibit in the spatial: "it is a discursive, epistemological, and dramaturgical space in which various kinds of temporality may be produced or shown to coexist."[3] This is to say, space conditions the experience of curated art, and the experience of a set of works stages a dialogue. Like Smith, Paul O'Neill argues the spatial and the performative are at the center of the modern curator's work, where exhibitions "produce temporary forms of order" and personal choice is converted into social and cultural capital.[4] This vocabulary of curatorial activities frames the polysemy made available by the set of texts owned by individual museums—or by playing companies. This model crucially can free literary critics from having to presume that there was a single individual guiding all of a company's purchasing choices and scheduling in advance.

David Balzer counters that to curate has become problematically synonymous with connoisseurship. His concerns for the contemporary art world point to how corporate entities have co-opted curatorial strategies as part of a larger *deskilling:* "the cost-cutting phasing-out of professional workers by machines or less-skilled workers" and consumers' complicity in it.[5] While Balzer points to the widespread deskillment curation promotes by way of "a self-fulfilling dependence on algorithms,"[6] theater historian Evelyn Tribble points, conversely, to the early modern repertory system as a venue in which curation promoted "enskillment."[7] Thus, curation provides a framework for exploring why it is that "we don't always click for the same reasons," "we don't always collect for the same reasons," and, by extension, playgoers did not always attend theater for the same reasons.[8]

Fire and Nuts, Chariots and Swords

Reading through the Strange's Men canon, it seems everyone is on fire. By using curation, one can trace the dramaturgical rather than the thematic features a company specialized in. Lawrence Manley demonstrates that many of this company's offerings called for the lighting of bodies, producing a trademark of theatrical experience—which then sent me looking for how one might actually light them.[9] Alongside recipes for toothpaste in early modern cookbooks, one can also find recipes for different cosmetics.[10] Some of these would safely allow one to immolate a part of the body, such as Abdelmelec's hand, made "a blazing brand of fire" (2.4.23) in *The Battle of Alcazar.* The odds that nut-based recipes were used

by actors increases when it is remembered that neighboring indus-
tries capitalized upon neighbors, and so perhaps the hazelnut
shells from a soap mill not two hundred yards from the Rose
theater were used both for flooring and to create pyrotechnic
makeup.[11]

Following Strange's calendar of plays adds an additional layer of
complexity to what might be considered distinguishable features of
the company's habits of playing. During the six months of Strange's
unrestrained (that is, not interrupted by censorship or plague) playing at the Rose between February 1592 and February 1593, the company staged 134 performances of 27 distinct playtexts. At least 11
(and as many as 15) of the 24 plays in repertory during that
season—approximately half of their active properties—featured at
least one contemporaneous Mediterranean figure.[12] As many as 20
of their 36 total known playtexts feature similar Mediterranean
figures and locales. The pie below on the left indicates the percentage of playtexts in the company's stock that included characters of
color, roughly less than half. If we take the same data and instead
measure the number of performances staged by the company that
included characters of color, the percentage was substantially more
than half. It may be that the company was investing in materials
and technologies, makeup and fire, to consistently provide an experience emphasizing the scale and cultural specificity of a range of
Mediterranean peoples.[13]

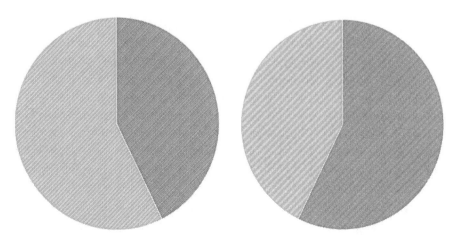

Fig. 1. The Lord Strange's repertory holdings, comparative: left, by number of
individual play-texts (47%); right, by number of discrete performances (67%).

While Strange's Men were playing with makeup, the Admiral's were playing with cars. As I have argued elsewhere, at least four of their plays in the late 1580s, including *The Wounds of Civil War, The Reign of Edward III,* and possibly *Tamar Cham,* made use of a chariot.[14] If a company was going to invest in such a complex prop, designed to be pulled by at least two men, perhaps they would be interested in other plays that might up-cycle that investment. While Matisse likely had the repetition of monstera leaves rather than a torture chariot in mind when he talked about their multiple roles, his observation that objects have their own parts to play distills the usefulness of repetition for organizing an audience's aesthetic experience.

Most exciting about applying this curatorial logic to early modern drama are the possibilities it presents for working with archaeologists. Since 1989, when the change in planning permissions meant that any new construction in London required an archaeological survey, several playhouse foundations have been discovered. Consider that during the 1592/93 plague closure, the Rose underwent significant renovation to include a balcony. While the Rose offered this new latitude, the Curtain, as archaeologist Heather Knight has shown, offered spectacular longitude.[15] Her dig this past year has not only revealed that the Curtain was both rect-

Fig. 2. Recent variations on 2 Tamburlaine's chariot: left, Shakespeare Theatre Company 2007, dir. Michael Kahn; right, Theatre for a New Audience 2015, dir. Michael Boyd.

angular and immediately across the lane from a pre-eminent fencing school, but that the width of the stage would have been the same length required of Olympic fencers today. Perhaps one went to the Curtain for a "fighty play," and plots were primarily a vehicle to such special feats. How might the ways in which scholars talk about Elizabethan drama change if projects were designed around such patterns of material uses rather than generic or thematic priorities?[16]

The early modern repertory system challenges the present-day appeal of the algorithm that prioritizes generic conventions as markers of aesthetic innovation, diversity, and intellectual development while prematurely foreclosing discussions of what was distinctive about an individual company's means of performance. A framework like repertorial curation helps underscore the factors specific to Elizabethan habits of theatergoing. If the offerings were relatively unknown until a playgoer got to the playhouse itself, and proximity was not a conditioning factor for selection, how did one choose? By curating distinctive house styles rooted in technical innovation and the ability to respond to their cultural moment, I contend it was through the repertory system that playing companies managed playgoer expectations in order to ensure their financial success.

Notes

I would like to thank John Kuhn, Daniel Pollack-Pelzner, and Misha Teramura for their feedback and support on early drafts of this presentation. This paper represents a snapshot of the theoretic framework for my forthcoming book, *The Repertory System before Shakespeare: Playing the Stock Market*.

1. Particularly innovative examples include Mary Bly, *Queer Virgins and Virgin Queans on the Early Modern Stage* (Oxford: Oxford University Press, 2000); Laurie Johnson, *Shakespeare's Lost Playhouse: Eleven Days at Newington Butts* (New York: Routledge, 2017); Roslyn L. Knutson, *The Repertory of Shakespeare's Company, 1594–1613* (Fayetteville, AK: University of Arkansas Press, 1991); James J. Marino, *Owning William Shakespeare: The King's Men and Their Intellectual Property* (Philadelphia, PA: University of Pennsylvania Press, 2011); Scott McMillin and Sally-Beth MacLean, *The Queen's Men and Their Plays* (New York: Cambridge University Press, 1998); Lucy Munro, *Children of the Queen's Revels: A Jacobean Theatre Repertory* (New York: Cambridge University Press, 2005); Michael Shapiro, *Children of the Revels: The Boy Companies of Shakespeare's Time and Their Plays* (New York: Columbia University Press, 1977); Brian Walsh, *Shakespeare, The Queen's Men, and the Elizabethan Performance of History* (New York: Cambridge University Press, 2009).

2. Hans Ulrich Obrist, *A Brief History of Curating* (Zurich, Switzerland: JRP / Ringier, 2008), 7.

3. Terry Smith, *Thinking Contemporary Curating* (New York: Independent Curators International, 2012), 30.

4. Paul O'Neill, *The Culture of Curating and the Curating of Culture(s)* (Cambridge, MA: Massachusetts Institute of Technology Press, 2012), 39; 87–88.

5. David Balzer, *Curationism: How Curating Took Over the Art World and Everything Else* (Toronto, ON: Coach House Books, 2014), 99.

6. Balzer, *Curationism*, 131.

7. Evelyn B. Tribble, *Cognition in the Globe: Attention and Memory in Shakespeare's Theatre* (New York, NY: Palgrave Macmillan, 2011), 115; 155.

8. Balzer, *Curationism*, 132.

9. Lawrence Manley, "Playing With Fire: Immolation in the Repertory of Strange's Men," *Early Theatre: A Journal Associated with the Records of Early English Drama*, 4 (2001): 115–29.

10. See Richard Blunt, "The Evolution of Blackface Cosmetics on the Early Modern Stage," in *The Materiality of Color: The Production, Circulation, and Application of Dyes and Pigments, 1400–1800*, eds. Andrea Feeser, Maureen Daly Goggin, and Beth Fowkes Tobin (Burlington, VT: Ashgate, 2012), 217–34.

11. See John Orrell, "Nutshells at the Rose," *Theatre Research International* 17, no. 1 (March 1992): 8–14.

12. Strange's repertorial holdings have been compiled from Henslowe's Diary and title page ascriptions. Mediterranean labels for non-extant plays drawn from *The Lost Plays* database and conventions within Mediterranean Studies. Mediterranean percentages based on total number excluding the three plays about which nothing of the content can be speculated upon.

13. Elizabeth E. Tavares, "A Race to the Roof: Cosmetics and Contemporary Histories in the Elizabethan Playhouse, 1592–1596," *Shakespeare Bulletin* 34, no. 2 (Summer 2016): 202–203.

14. Elizabeth E. Tavares, "Super Troupers; or, Supplemented Playing before 1594," *Shakespeare Studies* 45 (2017): 77–86.

15. Heather Knight, "What Can Archaeology Bring to the Party?," keynote presented at the Before Shakespeare Conference, University of Roehampton, UK, 24 August 2017.

16. I consider this question in greater detail in the post "Genre and the Elizabethan Troupe," for Before Shakespeare: The Beginnings of London Commercial Theatre, 1565–1595 (blog), May 11, 2017, https://beforeshakespeare.com/2017/05/11/genre-and-the-elizabethan-troupe.

Sultanic Drag in Ben Jonson's *Epicene*

CORINNE ZEMAN

Scholars of ANGLO-ISLAMIC CONTACT understandably focus on the so-called Turk plays—a dramatic corpus starring Muslim characters and set in Ottoman-occupied lands. Yet genre-specific portrayals of Islamic alterity offer an incomplete picture of global contact. We must broaden this archive to see the diversity of English responses to the Islamic world. I suggest that we look to a counterintuitive genre: the city comedy. London-based dramas fold Islamic cultural materials into the fabric of metropolitan life. These plays are not only littered with Levantine imports and Arabic loanwords, but include frequent moments of cross-cultural masquerade—scenes in which English characters make imaginative excursions across racial and religious boundaries. In the pages below, I look to Ben Jonson's *Epicene* to explore the comic displacement of a Turk-play stock character: the Ottoman sultan.[1] Jonson's comedy stars a cantankerous bachelor who sees the Ottoman monarch as an enviable model of heterosexist mastery. Spinning a fantasy of oriental dominion, this would-be sultan experiments in ethnic drag. He not only dons a turban, but establishes a seraglio in central London. *Epicene* offers insight into the counterintuitive identity experiments precipitated by global contact. More to the point, it permits us to consider the effects of genre on Islamic representation. The netted echoes of Turk plays past haunt the performance of this city comedy. But while Turk plays subject Muslim characters to the purgative logic of tragedy, city comedies defang but do not excise alterity.[2]

In its very first scene, *Epicene* introduces audiences to a turbaned Morose. Truewit reports, "I met that stiff piece of formality . . . yesterday, with a huge turban of night-caps on his head, buckled over his ears" (1.1.140–42).[3] On the early modern stage, turbans were used to designate Muslim characters.[4] This visual code would have registered with audiences in Whitefriars, for *Epicene* was performed in repertory with Turk plays like Robert Daborne's *A Christian Turn'd Turk*.[5] The repertory functions like a living, mnemonic palimpsest; it thickens performance by activating meanings across playscripts and genres.[6] In *Epicene,* Jonson activates the theme of conversion—or, more exactly, the turned-Turk topos. Like the renegades of Turk plays, Morose adopts the material signifiers of a Turkish identity to announce his withdrawal from the social and specifically auditory landscape of London. His costume indicates that he has a border-bridging identity; he, like his "turban of nightcaps," entangles the foreign and familiar.

In this early scene, *Epicene* toys with generic expectations, both playing upon and inverting the conventional portrayal of Turkish characters. Truewit first teases the arrival of the Ottoman scourge—a figure typically depicted as formidable and masculine. He declares Morose a "stiff piece," which could describe a durable firearm or well-protected fortress.[7] Relatedly, the term "to buckle" was often used to describe the donning of armor prior to a battle or expedition.[8] Morose is fashioning his body as a weapon or barricaded enclosure, his ears girded to withstand a metropolitan theater of war. Yet his makeshift armor highlights rather than obscures his vulnerability. Despite the obviously phallic connotations in "stiff piece," Morose's body reads as uniquely penetrable: his ears are under constant siege by the clamor of city life. Here, *Epicene* inflates, then immediately punctures an image of Turkish virility. The humor lies in the mishmash of conflicting generic cues—or, put differently, the jerk of thwarted expectations. Audiences must reconcile the potent image of a turbaned Turk with the comic reality of a noise-averse recluse. The play has smirkingly dismantled our flight of orientalizing fancy.

We next discover that Morose has begun construction on something like a seraglio—a term evocatively defined by lexicographer John Florio as "an inclosure, a close, a padocke, a parke, a cloister or secluse."[9] Morose "hath chosen a street to lie in so narrow at both ends that it will receive no coaches nor carts nor any of these common noises . . ." (1.1.166–68). He commands his servant to cover the walls, floors, and staircases with "thick quilt or flock-bed"—"nowhere worn out and bare" (2.1.11, 27). Visitors are required to remove their shoes, but are permitted to wear "socks, or slippers soled with wool" (1.2.187–88). This textile-lined home loosely evokes the carpeted, tapestry-strewn surfaces of an Islamic interior.[10] But Morose has chosen to Anglicize his seraglio. Both his textiles and footwear are made of wool, England's leading domestic export.[11] Morose's wool-draped cloister, like his "turban of night-caps," marries a foreign aesthetic to a domestic product. *Epicene* is gesturing to the contradictions plaguing English participation in the global marketplace. Morose neurotically embodies (a very literal) domestic protectionism, but both his clothing and living quarters hint at the exchange and naturalization of foreign imports. Morose, then, occupies a selectively hermetic home. Put simply, this is a seraglio with porous borders.

When Morose takes the stage in the play's second act, his identification with Ottoman culture leaves the realm of oblique reference. He immediately declares his home the monological space of a Muslim despot: "The Turk in this divine discipline is admirable, exceeding all the potentates of the earth; still waited on by mutes . . . most of his charges and directions given by signs and with silence: an exquisite art! . . . I will practise it hereafter" (2.1.30–38). Morose is referring to the Ottoman *dilsiz,* deaf-mutes employed as salaried pages in Constantinople's Topkapi Palace.[12] Hoping to flesh out the stage of his orientalist theater, Morose enlists his servant in a pantomime of genuflection. He requires the aptly named Mute to ape the proto-sign language of the Ottoman *dilsiz.* Over the course of 2.1, Mute performs seven consecutive bows in answer to Morose's queries. These bows and gesticulations visually incarnate Morose's designs on sultanic mastery. This recurring comic gag elongates the initial spectacle of obeisance, keeping in the minds of theatergoers Morose's status as a would-be Turk.

These early, tangible engagements with Ottoman culture attune audiences to the flickers of Islamic alterity in subsequent scenes. Much as the Ottoman sultan was said to use procurers to locate his concubines, Morose employs the barber Cutbeard to identify his prospective wife. Audiences learn that Cutbeard is aiding Morose's nephew in laying an elaborate trap to emasculate his uncle. Which is to say, a barber—a term interchangeable with surgeon and circumciser—labors to unman a pseudo-sultan. This is a plot twist that calls to mind the castration anxiety so pervasive in Turk plays.[13] The irony, of course, is that the sultan in a Turk play is never at risk of gelding. Once more, the play's generic baggage serves to deflate Morose's pretensions to Turkish masculinity.

Islamic resonances similarly thicken Morose's decision to divorce his bride. In the year *Epicene* was first staged, anti-divorce tracts circulating among Londoners decried the westward spread of the "Turkish libertie of putting awaie such wiues as [husbands] like not."[14] The divorce proceedings culminate in a telling moment of rhetorical misprision. When Morose insists that he suffers from impotence, the mock-curate is expected to say, "Your *impotentes . . .* are *minime apti ad contrahenda matrimonium,*" or "impotent men are least suited to contracting marriages" (5.3.188–9). Yet he inadvertently exchanges "*impotentes*" for "*omnipotentes*" (5.3.186). The mock-curate's error strikes at a core contradiction in the English construction of the Ottoman sultan. Though supposedly a figure of unlimited sovereignty, the Muslim potentate was said to be rendered impotent by the very potency of his desires. Morose neatly embodies this self-defeating paradox. It is his fantasy of hypermasculine control which sets in motion his emasculation. The play's conclusion reveals Morose's bride to be a boy in drag—a plot point that places Morose in a potentially sodomitical relationship.[15] And to be sure, sodomy was widely considered a Turkish and specifically sultanic vice.[16]

In close, the sultan accrues new facets when transposed into the city comedy. It has previously been argued that emasculation "overrides" Morose's brief "Turkification," but these processes are in fact simultaneous.[17] Morose is at once a Turk, an agoraphobe, a melancholic, an impotent spouse, and an unwitting sodomite. These are coincident, not discrete, vectors of his identity, for characterization is always an additive process. *Epicene* shows the flexibility with which the theater reconfigures available types, forging stock characters who impose a provisional coherence over discontinuity and difference. Though we are accustomed to thinking that Jonsonian characters are merely types—monadic and one-dimensional—we need to recall that types are by no means static facts. They are flexible composites. The product of generic and discursive bleed, Morose emerges as an identity bricolage. Cobbled from a mixed inventory of urban and Turkish types, his characterization is a testament to the burgeoning cosmopolitanisms of seventeenth-century London.

Epicene relies on the use of anti-Islamic tropes to disempower and therefore quell the threat of an imagined sultanate, but there is an additional, equally significant process at work. At the level of plot, we are witnessing the humiliation of a self-styled sultan, but as a matter of form, Morose's layered identity works implicitly to inscribe Islamic alterity in the social world of London. The Turk proves malcontent, gull, and sodomite—all identifiable types on the English stage. The foreign settles within the accreted layers of the familiar. We should construe *Epicene*'s revisions to sultanic characterization as both the comic deflation of an historically imposing other and, less obviously, the neutralization of alterity by its formal or discursive inclusion. Jonson's comedy fragments and remediates Islamic representation, placing unobtrusive allusions on the very threshold of visibility. Absorbed into the layered languages of London's streets and stages, the Turk ceases to be wholly *xenos,* or an unassimilated stranger in urban space. The city comedy neither generically nor geographically sequesters difference. In lieu of pitting London in opposition to a discrete, exogenous "East," *Epicene* works to erode borders—generic, national, and characterological. Jonson's audiences both breach the sultanic cloister and witness the trespass of Turkish types into the imaginative landscape of metropolitan fiction. By play's end, we have entered and demystified the seraglio, denying its status as a world apart.

Notes

1. While few have commented on Jonson's engagement with Islamic culture, important exceptions include: Justin Kolb, "'A Turk's Mustachio': Anglo- Islamic Traffic and Exotic London in Ben Jonson's *Every Man Out of His Humour* and *Entertainment at Britain's Burse,*" in *Early Modern England and Islamic Worlds,* ed. Bernadette Andrea and Linda McJannet (New York: Palgrave Macmillan, 2016), 197–214; Barbara Sebek, "Morose's Turban," *Shakespeare Studies* 35 (2007): 32–38; Daniel Vitkus, "'The Common Market of All the World': English Theater, the Global System, and the Ottoman Empire in the Early Modern Period," in *Global Traffic: Discourses and Practices of Trade in English Literature and Culture from 1550 to 1700,* ed. Stephen Deng and Barbara Sebek (New York: Palgrave, 2008), 19–37.

2. In the early twentieth century, Louis Wann identified 47 Tudor and Stuart dramas starring "oriental" characters. Wann lists 19 tragedies, nine conqueror plays, seven travel plays, five tragicomedies, and only four comedies. (Three non-extant plays are of unknown genre.) "The Oriental in the English Drama of the Sixteenth and Seventeenth Centuries" (PhD diss., University of Wisconsin–Madison, 1919), 168.

3. Ben Jonson, *Epicene, or The Silent Woman,* ed. Richard Dutton (Manchester: Manchester University Press, 2003). All quotations from *Epicene* refer to this edition.

4. For the use of turbans on the early modern stage, see Matthew Dimmock, "Materialising Islam on the Early Modern English Stage," in *Early Modern Encounters with the Islamic East,* ed. Ralf Hertel, Sabine Lucia Müller, and Sabine

Schülting (London: Routledge, 2012), 115–34; and "Old Mahomet's Head: Idols, Papists and Mortus Ali on the English Stage," in Matthew Dimmock, *Mythologies of the Prophet Muhammad in Early Modern English Culture* (Cambridge: Cambridge University Press, 2013), 116–25.

5. We do not have a precise date of composition for *A Christian Turn'd Turk,* though it was likely produced between 1609 and 1612. See Daniel Vitkus, introduction to *Three Turk Plays from Early Modern England* (New York: Columbia University Press, 2000), 24.

6. For the intertextuality of the repertory theater, see Gina Bloom, Anston Bosman, and William West, "Ophelia's Intertheatricality, or, How Performance Is History," *Theatre Journal* 65, no. 2 (2013): 165–82; Marvin Carlson, *The Haunted Stage: The Theatre as Memory Machine* (Ann Arbor: University of Michigan Press, 2006); William West, "Intertheatricality," in *Early Modern Theatricality,* ed. Henry Turner (Oxford: Oxford University Press, 2013), 151–72.

7. *OED Online,* s.v. "piece, n," accessed June 13, 2017, www.oed.com/view/Entry/143547.

8. *OED Online,* s.v. "buckle, v.," accessed June 13, 2017, www.oed.com/view/Entry/24189.

9. John Florio, *A Worlde of Wordes, or Most copious, and exact dictionarie in Italian and English* (London: Arnold Hatfield for Edw. Blount, 1598), 366. Through Morose does not explicitly refer to his home as a "seraglio," we know Jonson was familiar with and saw the theatrical potential inherent in this term. In *The Alchemist,* Sir Epicure Mammon is, like Morose, prone to orientalizing fantasies. He muses that he means to make the city's gallants the "eunuchs" in his "seraglio." Ben Jonson, *The Alchemist,* ed. Elizabeth Cook (London and New York: A&C Black, 1991), 2.2.68, 34.

10. For a description of Islamic interiors, see Sebastian Münster, *A Briefe Collection and Compendious Extract of the Straunge and Memorable Things,* trans. Richard Eden (London: Thomas Marshe, 1572), F3v.

11. That said, Truewit specifically notes that Morose owns a "carpet" (4.5.242)—a term often used in reference to the knotted pile weaves imported in large numbers from the Ottoman Empire or, alternatively, produced in Europe but modeled on Anatolian design. For the emblematic significance of carpets in Jacobean London, see Gerald M. MacLean, *Looking East: English Writing and the Ottoman Empire before 1800* (Houndmills: Palgrave Macmillan, 2007), 30–42.

12. M. Miles, "Signing in the Seraglio: Mutes, Dwarfs and Jestures at the Ottoman Court 1500–1700," *Disability and Society* 15, no. 1 (2000): 115–34. For contemporaneous accounts of the Ottoman mutes, see Michel Baudier, *The History of the Imperiall Estate of the Grand Seigneurs,* trans. Edward Grimeston (London: William Stansby for Richard Meighen, 1635), 126; Ogier Ghiselin de Busbecq, *The Life and Letters of Ogier Ghiselin de Busbecq,* ed. C. T. Forster and F. H. B. Daniell (London: Kegan Paul, 1881), 156, 303.

13. For references to circumcision and representations of the Ottoman eunuch, see Dennis Britton, "Muslim Conversion and Circumcision as Theater," in *Religion and Drama in Early Modern England: The Performance of Religion on the Renaissance Stage,* ed. Elizabeth Williamson and Jane Hwang Degenhardt (New York: Routledge, 2016), 71–88; Jonathan Burton, *Traffic and Turning: Islam and English Drama,* 1579–1624 (Newark: University of Delaware Press, 2005), 106–26.

14. Edmund Bunny, *Of Diuorce for Adulterie, and Marrying Againe: That There Is No Sufficient Warrant so to Do* (Oxford: Joseph Barnes, 1610), A.

15. For Morose's associations with sodomy, see Mario DiGangi, *The Homoerotics of Early Modern Drama* (Cambridge: Cambridge University Press, 1997), 74.

16. Joseph Boone, *The Homoerotics of Orientalism* (New York: Columbia University Press, 2014), esp. 27–43.

17. Sebek, "Morose's Turban," 33.

ARTICLES

Staging Rhetorical Vividness
in *Coriolanus*

KATHARINE A. CRAIK

I

S HAKESPEARE'S CORIOLANUS is a man of action rather than words. As Menenius explains to Sicinius, he "talks like a knell and his hum is a battery" (5.4.20–21).[1] Nevertheless, many scholars have explored the centrality of rhetoric in the Roman plays, and have commented on Coriolanus's particular aptitudes as an orator. Some have found his eloquence "remarkable" and "brilliant," noting its complex affinities to Ciceronian, anti-Ciceronian, or Attic style.[2] Others have argued that his overpacked, dense manner of speaking—not to mention his failure to utter when it matters most—represent his contempt for the civilizing resources of language; or, at best, his eloquent inarticulacy.[3] Critics interested in the play's rhetorical landscape have all however tended to agree that Coriolanus's own accomplishments or deficiencies as an orator lie at the heart of the drama. This essay aims to shed new light on the place of rhetoric in *Coriolanus* by looking beyond the hero's own speaking voice, concentrating instead on moments where language—informal report as well as formal declamation—calls Coriolanus vividly to mind when he is not present onstage. Cominius and Lartius, among others, sketch absorbing word pictures of Coriolanus in front of attentive onstage Roman audiences; and these word pictures are considered here as examples of the "rhetoric of immediacy" that summons up absent, remembered, or imagined people as if they were truly before our eyes.[4] I argue that Shakespeare was drawing on both classical and Christian ideas of rhetorical vividness, and that *Coriolanus* (as well as his earlier Roman play, *Julius Caesar*) set out to explore how and why such pictures

143

stir up strong responses, especially pity, among susceptible groups of listeners. As we will see, the Roman citizens' responses have consequences for the dramatization of *Romanitas.* More importantly, they also allow Shakespeare to explore more broadly the place of rhetoric in early modern theatrical representation.

It is not difficult to see why Coriolanus's own rhetorical prowess has so often been regarded as the play's central animating force. Coriolanus is a colossal machine of a man, with a thunderous voice to match. Fearing his avenging wrath in the play's final act, Menenius describes how he "moves like an engine and the ground shrinks before his treading" (5.4.18–20). To audiences in the theater, Coriolanus's character tends to prove exceptionally compelling—not least because of what he says, and how he says it. As A. C. Bradley memorably remarked, when Coriolanus is cut off by the conspirators in the play's final moments, it is as though "life has suddenly shrunk and dwindled, and become a home for pygmies."[5] But Bradley's comment misses a different and more complex kind of shrinking, or dwindling, which is felt by Coriolanus's *Roman* audiences not when he leaves the stage but rather when he takes to it. Coriolanus is often evoked by others in his absence, especially the outstanding orator Cominius, and their words summon him into lively, imaginative presence in the citizens' minds as the "best man i'th' field" (2.2.95). Here, in accordance with rhetorical theories of *enargeia,* Coriolanus is brought brightly alive, through words, as Rome's most "rare example" (2.2.102). I argue that Shakespeare is, however, centrally interested in the shortfall between such versions of Coriolanus, drawn in words, and the man who appears in person before the Roman citizens. Coriolanus fails, in person, to live up to his off-stage reputation—especially when he resolutely refuses to display his wounds. The play's exposure of this shortfall contributes to broader cultural debates about the place and value of rhetoric, especially sacred rhetoric, in early modern culture. As often as rhetoric was endorsed as an essential tool of persuasion, not least because of its ability to create lifelike presence, it was criticized for its propensity to foster deception and error.[6] The Roman plays prove a surprisingly rich site for exploring this problem.

Rhetoric and Rome were inseparable in Shakespeare's imagination. As Dan Hooley has written, "rhetoric itself, the acculturating, identity-imprinting system of education and language of civic discourse, is part and parcel of *Romanitas.*"[7] Shakespeare's familiarity with the ancient rhetorical tradition has long been recognized, and he would have absorbed from Livy's *Ab Urbe Condita* the importance of exemplary oratorical performance to the *res populi*.[8] A recent surge of critical attention to the schoolroom experiences of Shakespeare and his contemporaries has uncovered the rhetorical habits of mind that animate early modern drama, especially plays set in ancient Rome. Scholarship has often focused on the ways in which rhetorical exercise fostered stoical resolution and emotional self-management, leading toward a robust sense of solidarity among like-minded learners.[9] More recently Lynn Enterline has suggested in *Shakespeare's Schoolroom* that theater was capable of challenging the "socially normative" practices that generally served to shore up the political status quo in England.[10] The present essay agrees with Enterline and others that dramatizing the early modern rhetorical inheritance provided Shakespeare with an opportunity to problematize the relationship between good speaking and right action. But rather than seeing the Roman plays as acts of resistance to the gestural, expressive, and bodily constraints of the schoolroom, I argue here that their focus on eloquence forms part of a broader, more radical experiment with theatrical representation itself. Shakespeare was deeply interested in the boundaries between language's power to stimulate the mind's eye, and drama's ability to bring matters literally before us. These boundaries are a prominent feature of his later works, perhaps most memorably in act 4, scene 6 of *King Lear* where, on Dover cliff, the blinded Gloucester finds Edgar's description of events ("Ten masts at each make not the altitude / Which thou hast perpendicularly fell") more persuasively real than the smaller fall he has enacted onstage.[11] *The Winter's Tale* returns to this same problem, not only in the final "statue scene" but also in the two versions of Antigonus's unfortunate death—one narrated by the Clown to his father the shepherd ("I have seen . . . such sights"), and the other not quite witnessed by the audience ("*Exit, pursued by a bear*").[12] It is the Roman plays, especially *Julius Caesar* and *Coriolanus,* which, on the face of things, seem most explicitly concerned with rhetoric rather than theatrical effects; it is here, however, that Shakespeare interrogated most thoroughly the difference between seeing and believing.

The rhetorical landscape of *Coriolanus* is as Christian as it is Roman, and this has always seemed strangely at odds with the fact that the warlike Coriolanus is self-evidently not Christlike. Schol-

arship has accounted for this problem by discussing the play's
exploration of the differences between classical and Christian politics, or between Roman *honestas* and Christian patterns of sacrifice.[13] Attending more specifically to early modern debates about
rhetoric allows a fresh perspective on this difficult question. Shakespeare was writing at a time when theologians were debating ways
to make Christ's sacrifice more directly apprehensible to believers
through the sacraments, and more especially through preaching
from the pulpit. Here the stakes involved in rhetorical vividness
could scarcely have been higher as the preacher's invocation of
the Holy Spirit—brought through language before the faithful—
ravished, uplifted, and exhilarated communities of believers, reinforcing their devotion to something vastly greater.[14] In the Catholic
tradition of identifying with the suffering Christ, emotional intensity became a spiritual tool as each believer's pity for the broken
body of Christ, and suffering Christians more generally, pricked the
desire to perform good works.[15] But even as an innovative Christian
grand style was developing in England, pulpit eloquence was criticized as an affront to unadorned spiritual expression—and sacred
rhetoric eventually became "a polemical issue, possibly even a her-
esy."[16] The tension that arose was expressed through debates about
the legitimacy of painting vivid word pictures in the imagination;
and, relatedly, about the role of compassion as a crucial duty
among and between Christians.[17] When Shakespeare's Roman
citizen audiences encounter verbal tableaux of Coriolanus, they
long to witness his Christian martyrdom—but also to participate
vicariously in his military honor and heroism. The play's rhetorical
landscape therefore emerges as a combustible blend of sacred and
ancient traditions that sheds new light, especially in its second
half, on the limits of theatrical representation.

II

   Shakespeare and his contemporaries would have encountered
ancient theories about rhetorical vividness from a variety of
sources. As part of an account of the value of metaphor, Aristotle
describes in *The Art of Rhetoric* how speakers can effectively bring
matters "before the eyes" of an audience.[18] Later Quintilian makes
clear the close relationship between *enargeia* and *phantasia,* the
rhetorical methods "by which the images of absent things are pre-

sented to the mind in such a way that we seem actually to see them with our eyes and have them physically present to us." As part of this same discussion, Quintilian ascribes to Cicero the terms *illustratio* and *evidentia;* these are capable of stirring emotions in an audience which feel "very like the real thing."[19] Such speech makes people sense they are experiencing events directly rather than merely hearing them described, for they have "a quality which makes us seem not so much to be talking about something as exhibiting it. Emotions will ensue just as if we were present at the event itself."[20] Besides referencing these key sources, scholars have also recently detected in early modern culture the influence of Longinus's discussion of *phantasia* in *Peri Hupsous,* published in the mid-sixteenth century although not translated into English until 1652.[21] Together these ancient rhetorical ideas were filtering into early modern aesthetic and literary theory, along with surviving accounts of ancient (especially Stoic) philosophies of cognition where the quality of an "impression" allows the soul to determine the difference between appearance and reality.[22] Early modern literary theorists accordingly often praised writing in which the people or events described seemed indistinguishable from their real-life presence. As George Puttenham puts it in his account of *hypotyposis* in *The Art of English Poesy* (1589): "the matter and occasion leadeth us many times to describe and set forth many things in such sort as it should appear they were truly before our eyes though they were not present."[23] These various "visualizing" techniques (*evidentia, phantasia, hypotyposis*) are difficult to distinguish from one another in early modern writing—and, indeed, from *ekphrasis,* the creation of pictures in words.[24] All such aspects of rhetorical *techne* should appear effortless, even if they are extraordinarily difficult to achieve, bringing matters urgently before us rather than delineating them carefully and accurately. They secure the strongest possible emotional engagement of the audience who feel they are apprehending matters directly, rather than listening to them at one remove.

Shakespeare's Roman orators often powerfully deploy such *techne,* including Antony in his elegiac description of Caesar's death in *Julius Caesar.* Part of this episode's effectiveness lies in the fact that the audience has already witnessed in the previous scene the events Antony so vividly recreates. The citizens' immediate response to this spectacle, however, had been dismayed confusion: "Men, wives and children stare, cry out, and run." As Cassius

warns Brutus, Antony's speech at Caesar's funeral will have altogether more subtle, profound, and politically dangerous consequences: "the people may be moved / By that which he will
utter."[25] Antony goes on to describe the moment that Brutus, "Caesar's angel," betrays him:

> If you have tears, prepare to shed them now . . .
> For when the noble Caesar saw him stab,
> Ingratitude, more strong than traitor's arms,
> Quite vanquished him: then burst his mighty heart;
> And in his mantle muffling up his face,
> Even at the base of Pompey's statue,
> Which all the while ran blood, great Caesar fell.
> O, what a fall was there, my countrymen!
> Then I, and you, and all of us fell down,
> Whilst bloody treason flourished over us.
> O, now you weep, and I perceive you feel
> The dint of pity.[26]

Despite Antony's claim a few lines later that he is unskilled in rhetoric ("I have neither wit, nor words, not worth, / Action, nor utter-
ance, nor the power of speech / To stir men's blood" [3.2.214–16]),
this speech is a deft example of *evidentia* that brings a vivid tableau
of Caesar's murder before his audience. The citizens' pity is
aroused through Antony's description of Caesar muffling his face
with his mantle at the very moment when Brutus's ingratitude
"burst his mighty heart," but also by his nostalgic sketch of Caesar
first wearing that same mantle "on a summer's evening in his tent, /
That day he overcame the Nervii" (170–71). If the bloodied mantle
is a powerful prop, so is Caesar's body: "Here is himself, marred as
you see with traitors" (195). But it is Antony's rhetoric, rather than
the corpse, which impresses itself irresistibly on the plebeians so
that they "feel / The dint of pity." And it is Antony's moving word
picture, rather than the staged spectacle of Caesar's murder, which
ignites the play's pivotal events.

Shakespeare's main source for *Julius Caesar* was Plutarch's *Parallel Lives,* which he read in Thomas North's 1579 translation, *The
Lives of the Noble Grecians and Romans.* Besides the "Life of Marcus Antonius," Shakespeare surely also had Plutarch's "Life of
Marcus Brutus" in mind:

> Afterwards, when Caesar's body was brought into the marketplace,
> Antonius making his funeral oration in praise of the dead, according to

the ancient custom of Rome, and perceiving that his words moved the common people to compassion, he framed his eloquence to make their hearts yearn the more.[27]

In Plutarch's original, it is Antony himself who feels, or at least feigns, pity (*oiktos*) after his eulogy has moved the people.[28] Here, as elsewhere, North works closely with Jacques Amyot's 1559 French translation: "Antoine . . . voyant que la commune s'émouvait à compassion par son dire."[29] The "ancient custom" described is the *laudatio funebris,* or funeral eulogy, which formed an important part of the public funerals of the elite. Such eulogies traditionally celebrated the exploits (*exempla*) of the deceased that had impacted most profoundly upon political life, shoring up mourners' affiliation to their community and encouraging young Romans to emulate admirable accomplishments.[30] In Shakespeare's play, Antony rouses among the citizens these "Roman" forms of participatory sympathy—as well as their "dint of pity"—with a political aim firmly in mind. But in a departure from standard eulogy's emphasis on the public achievements of the dead, Antony also makes his words easily accessible to the listening citizens. His vivid picture of Caesar indeed seems capable of moving them more profoundly than the embodied Caesar could ever have done while he was alive. As David Daniell has commented, "in a play given almost wholly to oratory and persuasion, the titular hero does not persuade."[31]

In *Coriolanus,* too, the Roman citizens encounter compelling word pictures of an absent hero. In this later and more complex example, however, Roman forms of pity are brought more explicitly into conversation with Christian ones. As part of another formal, elegiac occasion, the Roman general Lartius summons up Coriolanus in a striking tableau in front of the city of Corioles, believing he has perished during his single-handed pursuit of the retreating Volscian army. Lartius addresses his noble memory directly:

> Thou wast a soldier
> Even to Cato's wish, not fierce and terrible
> Only in strokes, but with thy grim looks and
> The thunder-like percussion of thy sounds
> Thou mad'st thine enemies shake, as if the world
> Were feverous and did tremble.
>
> (1.4.60–65)

If *Julius Caesar* dramatizes Rome's mortal world reflecting heavenly chaos, "when all the sway of earth / Shakes like a thing unfirm" (1.3.3–4), here, by contrast, it is Coriolanus himself who is remembered—in all his vastness—as a new version of the thundering skies. Cominius will later remark that Coriolanus's unmistakable manner of speaking "thunder-strikes" those who encounter it:

> The shepherd knows not thunder from a tabor
> More than I know the sound of Martius' tongue
> From every meaner man.
>
> (1.6.25–27)

His voice is a weapon on a huge scale commanding silence and surrender, comparable to everyone else's voice only insofar as thunder is comparable to a snare drum. It does not so much persuade people as overwhelm them—as though Coriolanus is a brutal new world order before which they must fall silent. As Lartius makes clear, Coriolanus outdoes nature by outsizing it: "A carbuncle entire, as big as thou art, / Were not so rich a jewel" (1.4.59–60). Coriolanus's wounded person is elementally impressive, a human-sized red gemstone which shines in the dark. Lartius's elegy is interrupted, however, by Coriolanus's abrupt and unanticipated re-entry ("*Enter Martius bleeding*"):

> 1 SOLDIER   Look, sir.
> LARTIUS   O,'tis Martius
>
> (1.4.65).

As though it were impossible for his voice to live up to Lartius's promise, Coriolanus here says nothing at all. In the second half of the play, Shakespeare will explore more fully the variance between such versions of Coriolanus that are vividly conjured in the mind's eye and his embodied reality.

Another extraordinarily powerful evocation of the absent Coriolanus comes as the officers are making ready for his election as consul at the Capitol. This time it is Cominius who prepares "to report / A little of that worthy work" (2.2.42–43) that Coriolanus has performed. He puts forward a formal oration listing Coriolanus's victories on the battlefield before and since his "pupil age / Man-entered" (96–97), his subsequent inexorable waxing "like a sea" (97), and his eventual martial invincibility:

                    As weeds before
A vessel under sail, so men obeyed
And fell below his stem. His sword, death's stamp,
Where it did mark, it took; from face to foot
He was a thing of blood, whose every motion
Was timed with dying cries.

                                        (2.2.103–8)

Cominius's powerful evocation of Coriolanus's ruthlessness as a
death machine makes it easy to forget that this speech did not start
well. Just before Cominius had begun, Coriolanus had raised the
stakes by stalking offstage rather than consenting to "idly sit / To
hear my nothings monstered" (74–75). At the start of his oration
then, Cominius had seemed acutely aware of the high stakes
involved in bringing Coriolanus vividly back to mind, through
rhetoric, and had labored to find words to do justice to the occasion:

            I shall lack voice: the deeds of Coriolanus
            Should not be uttered feebly. It is held
            That valour is the chiefest virtue and
            Most dignifies the haver. If it be,
            The man I speak of cannot in the world
            Be singly counterpoised.

                                        (2.2.80–85)

The metrical irregularity of his first line suggests Cominius's struggle to match his own voice to Coriolanus's (reportedly) singularly
powerful one. And despite Menenius's confidence in his eloquence, Cominius himself fears he cannot hope to "counterpoise"
the enormity of Coriolanus's military accomplishments by speaking about them. He fears he will be unable properly to summon
Coriolanus into presence before the citizens: "I cannot speak him
home" (101). While Cominius's set piece surely impresses the audience in the playhouse, particularly those familiar with Roman epi-
deictic rhetoric, it leaves his onstage audience more or less
speechless. Even the usually prolix Menenius can respond only
with "Worthy man" (120). It is left to nameless characters to
retrieve matters by calling Coriolanus back onstage:

        1 SENATOR Call Coriolanus.
        OFFICER   He doth appear. (129)
                    Enter Coriolanus

Coriolanus's awkward mid-scene exit and re-entrance only reinforces the effort behind Cominius's attempt, exposing the fissure
between rhetoric's potential to stimulate the mind's eye, and Coriolanus's personal "form" (143). Indeed in the following scene the
unscrupulous tribunes Brutus and Sicinius will make political capital out of the citizens' dawning awareness of the difference
between listening to "lectures" (2.3.232) about Coriolanus's worthiness on the one hand, and the real-time and potentially more moving "apprehension of his present portance" (2.3.221) on the other.
Cominius's struggle to bring Coriolanus back into vivid presence
by talking about him signals Shakespeare's bold, metatheatrical
experiment with on- and off-stage presence across the action of the
play as a whole. Now the rhetorical landscape of Rome has emerged
as an ideal backdrop to explore a specific, human problem rich
with dramatic possibility: what happens when vivid description
does not neatly match but instead embarrassingly exceeds, or
indeed falls short of, the person it aims to represent? As Coriolanus
himself objects to Lartius and Cominius, his two most ardent picture makers, "you shout me forth / In acclamations hyperbolical"
(1.9.49–50).

Much later, in act 4, scene 5, the First and Second Servingman
encounter the same problem. Striving to find words to describe
Coriolanus outside Aufidius's house, the servingmen seek a formulation that might approximate and so do justice to the extraordinary
experience of actually seeing or hearing Coriolanus in person:

2 SERVINGMAN   Nay, I knew by his face that there was something in
               him. He had, sir, a kind of face, methought—I can-
               not tell how to term it.
1 SERVINGMAN   He had so, looking, as it were—would I were
               hanged but I thought there was more in him than I
               could think.
2 SERVINGMAN   So did I, I'll be sworn. He is simply the rarest man
               i'th'world.

                                              (4.5.156–61)

The servingmen's inarticulacy is part of the play's broader exploration of whether and how it is possible to capture, through words, a
powerful presence; and the consequences, personally and politically, when such efforts succeed or fail.[32] Here the difficulty resides
in what the second servingman calls Coriolanus's incomparable
rarity. How can language invoke a person who is absent—not just

as a typology, or a "kind of face," but rather as someone singular and particular? The additional problem here is that recalling Coriolanus's face conjures up only a fraction of the colossal man he is: "I thought there was more in him than I could think." Now Coriolanus seems not only beyond words, but also miraculously beyond comprehension. As we will see in the next section, the Romans' intense investment in making and receiving Coriolanus as a word picture—as well as their longing to feel his literal presence—suggests that Shakespeare's investment in vivid rhetoric was as Christian as it was Roman.

III

As many readers have noted, the ostensibly pre-Christian landscape of *Coriolanus* is freighted with Elizabethan and early Jacobean theology.[33] Coriolanus's story has Christological resonance, not least because of the spectacular wounds he receives after the battle at Corioli which the commoners will insist "he should have showed us" (2.3.160). As Stanley Cavell famously argued, these suggest Coriolanus's "connection with the figure of Christ," calling especially to mind Thomas's need to witness His wounds in order to believe in the Resurrection. Thomas was not present at the first showing, and would not believe until he had actually seen; to him, Christ said "because thou hast seen me, thou hast believed: blessed are they that have not seen, and yet have believed" (John 20:29).[34] These same questions of seeing, hearing, and believing also lie behind the fraught early modern debate about how best to make Christ vividly present to believers—even as post-Reformation thought was marginalizing symbolic ceremony from churches, and jettisoning "visual memory-systems from the imagination." Through the concept of *fides ex auditu* ("faith is by hearing") God was assumed to become present through the ear rather than the eye, the preacher's "visible words" circumventing, at least in part, the theological problems posed by images and symbols.[35] There was no greater early modern project of *praesentia* than the forms of sacred rhetoric that sought to bring Christ into proximity with the believer as a felt presence. When such rhetoric focused especially on Christ's suffering in the Passion, it was not intended to promote understanding through the rational faculties, nor indeed through straightforward sensory perception, but instead to ignite through pity a deep sense of faith, commitment, and assurance. In the Roman context of Shakespeare's play, the problem of how to foster, succumb to, or resist such responses becomes particularly pressing when Coriolanus finally and reluctantly accepts Cominius's invitation to display his wounds in front of the citizens at the Roman marketplace.

Coriolanus's reputation is secured in the minds of the citizens by word paintings with a distinctively Christological luster. As we have seen, "there's wondrous things spoke of him" (2.1.134), and Coriolanus's legend thrives, in the minds of the citizens, through his pierced body whose "wounds become him" (2.1.120). The spiritual intensity of the citizens' attentiveness contributes to what Hannibal Hamlin calls Shakespeare's creative anachronism in the Roman plays which tend to pay "frequent, deliberate and significant" attention to the bible, even as their classical settings are specifically elaborated.[36] According to the messenger, the citizens received the war-torn Coriolanus rapturously back into Rome after his victory at Corioli:

> I have seen the dumb men throng to see him, and
> The blind to hear him speak. Matrons flung gloves,
> Ladies and maids their scarves and handkerchiefs,
> Upon him as he passed. The nobles bended
> As to Jove's statue, and the commons made
> A shower and thunder with their caps and shouts.
>
> (2.1.256–61)

People flock to see and hear Coriolanus for themselves, even if they cannot hear or see. Indeed, the messenger recognizes that the citizens are uniquely receptive to their hero's presence by virtue of their very deafness and blindness. As the Second Officer will later make clear, Coriolanus's great "estimation" (2.2.27) has been firmly planted not only in the citizens' eyes, but also in their hearts. The first two lines quoted above may echo the description in Matthew 15:30 of Christ at Galilee where, after the story of His miracles has spread far and wide, "great multitudes came unto him, having with them those that were lame, blind, dumb . . . and cast them down at Jesus' feet."[37] Like those biblical multitudes, Shakespeare's plebeians have absorbed Coriolanus's legend in an intimate, transcendent way beyond the dull embodied senses of perception, and long to do so again, suggesting something of the spiritual rapture ignited by Coriolanus's own "good report" (1.3.20). In turn, this rapture is accompanied by their fervent desire to feel, and to share in, his personal aura—even as the Roman noblemen set about worshipping him like "Jove's statue."

The tension between hearing about Christ and actually seeing or feeling His presence was of course central to early modern spiritual practice. Like many of his contemporaries, Shakespeare would have encountered firsthand the expectation that powerful eloquence might conjure Christ in the imagination. But preachers found themselves wrestling with the problem of how to reconcile rhetoric's necessary artifice with grace—for, as John Ludham had written in his 1577 translation of Andreas Hyperius's *The Practis of Preaching*, "the maner of mouinge of affections assigned vnto Preachers in the Church, is not altogether lyke vnto that, that the Orators vse in their *Forum* or Consistory."[38] Not altogether like, perhaps, but also not altogether unlike. Most ministers were obliged, as Debora Shuger has argued, to "accept the paradox, already present in Augustine, that passionate oratory both is and is not a human art." Figures familiar from ancient rhetoric such as *apostrophe, admiratio* and *exclamatio* were all regarded as capable of capturing divine greatness, and of articulating "the soul's ardent response to God's presence."[39] The grand style of Christian rhetoric, or *Christiana Rhetorica,* relied fundamentally on conveying emotion—not least "pitie and compassion" for Christ's suffering—through the careful fashioning of words, countenance, and gesture. Like the orator, the minister was expected first to stir up in himself "such lyke affections" as he hoped "to bee translated into the myndes of his auditors," striving to master a passionate plain style commensurate with the Holy Spirit and repudiating rhetorical flourishes while still privileging the passion and expressivity necessary to foster Christian service.[40] John Donne summed up these aims succinctly in a sermon preached on Easter Day 1622: "Rhetorique will make absent and remote things present to your understanding."[41] It remained important to emphasize, however, that the source of this presence did not lie within the rhetorical figures themselves, nor entirely within the speaker—for, as John Norden suggests in *A Pensiue Mans Practise* (1596), "without the help of the holy Ghost, the voice of the preacher vanisheth, and the hearers profit nothing at all."[42] An accomplished preacher capable of mastering the appropriate rhetorical devices would need God's blessing before he could bring Christ vividly before the faithful.

Perhaps surprisingly, the marketplace at Rome proved a fitting place for Shakespeare to test these ideas on the early modern stage. Here, at last, Coriolanus appears in person in front of the citizens— although the action will still pivot around the question of exactly how much this onstage audience will literally witness, and how much will be left to their imagination. In accordance with Roman law, Coriolanus's appointment as Consul can be ratified only if he entreats the plebeians' acceptance by suing for their favor and publicly displaying his wounds. Coriolanus is here required to match, in person, the image of the wounded martyr that the plebeians already cherish in their imagination; but also to speak convincingly, for the first time, as his own advocate. The plebeians may accept or reject him by bestowing or withholding their voices in response to his. They are eager to "give . . . voices heartily" (2.3.103), seeking the rapturous sympathy that might re-create Coriolanus's euphoric entry into Rome in act 1, when their shouts (according to Lartius's report) had absorbed and then echoed "the thunder-like percussion" (1.4.63) of his voice. Speaking *for* Coriolanus's wounds, the plebeians will make them their own; recognizing his noble deeds, they will sympathetically share his nobility. They long to take some part in Coriolanus's epic "deed-achieving" (2.1.168), but also to undertake enthusiastic self-surrender much like the ardent, faithful volition the messenger had described in act 2, scene 1. For as the Third Citizen puts it, denying Coriolanus's voice "is a power that we have no power to do" (2.3.4–5). To borrow North's word from his "Life of Marcus Brutus," theirs is a kind of "yearning" for sympathetic involvement that blends Roman participation in Coriolanus's wounded nobility with Christian pity for his suffering. But their more particular yearning is to match this newly visible (and pitiable) Coriolanus, in the flesh, to the vivid impression they have already gathered of his wounded person.

The Fourth Citizen accordingly prompts Coriolanus: "You have received many wounds for your country"; but Coriolanus immediately rebuffs him: "I will not seal your knowledge with showing them" (2.3.105–7). He must nevertheless wear a "napless [threadbare] vesture of humility" (2.1.228) more clearly related to shame than the garment described in Plutarch, thanks to its resemblance to the sheet worn by public penitents. In displays of contrition resembling those that had occurred in marketplaces since the Middle Ages, early modern sinners were sometimes obliged to stand in church draped in a "meane simple cloathe," usually a white sheet, which made their wrongdoing starkly visible.[43] Shakespeare's line indeed recalls 1 Peter 5:5 where humility is worn as a garment: "be clothed with humility: for God resisteth the proud, and giveth grace to the humble." The word "vesture" may also reference the scene of the Crucifixion where the soldiers "cast lots upon the vesture of Christ."[44] Even donning the gown is a gesture Coriolanus can scarcely countenance: "I cannot / Put on the gown, stand naked and entreat them, / For my wounds' sake, to give their suffrage" (2.2.135–37).

In Lartius and Cominius's earlier reports, Coriolanus's thundering voice had inspired rapturous fellow feeling, establishing Roman solidarity, or *metropolitana civitas.* Now that Coriolanus is literally present before them, however, the plebeians long to see their colossus humbled, and to hear him begging for their voices like alms.[45] They seek in fact to participate in a Roman *imitatio Christi* whose aura resides in its portrait of infinite power rendered utterly vulnerable. At the beginning of the play, Coriolanus had regarded pity as his own to bestow on his poor host at Corioles (1.9.85). But to be pitied himself by "the beastly plebeians" (2.1.92) with their "children's voices" (3.1.31) would involve a devastating loss of Roman authority, suggesting his personal pain like the suffering Christ's.

Shakespeare's Coriolanus (unlike Plutarch's) therefore flatly refuses to reveal his wounds, and the plebeians' ardency soon comes to an aggrieved halt: "He said he had wounds" (2.3.163).[46] To Coriolanus, revealing himself in this way seems both an absurd deference to ancient custom and a shameful postponement of more purposeful action. The notion that his wounds were received "for the hire / Of their breath only" (2.2.148–49) is anathema to him; and, in any case, the Senate has already confirmed his appointment as Consul. Coriolanus goes on to disappoint his onstage citizen audience a second time in his manner of speaking—for he can imagine his voice meeting with theirs only in a way that involves disease: "so shall my lungs / Coin words till their decay against those measles / Which we disdain should tetter us" (3.1.79–81). Coriolanus spits forth language that decays the moment it is received, and the words he offers work like incantations against lepers ("measles").[47] The imagery of this passage turns on the resemblance between the tettered (blistered) human body and the divided state. But it also serves to prohibit the ardent pity which early modern sacred rhetoric sets out to foster among the faithful. Public speaking is here instead exposed as the lungs' dirty work.

Coriolanus imagines a terrible world where the plebeians are given too much credence by the patricians so that, when "both your voices blended" (104), there is nothing but "confusion" (111). The citizens had unanimously concluded in the very first scene that Coriolanus is "a very dog to the commonalty" (1.1.26). This doggishness, unequivocally proven by act 3, suggests not only casual cruelty but also Coriolanus's unwillingness to cultivate, through language, the consensus which might hold Rome peaceably together. And since the rhetorical landscape of this play is sacred as well as Roman, it also suggests his absolute rejection of affective Christian solidarity.

One particular aim of sacred rhetoric, as we have seen, was to stir up pity for Christ through vivid description. This in turn created a sense of intimate responsiveness shared and strengthened among the Christian faithful. Shakespeare's play painfully exposes the shortfall between an ecstatically vulnerable, imagined Christ figure and Coriolanus's stubborn presence in reality. And when Coriolanus does himself speak, his rhetorical performance is a much more wretched failure even than Cominius's in act 2, scene 2. As Menenius affirms, Coriolanus is "ill-schooled / In bolted language" (3.1.323–24). North's Coriolanus has an "eloquent tongue," but Shakespeare's would rather act than converse: "When blows have made me stay I fled from words" (2.2.70).[48] Menenius records Coriolanus's dramatic failure to set his emotions in order: "His heart's his mouth. / What his breast forges that his tongue must vent" (3.1.259–60). The heart stands in these lines for emotional authenticity: Coriolanus says what he feels.[49] On the face of it, this marks out Coriolanus as an effective orator—for, as Horace makes clear, the best speakers first feel the emotions they seek to stir among their auditors: "si vis me flere, dolendum est / primum ipsi tibi" ("If you would have me weep, you must first feel grief yourself").[50] But here the language of forging and venting suggests that if the raw stuff of Coriolanus's voice is heat and metal, as befits a colossus, his words are coined through a painful process of smelting which seems expressly to forbid pity.

Summoned back to the marketplace, and accused by Sicinius of treachery, Coriolanus retorts

> I'll know no further.
> Let them pronounce the steep Tarpeian death,
> Vagabond exile, flaying, pent to linger

But with a grain a day, I would not buy
Their mercy at the price of one fair word[.]

                                                           (3.3.86–90)

The nuts and bolts of language here fail Coriolanus, as they often do at crucial moments. Switching inexplicably from the parallel nouns "death . . . exile . . . flaying" to the past-participle construction "pent to linger," Coriolanus cannot encompass his fury within the strictures of blank verse. This stuttering effect contributes to the play's major achievement according to R. B. Parker who notes "the sense it gives of overpackedness, of details over-riding the regular patterns of metre, syntax, and grammar."[51] As Coriolanus imagines his "vagabond exile" on the Tarpeian rock, the emotion behind his words appears raw and improvised. It is also startlingly and riskily embodied through Coriolanus's willing preparedness for "flaying"—recalling Cominius's earlier visualization of his return from the battlefield as if "he were flayed" (1.6.22). It is true that Coriolanus's uncompromising resistance to the clamorous demands of the plebeians—and, more especially, to the manipulative schemes of the tribunes—are often thoroughly persuasive to an audience in the theater. Amongst his *onstage* citizen listeners, however, Coriolanus's words fall flat: "He's banished and it shall be so!" (3.3.106). When these Roman audiences directly see and hear Coriolanus, rather than experiencing him as an imaginative tableau through the words of other people, he no longer elicits impassioned feeling or self-sacrificing loyalty. The plebeians may be seeking "salvific intimacy" at the marketplace, but Coriolanus is unable or unwilling to live up their demands. Instead he experiences the citizens' attentiveness as one more act of flaying.[52]

Coriolanus by now offers far more than a portrait of a bluntly inarticulate (or obscurely eloquent) soldier orator. Instead, Shakespeare seems particularly focused on experimenting with how Coriolanus's character emerges through—and in conflict with—the story that has been told while he is offstage. In person, to the plebeians, Coriolanus resembles neither the deeply impressive "thing of blood" which Lartius and Cominius have eulogized; nor a wondrously pitiable Christ on the Cross. Readers have found it impossible to reconcile Coriolanus's notional Christlikeness with the man he is, but Shakespeare reveals that this irreconcilability is precisely the point. In person, Coriolanus brutally punctures the plebeians' expectations that they can bestow Christian pity on their wounded colossus, staging his own "vagabond exile" from the versions of himself that have been flourishing in the commoners' eager imaginations. As long as his presence is hoped for, remembered, or eulogized by others, Coriolanus seems capable of igniting powerfully compassionate fervor. But when he appears in person, this prowess, and the capacity of his plebeian audience to feel ardent sympathy for him, both stop abruptly. Shakespeare's radical experiment with rhetoric, in the early modern theater, is to make Coriolanus more compelling in the minds of the Roman citizens (if not the audience in the playhouse) when he is spoken *about* than when he speaks. And as Coriolanus is increasingly required to take center stage, and to play his own part, he begins himself to recognize—devastatingly—that these earlier lifelike tableaux were only a temporarily satisfying simulacrum. But theatrical representation scarcely emerges as a reliable or stable alternative.

IV

In act 3, Coriolanus's inability to move and persuade his onstage audience becomes not only a rhetorical problem but also an explicitly metatheatrical one. This is partly because, in Coriolanus's mind, to speak in front of the plebeians is inevitably to "perform a part" (3.2.110). Early modern theories of oratory and acting were in fact inseparable from one another since, as Joseph Roach has written, "the rhetoric of the passions, derived from the work of Quintilian and his successors, dominated discussions of acting."[53] This poses a new problem to Coriolanus, however, who sees the potential overlap as one more looming threat to his authority. He comes to the marketplace a second time, having been implored by Menenius, and then Volumnia, to make a more convincing show of humility by speaking

> not by your own instruction,
> Nor by th' matter which your heart prompts you,
> But with such words that are but roted in
> Your tongue, though but bastards and syllables
> Of no allowance to your bosom's truth.
>
> (3.2.54–58)

Coriolanus's earlier, surly outrage at the prospect of humbling himself had come from the heart, but Volumnia now encourages him to speak from a script. Coriolanus recognizes however that speaking an actor's "roted" words would involve a terrible compromise of his force:

> My throat of war be turned,
> Which choired with my drum, into a pipe
> Small as an eunuch or the virgin voice
> That babies lull asleep!
>
> (3.2.113–16)

To speak with such smallness would be to assume the plebeians' own weakness and childishness—and, for Coriolanus, "It is a part / That I shall blush in acting" (2.2.143–44). It is not only acting *per se* that seems threatening to Coriolanus, but more especially the prospect of disgracing himself "like a dull actor" (5.3.40) who cannot effortlessly engage the audience's emotions and so tries instead mechanically to "cog their hearts from them" (3.2.134).[54] Only actors who seem to speak the "bosom's truth" are persuasive and moving. Their speech only is truly "to th'life" (3.2.107), presenting a part which chimes recognizably with off-stage reality. Our most profound experiences of art (and especially of theater) are indeed surely those which are as vivid as our lived experience in the world. In these cases, the emotions we feel are, as Quintilian says of *enargeia,* "very like the real thing." But a poor actor slips (as Coriolanus dreads he will) into contemptible lowness and mechanical artifice.[55]

Act 2 dramatizes the friction between Coriolanus's potency as a rhetorical creation, conjured in the Romans' minds while he was offstage, and the reality of his embodied presence. In act 3, the theatrical consequences of this friction become increasingly apparent as Volumnia encourages Coriolanus not so much to match the oratorical accomplishments of Lartius, Cominius and the others, but instead to deploy the more flexible resources of acting in order to secure the plebeians' affection. To Volumnia, at least, Coriolanus's success at the marketplace hinges on his ability to play his own part, personating his own "motion, spirit and life" which, until now, has flourished best (from the plebeians' perspective) as a rhetorical effect in the speech of others. But, as Coriolanus objects to Cominius, "You have put me now to such a part which never / I shall discharge to th'life" (3.2.106–7). Cominius promises assistance—"Come, come, we'll prompt you" (3.2.107)—but even with the most generous prompting, what actor could convincingly personate the supersized machine Cominius had earlier summoned into presence? Part of the problem, well-documented in scholarly responses to the play, is Coriolanus's inability to master himself, and so to fall in with either a Christian or an ancient pattern of virtue and right action. But the more subtle and serious difficulty, as Coriolanus sees it, is that he cannot, in person, "discharge" his own part convincingly, which is to say affectively, in order to foster the citizen audience's sympathetic involvement. Paradoxically, it may be precisely this failure to move the onstage audience of citizens, in tandem with his refusal to emolliate the manipulative tribunes, which has given Coriolanus such charismatic appeal to his audiences offstage.

In this strictest tragedy of Shakespeare's, however, it is Coriolanus's perceived failure as an actor, rather than as an orator, which signals his mortality. He predicts how those watching will eventually expose and scatter "This mould of Martius" simply by witnessing his pretended, actorly baseness: "they to dust should grind it / And throw't against the wind" (3.2.104–5). Volumnia advises her son to soften himself "as the ripest mulberry / That will not hold the handling" (3.2.80–81), and this pregnable, pliable Coriolanus bears scant resemblance to the fiery "carbuncle entire" Lartius had earlier described. And perhaps it is Volumnia who is most keenly aware of the risk Coriolanus is taking, for she seemed to foresee this moment when she tallied up her son's wounds in act 2, scene 1 upon his return from Corioli. Among the play's many word pictures of the absent Coriolanus, Volumnia's is surely the strangest and most disturbing:

> Before him
> He carries noise, and behind him he leaves tears.
> Death, that dark Spirit, in's nervy arm doth lie,
> Which being advanced, declines, and then men die.
>
> (2.1.153–56)

Like her son, Volumnia sometimes slips into rhyming couplets when facing a difficult reality.[56] On the face of it, Coriolanus's "nervy arm," strung tight with sinews, stands for his unimaginably pitiless deeds on the battlefield. But the phrase is a strange one, and reveals not only Coriolanus's physical power but also how his skin contains and then brutally spills out the darkness of mortality itself. The uncomfortable resolution implied by the flat, masculine rhyme of Volumnia's closing couplet suggests however that she, like Coriolanus, knows that a warrior as spectacularly threatening as death itself could only ever be conjured through words in the imagination. Coriolanus will find such conjuring impossible to live up to, in person, through theatrical "dissembling" (3.2.63). To borrow another phrase from A. C. Bradley, Coriolanus is "an impossible person"—but he is not simply impossible to bear, as Bradley's remark implies. The graver difficulty lies in the impossibility of his performing, in person, his own reputed enormity.[57]

And of course it is Volumnia, rather than Coriolanus, who ends the play with an astonishingly powerful rhetorical performance. Her son's departure and triumphant return have already been made into orations by Volumnia. And as Coriolanus contemplates burning Rome and all it stands for, Volumnia insists he is not his own man—"Thou art my warrior. / I holp to frame thee" (5.3.62–63)—until Coriolanus, bewildered, concedes her victory: "it is no little thing to make / Mine eyes to sweat compassion" (195–96). The fact that his eyes "sweat" compassion makes Coriolanus's tears look assertive, but it is at this moment that he loses his voice altogether. In North's Plutarch, Coriolanus's compassion is highlighted in italics in the margin as the episode's central, organizing theme: "*Coriolanus compassion of his mother.*" Here, as in Shakespeare's play, Coriolanus responds helplessly to Volumnia's words "as if he had been violently carried with the fury of a most swift-running stream," calling to mind Quintilian's description in *Institutio Oratoria* of the ability of high or grandiloquent style to overcome listeners, regardless of their intentions, like "the river that can roll rocks along . . . will carry the judge away with its mighty torrent however much he resists."[58] Coriolanus's compassion for Volumnia is not, however, the Roman, participatory sympathy his own "rare example" had inspired in the plebeians' minds at the start of the play, nor is it the ardent Christian-seeming pity which the plebeians had longed to bestow upon their wounded martyr at the marketplace. It resembles instead a more private feeling which confirms both Volumnia's vulnerability and Coriolanus's own. Speaking for himself in front of his mother, rather than remotely evoked by others, Coriolanus looks as pitiable as any "corrected son" (5.3.57) as his inability to play his own part again becomes painfully evident: "I melt, and am not / Of stronger earth than others" (5.3.28–29). Coriolanus recognizes himself as a member of the commons not only because he feels himself slipping into a lower social order but also, more dreadfully, because his life (like most lives) is now revealed as something less than the miracle it had appeared by repute.

So long as Coriolanus was spoken about in his absence, he remained singular and celebrated. Lartius's premature elegy and Cominius's eulogy, in particular, had celebrated his miraculous potency through rhetorical pictures that Coriolanus himself had shrunk from as "acclamations hyperbolical" (1.9.50). But when he appears in person, Coriolanus's furious rejection of the citizens reflects larger denominational pressures that center on the power of word pictures to conjure up godly presence, and the attendant danger that they might instead create foolish (or heretical) error. And when Coriolanus steps unwillingly into his theatrical role at the marketplace, which explicitly relies on being directly perceived by his onstage audience's eyes and ears rather than only in their imagination, his potency proves impossible to sustain. The plebeians demand that Coriolanus "show us his wounds" (2.3.6), longing for a moving encounter that might outdo, or at least match, the heights of rhetorical *phantasia.* Such an encounter promises, momentarily, to foster the kind of compassionate fervor that Shakespeare had designated Roman in *Julius Caesar,* or the congregational forms of pity that seem so Christian in *Coriolanus.* But theater depends on the visible and vulnerable body of the actor, and appearing in this way involves exposure to different sorts of scrutiny. *Coriolanus* may seem charismatic, even uncompromisingly virtuous, to an audience in the playhouse. To his onstage citizen audience, however, he cannot persuasively "play / The man I am" (3.2.16–17). Exploring the place of both ancient and sacred rhetoric in the early modern theater, *Coriolanus* dramatizes what is gained, or more often lost, when cherished figures are no longer conjured vividly in the mind, but are instead brought nakedly before us. Shakespeare's engagement with rhetoric in this play therefore goes far beyond anatomizing either Coriolanus's oratorical proficiency or the tragic shrinking, or dwindling, which takes place when he is silenced. *Coriolanus* instead scrutinizes the more wide-reaching tension between rhetorical vividness and theatrical representation—and the mortal risks involved in speaking, rather than being spoken about.

Notes

1. All quotations from *Coriolanus* refer to Peter Holland's Arden edition (London: Bloomsbury, 2013).

2. Yvonne Bruce, "The Pathology of Rhetoric in *Coriolanus,*" *Upstart Crow* 20 (2000): 93–115 (107); Jonathan Crewe, ed., *Coriolanus* (New York: Penguin, 1999), xxxv. See also Michael West and Myron Silberstein, "The Controversial Eloquence of Shakespeare's Coriolanus—an anti-Ciceronian Orator?," *Modern Philology* 102, no. 3 (2005): 307–31 (309).

3. See Cathy Shrank, "Civility and the City in *Coriolanus,*" *Shakespeare Quarterly* 54, no. 4 (2003): 406–23 (419–20); Aleksandar Brlek, "Ill Seen, Well Said: On the Uses of Rhetoric in *Julius Caesar* and *Coriolanus,*" *Studia Romanica et Anglica Zagrabiensia,* 43 (1998): 161–71 (168); and Jarrett Walker, "Voiceless Bodies and Bodiless Voices: the Drama of Human Perception in *Coriolanus,*" *Shakespeare Quarterly* 43, no. 2 (1992): 170–85.

4. The term is Heinrich F. Plett's, from *Rhetoric and Renaissance Culture* (Berlin: Walter de Gruyter, 2004), 498.

5. See Bradley's 1912 essay, "Character and the Imaginative Appeal of Tragedy in *Coriolanus,*" in *Coriolanus: A Casebook,* ed. B. A. Brockman (London: Macmillan, 1977), 53–72 (67).

6. Neil Rhodes, *The Power of Eloquence and English Renaissance Literature* (New York: Harvester Wheatsheaf, 1992), 12–19; 64.

7. Dan Hooley, "Rhetoric and Satire: Horace, Persius, and Juvenal," in *A Companion to Roman Rhetoric,* ed. William Dominik and Jon Hall (Oxford: Blackwell, 2007), 396–412 (412).

8. See Anne Barton, "Livy, Machiavelli and Shakespeare's *Coriolanus,*" in *Shakespeare Survey* 38 (1985): 115–29.

9. See for example Stefan Daniel Keller's *The Development of Shakespeare's Rhetoric: A Study of Nine Plays* (Tübingen: Francke, 2009), 15–17.

10. Lynn Enterline, *Shakespeare's Schoolroom: Rhetoric, Discipline, Emotion* (Philadelphia: University of Pennsylvania Press, 2012), 1 and 8.

11. *King Lear,* ed. R. A. Foakes (London: Bloomsbury, 1997), 4.6.53–54.

12. *The Winter's Tale,* ed. John Pitcher (London: Bloomsbury, 2010), 3.3.81 and 3.3.57 [SD].

13. See for example Hannibal Hamlin, *The Bible in Shakespeare* (Oxford: Oxford University Press, 2013), 198–99.

14. Debora Shuger, *Sacred Rhetoric: The Christian Grand Style in the English Renaissance* (Princeton: Princeton University Press, 1988), 28–54.

15. Jan Franz Dijkhuizen describes how compassion's generally "relational dimension" was integrated into an overarching theology in *Pain and Compassion in Early Modern Literature and Culture* (Cambridge: D.S. Brewer, 2012), 7.

16. Shuger, *Sacred Rhetoric,* 3.

17. See Khen Lampert's discussion of "the compassionate God" in *Traditions of Compassion: From Religious Duty to Social Activism* (Basingstoke: Palgrave, 2005), 3–24.

18. Aristotle, *The Art of Rhetoric,* trans. John Henry Freese (Cambridge, MA: Harvard University Press, 1926), 398–99. Aristotle provides a further account, in

On Memory and Recollection, of the memory's capacity to "see and hear what is not present." See *Parva Naturalia,* trans. W. S. Hett (Cambridge, MA: Harvard University Press, 1986), 294–95.

19. Quintilian, *Institutio Oratoria,* trans. Donald A. Russell, 5 vols. (Cambridge, MA: Harvard University Press, 2001), Book 6.2.32–36 (3.60–65). Quintilian also discusses *enargeia* in Book 4.2.63–65 (2.250–51) and Book 8.3.61–71 (3.374–81).

20. Quintilian, *Institutio Oratoria,* 3.60–61. See also Cicero, *De Inventione,* trans. H. M. Hubbekk (Cambridge, MA: Harvard University Press, 1976) who describes in Book 1 how an auditor may be moved "as if he were present, and not by words alone" (158–59). For a summary of this strand of rhetorical thinking, see Ruth Webb, "Imagination and arousal of the emotions in Greco-Roman Rhetoric," in *The Passions in Roman Thought and Literature,* ed. Susanna Morton Braund and Christopher Gill (Cambridge: Cambridge University Press, 1997), 112–27.

21. *Peri Hypsous (On the Sublime),* trans. W. H. Fyfe and rev. Donald Russell (Cambridge, MA: Harvard University Press, 1995; rev. 1999), 214–17. On the dissemination of Longinus's ideas in early modern culture, see *The Early Modern Reception and Dissemination of Longinus' 'Peri Hupsous' in Rhetoric, the Visual Arts, Architecture and the Theatre,* ed. Caroline Van Eck et al. (Boston: Brill, 2012); and Patrick Cheney, *English Authorship and the Early Modern Sublime* (Cambridge: Cambridge University Press, 2018).

22. Diogenes Laertius makes an account in his life of Zeno of such "impressions." See *Lives of Eminent Philosophers,* trans. R. D. Hicks, 2 vols. (Cambridge, MA: Harvard University Press; London: W. Heinemann, 1950), 2.158–63. Diogenes's Greek text was available in Latin translation from 1570. On Stoic *phantasia* more generally, see Steven K. Strange, "The Stoics on the Voluntariness of the Passions" in *Stoicism: Traditions and Transformations,* ed. Steven K. Strange and Jack Zupko (Cambridge: Cambridge University Press, 2004), 32–51 (47–48).

23. *The Art of English Poesy,* ed. Frank Whigham and Wayne A. Rebhorn (Ithaca: Cornell University Press, 2007), 323.

24. As Richard Meek explains in *Narrating the Visual in Shakespeare* (Farnham: Ashgate, 2009), *ekphrasis* is one way "Shakespeare's plays beguile us with vivid descriptions of things unseen" (2). See also Alison Thorne, *Vision and Rhetoric in Shakespeare: Looking through Language* (Basingstoke: Palgrave, 2000), esp. 57–103.

25. *Julius Caesar,* ed. David Daniell (London: Bloomsbury Arden, 1998), 3.1.97 and 234. All quotations follow this edition.

26. *Julius Caesar,* 3.2.179, 167, and 182–92.

27. T. J. B. Spencer, ed., *Shakespeare's Plutarch* (Harmondsworth: Penguin, 1964), 128–29.

28. *Plutarch's Lives,* trans. Bernadotte Perrin, 11 vols. (London: Heinemann, 1918), 6.168–71; 9.168–69.

29. "Vie de Marcus Brutus" in *Les Vies des Hommes Illustres,* ed. Gérard Walter, 2 vols. (Paris: Éditions Gallimard, 1951), 2.1062. On North's dependence on Amyot, see "The Main Sources of *Julius Caesar*" in *Shakespeare's Plutarch,* ed. C. F. Tucker Brooke, 4 vols. (London: Chatto & Windus, 1909), 1.xv

30. See Catherine Edwards, *Death in Ancient Rome* (New Haven: Yale University Press, 2007), 19.

31. Daniell, ed., *Julius Caesar,* 47–48.

32. For an account of inarticulacy's cultural work in Renaissance drama, see

Carla Mazzio, *The Inarticulate Renaissance: Language Trouble in an Age of Eloquence* (Philadelphia: University of Pennsylvania Press, 2009).

33. Hamlin explores the "Christlike" Coriolanus in *The Bible in Shakespeare,* 200–214 (204). See also Peter Lake, "Shakespeare's *Julius Caesar* and the search for a usable (Christian) past" in *Shakespeare and Early Modern Religion,* ed. David Loewenstein and Michael Witmore (Cambridge: Cambridge University Press, 2015), 111–30.

34. *Disowning Knowledge in Six Plays of Shakespeare* (Cambridge: Cambridge University Press, 1987), 158–59. Cavell finds further parallels between certain actions of Coriolanus and the biblical Revelation. The other disciples, too, are slow to believe when Christ "shewed them his hands and his feet" in Luke 24:38–41. All biblical quotations follow the King James version (1611); https://www.kingjamesbibleonline.org

35. These three quotations come from Arnold Hunt, *The Art of Hearing: English Preachers and their Audiences, 1590–1640* (Cambridge: Cambridge University Press, 2010), 20–23.

36. Hamlin, *The Bible in Shakespeare,* 1.

37. See Holland, ed., *Coriolanus,* 256–62n. Further biblical references are explored in Naseeb Shaheen, *Biblical References in Shakespeare's Plays* (Newark: University of Delaware Press, 1999), 658–69.

38. Andreas Hyperius, *The Practis of Preaching, Otherwise Called the Pathway to the Pulpet,* trans. John Ludham (1577), sig. G1v.

39. Shuger, *Sacred Rhetoric,* 231, 239.

40. Ludham, *The Practis of Preaching,* 127.

41. *The Sermons of John Donne,* ed. Evelyn M. Simpson and George R. Potter, 10 vols., (Berkeley: University of California Press, 1953–62), 4.87.

42. Norden, *A Pensiue Mans Practise,* sig. G1v.

43. See William Stanley, *A Treatise of Penance* (1617) in *English Recusant Literature, 1558–1640,* ed. D. M. Rogers, vol. 92 (London: Scolar Press, 1972), 230; Alison Shell, *Shakespeare and Religion* (Bloomsbury: London, 2010), 53. On the medieval public "performance of penitence," which sometimes required sinners to appear "nude except for a white sheet," see Dave Postles, "Penance and the Market Place: a Reformation Dialogue with the Medieval Church (c. 1250 – c. 1600)," in *Journal of Ecclesiastical History* 54, no. 3 (2003): 441–68 (442 and 445).

44. Matthew 27:35; see Hamlin, *The Bible in Shakespeare,* 202–3.

45. *Coriolanus,* 2.3.69, 80.

46. Spencer, ed., *Shakespeare's Plutarch,* 319. For comparison of this episode in Plutarch and Shakespeare, see David C. Green, *Plutarch Revisited: A Study of Shakespeare's Last Roman Tragedies and their Source* (Salzburg: Salzburg Studies in English Literature, 1979), 146–47.

47. Compare *Hamlet,* 1.5.71–73. Gina Bloom discusses the material properties of the early modern voice in *Voice in Motion: Staging Gender, Shaping Sound in Early Modern England* (Philadelphia: University of Pennsylvania Press, 2007), 2.

48. Thomas North, *The Lives of the Noble Grecians and Romanes* (1579), sig. Y4r. John Wesley has recently explored the tension between eloquence and embodied expression in early modern rhetorical training. See "Rhetorical Delivery for Renaissance English: Voice, Gesture, Emotion, and the Sixteenth-Century Vernacular Turn," *Renaissance Quarterly* 68.4 (2015): 1265–96 (1266).

49. According to Thomas Wright, "all passions may be distinguished by the

dilation enlargement, or diffusion of the heart." See *The Passions of the Mind in Generall,* ed. Thomas O. Sloan (Urbana: University of Illinois Press, 1971), 24.

50. *Satires, Epistles, Ars Poetica,* trans. H. R. Fairclough (Cambridge, MA: Harvard University Press, 1991), 458–59.

51. *Coriolanus,* ed. R. B. Parker (Oxford: Oxford University Press, 1998), 74.

52. See James M. Bromley, "Intimacy and the Body in Seventeenth-century Religious Devotion," *Early Modern Literary Studies* 11.1 (May, 2005) http://purl .oclc.org/emls/11-1/brominti.htm

53. Joseph Roach, *The Player's Passion: Studies in the Science of Acting* (Ann Arbor: University of Michigan Press, 1993), 26.

54. Eve Rachele Sanders explores Coriolanus as "an antitheatrical ideologue" in "The Body of the Actor in *Coriolanus,*" *Shakespeare Quarterly* 57, no. 4 (2006): 387–412 (388).

55. Tracing a different classical genesis for this same episode, Emily Griffiths Jones argues that Coriolanus's conversation with his mother—and especially his fear of appearing "ignoble, feminized, and whorish"—is selectively derived from Xenophon's *Oeconomicus.* See "'Beloved of all the trades in Rome': Oeconomics, Occupation and the Gendered Body in *Coriolanus,*" *Shakespeare Studies* 43 (2015): 154–78 (172).

56. Compare Coriolanus's six rhyming couplets as he squares up to begging for the plebeians' voices at 2.3.111–22.

57. Bradley, "Character and the Imaginative Appeal," 60.

58. Spencer, *Shakespeare's Plutarch,* 353; Quintilian, *Institutio Oratoria,* Book 12.10.61 (5.314–15).

Thunderings, Not Words: Aspects of Pauline Style in *Pericles* and *The Winter's Tale*

DANIEL KNAPPER

Introduction: Shakespeare's Biblical Styles

IT IS ONE OF THE STRANGE IRONIES of Shakespeare's dramatic art that its distinctiveness resides in the playwright's ability to divest himself from his characters. Unlike the plays of Jonson or the poetry of Donne, a singular feature of Shakespearean drama is precisely its lack of Shakespearean personality—he generally prefers to separate his own values and attitudes from the thinking, speaking, and acting of his *dramatis personae,* who exhibit, as a result, a powerfully realized awareness of and responsiveness to themselves, their fellow characters, and their dramatic environments. Critics have recognized how this separation informs other aspects of Shakespeare's dramatic practice, including his use of language: "[Characters'] styles are individualized," observes Brian Vickers, "to a degree that no other dramatist ever achieved, and within their idiolects their registers vary according to the changes in their situation."[1] Shakespeare's characters, in other words, express their styles as fully as their religious beliefs or political commitments, and these styles evolve as the characters grow and their stories unfold.

If Shakespeare's characters bear unique and dynamic relationships to their modes and habits of expression, the development of these relations nonetheless depends on the patterns and processes of literary inspiration, imitation, and adaptation. As he fashions his dramatic speeches, Shakespeare draws verbal tropes and techniques from a variety of stylistic models, from classical authorities like Ovid and Seneca to contemporary professionals like Christopher Marlowe and John Fletcher.[2] And as in his approach to his narrative sources, Shakespeare consistently absorbs and transforms those stylistic sources in fresh and complex ways. According to Jessica Wolfe, "Shakespeare often employs several different modes of imitation in the same play and even in the same scene; he competes with his source texts by altering and interrogating them . . . he reads 'eclectically' by conjoining texts 'freely and unpredictably.' "[3] Gaps remain, however, in our map of Shakespeare's stylistic influences, especially in relation to one of his favorite sources of creative inspiration, the Bible. Scholars have recently begun to reassess how Shakespeare engages with the Bible to shape and enrich his dramatic work, emphasizing the extent to which he appropriates biblical and exegetical texts to develop the characters, themes, and poetic textures of his plays.[4] Yet questions persist concerning Shakespeare's knowledge and use of biblical styles. Did he read biblical texts for style, as he read and responded to the styles of other ancient and modern texts? And if so, did a biblical style inspire and inform his approach to any particular speeches?

In an essay on Shakespeare's interactions with the Bible in his later tragicomedies, Helen Wilcox explores "the difficult question of biblical style" and its influence over the diction, turns of phrase, and rhetorical forms of plays like *Measure for Measure* and *Cymbeline,* arguing that Shakespeare employed a "cumulative biblical style" to compose their "serious songs" and other "special moments of intensity." For Wilcox, a relatively coherent biblical style develops from "the recurring spiritual questions, the shared symbolism, and the webs of intertextual references" that bind together the books of the Bible, and Shakespeare practices this style when his language and ideas are "related to the Bible with such intertextual density that the effect itself becomes biblical."[5] I agree that Shakespeare occasionally synthesizes material from a variety of biblical texts to evoke a broad sense of 'the biblical,' without necessarily imitating the style of any biblical text in particular.[6] In this essay, though, I am going to argue that Shakespeare recognized and occasionally imitated the styles associated with individual biblical texts and authors. Specifically I will argue that Shakespeare studied and adapted the prose style of Saint Paul's New Testament letters to develop the verse and prose of two late plays, *Pericles, Prince of Tyre* and *The Winter's Tale.* Though distinctive in its strong focus on the rhetorical dimensions of Paul's texts, Shakespeare's adaptation of Pauline style in these plays reflects, even as it extends and deepens, his career-long interest in the life, language, and ideas of the apostle. In *The Comedy of Errors,* for instance, he sets the action in an Ephesus rumored to be infested with supernatural forces, a reputation established by Luke in his account of Paul's visit to the city in the book of *Acts;* at the same time, he explores themes in the play with direct relevance to Paul's letter to the Ephesians.[7] Shakespeare also engages with Paul in *A Midsummer Night's Dream,* where he caps a night of wonder and metamorphosis in the Athenian wood with a ridiculous travesty of Paul's visionary description of God's love in 1 Corinthians.[8] And in *Richard III,* he tightens the troubling identification between the villainous, hypocritical Richard and Paul, by whom Richard habitually swears and on whom Shakespeare bases his duplicitous, shape-shifting selfhood.[9]

Critics have traced Shakespeare's interest in Paul to different aspects of *Pericles* and *The Winter's Tale* as well, from characters and settings to themes and speech acts.[10] They have not recognized, however, Shakespeare's efforts to repurpose the rhetorical forms and effects of Paul's prose for the dramatic verse of the plays. As I will show, Shakespeare engages not only with the language of Paul's texts but also with humanist discussions of Paul's style, which ground the definition of his prose in a set of formal properties, and which characterize its artistry with reference to a pair of Greco-Roman figures: Pericles, the Athenian statesman and military general; and Mercury, the Roman god of eloquence.

Shakespeare draws on this humanist discourse as he experiments with Pauline style in each play. In *Pericles,* he casts Pericles as the hero and protagonist of the play, and he adapts a set of speech acts and rhetorical forms from Paul's letter to the Ephesians to compose a sequence of Pericles's speeches at sea, including different species of syntactical inversion and transposition (*hyperbaton*); divagation and digression (*anacoluthon*); and verbal and phrasal omission (*ellipsis*).[11] Then, in *The Winter's Tale,* he includes Autolycus, the mythological son of Mercury, as a prominent foil to Paulina, the apostle's namesake in the play, and he expands his earlier engagement with Paul's style to develop a series of Paulina's speeches at the Sicilian court, combining *hyperbaton, anacoluthon,* and *ellipsis* with other forms and techniques from Paul's letters to the Romans, Corinthians, and Galatians. These techniques include the heaping up of words (*congeries*) and verbal repetitions (*epanalepsis*) of Paul's diatribes; his angry rhetorical questions (*interrogatio*); and his blunt outspokenness on personally embarrassing or socially taboo topics (*parrhesia*).[12] In both plays, as we will see, Shakespeare's principles of dramatic decorum guide and delimit his use of Paul's style—Pericles and Paulina employ, that is, a Pauline style in response to the unique demands of their dramatic situations, and Pauline style itself conforms and contributes to the broader development of character and theme.

Pericles and the Rhetoric of Mystery

As Pericles sails near the coastlines of Ephesus and Tarsus, he delivers a trio of powerful speeches, each manifesting the distinctive tones and textures of Pauline style. In the first speech, he prays to the Olympian gods to calm a violent sea storm for the sake of his wife Thaisa, who lies in labor below deck. In the second, he speaks a benediction over his newborn daughter Marina, blessing her with a life of peace and happiness in lieu of her tumultuous birth aboard their ship. In the third, he gives a eulogy upon the apparent death of Thaisa. The speeches thus call for a style adequate to address major thresholds of human experience, the liminal points of being and reality: birth, death, and the divine. For most critics, the speeches signal a sea change in the quality of the play's verse: whereas the verse in most of the earlier speeches seems plodding and perfunctory, the verse in these speeches exhibits, according to MacDonald Jackson, the "lively imagery, expressive phrasing, and vigorous rhythms" of Shakespeare's late style.[13] But if the interplay of image, phrase, and rhythm reflects the influence of Shakespeare's late style, the interplay of form and effect reflects Shakespeare's use of Pauline prose to craft this style, specifically his use of syntactical inversions (*hyperbaton*), rhetorical digressions (*anacoluthon*), and verbal omissions (*ellipses*) to maximize the power, speed, passion, and profundity of the speeches.

Perhaps no Pauline epistle captures these dynamics as vividly as Ephesians, which produces the same palette of impressive effects as the other epistles, but which poses, at the same time, an exceptional degree of formal complexity. "In this Epistle of Paul," as Erasmus observes in his annotations on Ephesians, "there is the same fervor, the same depth of thought [*profunditas*], the same spirit and passion [*pectus*] throughout, but nowhere else is the language more troublesome because of *hyperbata, anapodota* [a species of *anacoluthon*], and other inconveniences."[14] Consider, for instance, the dynamics of *hyperbaton* and speed in Ephesians 2:1–3, where Paul discusses the benefits of God's mercy towards the Ephesians. Here and throughout the essay, I quote from an English translation of the text that Shakespeare is likely to have read privately, regularly, and carefully, the 1595 Geneva-Tomson Bible, a version that maintains the formal features of Paul's prose as they appear in his original Greek texts.[15] This formal equivalence reflects the theoretical principles of Renaissance English transla-tors, who maintained the lexical details, syntactical arrangements, and literal phrasing of their base texts out of respect for their sanc-tity, even at the expense of semantic clarity or stylistic elegance.[16] Like his engagements with the rest of scripture, translation gener-ally mediated Shakespeare's engagement with Paul's texts; but through translation Shakespeare could still discern and assess the features of Paul's style in action, including the influence of *hyper-baton* in the following passage.

1. And you *hathe he quickened,* that were dead in trespasses and sinnes,
2. Wherein, in time past ye walked, according to the course of this worlde, *and* after the prince that ruleth in the aire, *even* the spirite, that now worketh in the children of disobedience,
3. Among whome we also had our conversation in time past in the lustes of our flesh, in fulfilling the will of the flesh, and of the minde, & were by nature the children of wrath, as well as others.[17]

As he reminds the Ephesians of their former spiritual condition, Paul weaves a variety of inversions and transpositions into his sen-tence, quickening its pace and invigorating its rhythms.[18] Verse 1, for instance, reverses typical subject-object order, placing the direct object "you" at the head of the initial clause to arrest the attention of the audience. It also splits the past participle with the subject ("hathe he quickened"); and separates the object from its modifier ("And you . . . that were dead in trespasses and sinnes"), which increases the modifier's proximity to "quickened" and sharpens, as a result, the contrast between the sentence's metaphors of death and revival. Other hyperbatonic expressions accentuate the sen-tence's irregular syntax, accelerate its tempo, and sustain its breath-less accumulation of subordinate, relative, and appositive clauses.

Verse 2, for example, positions the subject and verb after a prepositional phrase ("in time past ye walked"), which itself includes a postpositive adjective ("time past"); and verse 3 again positions a prepositional phrase ahead of the subject and verb ("among whome we also had"), which extends the sentence for another round of clauses and leads to another pair of light transpositions ("time past," "and were by nature the children of wrath"). Along with its keen sense of alacrity, the free arrangement of words and phrases fosters the agile rhythms of the sentence, particularly the oscillation between short and long clauses in verse 3, which maintains its nervous energy in spite of its awkward length.

If Paul's use of *hyperbaton* builds an impression of discursive speed and agility in Ephesians 2:1–3, his use of *anacoluthon* strengthens the sense of passion and profundity in Ephesians 2:4–7, the next sentence, which celebrates the sanctification and glorification of the Ephesians "in Christ."

4. But God which is riche in mercie, through his great love wherewith he loved us,
5. Even when we were dead by sinnes, hathe quickened us together in Christ, *by whose* grace ye are saved,
6. And hathe raised us up together, and made us sit together in the heavenlie *places* in Christ Iesus,
7. That hee might shewe in the ages to come the exceeding riches of his grace through his kindnesse toward us in Christ Iesus.

From his depressing description of life without Christ Paul ascends to an ecstatic vision of Christian communion in "the heavenly *places*," strengthening his sentence with a flurry of loosely related theological assertions. Verse 5, for instance, disrupts the upward trajectory of the main predicate with an interpolated clause ("*by whose* grace ye are saved"), jumping to the subject of the next sentence prematurely and shifting rapidly between first- and second-person perspectives. Verse 6, moreover, disturbs the coherence of the sentence's rhetorical climax with an unexpected leap in figurative logic (*metalepsis*): whereas verses 1–5 use the idea of resurrection ("quickened") as a metaphor to describe the experience of moral and spiritual renewal under Christ, verse 6 suggests that Christ has somehow already "raised" (i.e., lifted) Paul and the Ephesians into paradise and seated them together in mystical fellowship.[19] These kinds of grammatical and logical inconsistency certainly test the reader's ability to discern the proper relations between and potential implications of Paul's ideas, but they also enable Paul to compose some of his most rhetorically bold and semantically rich sentences, which imbue the epistle, in turn, with an aura of mystery and exuberance. "[This] Epistle is full of high sentences," as John Chrysostom writes in his homilies on Ephesians, citing 2:6, "it is full of matters of very high sense, and exceding waightie."[20]

In addition to *hyperbaton* and *anacoluthon,* Paul employs different species of *ellipsis* to produce stylistic effects in Ephesians, particularly its sense of sublimity and profundity. In Ephesians 3:14–19, for instance, he incorporates a set of elliptical expressions into a complex prayer for and exhortation to the Ephesian community.

14. For this cause I bow my knees unto the Father of our Lord Iesus Christ,
15. (Of whome is named the whole family in heaven and in earth)
16. That he might graunt you according to the riches of his glory, that ye may be strengthened by his Spirit in the inner man,
17. That Christ may dwell in your heartes by faith:
18. That yee, being rooted and grounded in love, may be able to comprehend with al Saintes, what is the breadth, and length, and depth, and height:
19. And to knowe the love of Christ, which passeth knowledge, that ye may be filled with all fulnesse of God.

As he prays for the Ephesians to mature in faith and knowledge, Paul infuses the prayer with an array of cryptic phrases, ineffable images, and clauses lacking connective particles (*asyndeton*), striving both to express "the love of Christ, which passeth knowledge" and to inspire a commensurate zeal in his audience.[21] With few exceptions, for instance, the clauses connect, not through coordinating conjunctions like "and" or "so," but through the vague relative pronoun "that," which creates ambiguous relations between each clause—do the clauses represent a series of more or less discreet benedictory statements, or do they build upon each other into a larger, more meaningful whole? The clauses also persistently withhold information necessary for a precise interpretation of their meaning, prompting Renaissance critics to supplement them with possible glosses. Perhaps the most contested example occurs in verses 18 and 19, where Paul prays that the Ephesians "May be able to comprehend with all Saintes, what is the breadth, and length, and depth, and height"—of what, exactly? The Geneva marginalia suggest that Paul is describing "how perfite the worke of Christ is in every part," while Erasmus offers "the goodnesse of God" in a paraphrase of the passage.[22] But whatever reading Renaissance audiences preferred, the very proliferation of such glosses reflects the power of Paul's *ellipses* to cultivate an impression of surplus meaning, their ability, in other words, to provoke wonder and awe at the numinous contents seemingly concealed in the gaps of the epistle's sentences. "For there is none of [Paul's] Epistles," as Erasmus writes in his paraphrase, "that hath so darke and hidde sentences in it, as this to the Ephesians."[23]

Shakespeare's creative response to Paul's high and mysterious sentences emerges in the rhetorical dynamics of Pericles's major speeches during the sea storm, which adapt the key forms of Paul's prose to produce a similar constellation of effects. In his prayer for deliverance, for instance, Pericles makes frantic use of *anacoluthon* to heighten the force and speed of his appeal to the gods.

> The god of this great vast, rebuke these surges
> Which wash both heaven and hell, and thou that hast
> Upon the winds command, bind them in brass,
> Having called them from the deep. O, still
> Thy deafening dreadful thunders; gently quench
> Thy nimble sulphurous flashes! [*Calls*]
>   O how, Lychorida!
> How does my queen?—Thou stormest venomously;
> Wilt thou spit all thyself? The seaman's whistle
> Is as a whisper in the ears of death,
> Unheard. [*Calls*]
>   Lychorida!—Lucina, O,
> Divinest patroness, and midwife gentle
> To those that cry by night, convey thy deity
> Aboard our dancing boat, make swift the pangs
> Of my queen's travails!—Now, Lychorida![24]

Given its cosmic invocations ("god," "heaven and hell"), primordial imagery ("surges," "winds"), and expansive spatial dimensions ("this great vast," "from the deep"), Pericles's speech clearly manifests a broad relation to other grand styles in content. Critics have also detected biblical resonances in the speech's diction and imagery, including echoes of Psalm 104, where the seas are said to flee at the Lord's rebuke, and the Gospels, where Christ rebukes a storm on the Sea of Galilee.[25] These broad relations and resonances serve to enhance the speech's complex meanings and effects, even as the speech's formal properties reflect its specific relation to Pauline style, particularly its turbulent sequence of *anacolutha*. Pericles makes little effort to tighten the links between his thoughts and words as they ricochet between the gods, Thaisa's servant and midwife Lychorida, and the storm, directing and redirecting his discourse with rhetorical questions, real questions, and vocative outbursts. After an abrupt call to Lychorida in line 6, for instance, line 7 suddenly swerves to address the storm itself ("Thou stormest venomously"); line 10 then interjects another call to Lychorida, which interrupts the development of an analogy; and it pivots again with a cry to Lucina, goddess of childbirth ("The seaman's whistle / Is as a whisper in the ears of death / Unheard / Lychorida!—Lucina, O"). The successive overtures and complex directional shifts not only heighten the Pauline intensity and velocity of the speech but also conjure a frisson of numinous activity on the stage, crowding its imaginative space with powerful deities and personified figures. In addition, the audacious tone of the prayer fulfills Paul's prescriptions for prayer as a speech act: prayers should be spoken, according to Paul, with "boldness" and "confidence," a claim he makes in Ephesians 3:12 before modeling the approach in 3:14–19.

Various aspects of Pericles's dramatic environment also reflect Shakespeare's engagement with Pauline style in the speech. On the one hand, Pericles performs the prayer in view of two Mediterranean cities that Renaissance audiences strongly associated with Paul's life and writings: Tarsus (his birthplace) and Ephesus itself. On the other hand, Pericles performs the prayer in the midst of a storm full of "deafening dreadful thunders" and "nimble sulphurous flashes," which evoke Renaissance characterizations of Paul's style as 'thunder and lightning,' traditional metaphors for his discursive power and speed. These metaphors reflect, in turn, deeper cultural links between Paul and another figure named Pericles, the ancient Athenian military general, whose oratorical style was also described as thunder and lightning.[26] Saint Jerome was the first to claim that "whenever I read [Paul's letters], I seem to hear, not words, but peals of thunder [*tonitrua*]" and that "wherever you look, they are lightning bolts [*fulmina*]."[27] But as biblical humanists recognized, Jerome took these metaphors from classical accounts of the political speeches of Pericles, who "farre passed," according to Plutarch, "all the orators in his time . . . For it is reported, that he thundered and lightened in his oration to the people, & that his tongue was a terrible lightning."[28] Erasmus, for instance, acknowledges Jerome's borrowing in his paraphrase of the Corinthian letters, even as it inspires him to develop parallels between Paul and Pericles in terms of character and action. "These were the weapons and these the forces," Erasmus writes, referring to faith, prayer, and preaching,

> with which Paul, that invincible warrior, conquered Greece and a great part of Asia Minor and proceeded to attack and take possession of the Roman empire . . . of him it is true, as was once said of Pericles, if I mistake not, that with thunder and lightning he confounded, not Greece alone, but the whole world.[29]

After gesturing to Jerome's debt, Erasmus embeds his allusion to Paul's style, the "thunder and lightning" with which Paul "confounded" (*miscet*) the world, within a matrix of Pericles-inspired martial imagery, fashioning him into a kind of romance hero and his missionary journeys into imperialist military campaigns. The marginal note to the 1522 edition of Erasmus's New Testament paraphrases underscores the identity between Paul and Pericles that Erasmus seeks to establish in the passage: Paul, according to the note, is "the Pericles of our religion" (*Periculum nostrae religionis*).

Other biblical humanists make the stylistic basis of the connection between Paul and Pericles more explicit. The Jesuit scholar Nicolas Caussin, for instance, compares Paul to Pericles on the basis of style in his textbook on sacred and secular rhetoric: "What on Paul's part is lacking?" asks Caussin, "Who far more than Pericles, with thundering, lightning, and confounding speeches preached to the whole world?"[30] The Lutheran Victor Strigel also invokes the connection in one of his commentaries on the Psalms; referring to Paul's use of Psalm 32 in Romans 4, Strigel writes that "*Paule,* an Orator more rightly then *Pericles,* thundering and lightning in the midst of his auditorie, used the testimonie of thys Psalme in a most weighty cause."[31] Myriad other biblical humanists similarly characterize passages from Paul's letters as thunderous or lightning-like in their effects, emphasizing the power and speed of his style and reinforcing, at the same time, his cultural links with Pericles.[32]

Shakespeare exploits, then, the cultural links between Paul and Pericles as he coordinates the dramaturgical relations between Pericles's grand speech, stormy setting, and dire situation, harnessing the thunder and lightning of Paul's style to create an appropriate response to the thunder and lightning of the tempest. Other aspects of the dramatic environment shed similar light on Shakespeare's engagement with Pauline style in the next major speech of the scene, where Pericles combines different species of *hyperbaton* and *ellipsis* to bless his newborn daughter Marina.

> Now, mild may be thy life!
> For a more blusterous birth had never babe;
> Quiet and gentle thy conditions, for
> Thou art the rudeliest welcome to this world
> That ever was prince's child. Happy what follows!
> Thou hast as chiding a nativity
> As fire, air, water, earth, and heaven can make
> To herald thee from the womb.
> Even at the first thy loss is more than can
> Thy portage quit, with all thou canst find here.
> Now the good gods throw their best eyes upon't!
>
> (3.1.27–37)

Even as he hopes for a reversal in Marina's fortunes, Pericles employs a series of syntactical reversals and verbal omissions to manage a stark shift in tone, from a forceful appeal to the gods to a compassionate paternal benediction. Lines 27 to 31, for instance, consistently position complements ahead of verbs and subjects ("Now, mild may be thy life . . . Quiet and gentle thy conditions . . . Happy what follows"); line 28 reverses subject-verb-object order ("blusterous birth had never babe"); and lines 29 and 31 omit substantive verbs from their main clauses. In comparing, moreover, Marina's present experiences of "loss" (of her mother in particular) with her "portage" or remaining earthly possessions (her father, life, royal status), lines 35 to 36 divide an auxiliary verb from its main verb ("can/thy partage quit"), and they obscure Pericles's points of comparison with vague diction and elusive phrasing ("the first," "thy loss," "with all thou canst find here"). If these hyperbatonic and elliptical constructions combine to reproduce the discursive speed and affective power of Pauline style, they also perform distinct rhetorical functions in their new dramatic context: to keep the storm, for instance, from drowning out his speech, Pericles arranges words to emphasize key terms, and to keep the "dancing boat" from throwing the speech off balance, he positions or eliminates words and phrases to maintain a pliant rhythm, alternating between shorter declarative and longer comparative clauses in each of the hypotactic sentences. Finally, the speech's syntactical reversals reflect the dialectical development of its ideas and imagery, which draws, in turn, on Paul's use of dialectical patterns throughout his writings, including his juxtaposition of sin/death and grace/life in Ephesians 2:1–7. The benediction thus highlights Shakespeare's engagement with the rhetorical dimensions of Paul's style even as it provides evidence for what Kenneth Gross describes as Shakespeare's "deep fascination with the dialectical mode of Paul's writing, his oppositional imagery, his framing of opposed worlds, texts, persons, and churches."[33]

Pericles's Pauline style appears all the more prominently in contrast to speeches that other Shakespearean characters deliver under similar dramatic circumstances. Critics have noted, for instance, the resemblance between Pericles's prayer and King Lear's first speech after abandoning the houses of his treacherous daughters, where he rails against a violent storm while wandering on a barren heath.[34]

> Blow winds and crack your cheeks! Rage, blow!
> You cataracts and hurricanoes, spout
> Till you have drenched our steeples, drowned the cocks!
> You sulphurous and thought-executing fires,
> Vaunt-couriers of oak-cleaving thunderbolts,
> Singe my white head! And thou, all-shaking thunder,
> Strike flat the thick rotundity o'the world,
> Crack nature's moulds, all germens spill at once
> That make ungrateful man![35]

Lear's angry cries anticipate certain aspects of Pericles's prayer, from its chaotic setting and imperative mode to its strong diction and sublime imagery. But Lear's grand style differs significantly from Pericles's Pauline style in its surprising degree of structural coherence and visual clarity: whereas Pericles's speech fractures its focus and obscures its content through *anacolutha,* Lear's speech addresses the stormy elements in an orderly progression of commands; it casts these commands in straightforward syntactical arrangements; and it fills them with fully developed figures. Such rhetorical stability amid the "cataracts and hurricanoes" of the heath suggests that Pericles's rhetorical *instabilities* derive, not merely from the tumult of his environment, but from Shakespeare's creative adaptation of Pauline prose features. Similar evidence appears in one of Lear's later heath speeches, where he prays for the marginalized subjects of his kingdom. "Nay get thee in," he begins, instructing his fool to take shelter in a nearby hovel,

> I'll pray, and then I'll sleep.
> *[Kneels]* Poor naked wretches, wheresoe'er you are,
> That bides the pelting of this pitiless storm,
> How shall your houseless heads and unfed sides,
> Your looped and windowed raggedness, defend you
> From seasons such as these? O, I have tae'en
> Too little care of this. Take physic, pomp,
> Expose thyself to feel what wretches feel,
> That thou mayst shake the superflux to them
> And show the heavens more just.
>
> (3.4.27–36)

Lear combines a petitionary speech act with traditionally Christian subject matter to express a moving vision of socio-economic justice. If the speech, however, takes certain cues from Christian teachings and writings, it exhibits no relation to Pauline style—along with its lack of engagement with Pauline formal features, its tone of humility and contrition contrasts sharply with the Pauline boldness and confidence of Pericles's prayer at sea. And once again, the immediate clarity of Lear's speech underlines the need for explanations beyond setting and situation to account for the challenging, irregular features of Pericles's speeches.

Pericles's last major speech at sea substantiates Pauline style as the primary source of these challenging features, even as it culminates Shakespeare's experiments with them. After Pericles blesses his newborn daughter, two sailors enter and urge him to bury Thaisa at sea, who appears to have died in labor, and whose postmortem presence on board the sailors consider bad luck. Pericles reluctantly consents to the request, but not before combining different forms of *anacoluthon, hyperbaton,* and *ellipsis* into a poignant eulogy for his wife.

> A terrible childbed hast thou had, my dear,
> No light, no fire. Th'unfriendly elements
> Forgot thee utterly, nor have I time
> To give thee hallowed to thy grave, but straight
> Must cast thee, scarcely coffined, in the ooze,
> Where, for a monument upon thy bones
> And aye-remaining lamps, the belching whale
> And humming water must o'erwhelm thy corpse,
> Lying with simple shells. O Lychorida,
> Bid Nestor bring me spices, ink, and paper,
> My casket and my jewels, and bid Nicander
> Bring me the satin coffer.
>
> (3.1.56–67)

Though the roiling ship and panicking sailors prevent Pericles from sending Thaisa "hallowed" to her grave, a series of Pauline forms enables him to bid her a remarkably intimate farewell, including syntactical transpositions ("A terrible childbed hast thou had, my dear / No light, no fire"); dropped conjunctions ("No light, no fire") and condensed imagery ("aye-remaining lamps"); and finally, a sudden break in the direction of the discourse ("Lying with simple shells. O Lychorida"). But perhaps the clearest sign of Pauline influence is how these features prolong the steady swell of restrictive and non-restrictive clauses, which, depending on how editors punctuate the speech, stretch just one or two complete sentences across the opening eleven lines.[36] Just as Paul often fervently traverses a dense cluster of ideas, images, and emotions in the span of a single, highly-wrought sentence, so Pericles obsessively pursues the fantasy of his spouse lying "in the ooze" of the ocean floor, diving deeper and deeper into the details of her watery grave before snapping back to reality and issuing a series of commands to Lychorida. The result is a speech as rhetorically ambitious and emotionally layered as some of Paul's finest prose, by turns sensitive and aggressive, grief-stricken yet full of *gravitas,* visually concrete yet somehow entrancing and otherworldly. Above all, the speech exploits the elements of Pauline style to achieve the primary stylistic effect of Ephesians—feelings of mystery and awe—and it anticipates, as such, what Suzanne Gossett describes as Shakespeare's "deliberate attempt to dramatize wonder through words" in the play's later scenes of recognition and reunion.[37]

If Shakespeare's engagement with Pauline style contributes to the power and complexity of the storm scene, we might still wonder, what inspired Shakespeare to engage with Pauline style in *Pericles* in the first place? Responses to such a question will ultimately remain speculative, but Shakespeare's decision to experiment with Pauline style may relate to his decision to experiment with literary romance, a genre traditionally associated with Paul's life and letters. As critics have recognized, Shakespeare models Pericles's painful adventures at least partially on Paul's adventures as an itinerant missionary in the Mediterranean, which Luke represents in Acts using the generic formulae of Greek romance.[38] Luke was not, however, the only authority to link Paul to the romance tradition— Paul himself develops the connection in Ephesians, where he exhorts readers to transform themselves into Christian knights, instructing them to "Put on the whole armour of God, that ye may be able to stand against the assaults of the devil"; this allegorical armor, according to Paul, includes "the shield of faith, wherewith ye may quench all the fyrie dartes of the wicked," as well as "the helmet of salvation, and the sworde of the Spirit, which is the worde of God" (Eph. 6:11–17). For Renaissance authors, Paul's statements crystalized a broad relationship between literary romance and Christian allegory—Edmund Spenser, to take only one example, highlights the role of Ephesians in the development of English romance in a letter to Walter Raleigh, where he presents Paul's discussion of the armor of God as key to the allegory of *The Faerie Queene* book one. "In the end," Spenser writes, discussing Red Cross Knight's adventures, "the lady told him, that unlesse that armour which she brought would serve him *(that is, the armour of a Christian man specified by Saint Paul, vi. Ephes.),* that he could not succeed in that enterprise."[39]

The associations, then, between Paul, Ephesians, and romance may have inspired Shakespeare's decision to employ a Pauline style in a romance play, the possibility of which increases in light of the play's strong Pauline themes. Shakespeare develops one of these Pauline themes in close relation to his engagement with Pauline style: the problems and possibilities of practicing patience in the midst of trials, suffering, and loss. The theme itself emerges early in the play, when Pericles's closest advisor, Helicanus, counsels the prince to practice patience under the threat of siege and ruin from a foreign king: "[B]ear with patience," Helicanus advises an anxious Pericles, "Such griefs as you do lay upon yourself." (1.2.63–64).[40] The theme returns during the storm scene, when Lychorida urges Pericles to maintain fortitude in the face of his wife's apparent death, presenting his daughter to him as a source of consolation and new responsibility: "Patience, good sir," Lychorida admonishes in response to Pericles's anguished cries, "For the sake of [your daughter] / Be manly, and take comfort." (3.1.19–22) She repeats the charge a few lines later, when Pericles hesitates to accept the child, choosing instead to challenge the gods with the injustice of his own suffering.

> PERICLES   O you gods!
> Why do you make us love your goodly gifts,
> And snatch them straight away? We here below
> Recall not what we give, and therein may
> Use honour with you.
> LYCHORIDA   Patience, good sir,
> Even for this charge.
>
> (3.1.22–27)

Pericles's loss of faith in the goodness of the gods coincides and interacts with his struggle to find meaning and purpose in the traumatic vagaries of his life, a spiritual crisis that seriously endangers his willingness to receive his daughter. If the gods, after all, gave Thaisa as a gift to Pericles only to cruelly "snatch" her away, might they not intend to snatch away his daughter too? From Pericles's despairing point of view, Marina's birth looks less like a blessing and more like a curse, another torture instrument the gods will eventually use to inflict pointless misery on him.

Lychorida's answer to this despair represents, in effect, a crucial rereading of Marina—the child is a "goodly gift" to Pericles, not a curse—even as her references to "Patience" recall Paul's attempts to describe the divine purposes behind human suffering. One of Paul's strongest formulations on the positive value of suffering occurs in Romans, where he integrates "patience" into a process of spiritual transformation leading from suffering to hope: the church should "rejoice in tribulations," according to Paul, "knowing that tribulation bringeth forthe patience, and patience experience, and experience hope, and hope maketh not ashamed" (Rom. 5:3–5). Paul also affirms the value of suffering to the Ephesians, particularly when he encourages the church to "faint not at my tribulations for your sakes, which is your glorie" (Eph. 3:13). For Renaissance readers, Paul's reflections on and practice of patient suffering cast him as a "patern of patience," teaching them how to recognize hardship and loss as opportunities for Christian growth, and how to sustain a sense of God's nearness and goodness in the midst of adverse circumstances.[41]

By consistently invoking patience in relation to Pericles's experiences of stress and death, Shakespeare fashions his hero into a Pauline exemplar of the virtue, inviting his audiences to reflect on a range of delicate issues using Pericles as a point of reference, issues like the difficulty of choosing patience and faith over anger and despair; God's disturbing silences in the face of human tragedy; and the possibility of finding comfort in the present and hope for the future. That Pericles fails to perfectly embody patience himself hardly disqualifies him as an exemplar of the virtue. Indeed, his impulsiveness and quick temper, his lapses into apathy and doubt, his need for others to deal patiently with him and to inspire a patient spirit in him make him all the more compelling as a case study, and they cast his moments of achievement in the discipline into much sharper relief, including his decision to embrace his daughter and bless her by the " best eyes" of the "good gods."[42] Ironically, the same qualities also draw Pericles closer to his apostolic model—Paul himself, as we will see in the next section, was not always the ideal pattern of patience that his Renaissance readers preferred to imagine.

Paulina and the Rhetoric of Rebuke

In addition to the prayer-benediction-eulogy sequence in *Pericles,* Shakespeare engages with Pauline style to fashion an important speech act in *The Winter's Tale,* the rebuke. Paulina, as critics have recognized, recalls her apostolic namesake as much in her fierce chastisements of Leontes in the early sections of the play as in her appeals to faith and redemption in the later sections. It is "precisely her intemperate diatribes," according to Huston Diehl, "and the discomfort they arouse in both the on-stage and theatrical audiences that link Paulina most closely . . . to Paul," especially to Reformation conceptions of Paul as an incisive moral critic.[43] Diehl demonstrates how Reformers like Luther and Calvin sought to justify Paul's belligerent uses of the rebuke, and she also notes how Paulina vocalizes their metaphors to justify her rebukes of Leontes, particularly the metaphor of a physician applying painful but necessary remedies to restore a patient to health. Diehl does not, however, explore how Paulina's speeches adapt from Paul's letters, not

just the rebuke itself, but also the formal techniques that Paul uses
to strengthen his rebukes, techniques like the heaping up of words
(*congeries*) and verbal repetitions (*epanalepsis*) of his diatribes; his
angry rhetorical questions (*interrogatio*); and his blunt outspokenness on personally embarrassing or socially taboo topics (*parrhesia*).

Paul puts *interrogatio* and *parrhesia* into particularly severe
practice in 1 Corinthians, where he both condemns a member of
the Corinthian church for committing incest and rebukes the rest of
the church for tolerating the sin. "Shal I come unto you with a
rod?" Paul asks before raising the issue of incest directly, "It is
heard certeinly *that there is* fornication among you: and such fornication as is not once named among the Gentiles, that one should
have his fathers wife" (1 Cor. 4:21–5:1). After admonishing the
Corinthian church for their collective failure, Paul delivers a rhetorically tangled and emotionally fraught condemnation of the
incestuous man.

3. For I verily as absent in bodie, but present in spirite, have
   determined alreadie as though I were present, that he that
   hath thus done this thing,
4. When ye are gathered together, and my spirite, in the Name of
   our Lord Jesus Christ, that such one, I *say,* by the power of our
   Lord Jesus Christ,
5. Be delivered unto Satan, for the destruction of the flesh . . .

The condemnation's strength partially consists in the court of spirits Paul convenes to pronounce it, including his own spirit; Christ,
who authorizes his verdict; and Satan, who carries out the punishment, "the destruction of the flesh." Equally as integral, however,
to the strength of the condemnation is the circuitous development
of the sentence: Paul employs a litany of qualifying phrases and
clauses, not only to deepen the impression of his moral outrage and
disgust, but also to heighten the climactic expression of condemnation, coiling the sentence with delays and deferrals in verses 3 and
4 before unleashing its sting in verse 5.[44]

Closely related to Paul's rebukes are his bitter diatribes, which
employ a variety of formal techniques to produce their force and
feeling. In Romans 1:28–30, for instance, he combines *congeries*
and *asyndeton* to compose a lengthy diatribe against Gentile unbe-
lievers.

28. For as they regarded not to acknowledge God, even so God delivered them up unto a reprobate minde, to doe those things which are not convenient,
29. Being full of all unrighteousnesse, fornication, wickednesse, coveteousnesse, maliciousnesse, full of envie, of murther, of debate, of diceite, taking all things in the evil parte, whisperers,
30. Backebiters, haters of God, doers of wrong, proude, boasters, inventers of evil things, disobedient to parents, without understanding, covenant breakers, without natural affection, such as can never be appeased, mercilesse.

As he critiques the lifestyle of the pagans at Rome, Paul heaps up a mountain of derisive names and destructive qualities (*congeries*) against them to shock his readers with the moral implications of godless living. The diatribe develops, moreover, without the use of conjunctions or connectives (*asyndeton*), which "adds wonderfully," as Erasmus observes, "to the speed and vehemence of the oration."[45] In another diatribe, Romans 3:9–12, Paul employs a forceful sequence of repetitions (*epanalepsis*) to stress the subjugation of Jews and Gentiles alike "under sinne."

9. What then? are we more excellent? No, in no wise: for we have already proved, that all, both Jewes and Gentiles are under sinne.
10. As it is written, There is none righteous, no not one.
11. There is none that understandeth: there is none that seeketh God.
12. They have all gone out of the way . . . there is none that doeth good, no not one.

Lest the Gentiles of the Roman church suspect an assumption of ethnic superiority in his critique of paganism, Paul returns to a doctrinal point "already proved," which he frames as an answer to the objections of an imaginary interlocutor. After affirming God's indifference to Jew-Gentile distinctions, he hammers home the universal scope of human sinfulness with a torrent of *no*'s, *none*'s, and *no not one*'s.

For biblical humanists, Paul's rebukes are trickiest to defend in his letter to the Galatians, where the tone is unusually punitive and the content transparently insulting. To justify these harsh qualities, humanists appeal, not only to the painful but necessary process of all moral correction, but also to the special challenge of correcting the Galatians, whose proverbial dullness demanded a ham-fisted approach. Erasmus, for instance, explains the disproportionate amount of time the letter spends castigating versus instructing with reference to Paul's foolish audience: Paul "more vehemently and sharpely reproveth [in Galatians], then in other of his Epistles," writes Erasmus in his paraphrase ,"to the intent that such, as could not with reason be brought to a better mynde, might yet with authoritie be called home and amended."[46] Probably the sharpest passage occurs in Galatians 3:1–3, where Paul reprimands their lapse into the "workes of the Law" with a series of mocking rhetorical questions.

1. O Foolish Galatians, who hath bewitched you, that ye shulde not obey the trueth, to whom Jesus Christ before was described in your sight, and among you crucified?
2. This onely would I learne of you, Received ye the Spirit by the workes of the Law, or by the hearing of faith *preached?*
3. Are ye so foolish, that after ye have begun in the Spirit, ye would now be made perfect by the flesh?
4. Have yee suffered so many things in vaine?

If Paul's allusion to the sufferings of the Galatians reflects his respect for their history of faith and perseverance, his insults ("Foolish") and sarcasm ("This onely wolde I learne of you") reflect his incredulity and scorn for their present inconstancy. The elliptical aspects of the questions, moreover, reflect Paul's tendency to passionately rebuke rather than patiently instruct in the letter. What does he mean, for instance, when he claims that Jesus Christ was "crucified" among the Galatians? What do phrases like "begun in the Spirit" and "made perfect by the flesh" mean, and how do they oppose each other? The ambiguities represent the cost of Paul's rhetorical techniques, which tend to generate a great deal of charisma and emotion, though typically at the expense of logical clarity.[47]

The same rhetorical techniques inform Paulina's approach to Leontes, whose irrational suspicion of his wife's fidelity compels Paulina to confront the king, not with tightly structured and coherently reasoned arguments, but with an improvisational battery of insults, curses, and threats. Paulina's use of Pauline tactics emerges in one of her earliest exchanges with Leontes at court, where she combines *parrhesia* and *epanalepsis* with *anacoluthon* and *hyperbaton* while presenting herself as an advocate for Hermione.

> Good my liege, I come—
> And I beseech you hear me, who professes
> Myself your loyal servant, your physician,
> Your most obedient counselor, yet that dares
> Less appear so in comforting your evils
> Than such as most seem yours—I say I come
> From your good Queen.

(2.3.52–58)[48]

Before making her purpose at court explicit, Paulina suddenly breaks off mid-sentence and inserts an appeal for Leontes's full attention, including a three-fold characterization of herself as his servant, plus a vague, periphrastic comparison of herself to the other counselors. The interjection serves to establish Paulina's credibility as a counselor, to set a tone of urgency and seriousness, and most importantly, to smooth the introduction of an extremely delicate subject. At the mention of Hermione, however, Leontes cuts Paulina off, scoffing at the epithet "good Queen," which drives Paulina, in turn, into a full-frontal verbal assault:

> LEONTES   Good Queen!
> PAULINA
> Good Queen, my lord, good queen, I say good Queen,
> And would by combat make her good, so were I
> A man the worst about you!

(2.3.58–61)

The explosive repetition of "Good Queen" (*epanalepsis*) enacts, in effect, a rhetorical version of the physical violence Paulina threatens here and elsewhere in the scene: Paulina seizes her description of Hermione back from Leontes and bludgeons him with it, marring her syntax in the process with a pair of light transpositions ("by combat make her good", "so were I a man") and a hanging modifier ("the worst about you"). In addition to empowering and impassioning her speech, the use of Pauline style serves to alter and exploit the prejudicial gender dynamics of her dramatic situation: on the one hand, she ventriloquizes what Randall Martin describes as Paul's "privileged apostolic language," a language typically coded as masculine and reserved exclusively for male authority figures, in order to preempt misogynist dismissals of her rebukes as the frivolous scolds of an old busy-body.[49] On the other hand, she leverages the misogynist assumptions of her courtly audience to motivate defenses of Hermione's honor, blending Paul's masculine apostolic voice with the combative language of chivalry and knighthood to emasculate the other counselors and present herself as the sole defender of a maiden in distress.

If Pauline style fuels the ferocity of Paulina's attacks on Leontes, it also inspires pity in other members of the courtly audience. In the same scene, for instance, Paulina adapts the rhetorical features of Paul's diatribes, particularly *congeries* and *asyndeton,* to develop an ekphrastic description of the newborn princess, whom Leontes has proclaimed illegitimate and sentenced to death. The child "is yours," insists Paulina,

> And might we lay th'old proverb to your charge,
> So like you, 'tis the worse. Behold, my lords,
> Although the print be little, the whole matter
> And copy of the father—eye, nose, lip,
> The trick of's frown, his forehead, nay, the valley,
> The pretty dimples of his chin and cheek, his smiles,
> The very mould and frame of hand, nail, finger.
>
> (2.3.96–102)

To protect the princess from Leontes's wrath, Paulina rapidly catalogues her physical features for the other Sicilian lords, highlighting her resemblance to the king and arousing sympathy for her weakness and helplessness. The Pauline pace and pathos of the speech derive largely from the lack of conjunctions in the *ekphrasis,* which creates a vivid impression of Paulina's mind at work, of her thoughts outstripping her words. In balancing, moreover, her rebukes of Leontes with appeals for the princess, Paulina suggests the indebtedness of her speech to the softer, more maternal dimensions of Pauline style, tempering her dependence on its punitive, paternal dimensions. Paul himself displays the maternal dimensions of his style in Galatians, where he complements his rebukes with intimate expressions of concern for "My litle children," as he refers to the Galatians, "of whome I travaile in birth againe, until Christ be formed in you" (Gal. 4:19).[50] For Renaissance critics, Paul's readiness to dress himself in maternal imagery and speak in highly emotional tones of voice underwrites the loving intentions behind his rebukes, and it contributes, at the same time, to the strength and variety of his style.[51] The same readiness inspires Shakespeare's maternalization of Paul with the character of Paulina, even as Paul's rhetorical shifts between apostolic severity and pastoral care inform Paulina's shifts between sharp reproofs and sympathetic appeals.

As with Pericles's speeches at sea, the Pauline character of Paulina's speeches at court emerges with sharper clarity in contrast to the styles of other Shakespearean rebukes. In *The Comedy of Errors,* for instance, Shakespeare composes a rebuke for another strong, religiously inflected female character, the Abbess Emilia, whom critics sometimes adduce as a prototype for Paulina.[52] Towards the end of the play, Emilia questions one of the heroines, Adriana, about her relationship with her husband Antipholus, seeking the source of Antipholus's apparent madness. When Adriana reveals how she has badgered Antipholus with suspicions of infidelity, Emilia reproaches her for jealousy.

> And thereof came it that the man was mad.
> The venom clamours of a jealous woman
> Poisons more deadly than a mad dog's tooth.
> It seems his sleeps were hindered by thy railing,
> And thereof comes it that his head is light.
> Thou sayst his meat was sauced with thy upbraidings:
> Unquiet meals make ill digestions.
>
> (5.1.68–74)[53]

And so on. After several more lines of point-by-point analysis the Abbess brings her argument to a sensible conclusion, the proverbial wisdom of which she flaunts with a neat pair of couplets.

> In food, in sport, and life-preserving rest
> To be disturbed would mad or man or beast.
> The consequence is, then, thy jealous fits
> Hath scared thy husband from the use of wits.
>
> (5.1.83–86)

The formal symmetries of the speech contribute significantly to its persuasive force. In reprimanding Adriana as the cause of her husband's madness, Emilia deploys a series of discreet claims, each supported with clear evidence, seasoned with a simple metaphor, and expressed in stable iambic pentameter; she develops and com-

pletes ideas at regular intervals; and she defines, finally, the logical
relations between her ideas ("And thereof comes it," "The consequence is, then," etc.). If, however, Emilia's cogent use of deductive
reasoning strengthens her indictment of Adriana's jealousy, it also
distances the indictment from Paulina's emotionally driven Pauline rebukes. The stylistic difference stems as much from the
demands of their audiences as from differences in temperament
and character: whereas Leontes refuses to hear, let alone rationally
consider, any evidence that contradicts his belief in Hermione's
infidelity, Adriana is capable of responding to rational argumenta-
tion, rendering the use of Pauline rebukes unnecessary, if not
counterproductive.

Paulina's need for and practice of Pauline rebukes appears most
clearly as part of the conclusion to the play's tragic half. After forcing Hermione to stand trial for adultery, Leontes orders an oracle
from Apollo to be read aloud in court, expecting it to substantiate
his claims. But when the oracle actually exonerates Hermione,
Leontes flatly denies its authority, triggering, in turn, a series of
tragedies that culminates in Hermione's apparent death. Hermione
herself is hurried offstage after Leontes's denial, leaving Paulina to
report her death to the court, but not before she combines *parrhesia, interrogatio,* and *congeries* with *asyndeton* and *anacoluthon*
into a brutal condemnation of Leontes:

> What studied torments, tyrant, hast for me?
> What wheels, racks, fires? What flaying, boiling?
> In leads or oils? What old or newer torture
> Must I receive, whose every word deserves
> To taste of thy most worst? Thy tyranny,
> Together working with thy jealousies—
> Fancies too weak for boys, too green and idle
> For girls of nine—O think what they have done,
> And then run mad indeed, stark mad; for all
> Thy bygone fooleries were but the spices of it.
>
> (3.2.173–82)

The force of Paulina's rebuke derives in part from her repeated
accusation of "tyranny," an accusation she refrains from making in
her earlier exchanges with Leontes (cf. 2.3.115–19). But her charges
of tyranny, jealousy, and foolishness acquire most of their Pauline
bitterness and violence from the provocative rhetorical questions
preceding them, which Paulina uses to acknowledge and embrace

the dire consequences of leveling such openly hostile remarks at a monarch ("whose every word deserves / To taste of thy most worst"). A tissue of torture scenes fills the questions themselves with horror and dread ("wheels, racks, fires," "flaying, boiling"), even as the digressive description of his jealousy laces the accusations with sardonic humor ("Fancies too weak for boys, too green and idle / For girls of nine").

How should we understand Shakespeare's decision to engage with Paul's style in *The Winter's Tale*? Compared to *Pericles,* Shakespeare makes far less use of traditional romance conventions in *The Winter's Tale,* weakening Paul's associations with romance as a source of inspiration for his use of Pauline style in the latter play. Shakespeare may have drawn inspiration, however, from Paul's similar (if less familiar) associations with *The Winter's Tale*'s more obvious generic rubric, tragicomedy.[54] Paul's associations with tragicomedy derive from his identification with Mercury, the Roman god of eloquence, interpretation, trickery, and travel, whom Renaissance critics saw as the spokesperson for tragicomedy, beginning with his role as the conniving protagonist in Plautus's tragicomedy *Amphitruo.* "I will set out the plot of this tragedy," Mercury announces in the prologue to the play:

> What? Did you pull a face, because I said it was going to be a tragedy? I am a god so I'll change it, if you want. I will make a comedy out of this tragedy . . . I'll make it mixed: a tragicomedy.[55]

Similar to the associations between Orpheus and lyric poetry, Mercury's facetious invention of "tragicomoedia," the only recorded use of the term in the classical tradition, established an association between the god and the genre for Renaissance literary theorists, who debated his comments as authoritative grounds for the development of tragicomedy as a legitimate dramatic form.[56] At the same time, biblical humanists drew broad parallels between the tragicomic plot of *Amphitruo,* a raucous farce in which Zeus and Mercury disguise themselves as humans to seduce the wife of a Theban military general, and a zany episode from the book of Acts, "the sacrifice at Lystra," a story in which citizens of the Mediterranean city of Lystra mistake Paul and his fellow apostle Barnabas for Mercury and Zeus. The biblical story, which features as much wonder, confusion, and slapstick as anything in Plautus, warrants a brief summary. While preaching to a crowd of Lystrans, Paul notices, according to Luke, a man "impotent in his feete . . . a creeple from his mothers wombe," to whom he successfully commands, "Stand upright on thy feete" (Acts 14:8–10). So amazed are the Lystrans, not only with Paul's miraculous powers of healing, but also with his eloquent powers of speech, that they come to believe Paul and Barnabas are really *pagan* deities in human disguise: "Then when the people saw what Paul had done," writes Luke, "they lift [*sic*] up their voyces, saying . . . Gods are come downe to us in the likenesse of men. And they called Barnabas, Jupiter, *and Paul, Mercurius, because hee was the chiefe speaker*" (Acts 14:11–12 my emphasis). Things go from bad to worse when the Lystrans report Paul's miracle to the priest of Jupiter, who quickly prepares a sacrifice of "bulles with garlands" to honor the apostles. Once Paul and Barnabas learn of the sacrifice, however, they rush to prevent it in a dramatic display of humility and zeal. "But when the Apostles . . . heard it," writes Luke,

> they rent their clothes, and ran in among the people, crying, And saying, O men, why do ye these things? We are even men subject to the like passions that ye bee . . . turne from these vaine things, unto the living God. (Acts 14:14–15)

From here the narrative gives over to a sermon on "the living God," which is "scarce" able to keep the Lystrans from sacrificing to Paul and Barnabas. But relent the Lystrans eventually do, to the apostles' relief—at which point, to their dismay, "certaine Iewes" from a group of neighboring cities appear and convince the Lystrans that Paul is, in fact, a religious charlatan, whereupon the Lystrans stone Paul in a mob rage and toss his lifeless body outside the city! As a last twist to an outrageous scene, Paul, now presumed dead even by his followers mourning nearby, suddenly stands to his feet and marches back into the city, "confirming," as Luke tells it, "the disciples heartes, & exhorting them to continue in the faith, affirming that wee must through many afflictions entre into the kingdome of God" (Acts 14:22). For biblical humanists, Paul's tragicomic experiences in Lystra prompted reflection on a variety of moral and spiritual themes, from the dangers of idolatry to the inevitability of suffering for the Gospel. But they could hardly miss the story's entertaining, Plautine spirit: "The *Apostles* before had a taske," preached the Oxford clergyman Edward Chaloner, comparing the story directly to Plautus's tragicomedy, "to teach the Gentiles that

Iupiter was nothing, and *Mercurie* nothing, and now as if *Amphi-truo* were to be re-acted, they must beginne a new with them, and hardly make good that *Paul* is *Paul,* and not *Mercurie,* that *Barnabas* is *Barnabas,* and not *Iupiter.*"[57]

It is possible, then, that Shakespeare's engagement with Pauline style in *The Winter's Tale* reflects a creative response to the cultural associations between Paul, Mercury, and tragicomedy. The possibility strengthens in view of the biblical episode's role in Renaissance discussions of Pauline style: for many humanists, the confusion between Paul and Mercury provided proof of Paul's eloquence, his ability to captivate and impress his early audiences. In his commentary on Romans, for instance, Peter Martyr Vermigli observes that Paul was "of the men of [Lystra] taken for Mercury, by reason of his eloquence of speach."[58] Andrew Willet makes the same observation: "*Chrysostome* saith . . . his tongue or speach was brighter then the Sunne," writes Willet, "whereupon he was of the Infidels called Mercurie, because the office of speaking was committed to him."[59] Like his patristic ties to Pericles, Paul's biblical ties to Mercury buttressed his reputation as an eloquent stylist in Renaissance literary culture, though somewhat ironically, they also served to link the apostle to his pagan counterpart in the minds of Christian audiences, perpetuating Paul's reputation as "a Christian Mercury" in the Renaissance cultural imaginary.[60]

If the associations between Paul, Mercury, and tragicomedy help illuminate Shakespeare's decision to engage with Pauline style in *The Winter's Tale,* they also help illuminate Shakespeare's decision to include as characters both Paulina and Autolycus, the mythological son of Mercury, neither of whom appears in Shakespeare's primary narrative source, *Pandosto.*[61] As critics have recognized, Shakespeare presents the roguish, ballad-peddling trickster Autolycus as an important foil to Paulina, who convinces Leontes of her miraculous ability to resurrect Hermione and restore their marriage as part of the play's comic finale. Autolycus's "ballads serve," observes Stephen Orgel,

> as indices to the nature of and capacity for belief. . . . They are also prototypes of Paulina's equally unlikely but pre-eminently artistic charade at the play's conclusion, for which she requires that 'You do awake your faith,' [requiring] what in any other context would be called gullibility.[62]

In using Autolycus's cons to shape and complicate responses to Paulina's healing art, Shakespeare plugs *The Winter's Tale* into a

network of themes that connects it with the relationship between
Paul and Mercury in 'the sacrifice at Lystra'—both the play and the
biblical story use their character foils to foreground the tensions
and tradeoffs between faith and skepticism; between the risks of
wonder and the safeties of irony; between knowing for yourself and
trusting others.[63] The stories resolve, however, these tensions in
very different ways: whereas the Lystrans repeatedly turn to different authorities (Jupiter's priest, Paul, "certain Iewes") to make
sense of the cripple's miraculous recovery, an inconstancy that ultimately devolves into violence, Leontes and his court submit their
chapel experience entirely to Paulina, trusting not only in her ability to bring Hermione back from the dead but also in her *authority
to interpret* the resurrection as "lawful" business, as opposed to
charlatanism or witchcraft.[64]

More than her appeals to "grace," "faith," and "redemption" in
the chapel, it is Paulina's dual role as the play's wonder-worker and
master-interpreter that suggests her direct relationship to Renaissance conceptions of Paul. Lancelot Andrewes, for one, makes
Paul's reputation as master-interpreter clear in a 1607 Easter sermon, a sermon that resonates with the ending of *The Winter's Tale.*
Andrewes's text is 1 Corinthians 15:20–58, where Paul confronts
certain members of the Corinthian church with their lack of faith
in Christ's resurrection: "Now if it be preached," Paul writes in
apparent exasperation, "that Christ is risen from the dead, how say
some of you, that there is no resurrection of the dead?" (1 Cor.
15:12). After affirming the historical truth of Christ's bodily resurrection, Paul turns to an explanation of how Christ's resurrection
actually prefigures the future resurrection of all Christian believers,
like "the first fruits" of a larger harvest (1 Cor. 15:20). For Andrewes, Paul's affirmation of the resurrection is relatively uninter-
esting, since it merely rehearses a truth that the Angel first spoke
outside of Christ's empty tomb: "[Paul's] words, 'Christ is risen,'
were first uttered by an Angel," Andrewes observes, "all the Evan-
gelists so testify."[65] But Paul's *interpretation* of the resurrection is
indispensible, making sense of the Easter-event and providing
Christians with a source of hope for their own salvation and future
resurrection: " 'Christ is risen,' " writes Andrewes, "is a good text,
but reacheth not us, unless it be helped with the Apostle's exposition . . . . The exposition is it that giveth us our hope, and the
ground of our hope. 'Christ is risen,' saith the Angel. 'Christ the first
fruits,' saith the Apostle." Christ, in other words, did indeed come

back to life, but the miracle only matters to Christians because Paul explained its profound implications to the Corinthians. Such an attitude reflects wider Renaissance perceptions of Paul as Christianity's foremost critic, or as Erasmus calls him, "the supreme interpreter of our religion."[66]

If Shakespeare draws on Paul's reputation as master expositor to craft Paulina's role as counselor and critic of the Sicilian court, he also draws on Paul's reputation as God's wonder-worker, a reputation innumerable Renaissance authors celebrate in their biblical commentaries and sermons. Like patristic uses, Renaissances uses of the term "wonder" and its variants to describe Paul derive from a variety of biblical texts, including 2 Corinthians, where Paul claims that he wrought the "signes of an Apostle" among the Corinthians "with all patience, with signes, and wonders, and great workes" (2 Cor. 12:12). To discern, however, the associations between Paul and wonder and determine their relevance to *The Winter's Tale,* we need look no farther than "Paul," the name itself, which translates as "wonderful" in Hebrew. According to Jerome's commentary on Philemon,

> Paul in Hebrew expresses 'wonderful.' In fact, it is wonderful that after being Saul—which is translated 'asked for,' because he had been asked by the devil to harass the church—he changed from being a persecutor to being a vessel of election.[67]

The significance of Paul's name was not lost on Shakespeare as he developed the character of Paulina, who not only works wonders herself but also provokes cries of wonder from others during the comic denouement. "Such a deal of wonder is broken out," claims a gentleman present at the reunion of Leontes and his daughter Perdita, "that ballad makers cannot be able to express it " (5.2.23–25; cf. 5.2.16 and 164). That the gentleman is not describing reactions to Paulina's primary work of wonder, the resurrection of Hermione, hardly weakens her connection to them. Paulina, after all, is as instrumental to the recovery of the princess as she is to the recovery of the queen, since the court relies on her authoritative interpretation of Perdita's tokens to establish her identity. "This avouches the shepherd's son," claims another witness to Perdita's recovery, reporting how a pair of Bohemian shepherds had rescued and adopted the newfound princess sixteen years earlier, "who has not only his innocence . . . to justify him, but a handkerchief and rings

of his *that Paulina knows*" (5.2.62–65 my emphasis). Paulina's initial recognition of Perdita's tokens anticipates her final reading of
Perdita herself for the resurrected Hermione—"Turn, good lady/
Our Perdita is found" (5.3.120–21)—even as it initiates the play's
movement towards an improbable, tragicomic conclusion, with its
attending experiences of wonder and joy.[68] Shakespeare creates
those experiences through his own recognition of and engagement
with Paul's ability to make wonder-wounded watchers and hearers
out of audiences, by virtue of his miracles, his interpretations, and
his style.

Conclusion: Shakespeare's Late Styles

In a recent assessment of the emergence and development of
Shakespeare's "late style," Bart van Es explores the "modish and
intellectually sociable" qualities that define Shakespeare's dramatic work after 1607. Contrary to conventional accounts of Shakespeare's late style as "distant," "dreamy," and excessively "self-
reflexive," van Es focuses on Shakespeare's enthusiastic participation in the evolving values and trends of Jacobean England's literary and theatrical cultures. Shakespeare's "late plays," van Es
observes, "are alive with the presence of other writers. . . . Not only
did the playwright frequently collaborate with other writers, he can
also be seen to imitate them much more closely than" in earlier
phases of his career. One aspect of Shakespeare's late style that
reflects his investment in the literary community is his tendency to
invoke or incorporate canonical authors in the plays, what van Es
describes as his "persistent representation of author figures, ranging from Gower as on-stage narrator in *Pericles* to the apostrophe to
Chaucer in the prologue to *The Two Noble Kinsmen*."[69]

Alongside Gower and Chaucer we should, I think, acknowledge
Paul's place within the company of canonical and contemporary
authors that inspires and informs the complex development of
Shakespeare's late style. Recognizing the Pauline precedents of
Shakespeare's verse in *Pericles* and *The Winter's Tale* contributes
to the larger critical project of accounting more carefully for Shakespeare's stylistic practices across his late work, especially as they
relate to his use of language. For as long as the language of Shakespeare's late plays is considered "unlike anything he (or anybody
else) had composed before," criticism will continue to mystify its

origins, ascribing its development to the transcendent genius of Shakespeare's singular imagination.[70] Gordon McMullan has highlighted this tendency: "The history of Shakespearean criticism," observes McMullan, "foregrounds the attribution to late style of the status of a kind of apotheosis, an almost mystical seal attached to the life of a genius."[71] McMullan explores how Shakespeare's biography, specifically his proximity to death, tends to promote a quasi-sacred conception of his late style as the sublime product of old age. But whether as cause or effect, an integral feature of this "discourse of lateness" is the hesitation to explore influences on or precursors to Shakespeare's late style, which could dispel its aura of timelessness, power, authority, and genius. The irony, of course, is that one of Shakespeare's models, Saint Paul, enjoyed a similar kind of critical reverence among intellectual elites across Renaissance Europe.

Notes

My thanks to the many colleagues and mentors who provided generous support and feedback on early versions of this essay, particularly Hannibal Hamlin, Richard Dutton, Alan Farmer, and James Siemon.

1. Brian Vickers, "Approaching Shakespeare's Late Style," *Early Modern Literary Studies* 13, no. 3 (2008), 2.

2. For Ovid, see Jonathan Bate, *Shakespeare and Ovid* (Oxford: Oxford University Press, 1993). For Seneca, Robert Miola, *Shakespeare and Classical Tragedy: The Influence of Seneca* (Oxford: Oxford University Press, 1992). For Marlowe and Fletcher, Bart van Es, *Shakespeare in Company* (Oxford: Oxford University Press, 2013), 21–36 and 263–77.

3. Jessica Wolfe, "Classics," in *The Oxford Handbook of Shakespeare* ed. Arthur Kinney (Oxford: Oxford University Press, 2011), 523. Cf. Robert Miola, *Shakespeare's Reading* (Oxford: Oxford University Press, 2000), 154.

4. The bibliography on Shakespeare's interactions with the Bible is vast. Modern scholarship begins with Naseeb Shaheen's three-volume catalogue of biblical references in Shakespeare's plays: *Biblical References in Shakespeare's Comedies* (Newark: University of Delaware Press, 1993), *Biblical References in Shakespeare's Histories* (Newark: University of Delaware Press, 1989), and *Biblical References in Shakespeare's Tragedies* (Newark: University of Delaware Press, 1987). Hannibal Hamlin helpfully surveys pre-Shaheen scholarship in his critical study of Shakespeare's biblical allusions. See *The Bible in Shakespeare* (Oxford: Oxford University Press, 2013), 43–77. Other post-Shaheen studies include *Early Modern Drama and the Bible: Contexts and Readings, 1570–1625* ed. Adrian Streete (New York: Palgrave MacMillan, 2012); *Shakespeare, The Bible, and the Form of the Book: Contested Scriptures* ed. Travis DeCook and Alan Galey (New York: Routledge, 2012); Steven Marx, *Shakespeare and the Bible* (Oxford: Oxford Uni-

versity Press, 2000); Piero Boitani, *The Gospel According to Shakespeare*, trans. Vittorio Montemaggi and Rachel Jacoff (Notre Dame: University of Notre Dame Press, 2013); Randall Martin, "Shakespearean Biography, Biblical Allusion and Early Modern Practices of Reading Scripture," *Shakespeare Survey* 63 (2010): 212–24; and Julie Maxwell, "How the Renaissance (Mis)Used Sources: the Art of Misquotation" in *How to Do Things With Shakespeare*, ed. Laurie Maguire (Oxford: Blackwell, 2008), 56.

5. Helen Wilcox, "Measuring Up to Nebuchadnezzar: Biblical Presences in Shakespeare's Tragicomedies" in *Early Modern Drama and the Bible*, ed. Adrian Streete, 59–63.

6. Patricia Parker explores how Shakespeare employs a similar kind of synthetic biblical style in *The Comedy Errors*. See *Shakespeare from the Margins: Language, Culture, Context* (Chicago: University of Chicago Press, 1996), 56–82.

7. For Paul as a source for the play, see Arthur Kinney, "Shakespeare's *Comedy of Errors* and the Nature of Kinds," *Studies in Philology* 85, no. 1 (1988): 29–52. Cf. *The Comedy of Errors*, ed. Charles Whitworth (Oxford: Oxford University Press, 2002), 37–42.

8. *A Midsummer Night's Dream*, ed. Peter Holland (Oxford: Oxford University Press, 1994), 4.1.207–10.

9. Geoffrey Carnall, "Shakespeare's *Richard III* and St. Paul," *Shakespeare Quarterly* 14, no. 2 (1963): 186–88.

10. Studies of Pauline material in *Pericles* include Martin, "Shakespearean Biography," esp. 220–24; Richard Finkelstein, "*Pericles*, Paul, and Protestantism," *Comparative Drama* 44, no. 2 (2010): 101–29; and Maurice Hunt, "Shakespeare's *Pericles* and the Acts of the Apostles," *Christianity and Literature* 49, no. 3 (2000): 295–309. Studies of Pauline material in *The Winter's Tale* include Roy Battenhouse, "Theme and Structure in *The Winter's Tale*," *Shakespeare Survey* 33 (1980): 123–38; Huston Diehl, " 'Does not the stone rebuke me?': The Pauline Rebuke and Paulina's Lawful Magic in *The Winter's Tale*" in *Shakespeare and the Cultures of Performance*, ed. Paul Yachnin and Patricia Badir (Burlington: Ashgate, 2008), 69–82; Randall Martin, "Paulina, Corinthian Women, and the Revisioning of Pauline and Early Modern Patriarchal Ideology in *The Winter's Tale*" in *Shakespeare, the Bible, and the Form of the Book*, ed. Travis DeCook and Alan Galey, 57–77; James Kuzner, "*The Winter's Tale*: Faith in Law and the Law of Faith," *Exemplaria* 24, no. 3 (2012): 260–81; and Ken Jackson, " 'Grace to boot': St. Paul, Messianic Time, and Shakespeare's *The Winter's Tale*" in *The Return of Theory in Early Modern English Studies: Tarrying with the Subjunctive*, ed. Paul Cefalu and Bryan Reynolds (New York: Palgrave Macmillan, 2011), 192–209.

11. For *hyperbaton*, see Quintilian, *The Orator's Education, Volume V: Books 11–12*, ed. and trans. Donald A. Russell (Cambridge: Harvard University Press, 2002), 8.2.14 (334–35) and 8.6.62–8.6.67 (461–65). Cf. George Puttenham, *The Art of English Poesy: A Critical Edition*, ed. Frank Whigham and Wayne A. Rebhorn (New York: Cornell University Press, 2007), 252. For *anacoluthon*, see Herbert Weir Smyth, *A Greek Grammar for Colleges*, rev. Gordon M. Messing (Cambridge: Harvard University Press, 1980), 3004. For *ellipsis* or "eclipsis," see Johannes Susenbrotus, *Epitome troporum ac schematum* (Zurich, 1540), 25. Cf. Puttenham, *The Art*, 247.

12. For *congeries* see Quintilian, *The Orator's Education*, 8.4.26–27 (404–5). Cf. Puttenham, *Art*, 321. For *epanalepsis*, see Susenbrotus, *Epitome troporum*, 30. Cf.

Puttenham, *The Art,* 284–85. For *interrogatio,* see Quintilian, *The Orator's Education,* 9.2.6 (36–37). Cf. Desiderius Erasmus, *Ecclesiastes sive de ratione concionandi* trans. James L. P. Butrica ann. Frederick J. McGinness in *Collected Works of Erasmus: Spiritualia and Pastoralia* (Toronto: University of Toronto Press, 2015), 818. For *parrhesia,* see Susenbrotus, *Epitome troporum,* 64. Cf. Puttenham, *Art,* 312.

13. MacDonald P. Jackson, *Defining Shakespeare: Pericles as Test Case* (Oxford: Oxford University Press, 2003), 150–53. Most critics consider *Pericles* a collaborative work, which Shakespeare co-wrote with the playwright George Wilkins. Generally speaking, acts 1 and 2 are attributed to Wilkins, while acts 3, 4, and 5 are attributed to Shakespeare. Cf. the note to Scene 11 in William Shakespeare and George Wilkins, *Pericles, Prince of Tyre,* ed. Roger Warren (Oxford: Oxford University Press, 2003), 153; and the note to scene 3.1 in *Pericles,* ed. Suzanne Gossett (London: Arden Shakespeare, 2004), 276.

14. *Erasmus' Annotations on the New Testament: Galatians to the Apocalypse: Facsimile of the final Latin Text with all earlier variants* ed. Anne Reeve (New York: Brill, 1993), 591 (sig. Dd2^{r}). On *anapodoton,* see Henry Peacham, *The Garden of Eloquence* (London, 1577), F1$^{v.}$ For Renaissance efforts to define and represent Pauline style, see my "In Praise of Bad Prose: Reading Pauline Style in the Reformation" forthcoming in *Renaissance Studies.*

15. For Shakespeare's use of the Geneva Bible, see Naseeb Shaheen, "Shakespeare's Knowledge of the Bible—How Acquired," *Shakespeare Studies* 20 (1988): 206; and Barbara Mowat, "Shakespeare Reads the Geneva Bible" in *Shakespeare, The Bible,* 25–40.

16. For these principles, see Kevin Killeen, "Immethodical, Incoherent, Unadorned: Style and the Early Modern Bible" in *The Oxford Handbook of English Prose: 1500–1640,* ed. Andrew Hadfield (Oxford: Oxford University Press, 2013), 510.

17. Biblical citations are from the "Geneva-Tomson Bible," *The Bible, that is, the Holy Scriptures, contained in the Olde and Newe Testament* (London, 1595).

18. Erasmus notes the "extensive hyperbaton" (*hyperbaton prolixius*) in *Erasmus' Annotations on the New Testament,* 596 (sig. Dd4^{v}).

19. For *metalepsis,* see Puttenham, *Art,* 267. The figure was difficult for Renaissance rhetoricians to consistently define and apply. See Brian Cummings, "Metalepsis: the Boundaries of Metaphor" in *Renaissance Figures of Speech,* ed. Sylvia Adamson, Gavin Alexander, and Katrin Ettenhuber (Cambridge: Cambridge University Press, 2007), 217–33.

20. John Chrysostom, *An exposition upon . . . Ephesians* (London, 1581), 2 (Ai^{v}).

21. For *asyndeton,* see Quintilian, *The Orator's,* 9.3.53–54 (130–31).

22. For the marginalia, see *The Bible,* 590 (F5^{v}). For Erasmus's paraphrase, see *The second tome or volume of the Paraphrase of Erasmus upon the New Testament* (London, 1549), sig. BBi^{v}

23. *The second tome,* sig. AAi$^{r.}$

24. All citations are from *Pericles,* ed. Suzanne Gossett. For the quote, see 3.1.1–14.

25. Jackson, *Defining Shakespeare,* 151. Cf. Naseeb Shaheen, *Biblical References in Shakespeare's Plays* (Newark: University of Delaware Press, 1999), 686. Pericles's use of the term "rebuke" also evokes Paul's writings (see below).

26. Critics have not explored the cultural associations between Paul and Pericles. For the play's sources, see Warren, *Pericles,* 13–20. Cf. Gossett, *Pericles,* 70–76; and the notes to the cast list of *Pericles, Prince of Tyre,* ed. Doreen Delvecchio and Antony Hammond (Cambridge: Cambridge University Press, 1998), 83.

27. Jerome, "Apologeticum ad Pammachium" (Letter 48) in Hilberg, *Sancti Eusebii Hieronymi epistulae* (Corpus Scriptorum Ecclesiasticorum Latinorum 54) (Vienna and Leipzig, 1910–18), 369–70.

28. Plutarch, *The lives of the noble Grecians and Romanes* trans. Thomas North (London, 1579), 171–72 (sig. Pii^r-Pii^v). Cf. Quintilian, *The Orator's,* 12.10.24 (295): "And what about Pericles? Are we to think that his oratory was at all like Lysias' slender grace, when the comic poets, in attacking him, compare him to the lightning and thunder of heaven." None of Pericles's speeches survive, but his reputation as an orator endures. Thucydides, for instance, describes Pericles as "the man most effective in speech," while Plato claims that "no one could beat Pericles as an accomplished orator." See *Thucydidis Historiae,* ed. H. S. Jones (Oxford: Oxford University Press, 1942), 1.139.4; and Plato, *Phaedrus,* trans. Robin Waterfield (Oxford: Oxford University Press, 2002), 61.

29. Desiderius Erasmus, *Paraphrases on The Epistles to the Corinthians and the Epistles to the Ephesians, Philippians, Colossians, and Thessalonians,* ed. Robert D. Sider, trans. and ann. Mechtilde O'Mara and Eward A. Phillips Jr. in *Collected Works of Erasmus: New Testament Scholarship,* ed. Robert D. Sider (Toronto: University of Toronto Press, 2009), v. 43, 11. Latin in *In universas epistolas apostolorum . . . paraphrasis* (Basil, 1522), sig. K7^r.

30. Nicolas Caussin, *Eloquentiae sacrae et humanae* (Paris, 1630), 936 (sig. 3C2c^v).

31. Victor Strigel, *A proceeding in the harmonie of King Davids harpe* (London, 1591), 124 (sig. R2^v).

32. See notes 44 and 46 below.

33. Kenneth Gross, *Shylock is Shakespeare* (Chicago: University of Chicago Press, 2006), 86.

34. Gossett compares the speeches in the note to lines 1–14 in *Pericles,* 276.

35. William Shakespeare, *King Lear,* ed. R. A. Foakes (London: Arden Shakespeare, 1997), 3.2.1–9. Subsequent citation appears internally.

36. Following the 1609 quarto, for instance, DelVecchio and Hammond present lines 55–63 as part of one continuous discourse, punctuating line 56, "No light, no fire, Th'unfriendly elements . . . " in *Pericles,* 137.

37. Gossett, *Pericles,* 9.

38. Peter Womack, "Shakespeare and the Sea of Stories," *Journal of Medieval and Early Modern Studies* 29, no. 1 (1999): 171. Cf. Gossett, *Pericles,* 118.

39. For the letter to Raleigh, see Edmund Spenser, *The Faerie Queene* ed. A. C. Hamilton et al. (New York: Pearson Education, 2001), 717.

40. The lines appear in a portion of the play that critics generally assign to Wilkins. This does not, however, preclude Shakespeare's role in developing the theme, which he may have recognized in Wilkins's sections and expanded in his own sections or else introduced into Wilkins's scenes in revision.

41. For Paul as a "patern of patience," see Thomas Bilson, *The suruey of Christs sufferings* (London, 1604), 72 (H1^r).

42. Marina later appears to Pericles as an emblem of this achievement, even as she herself patiently restores him to life: "[T]hou does look / Like patience," Per-

icles muses to Marina during their recognition scene, "gazing on kings' graves, and smiling / Extremity out of act" (5.1.128–30).

43. Diehl, "Does not the stone," 73.

44. Erasmus describes the condemnation as "a terrifying thunderbolt" (*fulmen terrificum*). See Erasmus, *In universas epistolas,* K4ʳ·

45. *Erasmus' Annotations on the New Testament: Acts—Romans—I and II Corinthians: Facsimile of the final Latin text with all earlier variants,* ed. Anne Reeve and M.A. Screech (Leiden: Brill, 1990), 350 (sig. Gᵛ).

46. *The second tome,* sig. aaiʳ· Martin Luther describes how Paul "bursteth out into plaine thunderings and lightenings" as he rebukes the Galatians. See Martin Luther, *A Commentarie . . . upon the Epistle of S. Paul to the Galatians* (London, 1575), 22 (Cviᵛ).

47. Luther comments on the passage that "here the simple reader haply may be deceived, if he be not circumspect, to thinke that Paule in teaching keepeth no order at all. And surely after the manner of the Rhetoricians he observeth none: but as concerning the spirite he useth a goodly order." See Luther, *A Commentarie,* 87 (sig. L7ᵛ). The Geneva editors heavily supplement Paul's questions with glosses and paraphrases.

48. All citations are from *The Winter's Tale,* ed. Stephen Orgel (Oxford: Oxford University Press), 1996).

49. Martin, "Paulina, Corinthian Women," 71.

50. For Paul's maternal metaphors and imagery, see Beverly Roberts Gaventa, *Our Mother of Saint Paul* (Westminster: John Knox Press, 2007).

51. The biblical philologist Salomon Glassius, for instance, describes how Paul wins sympathy from his readers with "many maternal appeals [*maternis blandimentis*]" in *Philologiae Sacrae* (Jenae, 1623), 310 (sig. 2R1ᵛ).

52. For the relations between Emilia and Paulina, see Dorothy Kehler, "Shakespeare's Emilia's and the Politics of Celibacy" in *In Another Country: Feminist Perspectives on Renaissance Drama,* ed. Dorothy Kehler and Susan Baker (Metuchen: The Scarecrow Press, 1991), 157–80.

53. All citations are from *The Comedy of Errors,* ed. Charles Whitworth.

54. For an introduction to the terms "romance" and "tragicomedy," see Barbara Mowat, "'What's in a Name': Tragicomedy, Romance, or Late Comedy" in *A Companion to Shakespeare's Works: The Poems, Problem Comedies, Late Plays,* ed. Richard Dutton and Jean Howard (Oxford: Blackwell, 2003), 129–50.

55. *Plautus,* ed. Paul Nixon (Cambridge: Harvard University Press, 1916), v. 1, pg. 1–122, ll. 51–63.

56. Giambattista Guarini, for instance, claimed *Amphitruo* as a precedent for his controversial pastoral tragicomedy *Il pastor fido.* See Allan Gilbert, *Literary Criticism: Plato to Dryden* (New York: American Book Company, 1940), 509 ff. Philip Sidney acknowledges *Amphitruo* as the genre's classical precedent in *An Apologie for Poetrie* (London, 1595), ff. K2r-K2v. For the Renaissance reception of tragicomedy, see Tanya Pollard, "Tragicomedy" in *The Oxford History of Classical Reception in English Literature: 1558–1660,* v. 2, ed. Patrick Cheney and Philip Hardie (Oxford: Oxford University Press, 2015), 419. For the relations between mythic figures and literary forms in Renaissance literary theory, see Heather Dubrow, *The Challenges of Orpheus: Lyric Poetry and Early Modern England* (Baltimore: The Johns Hopkins University Press, 2007), esp. 16–18.

57. Edward Chaloner, *Six Sermons Preached by Edward Chaloner* (London, 1623), 222 (sig. P7^v)

58. Peter Martyr Vermigli, *Most learned and fruitfull commentaries upon . . . Romanes,* trans. Henry Billingsley (London, 1568), sig. Biii^r

59. Andrew Willet, *Hexapla, that is, A six-fold commentarie upon . . . Romanes* (Cambridge, 1611), 8 (sig. A4^v).

60. Gabriel Harvey refers to Paul as "a Christian Mercury" in *Pierces Supererogation* (London, 1593), 81 (sig. L2^r).

61. Critics have not explored the relations between Paul and Mercury or their relevance to *The Winter's Tale.* For the sources of *The Winter's Tale,* see *The Winter's Tale,* ed. J. H. P. Pafford (London: Arden Shakespeare, 1963), xxvii–xxxvii. Cf. *The Winter's Tale,* ed. Susan Snyder and Deborah T. Curren-Aquino (Cambridge: Cambridge University Press, 2007), 66–73, and the notes to the cast list at 79.

62. Orgel, *The Winter's Tale,* 52.

63. For the importance of these themes across the late plays, see Raphael Lyne, *Shakespeare's Late Work* (Oxford: Oxford University Press, 2007), esp. 6–8 and 30–80.

64. Sarah Beckwith stresses the significance of Paulina's authority in the chapel in *Shakespeare and the Grammar of Forgiveness* (New York: Cornell University Press, 2011), 144.

65. For the sermon, see *The Works of Lancelot Andrewes* (Library of Anglo-Catholic Theology, Oxford, 1854), v. 2, 206–20.

66. Erasmus, *Paraphrases on The Epistles to the Corinthians,* 3.

67. *St. Jerome's Commentaries on Galatians, Titus, and Philemon,* ed. and trans. Thomas Scheck (Notre Dame: University of Notre Dame Press, 2010), 358.

68. For "wonder" as the play's dominant mood, see T. G. Bishop, *Shakespeare and the Theatre of Wonder* (Cambridge: Cambridge University Press, 1996), 125–76; and Peter Platt, *Reason Diminished: Shakespeare and the Marvelous* (Lincoln: University of Nebraska Press, 1997), 153–69.

69. van Es, *Shakespeare in Company,* 264–65.

70. Russ McDonald, *Shakespeare's Late Style* (Cambridge: Cambridge University Press, 2006), 1.

71. Gordon McMullan, *Shakespeare and the Idea of Late Writing* (Cambridge: Cambridge University Press, 2007), 5.

"A delightful Proteus": Humors, Disguise, and the Actor's Skill in *The Blind Beggar of Alexandria* and *1 Henry IV*

ALEXANDER PAULSSON LASH

THE FIRST TWO SURVIVING PLAYBOOKS to invoke the concept of humors on their title pages, both published in 1598, were George Chapman's *The Blinde begger of Alexandria, most pleasantly discoursing his variable humours in disguised shapes full of conceit and pleasure,* and Shakespeare's *The History of Henrie the Fourth . . . With the humorous conceits of Sir Iohn Falstalffe.*[1] This essay proposes that there is more than coincidence in this odd conjunction. At first glance Shakespeare's play, with its subtle exploration of the young Henry V's political education, hardly seems to exist in the same theatrical world as Chapman's successful farce,[2] which centers on a single character's use of four different disguises to end up as King of Egypt. The title-page references to humors, however, point to a shared theatrical frame of reference. When performed, the Blind Beggar's "variable humours" and Falstaff's "humorous conceits" would not simply have resided in their language. This terminology also signals something about the gestures and physical behavior of the actors who had first played these roles, and I will be focusing here on the ideas about acting captured by this innovation in title-page phrasing.

The Galenic medical theory that underlies the concept of humors assumes that humoral dispositions shape each person deeply, even as it leaves room for flux and development across a person's life.[3] In Chapman's play, however, the actor transforms himself instantaneously, switching between his different personas in "disguised shapes." The title-page linkage of these shapes with "variable humours" suggests that there is more to disguise than changes of costume, that the actor must rapidly transform his physical gait, bearing, and gestures. Instead of the subtle and complex changes described in Galenic theory, the actor's mastery of disguise seems to reveal that he has mastered his own bodily disposition. There is a similar mastery driving Shakespeare's Hal, who enters the play planning a disguise-trick with Poins and proceeds to proclaim that he will uphold the "unyoked humors" of his tavern companions. Those companions may be controlled by their unrestrained humoral dispositions, but Hal himself behaves more like the Blind Beggar, biding his time in theatrical games until he can appear as a victorious warrior. He can imitate the tics and actions of his humorous companions, and he can make himself unrecognizable to them, as he does again when he disguises himself as a tavern drawer in *2 Henry IV* or a common soldier in *Henry V.* In reading *1 Henry IV* alongside *The Blind Beggar,* my central claim is that the combination of humors discourse and disguise plots, when used in the public theaters, created a rich new language for showcasing the skills of early modern actors, especially their capacities for modulating their physical movements and appearances.

My brief description of *The Blind Beggar of Alexandria* should already have made clear the extent to which its presentation of varied humors relies on disguise and different costumes.[4] We know that clothing was one of the most costly investment for theater companies, and disguise allowed a greater number of these investments to be displayed to the audience.[5] Following the influential suggestion of Ann Rosalind Jones and Peter Stallybrass that "the theater was a new and spectacular development of the clothing trade," I will demonstrate how the plots of both Chapman's and Shakespeare's plays make a point of promising that their central figures will appear in especially impressive costumes in their concluding scenes.[6] But even as the actors' bodies are used to display these striking pieces of clothing, the costumes are put in the service of the actors' humoral transformations. To better understand the function of both costumes and humors discourse in theatrical contexts, our accounts of these phenomena need more fully to incorporate a sense of the actor's skill.[7] The stars who perform roles like Hal and the Blind Beggar enliven their costume changes through varying modes of speech and movement, and end up seeming to control the humoral processes of their own bodies.

Through their celebration of this capacity for rapid transformation, plays like *1 Henry IV* and *The Blind Beggar of Alexandria* probably contributed to the reputations of the two most famous individual actors of the 1590s, Edward Alleyn and Richard Burbage.[8] The documentary record of their acting styles remains quite thin, and most commentary is based on their association with specific roles—the former with Marlovian heroes like Faustus and Tamburlaine, the latter with Shakespeare's tragic figures such as Hamlet and Othello—but in some of the most famous descriptions of their work, recorded in the decades after their deaths, both actors are compared to the changeable sea-god Proteus.[9] They were most celebrated, that is, for their capacity to transform themselves, as in Thomas Heywood's prologue to a revival of *The Jew of Malta* at the Cockpit in 1633, which praises Alleyn as "peerelesse, being a man / Whome we may ranke with (doing no one wrong) / Proteus for shapes, and Roscius for a tongue, / So could he speake, so vary."[10] Alleyn was loved not simply for his famous stalking and roaring, Heywood implies, but also for his capacity to shift between parts. Richard Flecknoe, in a similarly Protean description of Burbage for his 1664 *Short Discourse of the English Stage,* goes even further in connecting the actor's art with transformations of his appearance: "he was a delightful Proteus, so wholly transforming himself into his part, and putting off himself with his Cloathes, as he never (not so much as in the Tyring-house) assum'd himself again until the play was done."[11] Here, Burbage's capacity to transform himself is tied specifically to his costume; he becomes his character by putting on a disguise. For Flecknoe, writing more than four decades after Burbage's death, this celebration is conventional, but the later association between Proteus and two of the most prominent actors of the 1590s is no accident. This linkage reflects not simply a general idea about their acting. Rather, their roles in certain plays were especially memorable because they allowed them to perform in "disguised shapes," and thereby to celebrate their capacities for physical transformation.

Although these two actors would take on an outsize reputation in early modern records, they were hardly alone in displaying protean skills. Disguises could be assumed by nearly half the cast, as in the notoriously madcap 1600 Admiral's play *Look About You,* which grafts the multiple disguises of the sort one finds in *The Blind Beggar of Alexandria* onto a historical plot clearly influenced by *1 Henry IV.* By having so many of its characters disguise themselves onstage, this play suggests that the capacity to perform the varying of shapes was a standard part of the actor's tool-kit. Along with these skills at disguise, actors were increasingly expected to convey singular humors, and the versatility of a central role would be heightened when the actor could play off of the comic types provided by his colleagues. In *The Blind Beggar,* for instance, the hero triumphs over a Spanish braggart and a deluded merchant. The comic figures of *1 Henry IV,* especially Falstaff and Hotspur, give actors greater opportunities for complex characterization, but they also prove significantly less able than Hal to modulate their behavior between court, tavern, and battlefield. The title-page reference to Falstaff's "humorous conceits" may thus point to how the actor consistently embodied a set of physical behaviors, and suggests that the capacity to take on and convey a single comic humor over the course of the play was an inverse version of the capacity rapidly to switch between humors in disguise.

The historical roots of these skills probably lay in the doubling practices of the smaller troupes that were the core purveyors of theater before the institutionalization of the playhouses. In such performative contexts, an actor must rely both on costumes and on transformations of physical presence to signal the change between different roles. Plays like *The Blind Beggar* and *1 Henry IV* assume that their actors possess these skills, and then go a step further, making the transformations a source of explicit commentary under the categories of disguise and humors. As the central figures describe their own disguise practice, or refer to the comic types around them according to humors, the actorly skills involved appear more clearly. These practices and discourses aroused particular interest in the mid-1590s. Plays with multiple-disguise plots first appeared, along with the genre of humors comedy, in that moment, and both sets of plays provide their actors with a new way of conceptualizing their art.[12] After two decades of increased professional stability, the playing companies were expanding on their medley of skills—songs, jigs, and clowning—with plots that emphasized the actors' protean natures.[13] By inviting actors to use their traditional skills in the service of presenting humors and disguises onstage, these plays reveal the growing confidence of early modern actors in the potentialities of their art.

Alleyn's Disguises

It is highly likely that Chapman wrote *The Blind Beggar of Alexandria* for Alleyn, and that the play's success rested on the star actor's opportunity winkingly to recreate his own most famous roles in a parodic and farcical register.[14] Scholars have observed that some of the characters taken on by Chapman's hero echo the famous roles that Marlowe had likely written with Alleyn in mind, including Barabas and Tamburlaine.[15] As the shepherd's son who rose to become emperor, Alleyn had drawn on his own impressive physique to create what appears to have been his most memorable character, stalking the stage with his booming voice. Chapman crafts a version of that same role for him, as the central character rises from a shepherd's son to become the King of Egypt, ruling over the Kings of Ethiopia and Arabia, as well as the imaginary kingdoms of Phasiaca and Bebritia. The audience, however, only gets to see Alleyn in the persona of this regal figure, named Duke Cleanthes, in the final scene of the play.[16] The hero is introduced, instead, as Irus, the fortune-telling Blind Beggar, discussing the fate of Cleanthes with Aegiale, the Queen of Egypt. As soon as she leaves the stage, the actor leaps up, likely removing his blind beggar disguise, and exults in his varied identity:

> See Earth and Heaven where her *Cleanthes* is.
> I am *Cleanthes* and blind *Irus* too,
> And more than these, as you shall soone perceaue,
> Yet but a shepheardes sonne at *Memphis* borne,
> And I will tell you how I got that name,
> My Father was a fortune teller and from him I learnt his art.
>
> (i.109–14)[17]

Neither identity, warrior Duke or fortune-telling beggar, is given clear precedence here, so it remains ambiguous which name the character means that he has "got"—he might be Irus disguised as Cleanthes, or vice versa, or his original name may be some other that he has left behind with his shepherd's childhood.[18] Assuming that Alleyn played the part, then, we see him stepping into a role with strong and clear echoes of *Tamburlaine,* parodying a key moment of his signature role with a wink to the audience, even though they are here only given the tantalizing information that this figure is yet to appear fully revealed onstage. Not unlike Robert DeNiro in the *Analyze This* movies, where the actor's classic gangster tough guy roles are repeated for laughs, Alleyn was provided an opportunity to look at his famous persona as if from outside, playfully reminding audiences of the theatrical transformations at

stake when he shifted from a shepherd's son to an eastern conqueror.

What the audience gets to see in the last scene, when the disguiser finally sheds his other roles and appears as Cleanthes, is
above all his spectacular costume. For a revival of the play in May
or June 1601, following the opening of the Fortune and Alleyn's
return to the stage, Henslowe records four payments for "dyvers
thing for the playe of the blind begger of elexsandrea," including
"iiij score ownce of cope lace."[19] As Jean MacIntyre has explained,
copper lace provided an affordable substitute for the gold and sil-
ver used in the most sumptuous garments of the period, and could
be used to touch up garments when they became worn and
shabby.[20] MacIntyre calculates that Henslowe's 1601 purchase of
copper lace for one suit and one gown in The Blind Beggar would
have added five pounds of weight to these two garments.[21] When
he finally casts off his other costumes and strides out in this shim-
mering suit, the association with Tamburlaine would be visible to
all, considering that Henslowe's 1598 inventory explicitly men-
tions "Tamberlynes cotte with coper lace."[22] Not only does the conquering hero of The Blind Beggar enter the final scene like
Tamburlaine, leading four captive Kings who pledge their allegiance to him, he also shows off the sparkling garment that makes
him look especially regal.

The theatrical revelation of this spectacular garment marks some
of the distance between Alleyn's disguiser and his most obvious
theatrical predecessor, the Vice. Just as the main character of The
Blind Beggar uses disguise to deceive those around him, Vice
figures—so central to drama throughout the preceding century—
constantly take on false personas in their attempts to mislead the
plays' various personifications of humankind.[23] In the early
Reformation-era interlude Lusty Juventus, for instance, the Vice
"Hypocrisy," distracting Youth from attending a sermon, presents
himself as "Friendship."[24] These modes of allegorical deception
lived on among the earliest plays written for the purpose-built public theaters. Robert Wilson's The Three Ladies of London (c. 1581),
probably performed by both Leicester's Men and the Queen's Men,
opens with "Dissimulation" passing himself off as an honest farmer
to "Simplicity."[25] As a Vice, Dissimulation has a direct comic connection with the audience, openly announcing his name to them
before Simplicity enters. Chapman picks up on this element of intimacy with the audience for his Blind Beggar, who is constantly

explaining his disguises and deceptions. This disguiser, however, goes much further than his stage predecessors in the attention he lavishes on the theatrical practicalities of changing his appearance. He repeatedly describes the specific props and pieces of clothing he uses for his different personas, while the language of humors is employed to signal the transformations of gait, bearing, and gesture that complete the disguises. Chapman has imported the theatrical energy of the Vice, but he has sublimated the moral threat of deception into a comedic celebration of his star actor's capacity for transformation.[26]

This capacity for transformation had been developed, in part, as a response to the material circumstances of the actors who performed in the earlier moral interludes. As David Bevington showed some time ago, practices of doubling were absolutely essential to the repertories of small playing companies earlier in the sixteenth century.[27] This meant that actors needed to switch rapidly between various roles and to find ways to distinguish between them. For the skilled actors who played the Vice, this doubling could blur the lines with disguise. In the *New Enterlude of Vice conteyning the History of Horestes* (c. 1567), the Vice "Revenge" disguises himself as a Messenger from the Gods and encourages Horestes to kill his mother.[28] The Vice gives surprisingly little spoken guidance to the audience when he disguises himself as the Messenger, so the audience must instead have depended on the actor's conveying, perhaps with winks and gestures, that he is still the Vice. According to the doubling scheme presented on the title page, the same actor also appears as the personifications who speak against revenge, suggesting that he might need to affect a more stately bearing to double as "Nature" or "Duty." Alleyn would have relied on a similar set of skills when switching between the four personas of *The Blind Beggar*. Since these disguises are all meant to be put on by the same character, Alleyn can comment on and make explicit what he is doing, showing himself to be in full control of doubling practices.

The marked control of theatrical transformation that Chapman gives Alleyn stands out in contrast to another tradition of onstage disguise from the preceding decade: the Ovidian metamorphoses experienced by the boy actors in John Lyly's comedies of the 1580s. The schoolboy actors of Paul's Boys and the Children of the Chapel, for whom Lyly wrote, must have been quite talented at enacting changed personas, as they switch genders (*Gallathea*), ages

(Endymion waxing to old age and then returning to his youthful state), and even, in *Love's Metamorphoses,* from human to plant. Unlike the adult actors who performed Vices or figures like the Blind Beggar, however, these boys were not portrayed as if in control of this process. Lyly's plots instead impose the disguise or transformation from outside. The case of *Gallathea* is paradigmatic in this regard; Phyllida and Gallathea are put in their page-boy disguises by their fathers, and this only happens so that they can avoid becoming sacrificial offerings. While the boys who perform these two roles would need to be highly capable of switching between male and female presentation, the plot presents these skills as seemingly subordinate to those of their teacher, Lyly, who highlights how the boy actors are guided and advised by their (ostensibly) adult fathers.[29] Chapman, meanwhile, scripts a plot that makes the Blind Beggar the driving force of all the play's events, allowing Alleyn to seem as if he is in complete control of this theatrical world.[30]

Chapman further emphasizes Alleyn's capacity for rapid transformations in the play's middle sections, filled with a variety of playful tricks that make little direct contribution to the plot that brings the central character to the throne. Speaking as Irus in the opening explanation of his various disguises, he invites the audience to take pleasure in the transformations he will perform in the coming play:

> For till the time that I may claime the crowne,
> I meane to spend my tyme in sportes of loue,
> Which in the sequell you shal playnely see,
> And Ioy I hope in this my pollicie.

> (i.123–26)

While the play is framed by the hero beginning as blind beggar and ending as ruler, most of the playing time is given over to his playful sports, as the audience watches what he is able to achieve through his two other roles, the "rich vserer" Leon and the "mad brayne *Count*" Hermes (i.143–44). In these two disguises, he courts two beautiful sisters, using the fortunes he gives them as Irus to trick them into marrying his other personas. Immediately after arranging these marriages, he goes on to proclaim that now he will "woe them crossely both" (iii.156), that is, he will seduce each woman in his opposite guise, cuckolding himself. As he successfully woos each woman again, the hero makes it abundantly clear that in this play, the winning of women is a game, played most successfully by the man who is able to modify his appearance and physical bearing to the extent that not even his own wife can recognize him. The Alleyn who could rival Proteus for changing his shape would be the perfect actor for this role, reminding the audience that while he might end up as a stalking conqueror, he could also switch at lightning speed between different characters.

The embodied nature of Alleyn's transformation from character to character is emphasized most strongly in relation to the Count Hermes persona, which is consistently associated with either his humors or his mad brain. At the end of the opening scene, the audience sees him change into his Count Hermes outfit in preparation for seducing Elimine. As he goes through his wardrobe for the Count's velvet gown, eye patch, and the pistol he keeps girded to his side, he uses variations on the word "humor" five times to describe this character. Putting on this disguise involves some discomfort for the actor, since he wears a heavy velvet gown, even on hot summer days, which "hides my persons forme from beeing knowne, / When I *Cleanthes* am to be descried" (i.338–39). The heaviness of the gown "doth not fit my frencie wel" (337), as calling himself Count Hermes involves "assuming / The humour of a wild and frantick man" (i.330–31). There is more to being Hermes than simply the gown and patch. When playing him the actor must be in a constant state of frantic motion, conveying an underlying energy. Here the humor is not, in accordance with Galenic tradition, one that can be identified with one of the four fluid substances that decide temperament. Rather, humor signals the lack of control and excessive energy for which the hero has made himself known in the guise of Hermes.

Alleyn himself was noted at the time for the excessive humors of his famous roles. In a well-known invocation of his style, published the same year as *The Blind Beggar* and two years after the play's first performance, Edward Guilpin's 1598 epigram on an unskilled imitator of Alleyn presents the actor in terms similar to those used of Hermes:

> *Clodius* me thinks lookes passing big of late,
> With *Dunstons* browes, and *Allens Cutlacks* gate:
> What humours haue possest him so, I wonder,
> His eyes are lightning, and his words are thunder:

What meanes the Bragart by his alteration?
He knows he's known too wel, for this fond fashion:
To cause him to be feard: what meanes he than?
Belike, because he cannot play the man.
Yet would be awde, he keepes this filthy reuell,
Stalking and roaring like to *Iobs* great deuill.[31]

As Jeremy Lopez has pointed out, this epigram is the only surviving instance of "stalking" being associated with Alleyn himself, whereas other references draw the association specifically to the character of Tamburlaine.[32] Here, Alleyn appears not as the Scythian conqueror but as the hero of the lost play *Cutlack the Dane,* performed by the Admiral's in the 1594 season, and while we know little about this character, Guilpin's epigram suggests the physical energy demanded by this role, in terms not at all unlike the language used about Count Hermes. The unfortunate Clodius has endeavored to alter his physical presence, trying to appear controlled by his humors, as loud and imposing as Alleyn in one of his most striking roles. Through his poor skill as an actor, however, Clodius unwittingly serves to emphasize how Alleyn can transform himself fully into a role. In his first scene as Hermes, Alleyn plays out such a comparison through an encounter with a Spaniard named Bragadino, who exclaims against him in language similar to Clodius's, asking the Count: "what art thou that hast the gust of thy braines gript with such famine of knowledge not to know me" (ii.24–25). Of course, Hermes knows that Bragadino is just a braggart, but he himself has been able to play Hermes in such a way that when he wears this disguise, Bragadino knows that he is rude, uncivil, and bloody. Along with the underlying character that he plays, Alleyn's difference from braggarts like Clodius and Bragadino begins with his capacity to make his eyes lightning and his words thunder, to seem so fully transformed that other characters have no suspicion that he might be anyone but the wild and frantic Count. The audience, of course, knows better, and the great pleasure of *The Blind Beggar* lies in getting to watch Alleyn's transformation, to be reminded that each character is another shape into which he can vary his physical presence.

Chapman and Alleyn further heighten this pleasure for the audience through the speed with which these skillful changes take place. They put this speed to its most effective use in relation to the other persona of the play's sportive middle, the usurer Leon, through whom Alleyn gets to celebrate the economic benefit of knowing how to perform a role. With his most important prop a bottle-nose, Leon allowed Alleyn to winkingly repeat another of his Marlovian heroes, *The Jew of Malta*'s Barabas, and he draws on that figure's association with usury.[33] In one key sequence, he deploys his different personas in a financial scheme. Appearing before the King with a debtor he has had arrested, Antistenes, Leon claims that he is owed four thousand pounds, but as the audience soon realizes, Antistenes did in fact pay his debt, only making the mistake of doing so "Vpon the stone before blinde *Irus* caue" (iv.72). Leon, challenging Antistenes's account, argues that his debtor had requested an extension of the loan against an interest of another thousand pounds, and backs up this claim with reference to a supposed witness, the Count Hermes. While an enraged Antistenes sputters that Hermes was hardly present, Leon suddenly falls ill and exits, and only four lines later the Count appears and hollers about having overheard the offer of an extended loan. The actor, that is, changes costume from Leon's bottle nose to Hermes' eyepatch with extreme rapidity, and to complete the effect he would presumably need to modulate his posture and tone of voice as well. This process continues soon thereafter, as the Count's testimony is not sufficient, so he exits the stage in search of Irus, in front of whose cave the whole transaction supposedly took place. Irus then enters six lines later, and considering his credit as a holy hermit, the King believes him and settles the case in Leon's favor. This scene allows Alleyn to give his most virtuoso display of protean skill, all in service of showing the character doubling the return on a financial investment. As we know from the play's extraordinary success, audiences were perfectly willing to pay for the privilege of watching these rapid transformations, and they seem to have been more than happy with a reminder that the actor who could so wittily transform himself was pulling in reams of money.

Hal's Comedy of Humors

The success of *The Blind Beggar of Alexandria* points to some key features of the theatrical culture in which *1 Henry IV* was first performed. We are accustomed to treating Shakespeare's play alongside other history plays, but we can more fully recover its extraordinary theatrical vitality by also reading it alongside the fashions for disguise-plots and humors comedy in the mid-1590s. The part of Hal, in particular, allows an actor to perform a variety of roles, ranging from tavern ruffian to repentant son and warrior, in a manner quite similar to *The Blind Beggar*'s disguiser. Shakespeare, however, centers *1 Henry IV* much less consistently on one figure than had been the case in Chapman's play, as he redistributes the varied humors performed by a single actor in *The Blind Beggar of Alexandria.* While Chapman used the idea of humors to distinguish between the central figure's four different personas, Shakespeare gives distinctive traits to the variety of figures Hal encounters both in the tavern and in the historical plot, most memorably in Falstaff and Hotspur.[34] Instead of simply having the actor who played the Prince show off his skill at humoral transformation, *1 Henry IV* contrasts Hal's variable shapes with the more fixed and comic humors conveyed by the actors who performed these other figures.

This difference between the two plays may have been caused by the composition of the acting companies in 1596–97, when the Chamberlain's Men appear to have been less dominated by a single star actor than was the case for the Admiral's Men immediately preceding Alleyn's retirement. Even as Burbage was on his way to becoming the company's undisputed star, the play balances the four key parts of King, Prince, usurping rebel, and reckless companion quite evenly. Burbage could have been equally well suited for the parts of Hal or Hotspur, and while those scholars and editors who have ventured potential cast lists have assumed that he played the former—an assumption I share as the most likely—there is no firm evidence for deciding with certainty which part the young tragedian might have taken.[35] Considering the popularity of the Prince's reformation as a dramatic subject, captured in *The Famous Victories of Henry the Fifth,* the part would have had an immediate interest for contemporary audiences, but within Shakespeare's play Hal at times seems to be playing second fiddle to the more extravagant parts of Falstaff and Hotspur. [36] In this regard, *1 Henry IV* likely contributed to the development of humors comedy, which often relies on an active commentator who draws out the comic quirks and obsessions of the proper humors characters.[37]

Hal does, however, move towards a final appearance as successful warrior that is very similar to the dramatic movement of *The Blind Beggar of Alexandria*'s protagonist. Within the structure of the two plays, Hal's soliloquy at the end of his first scene with Falstaff and Poins echoes the Blind Beggar's opening address to the audience. Just as Irus announces that he will spend his time in sports of love until he can claim the crown, setting up the action for the play to come, Hal explains his own plan to use "loose behavior," timed to "playing holidays," that will be thrown off at the end of the play (1.2.184, 179). In describing this theatrical plan, he treats humors as available to put on like a disguise, famously stating "I know you all, and will awhile uphold / The unyoked humor of your idleness" (170–71). There is an ambiguity here about who is being addressed. On the one hand, Hal speaks most directly of Falstaff and Poins, who have just exited. In upholding their humor, he presents himself as able to playact an inhabitant of the rowdy Eastcheap world, even as parts of him will remain hidden. Along with this address to characters in the fiction, on the other hand, the speaker also seems to address the audience directly, with clear echoes of Irus's recounting of his disguise-plot.[38] This element of direct address provides a certain amount of slippage between Hal and the actor who performed him. The humor of idleness, then, would refer to the audience sitting and standing around the stage, watching this actor transform himself into their beloved warrior king for the "while" that the play lasts. If the part was in fact taken by Burbage, there might have been an extra frisson of knowing pleasure for the most theatrically aware spectators in seeing the young son of the aging theater-owner start to take on meaty parts like this one.[39] Regardless of who played the part, Hal's soliloquy allows that actor to announce his arrival as a leading man. When Hal concludes with the promise that "My reformation, glittering o'er my fault, / Shall show more goodly and attract more eyes / Than that which hath no foil to set it off" (188–90), the actor intimates that the audience, before the play is over, will get to see him appear in garments glittering like the copper-lace coats worn by Alleyn.

Shakespeare continued to find this structural element—a central character who announces the theatrical transformations that he will enact throughout the play—useful as his career progressed. In a case where we have firm evidence of Burbage taking the role, Hamlet performs a change of identity that echoes Hal's.[40] He may not disguise himself in a literal way as does Hal with the buckram suit. When he promises Horatio that he will "put an antic disposition on," however, he describes the precise gestures with which he will perform this role, "With arms encumbered thus, or this head-shake" (1.5.173–75). Burbage would surely have demonstrated these motions while speaking the lines, and while we cannot know how consistently he then embodied them throughout the play, the speech does function as a promise to the audience of what they will see. There will be something "strange or odd" in how Hamlet bears himself (171). Even as audience members can expect to eventually see him take revenge, they will first get to enjoy his physical transformations. For Hal, the shapeshifting is named as part of "playing holidays," while Hamlet's assumed disposition is put on to evade danger, suggesting a darker view of this theatricality in the tragedy. In both cases, however, the actor collaborates with the playwright to highlight his control of his physical bearing and gestures, more fully conveying his skill.

As Hal's long-term planning focuses on his glittering reformation, his more immediate concerns at the beginning of the play are with disguise and playacting. Right before his soliloquy, the Prince exclaims that "once in my days I'll be a madcap" and discusses the mechanics of his disguise-trick with Poins, worrying that their companions "will know us" if they do not pay sufficient attention to their "habits" and "every other appointment" (1.2.124, 152–53). He enters the play, that is, with the desire to conceal and transform his identity so well that even Falstaff, supposedly his closest companion, will not recognize him. As he and Poins set their plan in motion, he revels in his mirth, "it would be argument for a week, laughter for a month, and a good jest for ever" (2.2.83–85), inviting the audience to take pleasure in his disguise, just like *The Blind Beggar*'s disguiser. Similarly to that figure, as well, Hal celebrates his capacity to vary his humors, to transform his bodily disposition. Waiting for Falstaff and the others to return, Hal imagines himself as able to take on any humor, and by extension, to play any character: "I am now of all humors that have showed themselves humors since the old days of Goodman Adam" (2.4.86–87). He proceeds, for the remainder of the scene, to propose new scenarios that he might act out. As Falstaff trundles in, the Prince exclaims about how "I'll play Percy, and that damned brawn shall play Dame Mortimer his wife" (100–101), before getting distracted by Falstaff's retelling of the Gadshill encounter. Once Hal and Poins reveal that they were the ones who robbed the robbers, Falstaff tries to change the subject by proposing "a play extempore," to which Hal replies that "the argument shall be thy running away" (255–56). The audience to Shakespeare's play has already watched Falstaff's one moment of vigorous physical activity, as well as hearing it recounted in his extremely exaggerated version, and now the Prince wants to put it back onstage, performing it in a parodic register.

The scene that the audience actually gets to see the pair act out, of course, is Hal's repentant return to his father. In their performance, Falstaff and Hal are attentive to questions of physical posture and bearing. Emphasizing the contrast between seated Kings and standing supplicants, Falstaff begins by announcing that "This chair shall be my state" (2.4.344), while Hal kicks off the performance with a bow: "Well, here is my leg" (353). When Hal deposes Falstaff and they switch roles, the change is marked by a reversal of posture, with the Prince "set" and Falstaff proclaiming "And here I stand" (398–99). In addition to fussing about the seating arrangements, Falstaff creates his version of the King by modulating the physical appearance of his face, asking for "a cup of sack to make my eyes look red, that it may be thought that I have wept" (350–51). Puffy eyes, Falstaff believes, will help him to capture "King Cambyses' vein" (352)—a term that Will West has recently included, along with humor and conceit, as theatrical terms for recognizable actions that invoked specific theatrical traditions and gestures in the minds of spectators.[41] Falstaff, then, approaches the acting of royalty in large part as the art of modulating bodily expression.

When Hal comes to replay the scene with his father, by contrast, the King delineates a view of kingship as tied to clothing and the timing of his appearances. Indeed, scholars have noted how insistently both Hal and his father see their royal identities as determined by external signs throughout the whole series of plays in which they feature.[42] Complaining that Hal, like Richard II, has made himself too visible, Henry counters that he himself has been dressed "in such humility / . . . / My presence like a robe pontifical, / Ne'er seen but wondered at" (3.2.51–57). By timing his appearances to be "Seldom but sumptuous" (58), the King aims to control the impression made by those robes on the few occasions when they are seen. Although he does not realize it, his son has learned this lesson surprisingly well. Hal's successful transformation, growing out of the dramatic structure that Shakespeare's play shares with *The Blind Beggar,* depends on his disguised appearance in a coarse buckram suit to visualize the loose behavior that he will throw off.

Along with revealing his protean capacities to insinuate himself throughout his realm, Hal uses the disguise-trick to put the

"humorous conceits" of Falstaff and his companions—their cow-
ardice, their tics and obsessions—on display. When Hal and Poins
again disguise themselves in *2 Henry IV,* this time as drawers, Hal
makes this goal explicit by wondering how they might "see Falstaff
bestow himself tonight in his true colors" (2.2.146–48). The Prince
proves strikingly confident at playing cruel jokes on his tavern fellows.[43] In *1 Henry IV,* examples include his punning on Bardolph's
red face or his trick to make the inexperienced tapster Francis cry
"Anon" over and over. The theatrical success of these moments
would depend on the appearance and comic timing of the supporting actors—the red cosmetics on Bardolph's face referenced in "Hot
livers" and "Choler," or the physical confusion of Francis when he
"*stands amazed, not knowing which way to go*" (2.4.293–94,
73.SD). Most importantly, Hal plays off Falstaff, whom he refers to
as a "trunk of humours" in the voice of his father in the play-
within-the-play (409). With the barrage of references to Falstaff's
corpulence and taste for sack, the language of the plays paints his
behavior as determined by his physical appetites and an associated
overflowing of humoral fluid. This language sets up expectations
about how the part of Falstaff would have been played, with the
actor perhaps using movements and gestures of an exaggerated
sluggishness. Scholars have long noted how the language used by
and about Falstaff suggests a sedentary nature, and some of his
most memorable moments include falling asleep behind the arras
and playing dead on the battlefield.[44] The consistency of these references suggests that the actor could have conveyed this sluggish
quality by means of a stylized deportment.

Shakespeare clearly assumed that the actor playing Hal would be
thinner than the one playing Falstaff, considering how often the
two characters tease each other for these qualities. This contrast,
however, would not depend simply on physiological differences
between the actors. In part, costumes could be used to make the
Falstaff-actor appear bigger, something like the "giant hose" Will
Kemp appears to have acquired for a performance of *Sir John Oldcastle* with Worcester's Men in August 1602, perhaps with an echo
of his earlier performance in Shakespeare's play.[45] The sense of Falstaff as fat and Hal as thin, and of Falstaff as the real butt of the
Prince's jokes, could be further heightened by having the Hal-actor
move in a more nimble fashion around the comparatively immobile
Falstaff. The linguistic exchanges between these two figures have
provided a key point for scholarly analyses of Shakespeare's psy-

chological and political complexities, but they also show Shakespeare developing a physical contrast that a pair of actors can play with together.[46]

This contrast between a nimble performer and figures who tend towards comic types appears to have been influential, as the display of comic figures in Mistress Quickly's tavern provides a close analogy with Chapman's *An Humorous Day's Mirth*. Typically seen as the first proper example of humors comedy, Chapman's play appears to have been a great success for the Admiral's Men in the summer of 1597, likely soon after *1 Henry IV* was first performed by the Chamberlain's Men.[47] Chapman's humors figures all end up in a private supper club, Verone's ordinary, which becomes the site for comic confrontations between jealous spouses, the appearance of a melancholy scholar, and even an assignation for the disguised King of France. The company supported the creation of these various characters by investing in new costumes, with Henslowe's 1598 inventory listing two items particular to this play, "Verones sonnes hose" and "Labesyas clocke, with gowld buttenes," and a stage direction in the play specifying that Lavele enters in "a paire of large hose" (2.2.49 SD).[48] The Chamberlain's Men may very well have made similar investments in new costumes for figures like Bardolph, Quickly, and Falstaff, with distinctive clothing heightening their comic impact. This staging of humors characters becomes the whole principle of Chapman's plot, which is guided by the witty courtier Lemot, who announces early on that he will "sit like an old King in an old fashion play . . . and point out all my humorous companions" (1.2.11–19), before using various tricks to time everyone's arrival at Verone's ordinary. Regardless of whether he was played by Alleyn or another popular actor, Lemot performs a role with some similarities to that of Hal, bringing the audience along and guiding their laughter at the fools paraded across the stage.

This comic structure is doubled by Jonson in his first play for the Chamberlain's Men, *Every Man in His Humour* (1598), in which the young wits Lorenzo Junior and Prospero, assisted by the disguised servant Musco, compete in trying to find the most ridiculous humors character. The audience is thus treated to figures like the violent country gull Stephano, the bad poet Matheo, and the cowardly soldier Bobadilla, who shares his laziness and evasiveness with Falstaff. Jonson may have written this role with the idea that it would be performed by the same actor who had played the fat knight in Shakespeare's plays, allowing the energy of the humors introduced by Shakespeare to carry over across plays.[49] The humors comedies of both Chapman and Jonson, then, as well as the comic scenes of Shakespeare's history, depend on one or two star actors who play witty and performatively flexible audience guides, while the other actors work to become clearly graspable types that more directly give rise to laughter.

Even as we can see Shakespeare developing this comic structure in the play's tavern scenes, he also extends this type of interplay to the historical plot, especially in the contrast between Hal and Hotspur. Lady Percy complains to her husband that he is "altogether governed by humors" (3.1.229), and the play seems to locate this "humor" both in the medical terminology of an excess of fiery choler and in an aggressive style that echoes *The Blind Beggar's* Count Hermes.[50] Just as Falstaff seems dominated by the excess of liquid humors that need replenishment from his bottles of sack, Hotspur's choleric humor constantly drives him on towards battle, leaving room for the young Prince to show himself more nimble, even as the extremity of Falstaff and Hotspur's humors make them mirror images of sorts. Hotspur's stage presence appears to be marked, above all, by a constant and frantic motion that far exceeds Hal's movement around Falstaff. The scene at the Welsh court builds much of its comedy through his inability to sit still. Glyndŵr begins by asking him to "Sit, cousin Percy. / Sit" (3.1.6–7), and then again requesting that he "Sit and attend" when the Welsh Lady sings (221), while Lady Percy has to repeatedly command him to "Lie still" (230). Mortimer, meanwhile, is perfectly happy to "sit and hear her sing" (217), his lethargy emblematically highlighting Hotspur's energy. Throughout the play, Hotspur's actions are marked by speed and impatience, creating in turn a distinctive physical presence for the audience, recalled in *2 Henry IV* when Lady Percy speaks of how he was "the glass / Wherein the noble youth did dress themselves / . . . in speech, in gait, / In diet, in affections of delight, / In military rule, humors of blood" (2.3.21–30).[51] This passage suggests the immediate and impressive impact that the performance of Hotspur may have had on theatrical culture in 1597. One implication of this speech could be that some audience members had begun ostentatiously imitating the speech and gait emphasized here. In short, Hotspur's energetic humor may have become a mode of being onstage that even those offstage hoped could be put on like a costume.

This fiery humor, never varying to accord with different situations, becomes an important source of the play's comedy, as Hotspur refuses to alter his behavior, regardless of his location. The only place he seems at home is the battlefield, and he enters the play full of contempt for those who do not dress appropriately for war, drawing a contrast in his first speech between himself, "Breathless and faint, leaning upon my sword," and "a certain lord, neat and trimly dressed," who has come to demand his prisoners "Fresh as a bridegroom," with a "chin, new reaped" (1.3.32–34). This effeminate "popinjay" (50), with his box of perfume, would seem to be more at home in Chapman's lost humors comedy of 1598, *The Fount of New Fashions.* When Hotspur is at home, meanwhile, the situation is reversed. Shakespeare builds the comedy of the scene around Hotspur's obsession with military matters, as Lady Percy describes how she has heard him murmur in his sleep, "Of sallies and retires, of trenches, tents, / Of palisadoes, frontiers, parapets," and so on (2.3.46–48). Hotspur responds to his wife's concerns by calling for his horse, famously crying out "when I am a-horseback, I will swear / I love thee" (94–95). The contrast with the more versatile Hal becomes clear when this scene is immediately followed by one in which the Prince imitates his Northern rival's rude style. Just after watching Hotspur respond to his wife with a non-sequitur about his crop-ear roan horse, the audience sees Hal imagine Hotspur's response to a question from her with "Give my roan horse a drench" (2.4.99). Shakespeare, that is, has both created a humorous obsession with military and equestrian matters for the Hotspur actor to perform, and given the actor who plays Hal a delicious opportunity to parody that obsession.

While Hal makes Hotspur another of the gulls in his own comedy of humors, the play also demands that they appear together on the battlefield. For an audience coming to a play that saw a star actor transformed into their much-loved warrior King, the expectation of finally seeing him in armor would be similar to the expectation of seeing Alleyn in his Tamburlaine-esque Cleanthes costume at the end of *The Blind Beggar.* Here, the contrast with Hotspur's myopic focus on battle allows both the character of Hal and the actor who plays him to display a superior capacity for transformation, and Shakespeare whets both Hotspur's and the audience's desire to see him in his full regalia. When Hotspur asks if the Prince and his companions have arrived for the battle, Vernon responds by describing their appearance:

All furnished, all in arms,
All plumed like ostriches . . .
I saw young Harry with his beaver on,
His cuisses on his thighs, gallantly armed,
Rise from the ground like feathered Mercury.

(4.1.96–97, 103–5)

In part, the ostrich feathers refer to the traditional heraldic badge of
the Prince of Wales, but for Hotspur, this combination of warlike
armor and resplendent feathers only serves as a further impetus for
direct confrontation, exclaiming "Let them come . . . like sacrifices
in their trim" (111–12). On an actual battlefield, of course, ostrich
feathers would presumably not provide much practical advantage.
On a stage, however, Hal's appearance, beautified in these feathers,
would strikingly convey his arrival as conquering warrior. Hotspur's reaction to Vernon's description suggests that the showdown
between the two Harrys could involve not just two different rhetorical styles, but contrasting types of armor, with Hotspur's perhaps
more solid and lacking feathers, and Hal's shinier and more
fashion-forward, including the visually striking plumes. Just as
Alleyn's copper-lace coat signaled his victory in the theatrical
world of Alexandria, the feathers here add to the audience's pleasure in seeing Burbage, or one of the other recognizable members
of the Chamberlain's Men, victorious at Shrewsbury.

Conclusion: Multiplying Proteus

Shakespeare's and Chapman's plays both invite one actor to display a capacity for transformation while the other actors aim to
embody singular types. There is no need to assume, however, that
the skills involved in disguise and varied humors were specific
only to certain actors. In the anonymous Admiral's play *Look
About You,* likely performed in 1599, seven different characters
appear in disguise, often as each other, revealing that the celebration of actors' protean qualities could extend throughout the company.[52] Andrew Gurr has recently taken this play, along with *The
Blind Beggar,* as especially representative of the Admiral's repertory in the 1590s.[53] *Look About You,* however, may also have been
influenced by *1 Henry IV,* as Anne Begor Lancashire has suggested.[54] Apart from the general similarity of both plays combining
historical material concerning medieval English courts from

sources like Holinshed with contemporary-seeming comic sub-plots, Lancashire notes how *Look About You* picks up the comedy of a young tavern Drawer who cries "Anon" repeatedly; its figure of Prince John, who rants like Hotspur; and the influence on young royals named Henry by Falstaff and this play's villain, Skinke. She also points to a verbal echo in moments of revealed disguise, with Falstaff's response to Poins and Hal—"By the Lord, I knew ye as well as he that made ye" (2.4.244)—repeated when the character Faulconbridge learns that he has been tricked by his wife and Robin Hood, "I knew thee Mall, now by my swoord I knew thee" (2425). In noticing the pleasure generated by seeing a popular historical figure disguise himself onstage, and then multiplying that pleasure through a dizzying plot, the anonymous authors of *Look About You* celebrate the capacity of the Admiral's company actors for theatrical transformation, a celebration encapsulated by one disguiser's exclamation that he "wil be a proteus every houre" (1510).

This celebratory view of protean behavior marks plays like *Look About You, The Blind Beggar of Alexandria,* and *1 Henry IV.* At the time when these plays were first performed, however, references to actors as Proteus were not uniformly positive. The 1590s saw no surviving description of individual actors as Proteus. It was only later, in the decades after their deaths, that Alleyn and Burbage could be praised in such terms. Instead, the protean changeability of actors tended to appear as a popular trope in antitheatrical discourse. Anthony Munday, for example, wondered if players are "not as variable in heart, as they are in their parts."[55] This fear about the moral risks of playing could even extend to playwrights. Shakespeare only refers to Proteus twice in his works, and in both cases the reference carries negative connotations. There is, of course, the character in *Two Gentlemen of Verona,* whose changeability puts both male friendship and romantic love at serious risk. More insidiously, the future Richard III tells the audience in a soliloquy that he "can add colors to the chameleon, / Change shapes with Proteus for advantages, / And set the murderous machiavel to school" (*3 Henry VI,* 3.2.191–93). Only a few years later, Shakespeare was crafting a portrait of another young future king, who would announce his own protean qualities without assuming that they were pure evil. Tracing what she sees as the second tetralogy's more positive view of Hal's performance of various roles, as opposed to Richard III's Vice-like machinations, Jean Howard has argued that this "shift registers the growing self-confidence of theatrical craftsmen such as

Shakespeare."[56] Among such craftsmen, of course, the actors were those most on display, Burbage chief among them, likely celebrating his own skill for transformation at precisely the same moment as Alleyn was acting in plays like *The Blind Beggar of Alexandria*. Reading these plays now, it is hardly surprising that their star actors would come to be compared to Proteus, filling their audiences with delight.

Notes

1. Jason Scott-Warren notes the "welter of titles and subtitles" that begin appearing with this term from 1598 onward, and lists some of the earliest examples; see "When Theaters Were Bear-Gardens; or, What's at Stake in the Comedy of Humors," *Shakespeare Quarterly* 54, no. 1 (Spring 2003): 63–82, 75.

2. The play's success is revealed in a chart that Holger Syme has compiled of entries in Henslowe's diary, showing that it was the third highest grossing in the Admiral's repertory for the years 1594–97; see "The Meaning of Success: Stories of 1594 and its Aftermath," *Shakespeare Quarterly* 61, no. 4 (2010): 490–524, 507.

3. Our understanding of the relationship between early modern drama and medical theory has been shaped over the last two decades by the work of Gail Kern Paster, especially in *The Body Embarrassed: Drama and the Disciplines of Shame in Early Modern England* (Ithaca: Cornell University Press, 1993), and *Humoring the Body: Emotions and the Shakespearean Stage* (Chicago: University of Chicago Press, 2004). While this scholarly tradition has helped us to develop a rich account of how thoughts and emotions can be figured as embodied, I aim here to consider the specifically theatrical usage of such references.

4. For disguise in early modern drama, see Peter Hyland, *Disguise on the Early Modern English Stage* (Burlington: Ashgate, 2011); Victor Freeburg, *Disguise Plots in Elizabethan Drama: A Study in Stage Tradition* (New York: Columbia University Press, 1915); and Kevin A. Quarmby, *The Disguised Ruler in Shakespeare and His Contemporaries* (Burlington: Ashgate, 2012).

5. S.P. Cerasano, "'Borrowed Robes,' Costume Prices, and the Drawing of *Titus Andronicus*," *Shakespeare Studies* 22 (1994): 45–57; Natasha Korda, "Household Property/Stage Property: Henslowe as Pawnbroker," *Theatre Journal* 48, no. 2 (May 1996): 185–95; and Ann Rosalind Jones and Peter Stallybrass, *Renaissance Clothing and the Materials of Memory* (Cambridge: Cambridge University Press, 2000), 175–206.

6. Ibid., 176.

7. Evelyn Tribble has made a series of arguments for studying the skills of early modern actors; see "Skill" in *Early Modern Theatricality,* ed. Henry S. Turner (Oxford: Oxford University Press, 2013), 173–88; her "Introduction" to a forum on skill in *Shakespeare Studies* 43 (2015): 17–26; and *Early Modern Actors & Shakespeare's Theatre: Thinking with the Body* (London: Bloomsbury, 2017).

8. In considering them together, I build on Jeremy Lopez's call to "rediscover some important similarities between the two actors" (167); see "Alleyn Resurrected," *Marlowe Studies: An Annual* 1 (2011): 167–80.

9. For the association between actors and Proteus, see B. L. Joseph, *Elizabethan Acting,* 2nd ed. (Oxford: Oxford University Press 1964), 1–24; and Joseph Roach, *The Player's Passion: Studies in the Science of Acting* (Ann Arbor: University of Michigan Press, 1993), 23–57.

10. Christopher Marlowe, *The Famous Tragedy of the Rich Jew of Malta* (London: 1633), A4v. Accessed via *EEBO.*

11. Richard Flecknoe, *Love's Kingdom, with a Short Treatise of the English Stage* (London: 1664), H2v-H3r. Accessed via *EEBO.* See also Simon Palfrey and Tiffany Stern on contemporary praise for Burbage that emphasizes his "absolute control of his passions: he can blush and blench at will" (*Shakespeare in Parts* [Oxford: Oxford University Press, 2007], 312); for a discussion of how these emotions could be cued in actors' parts, see "The Actor With His Part: History," 311–27.

12. The date of Anthony Munday's dueling-disguiser play *John a Kent and John a Cumber* has been hotly contested. Although it has been dated 1590, the last decade has seen strong arguments for the play as written in 1595. See Douglas H. Arrell, "John a Kent, the Wise Man of Westchester," *Early Theatre* 17, no. 1 (2014): 75–92. *The Blind Beggar* was first performed in 1596, followed by the rise of humors comedy in Chapman's 1597 *An Humorous Day's Mirth,* Jonson's *Every Man in his Humor* (1598), and *Every Man Out of his Humor* (1599). Andrew Gurr takes disguise plays as representative of the Admiral's Men repertory in the mid-90s, in *Shakespeare's Opposites: The Admiral's Company 1594-1625* (Cambridge: Cambridge University Press, 2009), 49–81. Humors comedy, however, traveled between the Admiral's and the Chamberlain's companies, and disguise was key in Chamberlain's plays as well. In treating the repertories of the two companies as porous, I am inspired by Roslyn Knutson, especially *Playing Companies and Commerce in Shakespeare's Time* (Cambridge: Cambridge University Press, 2001), and "What's so Special about 1594?" *Shakespeare Quarterly* 61, no. 4 (2010): 449–67; as well as Syme, "The Meaning of Success." See also Tom Rutter, *Shakespeare and the Admiral's Men: Reading Across Repertories on the London Stage, 1594-1600* (Cambridge: Cambridge University Press, 2017).

13. William Ingram gives a concise account of the shift, across the Tudor century, from actors as loosely organized entertainers to highly accomplished professionals, in *English Professional Theatre, 1530-1660,* eds. Glynne Wickham, Herbert Berry, and William Ingram (Cambridge: Cambridge University Press, 2000), 153–56. See also Muriel Bradbrook, *The Rise of the Common Player: A Study of Actor and Society in Shakespeare's England* (Cambridge: Cambridge University Press, 1962); Gerald Eades Bentley, *The Profession of Player in Shakespeare's Time 1590-1642* (Princeton: Princeton University Press, 1984); and John Astington, *Actors and Acting in Shakespeare's Time: The Art of Stage Playing* (Cambridge: Cambridge University Press, 2010). In associating an increase of professional stability with greater artistic integration between playwright and player, I am inspired by Bart van Es, *Shakespeare in Company* (Oxford: Oxford University Press, 2013), although I see this integration as less specific to Shakespeare than does van Es.

14. Gurr, in *Shakespeare's Opposites,* assumes this to be true (5). It remains possible that the role was played by another actor, who would thereby be parodying his famous colleague. In that case, members of the audience who were familiar with Alleyn's acting would still be able to take a similar pleasure in watching his

style parodied. For Alleyn's celebrity, see S.P. Cerasano, "Edward Alleyn, the New Model Actor, and the Rise of the Celebrity in the 1590s," *Medieval and Renaissance Drama in England* 18 (2005): 47–58.

15. See Ennis Rees, "Chapman's 'Blind Beggar' and the Marlovian Hero," *The Journal of English and Germanic Philology* 57, no.1 (January 1958): 60–63.

16. T. M. Parrott's 1914 edition of the play argued that textual corruption in the sole surviving quarto edition points to a more fully developed "romantic story of Aegiale and Cleanthes," but that this story was cut down in response to the public's delight at the disguises; see *The Plays and Poems of George Chapman: The Comedies* (London: Routledge, 1914), 674. Scholars who have written on the play tend to accept this interpretation, and while I see no need to deny the possibility of Chapman having originally conceived or written a longer version, I focus on what we might be able to figure out about performance practice from the existing text.

17. All quotations of Chapman from Allan Holaday's edition of *The Comedies* (Urbana: University of Illinois Press, 1970).

18. The confusion about the character's "real" name is reflected in the 1598 quarto published by William Jones, in which the stage directions treat him as four different characters, stating "*Enter* Irus," "*Enter* Count," "*Enter* Leon," or "*Enter* Cleanthes," as occasion demands, and the speech prefixes similarly reflect the existence of four different speakers. For Jones and his compositors, it seems, the star of the show cannot be restricted to a single name.

19. See *Henslowe's Diary,* ed. R. A. Foakes, 2nd ed. (Cambridge: Cambridge University Press, 2002), 169–70. Alleyn did not perform with the Admiral's between 1597 and 1600, but returned with the opening of the Fortune playhouse. *The Blind Beggar of Alexandria* was revived in that season, strengthening the claim that Alleyn was the star of the play. For Alleyn's retirement, see S.P. Cerasano, "Edward Alleyn's 'Retirement' 1597–1600," *Medieval and Renaissance Drama in England* 10 (1998): 98–112.

20. *Costumes and Scripts in the Elizabethan Theatres* (Edmonton: University of Alberta Press, 1992), 92–95. See also Jones and Stallybrass, *Renaissance Clothing,* 190–91.

21. Ibid., 94.

22. Foakes, ed., *Henslowe's Diary,* 321.

23. Bernard Spivack's classic study of the Vice focuses on the shift from Psychomachia as an open battle between the forces of Good and Evil to the intrigues used by Evil to deceive the innocent. (*Shakespeare and the Allegory of Evil: The History of a Metaphor in Relation to his Major Villains* [New York: Columbia University Press, 1958]).

24. See R. Wever, *An Enterlude Called Lusty Iuuentus,* ed. Helen Scarborough Thomas (New York: Garland, 1982).

25. See *The Three Ladies of London* in *Three Renaissance usury plays,* ed. Lloyd Edward Kermode (Manchester: Manchester University Press, 2009), 2.7.

26. A similar influence from the Vice also appears to have shaped the figure of Hal, who directly addresses the audience with his plan to deceive his companions. Of course, the figure in *1 Henry IV* who has traditionally been seen as a descendant of the Vice is Falstaff, whom Hal refers to as a "reverend Vice" in the voice of his father in the play-within-the-play (2.4.412). Hal goes on in the same speech to refer to Falstaff as "That villainous abominable misleader of youth"

(421), and it is precisely through his effect on the Prince that Falstaff most resembles the Vice. Falstaff's claim in *2 Henry IV* that "The young Prince hath misled me" (1.2.133), however, points to how Shakespeare has redistributed the Vice's deceptions, so that the figure (Hal) who seems like he will be misled by the Vice figure (Falstaff) himself becomes a deceiving Vice as well. In this regard, Shakespeare seems to move beyond his earlier and more straightforward use of the Vice tradition with Richard III, who shares with the audience that "Thus, like the formal Vice, Iniquity, / I moralize two meanings in one word" (3.1.82–3). Citations of Shakespeare follow *The Norton Shakespeare, 3rd Edition,* ed. Greenblatt et al. (New York: Norton, 2016).

27. See *From* Mankind *to Marlowe: Growth of Structure in the Popular Drama of Tudor England* (Cambridge: Harvard University Press, 1962), esp. 68–103.

28. See John Pickering, *Horestes,* in *Three Tudor Classical Interludes,* ed. Marie Axton (Cambridge: D.S. Brewer, 1982).

29. See John Lyly, *Gallathea and Midas,* ed. Anne Begor Lancashire (Lincoln: University of Nebraska Press, 1969).

30. Katherine Schaap Williams locates a similar conjunction of theatrical impersonation and self-assertion in *The Fair Maid of the Exchange,* wherein the disguiser Frank Golding uses his capacity for impersonation to mark himself as able-bodied, in contrast to the "Cripple" who always remains himself. See " 'More legs than nature gave thee': Performing the Cripple in *The Fair Maid of the Exchange,*" *ELH* 82, no. 2 (Summer 2015): 491–519.

31. Edward Guilpin, "Of Clodius, 43," in *Skialetheia, or a Shadow of Truth, in Certaine Epigrams and Satyres* (London: 1598), B2v. Accessed via *EEBO.*

32. Lopez, "Alleyn Resurrected," 169.

33. See Bradley Ryner, "The Usurer's Theatrical Body: Refiguring Profit in *The Jew of Malta* and *The Blind Beggar of Alexandria,*" in *Early Modern Drama in Performance: Essays in Honor of Lois Potter,* eds. Darlene Farabee, Mark Netzloff, and Bradley Ryner (Newark: University of Delaware Press, 2015), 25–34.

34. This contrast between *The Blind Beggar* and other humors plays has been developed by Martin Wiggins in *Shakespeare and the Drama of his Time* (Oxford: Oxford University Press, 2000), 64–71.

35. T. W. Baldwin assigned the part of Hal to Burbage in *The Organization and Personnel of the Shakespearean Company* (Princeton: Princeton University Press, 1927); John Dover Wilson finds this "very probable" in his Cambridge edition (Cambridge: Cambridge University Press, 1946), xxxi; and David Scott Kastan accepts it as "likely" in his Arden edition (London: Bloomsbury, 2002), 78. Scott McMillin, in his *Shakespeare in Performance* volume on the play (Manchester: Manchester University Press, 1991), points out that from the Restoration through the mid-20th century Falstaff and Hotspur were the two parts most sought out by important actors (1–2), and Roberta Barker builds on this claim towards a larger argument about Hotspur as the tragic center of the play, "Tragical-Comical-Historical Hotspur," *Shakespeare Quarterly* 54, no. 3 (Fall 2003): 288–307. James Loehlin, in *Shakespeare Handbooks: Henry IV, Parts I and II,* suggests that Burbage "probably played Hal, though he might also have played Falstaff or Hotspur," (New York: Palgrave, 2008), 6.

36. The theatrical influence of *The Famous Victories* on Shakespeare's play is discussed in William N. West, "Intertheatricality," in Turner, ed. *Early Modern Theatricality,* 151–72, esp. 151–54; and Janet Clare, *Shakespeare's Stage Traffic:*

Imitation, Borrowing and Competition in Renaissance Theatre (Cambridge: Cambridge University Press, 2014), 144–64.

37. Scholars have typically treated *The Merry Wives of Windsor* as Shakespeare's attempt at humors comedy, but I see the same energies at work in all the plays that feature figures like Falstaff, Pistol, Bardolph, and Nim. See Roslyn Knutson, *The Repertory of Shakespeare's Company, 1594–1613* (Fayetteville: University of Arkansas Press, 1991), 43; Wiggins, *Shakespeare and the Drama of his Time,* 71–73; van Es, *Shakespeare in Company,* 131–35; and Rutter, *Shakespeare and the Admiral's Men,* 138–47.

38. Marjorie Garber suggested that this speech could be seen as direct address to the audience in " 'What's Past Is Prologue': Temporality and Prophecy in Shakespeare's History Plays," in *Renaissance Genres: Essays on Theory, History, and Interpretation,* ed. Barbara Kiefer Lewalski (Cambridge MA: Harvard University Press, 1986), 301–31; this point is developed by Ellen Summers, " 'Judge, My Masters': Playing Hal's Audience," in *Shakespeare's Second Historical Tetralogy: Some Christian Features,* ed. Beatrice Batson (West Cornwall: Locus Hill Press, 2004), 165–78. Jonathan Lamb emphasizes Hal's relationship to the theater audience as part of a larger argument about how Shakespeare uses disguise and related techniques to create a privileged epistemological standpoint for audience members; see "William Shakespeare's *Mucedorus* and the Market of Forms," *Renaissance Drama* 46, no. 1 (2018): 57–86, esp. 63–68.

39. James Marino has asserted the likelihood that early modern audiences brought their knowledge of Burbage as celebrity performer with them, and further shown that Shakespeare was highly attuned to those expectations about the specific actor in creating the role of Hamlet. See "Burbage's Father's Ghost," *English Literary Renaissance* 44, no. 1 (Winter 2014): 56–77.

40. Marino, ibid.

41. West, "Intertheatricality," 157–59. See also Peter Womack's description of how early modern acting can be understood more as a series of "Actions That a Man Might Play" than as the performance of a character, in *English Renaissance Drama* (Malden, MA: Blackwell, 2006), 261–311. Womack develops his ideas about early modern plays as built out of "quotable gestures" from a reading of the *Henry IV* plays; see "*Henry IV* and Epic Theatre," in *Henry IV, Parts One and Two,* ed. Nigel Wood (Buckingham: Open University Press, 1995), 126–61.

42. See David Scott Kastan, *Shakespeare After Theory* (London: Routledge 1999), 109–48; Jones and Stallybrass, *Renaissance Clothing,* 2–3; and Lina Perkins Wilder, " 'My Exion is Entered': Anatomy, Costume, and Theatrical Knowledge in *2 Henry IV,*" *Renaissance Drama* 41 (Fall 2013): 57–84, esp. 69–72. For a discussion of Hal's disguise on the eve of Agincourt in *Henry V,* see Quarmby, *Disguised Ruler,* 40–60.

43. The cruelty of moments such as this is brought out by Jason Scott-Warren, who compares humors plays to animal baiting; see "When Theaters Were Bear-Gardens."

44. See David Wiles, *Shakespeare's Clown: Actor and Text in the Elizabethan Playhouse* (Cambridge: Cambridge University Press, 1987), 119; Robert Reid, "Humoral Psychology in Shakespeare's 'Henriad,'" *Comparative Drama* 30, no. 4 (Winter 1996–97): 471–502, esp. 482–85, who associates this sluggishness with a phlegmatic complexion; and Paster, *Humoring the Body,* 141.

45. In the same week that he records other preparations of Worcester's Men for

a performance of the play, Henslowe records that he "Lent unto Wm kempe the 22 of aguste 1602 / to bye buckram to macke a payer of gyente hosse the some of Vs," *Diary,* 214. David Wiles has taken this entry as proof that Kemp played the Falstaffian role of Sir John of Wrotham, in service of his larger argument that Shakespeare created the part of Falstaff with Kemp in mind; see *Shakespeare's Clown.* Kastan's Arden edition cautions against a too-certain identification of Kemp as the original Falstaff, suggesting that he may just as well have been played by Thomas Pope (78–79).

46. For an influential account of the psychological relationship between Hal and Falstaff, see Harry Berger Jr., "The Prince's Dog: Falstaff and the Perils of Speech-Prefixity," *Shakespeare Quarterly* 49, no. 1 (Spring 1998), 40–73. Hugh Grady discusses Falstaff's political valences and provides a clear overview of earlier readings, "Falstaff: Subjectivity between the Carnival and the Aesthetic," *The Modern Language Review* 96, no. 3 (July 2001), 609–23.

47. Although we cannot know of direct influence with certainty, I find it likely that Shakespeare saw *The Blind Beggar,* which opened in February 1596, while working on *1 Henry IV,* and that Chapman saw the latter play while working on *An Humorous Day's Mirth,* which is most likely the *Comedy of Humors* Henslowe records as opening in May 1597. Based in part on the Oldcastle controversy, editors have tended to date first performance of *1 Henry IV* to the early months of 1597. See A. R. Humphreys' Arden 2 edition of *1 Henry IV* (London: Methuen, 1961), xi–xv; Herbert and Judith Weil's New Cambridge edition (Cambridge: Cambridge University Press, 1997), 4–6; and Kastan's Arden 3 edition of *1 Henry IV* (76).

48. Foakes, ed., *Henslowe's Diary,* 318, 321.

49. For analogies between Bobadilla and Falstaff, see Russ McDonald, *Shakespeare and Jonson/Jonson and Shakespeare* (Lincoln: University of Nebraska Press, 1988), 47–49.

50. For a discussion of Hotspur as choleric, see Reid, "Humoral Psychology," 478–80.

51. In the *Norton 3* edition, portions of this passage, which appeared only in the Folio text, must be accessed in the Digital Edition.

52. Gurr asserts that the play is in fact the play Henslowe listed as *The Disguises,* first performed in 1595 (*Shakespeare's Opposites,* 57), picking up an argument first made by F.L. Jones, "*Look About You* and *The Disguises,*" *PMLA* 44 (1929): 835–41. Jones in part based his argument on a reading of the relationship between the portrayal of figures from the Robin Hood legend in *Look About You* and in Munday and Chettle's two 1598 Robin Hood plays, *The Downfall* and *The Death of Robert Earl of Huntington.* Modern editors of the play, however, provide convincing arguments that *Look About You*'s Robin Hood must have followed the Huntington plays, and thereby assign it to 1599. Lancashire adds that there are other perfectly good candidates for alternate titles *Look About You* might have taken in Henslowe, including the 1599 *Tis No Deceit to Deceive the Deceiver.* See Anne Begor [Lancashire], "Look About You: A Critical Edition," PhD dissertation, Harvard (1965), 28–35, 50–61; and R. S. M. Hirsch, *A Pleasant Commodie Called Look About You: A Critical Edition* (New York: Garland, 1980), xix–xx. Citations of the play are from Hirsch.

53. See n. 12.

54. Lancashire, 45–49. If Gurr's linkage of the play to *The Disguises* were to be

accepted, the direction of influence would presumably run in the opposite direction.

55. *A Second and Third Blast of Retrait from Plays and Theatres* (1580), in Wickham et al., *Professional Theatre,* 163. Jonas Barish has argued that Proteus was a powerful figure in the antitheatrical imagination, and surveys negative associations between that classical figure and actors in *The Antitheatrical Prejudice* (Berkeley: University of California Press, 1981), 99–106.

56. *The Stage and Social Struggle* (London: Routledge, 1994), 151.

The Winter's Tale and Revenge Tragedy

BAILEY SINCOX

IN THIS ESSAY, I consider the genre of *The Winter's Tale* by situating the play in the intertheatrical context of London in 1611.[1] Through comparison to the language, structure, and staging of plays by Kyd, Marston, Chettle, and Middleton, I argue that *The Winter's Tale*'s dramatic project stems from its close relationship to contemporaneous revenge tragedies.[2]

Of course, neither Shakespeare nor his audiences referred to plays as "revenge tragedies." A. H. Thorndike coined the term in 1902 to describe plays which, following Kyd's *The Spanish Tragedy* (1587) dramatize a disenfranchised hero's retribution for wrongs.[3] Mid-twentieth century critics, including Ronald Broude, Fredson Bowers, and Lily Campbell, identify the genre by certain recurring tropes: vendettas, corrupt courts, ghosts, madness, poison, plays-within-plays, etc.[4] Around thirty extant early modern tragedies fall into the category as it is most strictly defined.[5] More recently, scholars have pushed revenge tragedy's generic boundaries. Linda Anderson studies revenge as "a benignly punitive forgiveness that awakens the offender's conscience" in Shakespeare's comedies; Harry Keyishian classifies revenge as a psychological pattern across genres that can be either "redemptive" or "vindictive."[6] Linda Woodbridge, noting that the word "revenge" occurs in all but two of Shakespeare's plays, argues for a "revenge drama" inclusive of tragedies and histories.[7] Despite the fact that "revenge tragedy" is, like all genres, constructed and challenged by critics, it allows us to identify plays that derive meaning from the same materials arranged and rearranged in increasingly self-referential patterns. Though *The Winter's Tale* is not a revenge tragedy, the generic template is useful to think with when considering how Shakespeare constructed his play and, perhaps, construed its relationship to earlier works. Indeed, a close reading of the *The Win-*

ter's Tale with an eye to revenge tragedy's formal features reveals surprising continuities.

However, the purpose of this essay is neither to suggest a new generic label for the play nor to allege insight into Shakespearean "intentions." Rather, it is to consider *The Winter's Tale* as a link in a longer chain of events in theater history, to recuperate a sense of the play as a product of the creative and commercial networks of the Jacobean playhouses. Inherent in this claim is the contention that playwrights saw what we call "revenge tragedy" as a tradition—or at least as a particular breed of drama—not least because they consistently characterize themselves and their works in relation to it. Just as Marston parodies the excesses of poetry and passion in *The Spanish Tragedy* with his *Antonio and Mellida* and, in the induction to *Bartholomew Fair,* Jonson derides the indefatigable popularity of "*Andronicus*" and "*Hieronimo,*" in *The Winter's Tale* Shakespeare echoes a certain dramaturgy most often to point out what his play is not (Ind. 79–82).[8] He is among playwrights who approach revenge tragedy with a ludic, even revisionist touch: Marston's *Antonio's Revenge* (1600) might be seen as a burlesque and his *Malcontent* (1603) as a kind of revenge comedy, while plays closely abutting the premiere of *The Winter's Tale*—Tourneur's *The Atheist's Tragedy* (1611) and Chapman's *The Revenge of Bussy D'Ambois* (1610)—have been called "antirevenge tragedies."[9] As work by Marvin Carlson, Roslyn Knutson, Jeremy Lopez, Emma Smith, and William N. West has demonstrated, meanings reverberate among such plays in a company's repertory as well as throughout theater history. Placing a formalist analysis into conversation with their findings makes possible new interpretations of *The Winter's Tale.*[10]

Reading the play alongside Kyd's *The Spanish Tragedy,* Middleton's *The Revenger's Tragedy,* Marston's *Antonio's Revenge,* and Chettle's *The Tragedy of Hoffman,* I identify both typical tropes and moments of intertheatrical reference in Leontes's revenge. Shakespeare structures acts 1–3 around Leontes's mounting suspicion, his poisonous madness, and a dream-ghost, provoking the audience's awareness of how the playwright tinkers with the "materials" of the revenge tragedy genre. In Paulina—a character not found in his source, Robert Greene's *Pandosto*—Shakespeare reprises and subverts the revenger-role. Her quasi-vengeance culminates when she acts the part of Hermione's ghost, but her grudge gives way to grace when Paulina reveals Hermione as a living statue. This ending bears striking similarity to Middleton's *Second Maiden's Tragedy* (1611), a play performed by the King's Men around the same time and in the same space: the intimate, indoor Blackfriars theater.[11] In that play, a tyrant disinters the body of a woman he effectively killed, demanding it be made up and displayed in his throne room as if it were alive; unlike in *The Winter's Tale*'s statue scene, however, the tyrant kisses the corpse and, finding poison on its lips, dies. Even as the plays' affinity evidences participation in a shared tradition, their difference reveals Shakespeare's particular generic admixture.

The Winter's Tale is not just a play that contains revenge but ends happily; like Perdita's "gillyvors" it is a crossbreed of the "wildest stock" and a "bud of nobler race" (4.4.82–95). The "bud" of pastoral tragicomedy has long been accepted, as has its marriage to certain "wilder stocks" including Senecan tragedy, Euripidean tragedy, and the so-called "tragedy of the tyrant."[12] However, the "wilder stock" of early modern revenge drama has all but escaped notice—despite the fact that the play claims that genealogy for itself through language, structure, and performative echoes. Like the gillyvors, too, the play is notable for its "piedness." Though we may only speculate on audiences' responses to *The Winter's Tale,* it is worth considering that the particular pleasures of seeing the play in 1611 derived from recognizing such pied beauty—from recognizing not "nature's bastards," but art's blossoming from Shakespeare's familiar base.

Early modern revenge tragedies begin with a grudge: a murder, rape, or theft that instigates the hero's retaliation. *The Spanish Tragedy*'s Andrea wants to see his killer punished; Vindice of *The Revenger's Tragedy* stalks the duke who assaulted and poisoned his beloved Gloriana. Antonio of *Antonio's Revenge* seeks his father-in-law who murdered his own father and friend; *The Tragedy of Hoffman*'s titular hero plots to annihilate the family of the man who executed his father for piracy. These plays seem formulaic because they are; in Smith's words, genres (like all market commodities) balance "standardization and differentiation," familiarity and innovation.[13] With its black humor and stark political commentary, *The Spanish Tragedy* was perhaps the most popular play in the early modern period: it was revived several times by both the Admiral's Men and the King's Men, saw a prequel in 1604, "additions" (variously attributed to Shakespeare and to Jonson) in 1602, and nine print editions between 1592 and 1633.[14] Not surprisingly considering its ubiquity, it inspired numerous imitations ranging from homage to parody. With structural, visual, and linguistic echoes of Kyd, later playwrights situated themselves in a theatrical idiom well-known to their audiences. In addition to making the plays marketable, this practice made the plays meaningful.[15] As West writes, "early modern audiences seem to have understood what they saw" in the theaters as "a reverberant constellation of speeches, gestures, and interactions rather than neatly circumscribed plays."[16] Similarly Smith, by drawing on theories of cinematic genre, argues that "interconnected instantiations" of revenge tragedy "form a single composite text."[17] In short, these plays build on one another.

One such persistent echo in these plays is the revelation of a crime that happened in the murky, pre-play past; these revelations are characterized by the language of blood-debt, what Linda Woodbridge calls a "book–balancing devotion to equality."[18] In keeping with this central logic, revengers—typically in early scenes—point their accomplices (and the audience) to testaments of the violence done to them. Hieronimo does just this when he and his wife, Isabella, discover their son, Horatio, stabbed to death:

> See'st thou this handkercher besmear'd with blood?
> It shall not from me, till I take revenge.
> See'st thou those wounds that yet are bleeding fresh?
> I'll not entomb them, till I have revenge.
> Then will I joy amidst my discontent;
> Till then my sorrow never shall be spent.
>
> (*ST* 2.5.51–56)[19]

With repeated entreaties to "see," Hieronimo makes Isabella a witness to his crude investigation. The handkerchief and the boy's wounds, both wet with blood, are exhibits in his case for revenge, artifacts he insists on retaining until justice is served. The doubling of "See'st thou" and "till I take revenge" creates parallelisms between vision and action, grief and bloodlust, proof and motivation, like a macabre version of the two-column ledger.[20] The word "spent" in the final line reinforces this economic metaphor, figuring Hieronimo's own emotion—his "sorrow" and his rage—as a resource that will not be depleted, despite the difficulty of his project. So, then, the revenger's mathematical calculations give way to a near–inexpressible transformation in which Hieronimo's identity and all his faculties are subsumed into the role of revenger.

Chettle emulates Kyd's handling of this trope in the first scene of *Hoffman*. Hoffman vows to eliminate not only his father's murderer, but also any man with

> but one ounce of blood, of which he's part.
> He was my father: my heart still bleeds,
> Nor can my wounds be stopped till an incision
> I've made to bury my dead father in.
>
> (*Hoffman* 1.1.69–72)[21]

Hoffman surpasses a simple tally, commodifying his enemies as vessels of blood. Because, by his logic, every "ounce" of Luninberg's blood is owed him, his vendetta extends to Luninberg's son, Otho, his brothers, and his nephews. Strangely, hauntingly, Hoffman imagines the "incision" he makes in his enemy's flesh will be a grave in which to bury his father. Only once he sunders skin will he break the earth; until then, Old Hoffman remains above ground, the rotting corpse a stinking reminder of revenge's necessity. As Hoffman articulates, these displayed bodies are totems of a debt repaid through mimetic retribution. Revengers reiterate this notion obsessively. With his characteristic sarcasm, Vindice asks, "Hum, whoe'er knew / Murder unpaid? Faith, give Revenge her due" (*RT* 1.1.42–43).[22] In the same vein, one of Hoffman's enemies, Prince Mathias of Saxony, counsels those who would retaliate: "revenge should have proportion," for only then "the revenge were fit, just, and square" (*Hoffman* 5.1.279–82). As heroes devote themselves to vengeance, they necessarily count—or count on—bodies to validate emulative violence. By announcing an imbalance, revengers generate audience "expectations," which Carlson defines as "the residue of memory of previous such experiences," as to the dramatic action required for resolution.[23] In other words: with self-consciously familiar structure and language, playwrights signal that the present play is a revenge tragedy.

Leontes, too, establishes his grudge at the beginning of *The Winter's Tale;* however, his is precipitated not by the testimony of a rotting corpse, but by his own jealous suspicion. As Hermione—whom he has exhorted to convince Polixenes to stay—is "paddling palms" with the other king, Leontes exclaims, "Too hot, too hot. / To mingle friendship far is mingling bloods" (*WT* 1.2.108–9).[24] Though Hermione merely complies with Leontes's own demands (to embody hospitality to his childhood friend), Leontes inscribes their joined hands with a different narrative—betrayal, adultery, revenge.[25] He continues:

> Ha' not you seen, Camillo—
> But that's past doubt; you have, or your eye-glass
> Is thicker than a cuckold's horn—or heard—
> For, to a vision so apparent, rumor
> Cannot be mute—or thought—for cogitation
> Resides not in that man that does not think—
> My wife is slippery? If thou wilt confess,
> Or else be impudently negative,
> To have nor eyes, nor ears, nor thought, then say
> My wife's a hobby-horse, deserves a name
> As rank as any flax-wench that puts to
> Before her troth-plight. Say't and justify't.
>
> (1.2.267–78)

Like his revenger predecessors, Leontes presents evidence of wrong to a witness, Camillo, who he hopes will become his ally/agent. He appeals to Camillo's eyes, ears, and capacity for thought to corroborate that his wife is "slippery," "a hobby-horse," and a promiscuous "flax-wench," but Camillo remains unmoved. Unlike the bleeding corpse and stained handkerchief Hieronimo offers to Isabella, Leontes's exhibits are only credible according to his circular logic—Hermione's adultery is visible because eyes should see it, audible because ears should hear it, intelligible because minds should comprehend it. In an attempt to quantify his grievances, Leontes then catalogues alleged actions ("Whispering," "leaning cheek to cheek," "meeting noses," "kissing with inside lip"). A seasoned theater patron, conditioned by what Carlson (building on Hans Robert Jauss) calls the "codes and strategies that shape reception," would surely understand these speeches as a statement of Leontes's type: revenger.[26] This is not to say that Leontes is not identifiable with other types—he is also clearly a tyrant in the tradition of Cambyses, Tamburlaine, Richard III, and others, as well as a cuckold in the tradition of, to turn to Shakespeare's own works, Othello, or even Claudio in *Much Ado About Nothing*. However, as Emrys Jones writes, arguing for affinities between *The Winter's Tale* and Seneca's *Agamemnon,* "Leontes is not a true tyrant," and the play has no more than what he calls a "slight coloring," a "Senecan feel in the diction."[27] Indeed, as we will see, Leontes is not a true revenger, either; his "affection" merely prompts him to play that role, among others.

The language of counting and recounting many—most notably Stanley Cavell and Shankar Raman—identify in the play takes on a new significance when read as intertextually and intertheatrically linked to the revenge tragedy tradition.[28] These resonances are just as profound when Shakespeare conforms to precedent as when he departs from it. A Kydian parity characterizes Polixenes's description of Leontes's revenge-logic: since his "jealousy / Is for a precious creature," it must "be great," and as he believes himself "dishonored" by his best friend, "his revenges must / In that be made more bitter" (1.2.449–55). Unlike Hieronimo, however, Leontes (when Camillo effectively tells him his forensic accounting does not add up) forswears value itself, for "if this be nothing," the "world and all that's in't," including the "sky," "Bohemia," and his very "wife," are "nothing" (1.2.285–96). The same patron who recognizes Leontes-as-revenger would hear this as a darkly playful subversion of a decades-old discourse. We might speculate these linguistic parallels were amplified by performance details, fulfilling West's criteria for true intertheatricality, those "networks of traceable elements of action."[29] In an echo of Hieronimo's cries of "See'st thou?" the speech above implies a deictic gesture directed to Hermione and Polixenes (whether onstage or off). The similarities here to *Spanish Tragedy* and *Hoffman* go beyond mere allusion; the dramatic syntax (revelation of crime, followed by call to action) and the accent in which it is conveyed (figured as quantification and balance) promises the audience a kind of theatrical experience, an investment in characters and an expectation of typical outcomes. This promise is only partially fulfilled. Though Leontes acts as though he were in a revenge tragedy, he lacks a body of justificatory evidence, thus this fast-paced scene's irony. Early on in *The Winter's Tale,* Shakespeare alerts his audience to his project, simultaneously familiar and strange.

Word play and intertheatrical reference surround another point of dramatic dissonance: Leontes is neither marginalized nor powerless. Indeed, a defining feature of the genre is its heroes' necessary resort to extralegal means of retaliation. As Derek Dunne writes: "At its most basic, early modern revenge tragedy tells the story of someone from outside the ruling elite challenging the *status quo,* having been failed by the institutions designed to protect citizens."[30] Linda Woodbridge puts it more simply: "revengers are disempowered people, unjustly treated, who step up and take control."[31] Thus Hieronimo, unable to charge Lorenzo and Balthazar in court, cries, "Where shall I run to breathe abroad my woes, / My woes whose weight hath wearied the earth?" (*ST* 3.7.1–2). By contrast, though Leontes speaks the language of revenge, his sovereign status contradicts his identification with the "type" of the revenger. Leontes practically acknowledges this tension, saying:

> —Go, play, boy, play. —Thy mother plays, and I
> Play too, but so disgraced a part, whose issue
> Will hiss me to my grave. Contempt and clamor
> Will be my knell.
>
> (*WT* 1.2.186–89)

Leontes puns on "play," imagining himself an actor in the disgraced "part" of the cuckold forced on him by his wife's performance. Embedded in Leontes's language is an inkling that the "part" is, in fact, his own construction, the part of the revenger so inappropriate even in response to the alleged crime. The repeated, sibilant "s" in "issue" and "hiss me" performs the mockery he imagines others direct at him, and the harsh consonants of "contempt" and "clamour," followed by the barrage of monosyllables "will be my knell" embody the ominous death toll. In this speech, generic self-consciousness rises to the surface as a kind of in-joke with the audience. Again, we might imagine that a gesture physically linked Leontes to earlier stage revengers. As West has shown, "the most frequently remembered element" from *The Spanish Tragedy* was "*Hieronimo* beware, go by, go by" (*ST* 3.12.31).[32] Quotations of this unremarkable line appear in Marston's *Antonio and Mellida,* Jonson's *Every Man in His Humour,* Dekker's *Shoemaker's Holiday,* and elsewhere, prompting West to suggest that the true quotation might be a "distinctive way of walking across the stage"—namely Edward Alleyn's disdainful "stalking" as Hieronimo (and/or Tamburlaine).[33] Is it possible that the actor playing Leontes (Burbage, many speculate) stalked disdainfully à la Hieronimo as he barked "Go play, boy, play"? Accompanied with the right gestures, the line constituted a wink and a nod to one of the most well-trafficked theatrical gags in Shakespeare's London. In keeping with this friction between verbal-visual cues and plot, Camillo refuses to be complicit with Leontes's delusion. When the king declares Hermione to be "slippery" "past doubt," Camillo swears: "I would not be a stander-by to hear / My sovereign mistress clouded so without / My present vengeance taken" (*WT* 1.2.279–81). In a resonant turn of phrase, Camillo imagines himself a revenger against Leontes's unjustified violence (that is, his slander against Hermione and plot to murder Polixenes). As Leontes becomes a tyrant, the very force most revengers rebel against, the overturning of expectations creates a mounting sense of parody.

Isolated, frustrated, and disillusioned, revengers go mad; the trope is so prevalent that some identify it as the hallmark of the genre.[34] Hieronimo raves wildly to two unsuspecting "Portingals," his mind flitting from his son's slippers, which he wears, to the nature of fatherhood, to (when the two men ask for directions to the Duke's castle) rocky cliffs symbolizing "Despair and Death;" he asks, "What is there yet in a son / To make a father dote, rave, or run mad?" (*ST* 3.11.[1]–29).[35] Vindice says obliquely, "Surely we're all mad people, and they / Whom we think are, are not—we mistake those: / 'Tis we are mad in sense, they but in clothes" (*RT* 3.5.80–82). At the height of their madness, revengers select their means of retaliation; in many later plays (i.e., not in *The Spanish Tragedy* or in *Titus Andronicus*) they choose poison. In *Hoffman* and *The Revenger's Tragedy* particularly, madness and poison serve as metadramatic shorthand for the burgeoning revenge tragedy tradition. In the generic terms Smith adopts from film theory, these tropes become so "opaque" that they form a surface upon which later playwrights—including Shakespeare—may embellish new significations.[36]

Poison and madness are intertwined in the convoluted climax of *Hoffman* (as in *The Duchess of Malfi, The Changeling,* and numerous other revenge tragedies). Hoffman's henchman Lorrique, disguised as a French doctor, instructs Prince Jerome (son of Ferdinand, Duke of Prussia, both enemies of Hoffman) to poison "Otho" (that is, Hoffman disguised as the Duke of Luninberg's son) by lacing his father's cup. He offers Jerome an antidote so that he (as cupbearer) and his father will not also succumb to the dram. As Hoffman prepares the scheme, he instructs his servant: "Lorrique, now or never play thy part: / This act is even our tragedy's best heart" (*Hoffman* 3.2.195–96). As he reaches this, the self-proclaimed height of a self-aware dramatic arc, Hoffman becomes even more deranged, addressing Revenge directly as a goddess:

> Now scarlet mistress from thick sable clouds
> Thrust forth thy blood-stained hands, applaud my plot,

> That giddy wonderers may amazed stand,
> While death smites down suspectless Ferdinand.
>
> (3.2.210–13)

Hoffman, it appears, suffers hallucinations, arcane visions brought
on by his own designs to murder "suspectless Ferdinand" (one of
the aforementioned "vessels" containing Luninberg's blood).
Though Revenge does not appear on stage as in *The Spanish Tragedy,* Chettle's words recall Kyd's supernatural spectator, who
indeed "applauds" Hieronimo's "plot" from the "thick sable
clouds" of hell. In *Hoffman,* madness, because of its intertheatricality, becomes metatheatrical. That is, re-playing a passion associated
with this breed of "tragedy" draws attention to the performance as
such.

Middleton reworks Kyd's and Chettle's materials with striking
innovation. Moments after commenting on the nature of madness,
Vindice explains his plot to poison the Duke: the woman the Duke
himself poisoned will now, as an exhumed skeleton, "kiss his lips
to death" (*RT* 3.5.105). When the Duke enters the chamber, antici-
pating a sexual liaison with the country girl Vindice promised to
procure, he takes the skeleton (with its dress, wig, and gaudy
makeup) to be alive. Greedily, he kisses it, collapsing into death
throes as Vindice laughingly reveals his true identity. The scene's
metatheatricality is heightened by Vindice's declaration that he has
not "fashioned" the poisoned skeleton "only for show / And use-
less property," but rather, to "bear a part / E'en in its own revenge"
(3.5.100–102). Impossibly, Vindice promises to use Gloriana's
remains as more than a stage prop, reappropriating the reminder of
his loss as the means of his retribution. Vindice manipulates the
"props" and "parts" in his revenge just as Middleton manipulates
an identifiable dramatic idiom, relying on the audience's familiarity with it for the efficacy of his dialogue and his stagecraft. Poison
and madness, though hackneyed by 1606, continued to generate
possibilities for theatrical ingenuity. Indeed, the thickness of tradition makes possible Middleton's deliciously absurd construction:
his mad revenger lays poison on the poisoned to trap the poisoner.
As I will show below, Middleton recycles this scene in *Second
Maiden's,* a play closely related to *Winter's Tale.*

Shakespeare roots himself in this dramatic genealogy by tele-
scoping the tropes of madness and poison; his poetic language is
even more evocative when seen against the "opacity" of its generic

surface. Soon after Leontes's spontaneous exclamation of "Too hot!" he admits to what he calls "the infection of my brains," but later dismisses his counselors for declaring him "abused" (*WT* 1.2.145; 2.1.142). More explicitly, Paulina derides the "lunes i'th' king," claims the "root of his opinion" must be "removed" for it is "rotten / As ever stone or oak was sound," and labels him "mad" three times (2.2.31; 2.3.87–89; 2.3.71; 3.1.180). As we would expect, Leontes chooses poison as his means of retaliation. His attempt to literally poison Polixenes fails, for Camillo realizes the king is "in rebellion with himself" (1.2.354). However, Leontes's figurative, epistemological poisoning continues, as he describes in his "I have drunk and seen the spider" speech (2.1.37–49). Wishing for "lesser knowledge," Leontes explains that one who drinks from a cup containing a spider may "drink, depart, / And yet partake no venom, for his knowledge / Is not infected"; it is the sight of the spider that kills. Unlike Othello, who imbibes the idea of an unfaithful wife from Iago's incremental doses, Leontes plants the "spider" in his own "cup" and, glimpsing the evidence of his own delusion, "cracks his gorge, his sides," lapsing into paranoid paroxysms. Anne Barton compares him to Antonio in *The Tempest* who "to credit his own lie" believed "he was indeed the duke" (*Tempest* 1.2.102–3). Both Leontes and Antonio author "false and destructive fictions, credited only by their creators. And in both plays they can be countered only by another, and benevolent, kind of illusion: Prospero's restorative art, or the pastoral make-believe of Bohemia."[37] Like Antonio who, with "no screen between this part he played /And him he played it for" contrived to be "Absolute Milan," Leontes acts the "part" of the revenger until it is indistinguishable from his "tyrannous passion" (*Tempest* 2.3.107–9; *WT* 2.3.28). Here the metatheatricality that characterizes analogous moments in *Hoffman* and *Revenger's Tragedy* is apparent. Even so, Leontes partakes of the "venom," he says, because his "knowledge" is "infected," an ironic inversion of the madness revengers known to the audience of *The Winter's Tale* suffer because of their unacknowledged, bona fide grievances. By incorporating these devices, the stock-in-trade of the popular revenge tragedy genre, into the first three acts of his play, Shakespeare simultaneously constructs and demolishes this particular dramatic structure, playing, all the while, with closely related dramatic structures associated with the cuckold and the tyrant. Playgoers, we imagine, reacted to these changes—perhaps their experience was defined by them ("Leontes

shouldn't be taking revenge!" "He's not powerless, he's tyrannical!" "He's sick in the head!"). Dramatically, then, as Barton claims,
Leontes's poisonous madness requires an antidote. In this sense,
the "dram" or "remedy" is not simply, as Barton describes, the
"pastoral make-believe of Bohemia," but also the restorative
revenge of Paulina which culminates in the revelation of Hermione's body—not a cold, poisoned corpse, but a warm, forgiving
wife, as I show in this essay's final section (2.1.139; 5.1.77).

The re-presented body so critical to the revenger's vendetta often
appears in another form: the ghost, an early modern staple borrowed from Seneca's revenge plays. A symbolic echo of the rotting
corpse, specters like Don Andrea and Old Hamlet further justify the
revenger's quest, providing corroborating testimony from beyond
the grave. Jeremy Lopez, who discusses actors' bodies as "formal
devices not distinct from dramaturgical elements such as verse
style, subject matter, and staging habits," identifies stage deaths as
key sites for generating audience desire and disappointment. Such
moments, Lopez says, play "our sympathy for the characters"
against "understanding of generic form" as we long for the possibly
dead to revive, or the definitely dead to return as ghosts.[38] To
expand on this, we could say that, in a tragedy, the playgoers desire
the dead heroine to revive, though they know, according to generic
conventions, she will not; conversely, in a revenge play, a corpse
on the stage might provoke the expectation that the same actor will
return to haunt the remaining scenes. The template is not invari-
able; some revenge tragedies, including *Titus,* have no ghosts,
while others, including *The Spanish Tragedy,* see only some characters onstage as ghosts (Horatio's corpse remains a corpse). These
literal and metaphorical ghosts of theater history populate every
later performance.[39]

Hermione's ghost, unlike Don Andrea's or Old Hamlet's, does not
appear bodily. For this reason, comparison to another deferred
ghost, that of Andrugio in *Antonio's Revenge,* best elucidates
Shakespeare's intertheatrical engagement. The day after discovering his father and his friend Feliche slain, Antonio describes a
wakeful night:

Last sleep, my sense was steeped in horrid dreams:
Three parts of night were swallowed in the gulf
Of ravenous time, when to my slumbering powers,
Two meagre ghosts made apparition:

> The one's breast seemed fresh paunched with bleeding wounds,
> Whose bubbling gore sprang in my frighted eyes;
> The other ghost assumed my father's shape.
> Both cried "Revenge!", at which my trembling joints,
> Iced quite over with a frozed cold sweat,
> Leaped forth the sheets. Three times I gasped at shades,
> And thrice, deluded by erroneous sense
> I forced my thoughts make stand, when lo, I oped
> A large bay window, through which the night
> Struck terror to my soul . . . //
> 　　　　　. . . At which, my nose straight bled.
> Then doubled I my word, so slunk to bed.
>
> (*AR* 1.3.39–60)[40]

Andrugio and Feliche appear to Antonio in a dream, bearing, like the corpses of Horatio, Gloriana, and Old Hoffman described above, the signs of murderous abuse. Presenting their "bleeding wounds" and "bubbling gore" to Antonio's "frighted eyes," the ghosts speak, charging Antonio with a task: "Revenge!" Upon waking, Antonio doubts his vision, but an apparition rids him of his doubt; the combination of natural omen and his own altered physiological state convinces him that the ghosts' word is true. Because Andrugio and Feliche, as phantoms, provide supernatural validation for Antonio's revenge—and because they are advertised in such vivid language—the audience might well long to see them. This wish is soon answered. Andrugio appears to Antonio and to other characters, directing the retributive process: he assures Antonio that Mellida is faithful, reveals that Mellida's father, Piero, is the murderer, intervenes to stop Antonio from killing his own mother, Maria, and watches triumphantly as Piero dies during the final masque (5.5.79–86). Thus, while Marston defers the initial staging of Andrugio-as-ghost, the eventual (and repeated) revelation of the specter confirms Antonio's reading of the spiritual omen. The theatrical "exuberance" (Lopez's word) of these moments adds spectacle to generic satisfaction, recalling the first figures in Kyd's seminal drama.[41]

　　Shakespeare tips his cap to the ghost trope twice in *The Winter's Tale,* beginning with Antigonus who, shipwrecked in Bohemia, believes the queen visited him in a nightmare. Addressing the infant Perdita whom Leontes tasked him to abandon, Antigonus confesses:

I have heard, but not believed, the spirits o'th' dead
May walk again. If such thing be, thy mother
Appeared to me last night, for ne'er was dream
So like a waking. To me comes a creature,
Sometimes her head on one side, some another;
I never saw a vessel of like sorrow
So filled and so becoming. In pure white robes
Like very sanctity she did approach
My cabin where I lay; thrice bowed before me,
And, gasping to begin some speech, her eyes
Became two spouts; the fury spent, anon
Did this break from her: "Good Antigonus . . . //
          . . . thou ne'er shalt see
Thy wife Paulina more." And so with shrieks
She melted into air. Affrighted much,
I did in time collect myself and thought
This was so and no slumber.

                              (*WT* 3.3.15–38)

Antigonus's description matches that of earlier revenge tragedies' stage ghosts: sorrowful, shrieking, prophetic, immaterial. Like Antonio, Antigonus resolves his own skepticism, recounting his nightmare as a certain truth that justifies violent action (in Antigonus's case, the abandonment of Perdita, whom he claims is "indeed the issue / Of King Polixenes"). It is in contrast to Antonio that Antigonus's speech takes on hyper-narrative significance, for his description of Hermione vindicates neither Leontes's prosecution of the queen herself nor Antigonus's disposal of Perdita. In the previous scene (unknown to Antigonus), Apollo's oracle had pronounced that "Hermione is chaste, Polixenes blameless" and "the innocent babe truly begotten" (3.2.130–32). Thus Antigonus's interpretation of the ghost—that is, that "Hermione hath suffered death" and that Perdita is Polixenes's daughter contradicts divine prophecy, as well as Hermione's own testimony (3.3.41–43). This obvious incongruity notwithstanding, the timing of the dream alone—after retributive action has taken place, rather than prescribing action that has not yet been taken—is unusual. Shakespeare alters the familiar device, making Hermione's ghost not a bolster to Leontes's revenge, but the presage of, in Paulina's words, a "vengeance not dropped down yet" (3.2.198–99). Furthermore, according to established conventions, ghost-reports foreshadow ghost-sightings. By adumbrating—but deferring—the ghost, he simulta-

neously conforms his play to the tropes of revenge tragedy and prepares his audience for the palimpsest of Paulina's retribution,
culminating in the fantastic revelation of Hermione's body.

Throughout the first three acts of *The Winter's Tale,* Shakespeare
plays with the materials of revenge tragedy; the final two acts reas-
semble those materials into something new: a kind of revenge tragicomedy. His invention hinges on Paulina—a character not found in
Greene's romance—who is and is not a revenger. As Hermione's
loyal agent, Paulina vows vengeance on Leontes, reprising the
tropes discussed above: she announces a wrong that needs answering, castigates Leontes for his toxic "suspicions," and, finally, acts
the part of Hermione's ghost. However, Paulina's punishment is
also restorative, engendering reconciliation rather than annihila-
tion. The final scene—in which a seeming statue of Hermione turns
out to be Hermione's living, breathing body—strongly resembles
the end of Middleton's *Second Maiden's Tragedy,* which the King's
Men performed in the same year as *The Winter's Tale.*[42] In that play,
a Tyrant demands that a dead Lady be exhumed, painted, and set
up in his court; her lover poisons the paint and, when the Tyrant
kisses the Lady's lips, he dies. The two plays' commonalities show
Shakespeare's integration in the revenge tragedy tradition. Indeed,
his adaptation of a Middletonian device—the corpse-as-vehicle-of-
vengeance—satisfactorily sutures the first three acts to the final
two.[43] Early modern audiences experienced an unexpected reversal
as female characters, performing the visual/verbal cues of the period's most violent theater, ushered the play to a "wondrous" conclusion.

In the way of Hieronimo and Hoffman, Paulina identifies herself
as a revenger, announcing a vendetta she supports with evidence.
As news of Mamillius's death reaches the court and Hermione collapses, Paulina instructs the king to "look down and see what death
is doing," words not unlike Revenge's at the beginning of *The
Spanish Tragedy:* "thou shalt see the author of thy death" (*ST*
1.1.87). Addressing the "author of death," Leontes, Paulina gives
body to her vendetta with an itemized list of his crimes (*WT*
3.2.182–99).[44] Paulina justifies her "vengeance" on behalf of the
"sweetest, dearest creature" (Hermione). Employing an ironized
language of value and debt ("nothing," "much," "poor," "none or
little," "laid to thee"), Paulina refutes Leontes's earlier, parallel
declarations. He calls Polixenes a "traitor"; Paulina shows Leontes
it was Sicilia, not Bohemia who was "inconstant." Leontes enlists

Camillo to poison Polixenes; Paulina declares that Leontes "poisoned" Camillo's honor. Leontes argues that leaving Perdita to the
crows is "merciful," but Paulina rebuts that a "devil" would have
been more kind; Leontes attributes Mamillius's sickness to Hermione's crime; Paulina links it to Leontes's error. Reassigning worth
to that which Leontes nullified in his "nothing" speech, Paulina
arrives at the impetus for her retaliation: Hermione's death. The
bodies of the queen (just taken off stage), Mamillius (reported
dead), and Perdita (now lost) lend credibility to Paulina's project.
Like all revengers, she restructures her identity around her "new
role" as the "avenger of another's suffering," swearing by Hermione
that action is required (3.2.201–2; 225).[45] Thus even as she
denounces Leontes's words, she duplicates his function, demanding that witnesses recognize her accounting and validate her thirst
for reprisal.

Of course, Paulina in many ways departs from the revenger
template. First, she does not seek some distant foe, but rather confronts a tractable, regretful supplicant. By admitting "I have too
much believed mine own suspicion," being "transported by my
jealousies / To bloody thoughts and to revenge," the king discards
his own earlier identification with the revenger-character, allowing
Paulina to take up the role (3.2.148; 155–56). Second, in contrast to
the pervasive language of balance noted by Woodbridge and others,
Paulina articulates a problem of irremediability. She rejoins the
king, telling him "Do not repent these things" for even (to paraphrase) a thousand people praying and fasting naked for ten thousand years in a constant mountain blizzard would not make him
worthy of forgiveness (3.2.204–11). Contrary to the measure-for-
measure, tit-for-tat logic of revenge, Leontes can never satisfy his
debt, so, fittingly, Paulina prescribes him a daily regimen of self-
effacement, replicating the "grammar," as Sarah Beckwith has
shown, of Christian confession and penance.[46] Third, Paulina,
unlike most early modern revenge protagonists, is female (though
her gender is less surprising, perhaps, in light of the classical
revengers Medea, Clytemnestra, and, most especially, Hecuba, the
last of whom Tanya Pollard has identified as a crucial inspiration
for Shakespeare).[47] While Marguerite Tassi has argued these women
are direct models for figures like Tamora in *Titus Andronicus* and
Margaret in Shakespeare's first tetralogy, Paulina's actions are not
violent, but "benignly punitive," as Linda Anderson has described
Portia, Hero, and other comic heroines.[48] Thus Paulina's overriding

ethos presents simultaneously gendered and generic challenges to the first half of *The Winter's Tale*. Placing readings of Paulina according to Beckwith, Pollard, Anderson, and Tassi into conversation with the theater history work of Carlson, Lopez, and Smith allows us to see how Paulina's departures, rather than disqualifying her as a revenger, signify in relation to the revenge stage tradition.

We need not turn to Hieronimo or Hoffman, however, to see how Paulina's actions are, to use Carlson's coinage, "haunted." Shakespeare constructs parallels between Leontes's revenge and Paulina's, the dramatic efficacy of which stems from the repetition and reversal of familiar revenge tragedy tropes. On the one hand, Paulina enforces a "real" revenge, a castigation that Leontes undergoes as payment for his crimes, always—and explicitly—under her eye. On the other, as the metaphor of penance suggests, Paulina's project is not just penalizing, but also restorative, ameliorating Leontes for the moment Hermione deigns to return (having "preserved" herself, as she says, to "see the issue," i.e., Perdita). Thus, Paulina's counsel is a "remedy" for Leontes's epistemological poison; she uses the very word "remedy" to describe her role in preventing the king from remarrying (5.1.77). Leontes accepts Paulina's medicine, though it is "as bitter / Upon thy tongue as in my thought" (5.1.18–19). Indeed, Leontes's requests for more of Paulina's words permeate their dialogue from the moment of his first acknowledgement of guilt to their conversations in act 5: "Thou canst not speak too much. I have deserved / All tongues to talk their bitt'rest"; "Thou didst speak but well / When most the truth"; "Thou speak'st truth," (3.2.212–13; 3.2.229–30; 5.1.55). Sixteen years later, still contrite, Leontes continues his daily visits to the chapel where Hermione and Mamillius lie, despite the protestations of advisors who believe he has "performed / A saint-like sorrow" and "paid down / More penitence than done trespass" (5.1.1–4). Paulina responds that even if he "one by one wedded all the world" the sum "good" of them all would not equal the "unparalleled" Hermione (5.1.13–16).[49] The language of counting and balancing resurfaces, but Leontes professes his continuing need to remember his "blemishes" in the loss of his queen and daughter. In turn, the king's madness—that radical disbelief in his wife's fidelity and his children's paternity—erodes under the persistent pressure of Paulina's exhortations to patient belief. For, before Hermione returns and (apparently) forgives Leontes, Paulina instructs her penitent, "It is required / You do awake your faith" (5.3.94–95). Remaining within the linguistic realm of revenge tragedy even while overturning its structure, the play takes on a new tenor.

In the character of Paulina, where the play's intertextual and intertheatrical resonances converge, Shakespeare's aesthetic project becomes most apparent. As a quasi-revenger, Paulina enables that redemptive power of the feminine so characteristic of Shakespeare's late plays. Hermione and Perdita—like Marina, Imogen, and Miranda—bind, heal, and regenerate their fathers, lovers and communities. Yet it is Paulina who bridges the gap between Leontes's near-magical wife and daughter and the first three acts of revenge tragedy. In essence, Paulina's "remedy" functions in much the same way as the "pastoral make-believe of Bohemia" which, as Barton suggests, is a kind of dramatic antidote. In Bohemia, the threat of revenge becomes alternately an impossible fairy-tale and the punch line of a joke (albeit a genuinely threatening one); the coney-catcher Autolycus terrorizes Perdita's foster father and brother, describing the "vengeance bitter" Polixenes will unleash on the family of the girl who seduced his son, Florizel (4.4.756). Simultaneously, much of the language of the first three acts returns, repurposed and reimagined. As Perdita unknowingly makes her way to the father who bastardized her, she remarks, "I see the play so lies / That I must bear a part." Here, Perdita in all her Persephone-like vibrancy is not entirely unlike Gloriana, whose corpse acts a "part" in Vindice's revenge; she, too will be presented to the man who wronged her in a disguise, becoming instrument and emblem of other characters' response to his wrongs. Furthermore, to the princess' innocently ironic statement, Camillo replies "No remedy," identifying exactly that in which she participates (4.4.642–43). Though a full consideration of act 4 is outside the scope of this essay, it is sufficient to say that the action in Bohemia, in conjunction with Paulina's redemptive reprisal, constitutes a revenge against revenge. As West reminds us, "difference" between intertheatrically-linked plays is not "developmental," but "responsive"; the opacity of generic signification lends itself equally to parody and (as in this case) to reversal.[50] In accordance with this is the work of critics that have explored classical reception in *The Winter's Tale*. Identifying the play as an example of "light Seneca," Robert S. Miola writes that "Shakespeare varies the standard formula" of the Senecan tyrant play, in which reformation normally happens in the final act, in order to "portray forgiveness and redemption as well as sin and suffering."[51] Both Senecan drama and its imitators in early modern revenge tragedy are here over-turned. Time, as Chorus and as a motif surrounding Perdita's estrangement and Leontes's penance, also figures the gestation of a play unlike anything in theater history, even unlike its own first half; like a midwife, Paulina delivers a dramatic "gillyvor" fathered by revenge and mothered by pastoral comedy (4.4.79–98).

Shakespeare returns to the heart of revenge tragedy when he reprises the hallmark trope of the ghost to which Antigonus's dream earlier gestured. Unlike Andrugio, Don Andrea, and Old Hamlet who appear bodily, Hermione's ghost is performed by Paulina. In Sicilia, just before Perdita and Florizel's arrival, Leontes speculates that, were he to marry again, the sight of his new bride

> would make [Hermione's] sainted spirit
> Again possess her corpse, and on this stage,
> Where we offenders now appear, soul-vexed,
> And begin, "Why to me?"
>
> (5.1.57–60)

Paulina answers that to take offense so would be "just." Leontes agrees, and further ventures that the hypothetical ghost of his wife would "incense me / To murder her I married," effectively prompting him to take revenge on himself. Paulina replies:

> Were I the ghost that walked, I'd bid you mark
> Her eye and tell me for what dull part in't
> You chose her. Then I'd shriek that even your ears
> Should rift to hear me; and the words that followed
> Should be, "Remember mine."
>
> (5.1.61–67)

In this extraordinary moment, Leontes and Paulina "stage" a revenge tragedy ending. Paulina assumes the role of the ghost who, like Andrugio, bids the living to "remember" trespasses against the dead. In their speculative murder-suicide, Leontes's crimes would be avenged. So, too the language of penitence would be carried to its graceless conclusion, Leontes's despair and self-annihilation the mark of a "diseased opinion" fully remedied. Yet, confined in the grammar of the conditional, this playlet serves only as a symbolic echo, conjuring the audience's memories of past theatrical experiences, adumbrating a tragic end the play will not, in fact, reach. Loaded with the weight of this second deferral, the eventual revelation of Hermione's actual body resonates not just with ghosts past (in the revenge tragedy tradition and in Shakespeare's corpus, such as *Othello* and *Much Ado*), but also with ghosts present in the King's Men's repertory—namely, in Middleton's *Second Maiden's.*

Because the play only survives in manuscript (and remained seldom-studied until the 1990s, when some debated the play's identification as Shakespeare's lost *Cardenio*), its relationship to *The Winter's Tale* remains to be explored fully.[52] Sarah Beckwith, Suzanne Gossett, Raphael Lyne, and Andrea Stevens have begun this work; however, the plays' commonality has not yet been considered in light of the revenge tragedy tradition.[53] Furthermore, many studies remain focused on the priority of Shakespeare over Middleton. Lyne writes that "[i]t is in *The Second Maiden's Tragedy* that Middleton comes closest to late Shakespeare," for the play's conclusion "recalls, in a strange and parodic way, the invented story of the statue of Hermione in *The Winter's Tale*."[54] Similarly, Gossett's reading of the final scene in *Second Maiden's* as "uncanny" is predicated on its assumed premiere after *The Winter's Tale*.[55] Nevertheless, the question of precedent is less relevant here than the question of participation in a shared tradition. As both plays were performed by the King's Men in the Blackfriars theater toward the end of 1611 (and later in the Globe), their affinity epitomizes those concerns with shared formal structures and material conditions with which this essay began. Close comparison with *Second Maiden's* prompts a re-reading of *The Winter's Tale*'s statue scene as the climax of its project, embodying and transforming generic expectations.

Second Maiden's, as Sarah Beckwith shows, has a "sustained interaction" with *The Winter's Tale,* meditating on themes of tyranny and injustice, love and jealousy, art and artifice, death and rebirth.[56] When the Tyrant usurps Govianus's throne and demands Govianus's Lady become his mistress, she kills herself rather than give in to his demands; Govianus vows to avenge her. In the subplot, Govianus's brother Anselmus tests his wife's faithfulness; she falls in love with his friend Votarius, leading to a bloodbath that leaves Anselmus, his wife, his wife's lover, and her servant dead. Meanwhile, Govianus flies to court, swearing on the Lady's ghost: "I've plighted my faith to't. / 'T'as opened me the way to revenge" (*SMT* 5.1.190–91).[57] The Tyrant, not deterred by the Lady's suicide, exhumes her body, displaying it in his throne room as a stage direction gruesomely describes: "*They bring the body in a chair, dressed*

up in black velvet which sets out the paleness of the hands and
face, and a fair chain of pearl across her breast and the crucifix
above it" (5.2.SD). A simultaneously lifeless and lifelike female
form also, of course, appears at the end of *The Winter's Tale,* introduced with a comparable stage direction: *Enter . . . HERMIONE*
(like a statue) (WT 5.3.SD).

Shakespeare and Middleton's ensuing scenes follow one another
closely. The Tyrant invites a painter—Govianus in disguise—to
make up the Lady's face, simulating life. He explains that he will
"By art force beauty on yon lady's face / Though death sit frowning
on't" for "Our pleasure shall prevail" (*SMT* 5.2.96–98). Likewise,
ushering Leontes into the statue's chamber, Paulina intones:
"Prepare / To see the life as lively mocked as ever / Still sleep
mocked death" (*WT* 5.3.18–20). When Govianus-as-painter reveals
his work, the Tyrant exults: "O, she lives again! She'll presently
speak to me! / Keep her up" and "Does she not feel warm to thee?"
(*SMT* 5.2.100–103). In much the same way, Leontes exclaims: "Oh,
she's warm! / If this be magic, let it be an art/ Lawful as eating" (*WT*
5.3.109–11). In addition to using the same central device (the represented body), these scenes, when first staged, shared material
conditions. Besides being staged in the same physical space and
with, presumably, the same repertoire of costumes and props, the
Lady and Hermione may have been played by the same actor, Richard Robinson (as Eric Rasmussen, Andrea Stevens, and Julia Briggs
have argued); Briggs furthermore suggests that Richard Burbage
played both Leontes and the Tyrant.[58] Leontes recalls the Tyrant
and the Tyrant recalls Leontes; they both recall Hieronimo. An
actor's body, performing analogous roles in these plays in the intimate, candlelit Blackfriars, becomes the site of an intertheatrical
dialectic; this dialectic produces the very meaning of Hermione's
body at the culmination of *The Winter's Tale.*

Both these plays end with a stage device Middleton developed
in *The Revenger's Tragedy:* the victim's body itself, like Gloriana's
skeleton, becomes the means of response—whether that response
is revenge or reconciliation. In *Second Maiden's,* Govianus, like
Vindice, prepares his dead beloved's lips with poison, using a disguise to gain his enemy's confidence. Looking upon the "painter's"
handiwork, the Tyrant fulfills his necrophiliac fantasies with a kiss:

TYRANT   Our arms and lips
Shall labor life into her. Wake, sweet mistress,

> 'Tis I that call thee at the door of life! [*He kisses her*]
> Ha!
> I talk so long to death, I'm sick myself.
> Methinks an evil scent still follows me.
> GOVIANUS Maybe 'tis nothing but the color, sir,
> That I laid on.
> TYRANT   Is that so strong?
> GOVIANUS   Yes, faith, sir.
> 'Twas the best poison I could get for money. [*He reveals himself*]
>
>   (*SMT* 5.2.104–12)

This scene, of course, is remarkably like Shakespeare's, both in language and action:

> LEONTES
>   What fine chisel
> Could ever yet cut breath? Let no man mock me,
> For I will kiss her.
> PAULINA   Good my lord, forbear.
> The ruddiness upon her lip is wet.
> You'll mar it if you kiss it, stain your own
> With oily painting.
>
>   (*WT* 5.3.78–83)

The suspense, the danger, the bated-breath of this moment derive from its implicit echo of—transhistorically—Vindice and the Duke, and perhaps—in repertory—Govianus and the Tyrant. Paulina forbids Leontes's kiss, warning him that painted lips can have devastating consequences. Once again analogous to these male characters, Paulina displays the body of her enemy's victim, the tension between his tyrannical desire and her own dedication to avenge Hermione producing the spectatorial assumption that Leontes will indeed receive his due. But Paulina is Shakespeare's pseudo-revenger, and the body she displays is a vehicle of forgiveness, not death. Wondrously, Hermione appears neither as a ghost nor as a corpse; she is alive, with sixteen years' worth of wrinkles. It is unlikely, as Lyne argues, that Middleton is "travestying Shakespeare and his sources, resisting the romance version of the theme and transforming it into brutal tragedy."[59] Rather Shakespeare, like Middleton, takes the raw matter of revenge tragedy and creates something both familiar and wondrously new.[60]

Because Hermione's body in 1611 took on layers of meaning from earlier stage bodies, the teleology of revenge tragedy is re-made in her seeming resurrection. For, like all stage revenges, Hermione's embrace is symbolically satisfying, but to a different end. Hieronimo's playlet causes Andrea's ghost to exclaim, "Ay, these were spectacles to please my soul"; by contrast, the sight of Hermione satiates Leontes with an art as "lawful as eating" (*ST* 4.5.12; *WT* 5.3.111). Leontes invites the reunited families to a feast at which they will tell and re-tell the story, "like an old tale still," of the last sixteen years (5.2.58). Appropriately, Paulina has "one eye declined for the loss of her husband, another elevated that the oracle was fulfilled" (5.2.69–71). In her person meet the smiling and frowning masks emblematic of two genres, the very picture of Shakespeare's "pied" play.

Notes

1. This essay benefitted from the generous advice of Sarah Beckwith, Stephen Greenblatt, Diana E. Henderson, Harry R. McCarthy, Esther Osorio Whewell, James R. Siemon, Emma Smith, and Leah Whittington as well as that of participants at the Harvard Renaissance Colloquium, the Shakespearean Studies Seminar at the Mahindra Humanities Center, the 2017 University of Exeter Center for Early Modern Studies Conference, and the 2018 British Shakespeare Association Conference.

2. The question of *The Winter's Tale*'s genre is not new. Heminges and Condell group it with the "comedies" in the First Folio, but since then critics have oscillated between "romance" or the classically inclined "tragicomedy." Boas's term "problem play," popular for much of the twentieth century, has fallen out of favor, yet others continue to invent new terms (for example, Stanley Cavell calls it a "remarriage comedy"). Notably, John Pitcher, editor of the third Arden edition, classifies the play as a tragicomedy, establishing strong links to classical sources, including Euripides's *Alcestis*. See Stanley Cavell, *Pursuits of Happiness: The Hollywood Comedy of Remarriage* (Cambridge: Harvard University Press, 1981). See also John Pitcher, "Introduction" in *The Winter's Tale,* ed. John Pitcher (London: Arden, 2010).

3. Ronald Broude, "Revenge and Revenge Tragedy in Renaissance England" *Renaissance Quarterly* 28, no. 1 (Spring 1975): 39. Chris McMahon, *Family and the State in Early Modern Revenge Drama: Economies of Vengeance* (New York: Routledge, 2012), 20. Linda Woodbridge, *English Revenge Drama: Money, Resistance, Equality* (Cambridge: Cambridge University Press, 2010), 5.

4. Fredson Bowers, *Elizabethan Revenge Tragedy, 1587–1642* (Princeton: Princeton University Press, 1966). Lily B. Campbell, "Theories of Revenge in Renaissance England," *Modern Philology* 28, no. 3 (1931), 281–96.

5. Stevie Simkin provides a comprehensive list of revenge tragedies in the introduction to *Revenge Tragedy:* Kyd's *The Spanish Tragedy* (1587) and his lost *Hamlet* (c. 1589), Shakespeare's *Titus Andronicus* (1591), Marlowe's *The Jew of Malta* (1589), Marston's *Antonio's Revenge* (1600), Chettle's *Hoffman* (1602),

Mason's *The Turk* (1607), Chapman's *The Revenge of Bussy D'Ambois* (1610), Tourneur's *The Atheist's Tragedy* (1611), Middleton's *The Revenger's Tragedy* (1606), *The Second Maiden's Tragedy* (1611), *Women Beware Women* (1621), and *The Changeling* (1622), Beaumont and Fletcher's *The Maid's Tragedy* (1611), Webster's *The White Devil* (1612) and *The Duchess of Malfi* (1614), Fletcher's *Tragedy of Valentinian* (1614) and *The Bloody Brother* (1619), Drue's *The Bloody Banquet* (1620), Massinger's *The Duke of Milan* (1621) and *The Unnatural Combat* (1621), Goffe's *Orestes* (1623), Davenant's *Albovine* (1626), Heminge's *The Jew's Tragedy* (1628) and *The Fatal Contract* (1630), Shirley's *The Maid's Revenge* (1626), *The Traitor* (1631), and *The Cardinal* (1641), Ford's *'Tis Pity She's a Whore* (1630), and Henry Glapthorne's *Revenge for Honour* (1640). Stevie Simkin, "Introduction" in *Revenge Tragedy* (Basingstoke and New York: Palgrave, 2001). See also Woodbridge's list of plays that fit her idiosyncratic criteria for "revenge drama." Woodbridge, *English Revenge Drama*, xi–xiii.

   6. Linda Anderson, *A Kind of Wild Justice: Revenge in Shakespeare's Comedies* (Newark: University of Delaware Press, 1987), 4. Harry Keyishian, *The Shapes of Revenge: Victimization, Vengeance, and Vindictiveness in Shakespeare* (New York: Humanity Books, 2003), 2.

   7. "Revenge" does not appear in *Love's Labour's Lost* or *The Comedy of Errors* (Woodbridge, *English Revenge Drama*, 5).

   8. Ben Jonson, *Bartholomew Fair (1614),* ed. John Creaser in *The Cambridge Edition of the Works of Ben Jonson Online,* gen. ed. Martin Butler (Cambridge: Cambridge University Press, 2014).

   9. Katharine Eisaman Maus, "Introduction" in *Four Revenge Tragedies* (Oxford: Oxford University Press, 1995), xxiii.

   10. Marvin Carlson, *The Haunted Stage: The Theatre as Memory Machine* (Ann Arbor: University of Michigan Press, 2001). Roslyn Knutson, *Playing Companies and Commerce in Shakespeare's Time* (Cambridge: Cambridge University Press, 2001). Jeremy Lopez, "Imagining the Actor's Body on the Early Modern Stage," *Medieval and Renaissance Drama in England* 20 (2007): 187–203. Emma Smith, "Genres: Cinematic and Early Modern," *Shakespeare Bulletin* 32, no. 1 (2014): 27–43. William N. West, "Intertheatricality" in *Early Modern Theatricality,* ed. Henry S. Turner (Oxford: Oxford University Press, 2013).

   11. Middleton's authorship of this anonymous play is now generally accepted. The sole surviving manuscript (about which I say more below) is not titled; then Master of the Revels George Buc gave it the title "The Second Maiden's Tragedy" for its apparent similarity to Beaumont and Fletcher's *The Maid's Tragedy.* In this essay, I use the title "Second Maiden's" to remain consistent with the majority of scholarship on the play. Julia Briggs uses the title "The Lady's Tragedy" or "The Ladies' Tragedy," while Martin Wiggins uses "The Maiden's Tragedy." See Julia Briggs, "The Lady's Tragedy: Parallel Texts" in *The Complete Works of Thomas Middleton,* gen. eds. Gary Taylor and John Lavagnino (Oxford: Clarendon Press, 2007), 833–38. See also *Four Jacobean Sex Tragedies,* ed. Martin Wiggins (Oxford: Oxford University Press, 2009).

   12. Though Gordon Braden does not discuss *The Winter's Tale,* he discusses *The Spanish Tragedy, The Revenge of Bussy D'Ambois,* and numerous plays by Shakespeare—including *Hamlet, Othello* and *Titus Andronicus*—in terms of Senecan reception. Gordon Braden, *Renaissance Tragedy and the Senecan Tradition: Anger's Privilege* (New Haven, CT: Yale University Press, 1985), 153–223. Rebecca

Bushnell identifies *The Second Maiden's Tragedy* (along with more customary plays, like *Cambyses* and *Sejanus*) as a tragedy of the tyrant. Rebecca Bushnell, *Tragedies of Tyrants* (Ithaca, NY: Cornell University Press, 1990), 154–76. Blair Hoxby acknowledges the play's indebtedness to *Alcestis,* grouping both, with the likes of *Hercules Furens,* under the heading "simple pathetic tragedy." Blair Hoxby, *What Was Tragedy? Theory and the Early Modern Canon* (Oxford: Oxford University Press, 2015), 120–22. Emrys Jones details at length Shakespeare's use of Euripides, particularly in *Titus Andronicus;* he also suggests possible resonances in *The Winter's Tale* with Seneca's *Agamemnon*. Emrys Jones, *The Origins of Shakespeare* (Oxford: Clarendon Press, 1977), 270–71. Perhaps most importantly, Robert Miola finds a reworking of *Hercules Furens* in *The Winter's Tale*'s final scene. Robert Miola, *Shakespeare and Classical Tragedy: the Influence of Seneca* (Oxford: Oxford University Press, 1992), 175–214.

13. Smith, "Genres," 29.

14. Ibid., 37–38. West, "Intertheatricality," 162–63.

15. See Smith, "Genres," 28–29.

16. West, "Intertheatricality," 152.

17. Smith, "Genres," 31.

18. Woodbridge, *English Revenge Drama,* 270.

19. All Kyd citations are from: Thomas Kyd, *The Spanish Tragedy,* ed. Clara Calvo and Jesús Tronch (London: Arden, 2013).

20. My reading of quantitative revenge tragedy language is indebted to Woodbridge. See Part II of Woodbridge's book, "Economic Unfairness: Revenge and Money."

21. All Chettle citations are from: Henry Chettle, *The Tragedy of Hoffman or a Revenge for a Father* in *Five Revenge Tragedies: Kyd, Shakespeare, Marston, Chettle, Middleton,* ed. Emma Smith (London: Penguin, 2012), 243–324.

22. All Middleton citations are from: Thomas Middleton, *The Complete Works of Thomas Middleton,* gen. eds. Gary Taylor and John Lavagnino (Oxford: Clarendon Press, 2007).

23. Carlson, *Haunted Stage,* 5–6. Of course, Carlson builds on the reception theory of Hans Robert Jauss. See Jauss, *Toward an Aesthetic of Reception,* trans. Timothy Bahti (Minneapolis: University of Minnesota Press, 1982).

24. All Shakespeare citations are from: William Shakespeare, *The Norton Shakespeare* (3rd ed.), gen. ed. Stephen Greenblatt (New York: Norton, 2016).

25. Some scholars, of course, read Hermione as going beyond Leontes's demand. For an example of this argument, see Howard Felperin, " 'Tongue-Tied, Our Queen?': The Deconstruction of Presence in *The Winter's Tale*" in *Uses of the Canon: Elizabethan Literature and Contemporary Theory* (Oxford: Oxford University Press, 1992).

26. Carlson, *Haunted Stage,* 5.

27. Jones, *Origins,* 270.

28. Stanley Cavell, "Recounting Gains, Showing Losses" in *Disowning Knowledge in Seven Plays of Shakespeare* (Cambridge: Cambridge University Press, 2003). Shankar Raman, "Death by Numbers: Counting and Accounting in The Winter's Tale" in *Alternative Shakespeares,* ed. Diana E. Henderson (London: Routledge, 2008), 158–80. Of course, the language of counting occurs throughout Shakespeare's works; the attention here is to a particular use of the motif in conjunction with the tropes of revenge tragedy. For a relevant example of the broader

use of counting, see Patricia Parker, "Cassio, Cash, and the 'Infidel 0': Arithmetic, Double-Entry Bookkeeping, and Othello's Unfaithful Accounts" in *A Companion to the Global Renaissance: English Literature and Culture in the Era of Expansion,* ed. Jyotsna G. Singh (Oxford: Wiley-Blackwell, 2009), 223–41.

29. West, "Intertheatricality," 154.

30. Derek Dunne, *Shakespeare, Revenge Tragedy and Early Modern Law: Vindictive Justice* (Basingstoke: Palgrave, 2016), 4.

31. Woodbridge, *English Revenge Drama,* 2.

32. West, "Intertheatricality," 163.

33. West, "Intertheatricality, 164–65.

34. See particularly Charles A. Hallet and Elaine Hallett, *The Revenger's Madness: A Study of Revenge Tragedy Motifs* (Lincoln: University of Nebraska Press, 1980).

35. As Tronch and Calvo note, the first half of this scene is only in the 1602 Quarto (Q4).

36. See Smith's account of parody in the revenge tragedy tradition, Smith, "Genres," 32–35.

37. Anne Barton, "Leontes and the Spider: Language and Speaker in Shakespeare's Last Plays" in *Shakespeare's Styles: Essays In Honor of Kenneth Muir,* ed. Philip Edwards, Inga-Stina Ewbank, and G. K. Hunter (Cambridge: Cambridge University Press,1980), 147.

38. Lopez, "Actor's Body," 193–94.

39. Carlson, *Haunted Stage,* 1–15.

40. All Marston citations are from: John Marston, *Antonio's Revenge* in *Five Revenge Tragedies: Kyd, Shakespeare, Marston, Chettle, Middleton,* ed. Emma Smith (London: Penguin, 2012), 169–241.

41. Lopez, "Actor's Body," 195.

42. Of course, the returned wife also features in Euripides's *Alcestis.* See Pitcher, "Introduction" and also Tanya Pollard, *Greek Tragic Women on Shakespearean Stages* (Oxford: Oxford University Press, 2018).

43. A version of this device, as Linda Anderson notes, is also at work in Shakespeare's comedies, most notably in *Much Ado About Nothing.* However, in the comic mode death is feigned, while in the revenge tragedy mode a genuine corpse is used—Hermione's body can and should be read with attention to both these dramatic lineages. Anderson, *Wild Justice,* 82–90.

44. Again see Cavell, "Recounting Gains, Showing Losses," especially 199–201 and 209–10.

45. Keyishian, *Shapes of Revenge,* 2. McMahon, *Family and the State,* 30.

46. Sarah Beckwith, *Shakespeare and the Grammar of Forgiveness* (Ithaca: Cornell University Press, 2011), 127–46. There is, of course, much earlier scholarship that has explored Paulina's resonance with the Biblical Paul and Post-Reformation understandings of Pauline theology. See Roy Battenhouse, "Theme and Structure in *The Winter's Tale,*" *Shakespeare Survey* 33 (1980): 123–38. Huston Diehl, " 'Does not the stone rebuke me?': The Pauline Rebuke and Paulina's Lawful Magic in *The Winter's Tale*" in *Shakespeare and the Cultures of Performance,* ed. Paul Yachnin and Patricia Badir (London: Routledge, 2008). For an exploration of Catholic, Protestant, and Greco-Roman resonances at work in the play in general, see Julia Reinhard Lupton, *Afterlives of the Saints: Hagiography, Typology, and Renaissance Literature* (Stanford, CA: Stanford University Press, 1996), 175–218.

47. Tanya Pollard, "What's Hecuba to Shakespeare?" *Renaissance Quarterly* 65, no. 4 (2012): 1060–93.

48. See Marguerite A. Tassi, *Women and Revenge in Shakespeare: Gender, Genre, and Ethics* (Selinsgrove: Susquehanna University Press, 2011). Though Tassi's project—a feminist reconsideration of women's ethical roles in revenge drama—differs from my own, her identification of Paulina as a revenger in this vein harmonizes with my reading. Anderson, *Wild Justice,* 4.

49. Despite this language, Paulina is not literally "constructing herself as God's agent," becoming a "vehicle of God's grace," or "reflecting divine justice" as critics have characterized some revengers; Paulina neither claims Apollo's authority nor the Christian God's. Eileen Allman, *Jacobean Revenge Tragedy and the Politics of Virtue* (Newark: University of Delaware Press, 1999), 105. Keyishian, *Shapes of Revenge,* 8. Broude, "Revenge," 55.

50. West, "Intertheatricality," 107.

51. Miola, *Classical Tragedy,* 208.

52. On the verso of the manuscript's final page, three different attributions appear—the first, to Thomas "Goff" (Gough), the second to George Chapman, the third to "Will Shakspear." All are crossed out; the final observation being "A Tragedy Indeed." Anne Lancashire notes that, while these attributions are unlikely to be original to the manuscript, they predated Warburton's acquisition sometime in the early eighteenth century. See Charles Hamilton, *Cardenio, or The Second Maiden's Tragedy* (Lakewood, CO: Glenridge, 1994).

53. Beckwith, *Grammar of Forgiveness,* 138. Raphael Lyne, *Shakespeare's Late Work* (Oxford: Oxford University Press, 2007). Suzanne Gossett, ed. *Thomas Middleton in Context* (Cambridge: Cambridge University Press, 2011). Andrea Stevens, *The Invention of Skin* (Edinburgh: Edinburgh University Press, 2013). The similar use of cosmetics in the two plays is also mentioned in Farah Karim-Cooper, *Cosmetics in Shakespearean and Renaissance Drama* (Edinburgh: Edinburgh University Press, 2006), 80–86.

54. Lyne, *Shakespeare's Late Work,* 119.

55. Gossett, *Thomas Middleton,* 310.

56. Beckwith, *Grammar of Forgiveness,* 138.

57. Citations again come from the Oxford edition, in which the play is edited by Julia Briggs. More specifically, the citations come from the performance text, which appears in the right column of Briggs's parallel-text edition. However, in this essay I use the title *The Second Maiden's Tragedy,* while the Oxford supplies the title *The Lady's Tragedy.* For another serviceable edition that maintains the title originally given the play by George Buc (though it does not concede Middleton's authorship), see *The Second Maiden's Tragedy,* ed. Anne Lancashire (London: Revels, 1978).

58. A note on the surviving manuscript, which served as the King's Men's prompt copy, identifies Robinson as the actor who played the Lady. As Eric Rasmussen notes, Richard Robinson and Robert Gough are listed as "Principal Tragedians" in *Catiline* in the 1616 Jonson folio, and are listed next to each other in the list of actors in Shakespeare's 1623 folio. Eric Rasmussen, "Shakespeare's Hand in *The Second Maiden's Tragedy,*" *Shakespeare Quarterly* 40, no. 1 (1989), 1–26. Stevens also suggests another actor played the Lady's corpse. Stevens, *Invention,* 133. See Briggs, "The Lady's Tragedy," 834–35.

59. Lyne, *Shakespeare's Late Work,* 122.

60. Lyne later admits this, saying "Things highly characteristic of late Shake-speare are actually in evidence in other contemporary works to the extent that it is not always possible to identify Shakespeare as the inaugurator of key elements of his own style, and indeed to the extent that it is not feasible to assert a clear author-based priority in who did what first. *The Second Maiden's Tragedy* is not just aimed at *The Winter's Tale;* it is a different response to the same things Shake-speare's play is tackling." Lyne, *Shakespeare's Late Work,* 122.

REVIEW ARTICLE

Forms of Justice

SUBHA MUKHERJI

Regina Mara Schwartz, *Loving Justice, Living Shakespeare* (Oxford: Oxford University Press, 2016)

Marissa Greenberg, *Metropolitan Tragedy: Genre, Justice, and the City in Early Modern England* (Toronto: University of Toronto Press, 2015)

In her last testament, *Paradiso,* the philosopher Gillian Rose asserts "a refusal to adopt or affirm the opposition between law and love which has so marred the development of Christian theology," and, by implication, Western thought about justice.[1] It is in this courageous, revisionist tradition that Regina Schwartz's impassioned book *Loving Justice, Living Shakespeare* positions itself, and in turn locates Shakespeare's works, as it issues a clarion call for the integration of ethics and affect in creative as well as critical practice. But it is also an invitation to live a larger life, to operate in an economy of plenitude, not of scarcity, and to rethink the particulars of love in an age of suspicion and hardening insularity. Its agenda is unabashedly one of healing: healing a rupture between loving and judging, the personal and the political, textual and social practice, and between being critical and being human. And its central claim is that Shakespeare shows us how to do this: not through any resounding moral abstraction or impersonal doctrine of moral good, but through dramatizing specific human encounters and relations that invite us to recalibrate the 'justice imaginary' we inhabit (6). For it is in our negotiation of the need and worthiness of the other—Rose calls it "loveability," and Schwartz "intrinsic value" (7), to be contrasted with desert or merit— that we exercise justice, or fail to be just; it is in laying ourselves open to the risk of encounter that we practice equity, and bring truth into dialogue with love.[2] When, in securing protective walls around our own selves and interests at times of crisis, we refuse to engage with the reality of the other or to respond to their questioning, we miscarry quotidian justice and degrade the original gift of love by robbing another's dignity. Implicit in Schwartz's narrative—which begins with a deeply personal experience of care and ends with a daringly comparative analysis of Shakespeare's Juliet and Bizet's Carmen—is the inextricability of capacious living, loving, and reading.

There is a peculiar synchronicity about these interrelations. I have been reading *Loving Justice* at a café at the Piazza della Rivoluzione in Palermo, with the hum of life circling around me, and the statue of the Genio di Palermo right in front, diverting my gaze. Yet as I try to re-focus myself and return to the book, the sculpture turns out not to be a distraction but a strange, if challenging, objective correlative of the sentiment Schwartz begins with – the exhortation in the Hebrew Bible to love the alien, extended by the New Testament into an extension to love the enemy (Chapter II, "The Law of Love"). For the Genio—the *genius loci* and protective deity of Palermo (along with its patron saint, Rosalia)—is an elderly, bearded man who nurses a serpent at his breast, coiled around him in a gesture of familiarity. The iconography makes him an emblematic personification of the city itself, with its long history of plurality, exchange, and inclusiveness. The Genio exists in several representations across the city, dating back to the period between the fifteenth and the seventeenth centuries. The snake has been variously interpreted—including an identification of it with Scipio Africanus, the Roman general helped by Palermitans in a war against Hannibal's army, in thanks for which Scipio donated a *conca doro* (golden basin) to the city; the fertile basin on which Palermo stands was named the *conca doro* by the Arabs. But in almost all versions of the myth, the serpent is the other, the stranger, who is welcomed, housed and fed by this enchanting city to which foreigners have always been drawn, whether as traders, invaders, conquerors, travellers or refugees. But from guest to host or parasite is one small step, as Derrida reminds us (in his essay "Of Hospitality"), and welcoming the other has ever had its ambiguities, its inseparability from anxieties about making the self vulnerable. And so the Genio di Palermo has a tough motto on the basin that cradles the statue in Piazza Pretoria (and several others): *Panormus conca aurea suos devorat alienos nutrit,* which translates as follows: "Palermo (all-port), golden basin, devours its own and nourishes foreigners." A particularly difficult inscription, this, in our times, when Palermo is fashioning its own identity as the capital of the most diverse, multicultural, multi-ethnic and receptive part of a country dangerously veering towards building rather than breaking walls. But it is also heaving with immigrants arriving at its harbors, placing demands on love, hospitality, and resources. Thus, while this symbol of benevolent hybridity with its unassimilable adage is specific to Sicily, it is also synecdochic of the ambivalent world we live in, and resonant of the mixed affects it throws at us; not entirely unlike the plays Schwartz chooses as her examples. Love, like justice, is a difficult gift; and they both entail an absolute command. Schwartz is aware of this (35, 32).

It is in this context that we need to understand the urgency and fervor of her use of Shakespeare, not least of the play of *Sir Thomas More.* The additions by Hand D here, credibly ascribed to Shakespeare, offer a haunting portrayal of "wretched strangers, / Their poor babes at their backs and their poor luggage, / Plodding to the ports and coasts for transportation": lines more vivid than ever in our historical moment, when the increasingly familiar figure of the stranger arriving at shores unknown with their poor luggage and terrified babes evokes a tangle of intense feelings.[3] But Shakespeare puts the "strangers' case" eloquently, as the play turns anxieties about foreigners on their head and asks the xenophobic mobs of London to consider a scenario where they "must needs be strangers," and rethink their "mountainish inhumanity." At moments such as this, Schwartz hears—and makes us hear in turn—an echo of the biblical injunction to love the stranger, for the one who resists, fears and alienates was "once a stranger in the land of Egypt" (50; Deuteronomy 10:19 and Leviticus, 19:34). She argues that *King Lear* explores how to love the stranger and *Romeo and Juliet* takes up the question of loving the enemy (Chapter III, "The Power of Love").

Yet Shakespeare understood the difficulty of such love in more inward and more unflinching terms, than purely as the uncompromising ferocity of the love command. Schwartz's sensitive suggestion that in *Lear,* all inadequate understandings of justice are pared away "until only an implied vision, albeit extremely frail, is left" (39), is in tune with the play's simultaneous and principled refusal of both formal solace and metaphysical despair; its bleak affirmation of the capacities of the human fiber. The fiction of the play, containing many failures of judgment with tragic results, speaks to Schwartz's consciously Shakespearean refutation of some of the qualities we routinely value and observe in our hermeneutic and adjudicatory practices, whether out of a sense of duty or out of disciplinary cautiousness: the bland neutrality of universal rights, an infinite and sceptical relativism, a monolithic and literal equality, the logic of fair distribution, and the indecorum of love in the Kantian moral law of impartiality that has seeped into the very pores of liberal modernity. But violation and failure of justice are distinct, involving different agencies. For instance, poetic justice—which could be seen to be an aesthetic equivalent of "natural law"—is violated by the play itself (as Dr. Johnson protested), but its relation to the moral and juridical failures by characters within the play world is inverse, and its purpose is resolutely mimetic, effected through an ethically pointed harrowing of the tragic form: both its magnitude and its comforts. Schwartz's lists of the concepts of justice that the play "[chronicles] the violation of"— "distribution, retribution, restoration, and the kind of justice associated with natural law, positive law, the rule of the strong, virtue ethics, charity, equity, and *ordo amoris*" (39). But are these equivalents in the play's juridical economy? Some of these are valid and valued, but agents in the play fail to sustain them; others are flouted by the play itself and exposed to be the stuff of false comfort or piety. The play's "unique vision of justice," gleaned out of this wreckage, does not consistently reject "retribution," for instance, quite in the same way as it does "distribution." The "authentic love" that Schwartz shows Lear discovering (48) is comprehensive, complex and challenging, and very far from feel-good; it includes primal rage, and the pain that legitimizes it. It even accommodates the impulse to avenge—the sentiment this book rightly shows *Hamlet* critiquing. Just as empathy must not be sentimentalized as emotional identification though it must accommodate "fellow-feeling"—as Schwartz explores in a deeply interesting section on "the relation of feeling to justice"— the "remedial" impulse must not be solely identified with sympathy (41): "remedy" is as much a love-word as a plot-word and a revenge-word. Remember Duke Vincentio in *Measure for Measure*—"A remedy presents itself" (3.1.198)—followed shortly by his speech on the kind of justice he relishes dealing in:

> Craft against vice I must apply:
> With Angelo to-night shall lie
> His old betrothed but despised;
> So disguise shall, by the disguised,
> Pay with falsehood false exacting,
> And perform an old contracting.
>
> (3.2.277–82)[4]

This smacks of phonetic revenge and comedic ordering—eye for eye and tooth for tooth—and anticipates his smug judicial assertion at the finale of the play: "Like doth quit like, and measure still for measure" (5.1.411). This is exactly the calculus that Schwartz says Shakespeare rejects: no wonder this legally obsessed play is his last comedy before he returned to the form in his final tragicomic romances: by this time the genre had been transformed, having been filtered through the great tragedies. But *Lear* places the vengeful instinct in a context of savage pain—witness Lear's fantasy of justice in the Quarto mock-trial (3.6.16–52), leading to an eviscerating impulse: "let them anatomise Regan and see what breeds about her heart" (F 3.6.33–34; Q 3.6.70–71). But his vengefulness surely cannot be pinned down to the "onset of his madness" (112)? The repaired and restored Lear vows that anyone who tries to part him and Cordelia will be "[devoured]" by the "good years," "flesh and fell," before he can make them weep—"We'll see 'em starve first" (F 5.3.24).[5] At the tenderest moment with the dead Cordelia, Lear declares, "I killed the slave that was a-hanging thee" (F 5.3.248; Q 5.3.267).

The Folio play comes out of a reaction to the sentimental providentialism of the old chronicle play of Leir, where piety pre-empts the psychic reality of unassimilable grief.[6] But it is the Quarto that offers the alternative trial that Lear sets up on the heath, in a violent attempt to redress the world's violation of equity; equity was by no means reserved for the "landed nobility" as the book suggests (76), but that only lends force to the play's inset staging of a radical appellate jurisdiction organized by the dispossessed few. These optative visions of justice are not frail but fierce, and in the context they feel right, as responses to mad-making grief and loss—like Titus's absurd laughter in *Titus Andronicus*. This is a play that does not only challenge the assumed indecorum of love, but also its decorum—not to dilute but to try it by these admixtures. It does not so much heal as it probes the wound, testing its resources. If these unassimilables of love were addressed head-on, they would not detract from Schwartz's reading, but complicate it productively. The serpent coiled around the Genio is the uncanny other, both friend and foe; the old man Palermo is *hostis*—both host and enemy; like our unaccommodable feelings and resistant instincts. But the avoidance—perhaps unseeing—is itself curiously moving: a window, perhaps, on the author's own dream of justice, and of the love that seeks it "unmixed with baser matter," as Hamlet might say (*Hamlet* 1.5.104). In a joyful, inventive and moving story-telling workshop in Palermo in September—*Stories in Transit V*— the story of the Genio was variously rewritten collectively by migrant teenagers, but the motto was taken out.[7] But is not purity itself proved a fantasy by *Lear,* whether it pertains to feeling or form, both of which impact on judgment? Like Staretz Silouan, whom Gillian Rose quotes in her epigraph to *Love's Work,* the play seems to dare us: "Keep your mind in hell, and despair not."

Loving the enemy, however, might be a way out of Hell—not only personal but social chaos. The book offers a fresh reading of *Romeo and Juliet* as a parable of the political force of a love that is fully directed to the other, that can reframe the foe and embrace him, healing social rifts through its own ecstatic extremity. But a further idea is planted in this chapter, which resonates through the rest of the book: loving without evidence, and in excess of it (55). This makes Juliet's love sound like faith—the kind of faith that Richard Hooker calls "certainty of adherence," defined against the "certainty of evidence."[8] The necessary disproportion of such an affect points the way to the heart of the fourth chapter on "The Economics of Love," where the gift of love is shown to be assailed by the economics of reciprocity in *The Merchant of Venice.* This discussion opens up Shakespeare's awareness of the deep vexation of contract which dominates social concepts of justice, and even of love; and of the dubiousness of a promise based not on trust but on law, drawing on authority rather than faith as its guarantor. Schwartz's analysis of how the play pushes commensuration and measurability to a literalist parody in Shylock's "bond," and then to a further parody of literal interpretation in Portia's legal revenge on him, taps right into the intersection between diverse theological and legal traditions. Her reflection on the price of reducing life and love to economic calculus, however, evokes moments of affective ambiguity as much as critical clarity: when Portia says to Bassanio that since he is "dear-bought," she will "love [him] dear" (3.2.313), the contractual language is at once a sign of vulnerability and manipulative strategy, as with Helena's transactional economy in *All's Well that Ends Well*—at once potent and poignant. Shakespeare understood the deep mischief of "dear"—Bertram in that play swears in court that "if" Helena "can make [him] know" her improbable claims "clearly," he "will love her dearly, ever, ever dearly" (5.3.315–16). Bassanio's vocabulary is indeed laced with commerce, as Schwartz points out (80), but the double-entendres are contronymic and cut both ways: Portia is "a lady richly left": left enviably rich, as well as desolately abandoned to her riches. If this chapter's readings were fully extended to the internal conflicts of what Theodore Leinwand calls "affective economies," how might that inflect the notion of "price," or indeed of "economic thinking"?[9] Would the equation of Antonio's love for Bassanio with Bassanio's for Portia (82) still hold? Antonio operates in two economies: he manages risk by calculation when he invests in trade— "[his] ventures are not in one bottom trusted," but in love, he practices a reckless plenitude and hazards all: "My purse, my person, my extremest means / Lie all unlocked to your occasions" (1.1.42; 1.1.138–39). This love the play does not need to "long for" (84); it is available, but dissolved into abjection by the asymmetries of affect. Again, the binaries get blurred in an impure world.

Against the economics of "mutual benefit," Schwartz posits not only the gratuity of grace but also the surplus of unconditional forgiveness in human affairs. The pitfalls of conditional forgiveness are shown also to be perils of proportion in the imagination of justice. But, as Jacques Derrida and Vladimir Jankelevitch are shown to have admitted, such radically free forgiveness is almost an impossible condition for humans. In a surprising and unconventional move, Schwartz diverges from these thinkers in her fifth chapter ("The Forgiveness of Love") to suggest that conditional forgiveness may be the precise agent for reconciling unconditional love with the *work* of reparative justice. And here is the further edge to her advocacy of an economics of forgiveness after all, but one that is defined and legitimized by relationality: the productiveness of rebuke, rather than retribution, as an agent of restoration. Levinas meets Leviticus in her striking reading of *Hamlet* in terms of rebuke as a threshold of recognition, acknowledgement and communication, where justice stirs, and "comes into being" (97). The specter of an edgeless, soft-centred love is vanquished. The closet scene is analysed as Hamlet's shriving of Gertrude in an act of vigilance, of restorative love watching over justice. Expanding out from her reading of *Romeo and Juliet,* she brings social justice in dialogue with a closer encounter—that between offender and victim. The Shakespearean theater is shown to offer the possibility of attunement to the other as a basis for forgiveness which exceeds the offence, but rebuke ensures responsibility in responding to the unknowable other.

As moral recognition is cut loose from factual knowledge, does the twinning of violence and redress raise further questions about the ethics of response vis-à-vis its epistemic content? Joshua Oppenheimer's film, *The Look of Silence* (2014), posits the silent gaze rather than "[speaking] daggers" as its moral tool as it follows optician Adi's face-to-face meetings with the killers of his brother in the Indonesian genocide of 1955–56 (*Hamlet,* 3.2.396); when he looks his patients in the eye, care quickens into confrontation, and confrontation into a glimmer of redemption, as words fall away. How do articulate rebuke and resonant silence interact in Shakespeare? Does the resurrected Hermione's silence to her husband, or Virgilia's to Coriolanus, or Isabella's to the Duke's proposal, negotiate the dynamic between rebuke, recognition and absolution? This chapter's unpacking of the unavoidable temporality of forgiveness—its sequential position—in relation to remorse and apology in Christian as well as Judaic traditions is curiously suggestive for the drama of forgiveness not only in life but in art. It raises fresh questions, for example, about what counts as repentance in post-Reformation culture: one wants to ask why Marlowe's Faustus is not forgiven, and what that has to do with the foregrounded generic character of the play—a "Tragedy." It complicates the lack of divine forgiveness of the transgressive scholar—so many times on the brink of formal contrition in the play, and yet so often slipping back—in the light of the Thomist idea that forgiveness could almost precede and prompt remorse. In a purely Shakespearean context, Schwartz connects the "time of narrative" to the *process* of reparation. This rings true: if a live Hermione had been sprung on Leontes as Hero is on Claudio in *Much Ado about Nothing,* almost instantly after the injury, the recognition would have lacked authenticity, the agents would have lacked absorption and readiness. But prolongation, held up in the book as "the friend . . .

of injury" (101–3), can also be a space for perverse retardation—whether either Leontes or Hermione needed sixteen years is questionable, but the aesthetic agenda of the tragicomic plot certainly did. Joseph's elaborate and long tests of his errant brothers, a narrative fascinatingly used here, is full of false trials, like Edgar's trial of his already grief-crazed and freshly blind father on Dover Cliff. Prospero does indeed create the time for his "victimisers" to "experience remorse": but this is also the retardation that ensures productive wonder. The analysis brings up the question of the relation between generic affiliations and judicial paradigms, and what love has got to do with it.

These questions are not to gainsay the learning, ardor and commitment of this book, but to indicate the scope and resonance of its lucid but compressed argument, both in terms of Shakespeare's works, and of early modern literature; and yes, perhaps a longing to see these pregnant ideas tested out yet more strenuously, more extensively and over rougher terrain. That longing is a testimony to the provocative resonance of *Loving Justice, Living Shakespeare* against a progressively emaciated and utilitarian idea of justice. This is an important, urgent and humane book which affirms the theater's role as an alternative jurisdiction to political thought and legal practice or discourse. It should be of immense interest to historians of literature, theology and the law, as well as to philosophers of ethics.

*   *   *

If questions of genre are implicit and somewhat understated in Schwartz's book, they are at the heart of Marissa Greenberg's *Metropolitan Tragedy: Genre, Justice and the City in Early Modern England*. Through a set of astute, sprightly, historically informed, and theoretically adventurous close readings of selected judicial plays in relation to their urban context, Greenberg argues that London in its full, fluid, vital complexity did not only provide material for city comedy but for a specific kind of tragedy—one that was shaped by metropolitan justice and its sense of place, and which entwined performance and punishment through urban placement. The chapters focus on an unusual, engaging and cannily identified range of dramatic subgenres: domestic tragedy, revenge tragedy, "tyrant tragedy" in Stuart England, and what Milton called "that sort of Dramatic Poem which is call'd Tragedy," in the shape of Milton's *Samson Agonistes*. The book attempts to unearth the historically available responses to tragedy by drawing on an impressive range of historical sources, both dramatic, and non-dramatic—including crime reports, political pamphlets, religious tracts, plays, and accounts of the Great Fire—and suggestively brings into dialogue tragedy as lived experience and tragedy as genre. In doing so, it contributes fresh insights to the understanding of London literature in relation to urban geography, and succeeds in establishing its larger claim about "the imbrication of genre and experience" (17). But the place of the judiciary in this mapping is less clear in some chapters and analyses than in others.

Domestic tragedy, in particular, bears out Greenberg's thesis about the centrality of urban sensibility and experience to theatrical tragedy; because this genre is heavily invested in contemporary legal events, the link between the juridical, the theatrical and the metropolitan are clearly visible and productive. One need only think of an iconic scene in the anonymous 1590s play based on a contemporary scandal, *A Warning for Fair Women,* where Anne Sanders, city merchant George Sanders's wife, sits at the threshold of her marital home when she encounters wealthy Captain George Browne, her prospective seducer and murderer of her husband: what ensues is adultery, murder, trial, and execution. Various urban and often mercantile occupations impinge on the lives, crimes and fates of the protagonists—from palmistry to tailoring, from judging to punishing to shriving. This is one of the plays Greenberg addresses, and it serves her well in providing a perfect example of the city acting as a space where "genre and justice overlap" (10). It is a generically self-aware play which begins with the figure of "Tragedie," declaring: "My Sceane is London, native and your owne" (l. 95)—thus playing to understood relations and assumed familiarities. The entwining of performance and punishment is engagingly explored in the first chapter, which focuses on this play together with *Two Lamentable Tragedies* to establish the "fantasy of the metropolis as an effective force of justice" (42)—whether through a thinly disguising Italian location or a vividly localized London neighborhood such as Shooters Hill.

The second chapter offers a fascinating counter-model for the traditional narrative of *translatio imperii* for the period's Roman plays, by reading *Titus Andronicus* as an example of revenge tragedy's project of a *translatio metropolitae* by means of a return to Rome. This, it argues, becomes evident "when we shift the object of study from textual citation to embodied performance" (48).

While *polis* in "the ancient world" (48) did not connote "an urban setting" or necessarily (or even often) concern "urban issues," as assumed by this book (53; 108–9) but primarily carried the sense of a citizen state, the interpretation of the violent repetition of revenge as an enactment of "the movements of urban life, both formal ceremony and improvised activity," is provocative (55).[10] The suggestion that this makes it possible for law and order to return to the city through the experience of performance is welcome and salutary (given the book's overall association of justice with catastrophe or punishment), though its precise relation to the larger argument connecting law with the "tragic returns" of revenge (49) could have been clearer. The textual and the physical, the thematic and the performative, are in tense and fertile dialogue in the play: perhaps it is time to go beyond a "shift" to a syncretic approach which registers and makes sense of their dynamic. This chapter vivifies the civic pageantry and tragic violence of Shakespeare's London, but it does so at a price that the play neither pays nor owes; for *Titus* combines the specificities of "Rome" as imagined by the early moderns with the particularities of space and affect of London in the 1590s. Besides, Lavinia's rape and Bassianus's murder both take place in the "unfrequented plots" (at once literary and geographical) of "vast and gloomy woods," and are already acts of revenge (at once poetic and political); witness Titus's lament as the arm-less Lavinia struggles to inscribe her fate in sand by "quoting" with stumps her nephew's copy of *The Metamorphoses:* "(O, had we never, never hunted there!), / Pattern'd by that the poet here describes, / By nature made for murthers and for rapes" (4.1.53; 2.1.115; 4.1.50; 56–58).[11] Such entwinements—of nature and nurture, city and forest, savage and crafted, text and body—stretch the claim that in this play "the intersection of the form of revenge tragedy and the performance dynamics generated onstage takes place in an explicitly and insistently urban setting" (53): the return to the city motif here functions differently from, say, the recursive movements of *A Midsummer Night's Dream,* or even *The Tempest.* "Shakespeare's representations of the spaces and activities of the *polis* . . . render Rome a correlative to London" (69) is a claim that is at once useful and over-neat; Stow and Ovid jostle with each other in the textual and theatrical economies of this play; the humanist school-room is as "present" as a location here as London Bridge with its display of traitors' heads. The meditation on "motion and emotions," meanwhile, indicates what the book does at its best, recovering available responses suggested, shaped and made recognizable by the theater (62–63).

Tragic tyranny and tyrant tragedy are the protagonists of the third chapter, which focuses on Philip Massinger's *The Roman Actor* (performed 1626, published 1629) to move forward into the Caroline theater and Stuart London. Greenberg suggests that "defences of the stage present theatrical tragedy . . . as a source of 'actual' tragedy in the metropolis" (77), and proceeds to examine Massinger's representation of tragedy and tyranny. She reads the toppling of Emperor Domitian, his transition "from a figure for catharsis to its object" (78), as a refiguring of the execution of Charles I in a scathing critique of tragedy's own tyranny over the metropolis: an authority deployed to achieve the ameliorative ends of genre. This chapter is an effective reconsideration of the "flaw in the theory of tragedy in early modern England" (78) through the theater's critical engagement with it.

In the intriguing and inventive final chapter, Greenberg attends to poetic form in order to identify "auricular failure" as the tool through which Milton comments on the loss of measure in material, moral and civic life in *Samson Agonistes*. The "cacophony of a ruined metropolis" is shown to provide "a sense of tragic *mismeasure*" to explore urban catastrophe (124). The gesture towards Milton's Greek inheritance is less persuasive than the lively connection with the "rough music" of London, though a more informed appreciation of Milton's engagement with Greek texts, and the texts that mediated and shaped this legacy for the early moderns, could have brought alive the dialogue between the local habitation and the universal elements of the tragic genre.[12] But the reading of Samson's razing of the temple as an analogy of the Great Fire of 1666, with Gaza being a figure for London, is deftly done, and lends force to the proposal that this dramatic poem demands "a spatially local reading," attuned to sensory experience, to unpack the resonances of "the discourse of tragedy in the metropolis" (137).

The challenge this book sets itself is to identify a productive intersection between law, the tragic genre, and London as a metropolis. It is the relation between its three constitutive elements that seems at times less than organic. The centrality of disciplinary sites such as The Tower of London to the status of London as a royal chamber, and their imaginative and actual overlap with sites of civic pageantry, are well argued. But "places of justice in early modern London" (15) were far more various than places of punishment might suggest: these included not only the gallows and the scaffolds but Westminster, the Inns of Court, Inns of Chancery, the legal areas of London, prisons, taverns, and indeed even the household—as domestic tragedies such as Heywood's *A Woman Killed with Kindness* show, the home can become a site of both transgression and punishment, as well as a ground-plot for related judicial operations such as surveillance, detection and evidence-collection. The self-policing metropolis—the focus of the book's argument—is only separated porously from the self-policing household, as the location of Anne Sanders's encounter with temptation on the threshold between home and city shows. Theatrical culture defines "law"—and indeed "justice"—in terms that are significantly less narrow than this book's parameters might suggest. This makes the selection of texts look less than inevitable: why, when Heywood's *An Apology for Actors* is rightly and repeatedly used in exploring early modern tragic theory, is his *Woman Killed* — arguably one of the best-known domestic tragedies of the period, and one centrally concerned with adjudication—not addressed? Its brand of homegrownness has to do with domestic *oeconomy,* the social geography of the household, a crime and a punishment located in a country house and a "manor seven mile off" (scene xiii, 166), and the intangibles of a very English class-system spanning town and country, rather than with "metropolitan catastrophe" (46), urban knowingness or the conflicts and changes of London society or topography.[13] Symptomatic is a statement such as this, comparing a domestic tragedy and a tract on acting by possibly the most famous author of a domestic tragedy, bringing together unlikes and omitting the obvious and naturally called-for comparison: "Significantly, both *A Warning for Fair Women* and Heywood's *An Apology for Actors* take London as the explicit or implicit venue for theatrical tragedy" (86). The paragraph claims as much as it concedes that though the well-known example of tragic efficacy, in *Apology,* of the woman of (King's) Lynn having her conscience caught by the "mousetrap" of a play is located "in Lynn, a provincial town in Norfolk . . . [y]et London . . . remains the point of reference for Heywood's tribute to theatre as a definitive institution of the metropolis" (86–87). Perhaps what might have made it possible to avoid such selection and stretching is an adjustment of terminology and parameters.

Justice has its own range of genres, too, and calls for a wider

understanding, if only to sharpen the focus on the specific affiliations that law shares with tragedy. The law was not just an agent
of discipline and tyranny but also resolved conflicts, orchestrated
solutions and sometimes reconciled adversaries. Its comedic *telos*
is both ironized and enacted in the drama of the time; it is both the
object of satire and of play, and a principle of emplotment variously
adopted, adapted and assailed: from Lording Barry's romp of a
play, *Law Tricks,* to Shakespeare's *Measure for Measure,* the genres
of law are as plural as the genres of drama. Comedy-as-genre provided as much of a framework by which "writers, readers, and
playgoers might register and respond to" the experiences of crime
and punishment, as "tragedy-as-genre" is said to do (10). While this
book's focus on tragedy is partly meant to be corrective of the current critical orthodoxy which is perhaps partial to city-comedy as
the genre that is recognised as being manifestly urban, the book's
own thesis would have gained in nuance if the wider generic context and scope of legal action and judicial structures of thinking
had been accommodated. Justice also has its variety of locales:
while legal London was undoubtedly a productive hub for cultural
artefacts both emerging from and addressing it, the law travelled to
other parts of the country, in assize courts held in town-halls and
market-places, not to say local church courts. Thomas Arden was
very much a Kent man and those accused of his murder were
indicted and arraigned in the Faversham Abbey Hall. Despite the
claim of chapter 1 (in relation to *Warning*) that the precision of the
drama's locating of the *revelation* of crime in London, irrespective
of the *site* of its commission, makes domestic tragedies metropolitan, *Arden of Faversham* turns a middle-class house in Kent into
the labyrinthine site of both the crime and its discovery. It is the
Faversham Borough Records Archive that holds the bulk of the
legal documentation from the murder trial, as Patricia Hyde's monumental book has detailed.[14] The "court" itself, while increasingly
centralized, was still also a metaphor and a moveable feast, as legal
historian John Baker has demonstrated.[15] The early modern theater
had an intuitive understanding of this, and of the dangers of over-
placing justice.

The larger aim of *Metropolitan Tragedy* is to relocate tragedy "in
its rightful place as an urban genre," deriving its tragic energies
from the metropolis in transition (5). While the author is aware of
the "polysemy" of her two main terms— "metropolis" and "tragedy" (6)—this radical claim for "early modern English tragedy"

seems sweeping (6): there are many tragedies which feature urban settings that are incidental rather than constitutive, and many others that are not set in the metropolis—whether it is London or London in disguise—and are not about metropolitan crises and upheavals: think *Macbeth.* On a smaller scale, the claim that domestic tragedy takes the metropolis as its scene does not seem consistently tenable either: think *Arden.* On the latter, the claim that though the murder happens in Faversham, this is really a London play because several attempts are made on Arden's life on the route between London and Faversham and London is really not that far from Faversham (36), seems strained, and does injustice to the book's considerable research and its bold readings. That theatrical tragedy is "productive of the metropolis" (6) is an interesting but distinct thesis, but seams between these related arguments are sometimes slippery, like the definitions of what Greenberg repeatedly and emphatically identifies as her "eponymous terms."

One would have liked a fuller exploration of the polysemy too. For instance, the suggestion that "for scholars of urban geography, history, and literature, *metropolitan* and its cognate *metropolis* refer to the physical *metre,* or measurement, of the *polis* as a built environment" is novel and fascinating. But given that the etymology of *metro* in the word goes back to Greek *mētēr*, meaning "mother" (as opposed to Greek *metron* = measure), it would have been instructive to know the basis of this assumption, and how it relates to the more familiar and well-traced sense of the *metropolis* as a mother-state or founding citizen-state. Passing suggestions such as these are tantalizing, but there are missed opportunities, especially where such hints are grounded but unfamiliar. The strongest parts of the book, for this reader at least, are not so much the grand narratives as the intricate, contextualized readings of particular texts—ranging from obvious suspects such as *A Warning for Fair Women* to surprising ones such as Milton's *Samson Agonistes.* But the intuition that the experiences of urban crime, historical change, suffering and loss found a distinctive tragic focus, and that the drama of justice and punishment had a shaping power over the dramatic representation of these phenomena, is provocative, and argued with ingenuity and verve. This study restores to visibility a form—judicial metropolitan tragedy—which has been somewhat eclipsed in critical history by our attention to the form that took over: city comedy. Local vexations notwithstanding, this is a valuable and provocative study at the generative crossroads between cultural practice and literary form.

Notes

1. Gillian Rose, *Paradiso* (London: Menard Press, 1999), 18.
2. Gillian Rose, *Love's Work* (New York: NYRB Books, 1995; repr. 2011), 105.
3. *Sir Thomas More,* addition by Hand D, credibly ascribed to Shakespeare. Cf. Alfred W. Pollard, ed., *Shakespeare's Hand in the Play of Sir Thomas More* (Cambridge: Cambridge University Press, 1923).
4. All references to Shakespeare's works are to *The Riverside Shakespeare,* ed. G. Blakemore Evans (Boston: Houghton Mifflin, 1997, 2nd ed.; first published 1974), unless otherwise specified.
5. Note the Folio's alteration of the Quarto's more pious thought, "the good shall devour them . . . " (5.3.24). All references to *King Lear* are to *King Lear: A Parallel Text Edition,* ed. by René Weis (Harlow: Longman, 1993).
6. *The True Chronicle History of King Leir* (London, 1605).
7. This was part of a project created by Marina Warner; the Palermo workshops were co-organized with Valentina Castagna and in partnership with the Museo delle Marionette of Palermo: www.storiesintransit.org.
8. Richard Hooker, "Of the Certainty and Perpetuity of Faith in the Elect," sermon preached in 1585, but published in 1612, in "A Learned and Comfortable Sermon Of the Certainty and Perpetuity of Faith in the Elect. Especially of the Prophet Habakkuk's Faith," in *Tractates and Sermons. The Folger Library Edition of the Works of Richard Hooker: Books 1-5,* Gen. ed. W. Speed Hill, vol. 5. ed. Laetitia Yeandle (Cambridge, MA: Harvard University Press, 1990), 69–82 (71).
9. Theodore Leinwand, *Theatre, Finance and Society in Early Modern England* (Cambridge: Cambridge University Press, 1999), "Introduction," 1–12.
10. There is an established body of work on this, mainly in classics. For a start, see Paul Cartledge, *Democracy: A Life* (Oxford: Oxford University Press, 2016), esp. 15, 37–39, 316, for what is possibly the fullest study of the trajectory of the word *polis.* As Cartledge demonstrates, translating it as "city," or even "city-state," is potentially misleading: "citizens were the *polis,* a notion reflected in the ancient political terminology." Hence his warning against the "unwanted anachronistic associations of 'city'" (37–38).
11. "Quote" could mean both "to mark," and to "refer to"—bringing together Lavinia's physical use of Ovid, and Shakespeare's literary act of allusion.
12. The question of what associations Greek tragedy brought along with it to the Renaissance has been the subject of a great deal of recent probing. See, e.g., Tania Demetriou and Tanya Pollard, eds, *Milton, Drama and Greek Texts* (London: Routledge, 2017), a book that came out after *Metropolitan Tragedy,* but is instructive on earlier studies as well as sources.
13. Quotations refer to Thomas Heywood, *A Woman Killed with Kindness,* ed. Brian Scobie (London: New Mermaids, 1985; repr. 1991).
14. Patricia Hyde, *Thomas Arden in Faversham: The Man Behind the Myth* (Faversham: The Faversham Society, 1996).
15. J. H. Baker, "The Changing Concept of a Court," in J. H. Baker, *The Legal Profession and the Common Law* (London: The Hambledon Press, 1986), 153–69.

REVIEWS

Shakespeare and the Cultivation of Difference:
Race and Conduct in the Early Modern World
By Patricia Akhimie
New York: Routledge, 2018

Reviewer: Joyce Green MacDonald

The observation that conceptions of race were fluid enough to include not only the familiar modern marker of skin color, but religion, region, kinship, and climate has been a commonplace in early modern race studies. Patricia Akhimie's *Shakespeare and the Cultivation of Difference* (which I first read in an early manuscript form) sets out to complicate this truism by first pointing out its social implications: if race could inhere in so many different domains, then Shakespeare's England was deeply racialized in ways that we may not have noticed, and that have nothing to do with how many nonwhite, non-Christian people there actually were in the country. To such commonly recognized racial domains as somatic types or "blood," Akhimie adds her particular interest in doctrines of social cultivation—visible in documents ranging from *ars apodemica,* discussions of the art of foreign travel, to conduct books, records of country-house entertainments, and manuals on household management.

Akhimie argues that the belief in social mobility built into lessons on proper self-cultivation map over and are visible through race's multiple manifestations, in ways that make us see the pitfalls of losing one's essential Englishness, the limited possibility that some people have of improving themselves, and the bedrock intractability of racial identity despite its varied surface presentation. In her four chapters, she demonstrates her guiding conviction that the possession of a "mutable body"—one that could be trained and disciplined to comport itself in ways that gave it a new kind of social value—was in fact dictated by the period's conviction that differences in physical appearance were morally "indelible": the "stigma" attached to certain kinds of bodily markers polices "access to cultivation, impeding those who might otherwise be able to make themselves over into social elites" (9). Over and over again, she points us to places in the plays she studies where characters have markers of difference imposed on them, either because of who they physically are, as we see with the Moor of Venice, through force (as in the case of the unfortunate Dromios in *The Comedy of Errors,* who are constantly being beaten black and blue), or by the circumstances of their birth. Repeatedly, we see them try to navigate the ideological roles into which their marked bodies have thrust them.

Sometimes, trying to keep track of how race mutates in Renaissance drama feels like playing critical whack-a-mole; you pin it down in one place and it just pops up somewhere else with new whiskers and fake teeth. In contrast, Akhimie's connection of race to conduct and status provides a larger perspective. Rather than listing individual examples of where ideas about race or racial difference appear in a text, she concentrates on how a range of "fluctuating ideas about human differences" (9) intersect with structures of authority and hierarchy, and on the social effects that these intersections cause. Chief among these differences are bodily markers that include but are not limited to the color of one's skin. *Shakespeare and the Cultivation of Difference* wants to examine how a variety of marked bodies are used by these structures of authority to affirm and preserve existing social order, and how race can therefore become more materially available to our reading.

Its attention to bodies—bodies that are not only born a specific color, but laboring bodies marked by effects of the work they perform for the society that holds them in the place that will sustain its own operations—distinguishes Akhimie's discussion of race. Because of its interest in how certain bodies become the instruments through which a hierarchical order preserves its structures of privilege, Akhimie's book is also interested in the conjunction of race and class, which I think makes it stand out even more among current treatments of her subject. Despite the promise of upward social mobility held out by the doctrine of self-cultivation, she notes, the characters she studies are prevented from rising by the ways in which their bodies are marked—not only by color, but by the evidence of the work they are relegated to doing. The injustice these characters suffer and the physical and emotional pain they experience in their thwarted attempts to rise are where we can see race in action, Akhimie argues. For her, only "race," with the kinds of confining, exclusionary thinking it promotes, seems a protean enough term to account for the different stories of oppression her chapters detail.

Shakespeare and the Cultivation of Difference begins with a chapter on *Othello,* as so many books in early modern race studies must. Akhimie's understanding of the text details a story about the limits of cultivation. A traveler who has survived many strange adventures, Othello has both profited from his exposure to foreign worlds—his stories' wonder is what catches Desdemona's imagination—and, as Akhimie's reading of period debates over the value of travel reveals, been damaged by it. Travel analysts like Fynes Morrison believed that even if travel could make you polished and sophisticated, it also created the risk of eroding the national identity into which you were born, turning you into a stranger in your own land. Othello himself is already a stranger in Venice, as well as separated from his own native land, wherever that might be. Without a place of his own, he is vulnerable to the "new vices, new staines, new diseases" Morrison saw as the ill effects awaiting the traveller insufficiently bred to his own country's ways. But of course, Othello is already literally stained by his dark skin—marked, that is, in ways that already suggest his natural imperviousness to all attempts to cultivate his character and quality of discernment. His predicament is further complicated by what Iago calls the "curse of service." If we are all indeed condemned to serve a social order that rarely (he says) rewards us as we deserve, it may well be true that it does not make any difference how well we perform. Whether we are excellent or merely serving time until we are cashiered, the notion of a meritocracy that will fairly judge our accomplishments is a laughable fiction. When Othello compares himself to a "base Judean" (or Indian) before his suicide, Akhimie says, the more important term in the phrase is 'base,' because it speaks to this sense of irreparable relegation to an ordained place and role in society. Here, we see her combining her insights into the contradictory doctrine of cultivation with her interest in the social implication of racial markers, to subtle and persuasive effect.

The completely surprising second chapter, on *The Comedy of Errors,* shows the breadth and versatility of Akhimie's belief in the flexibility of racial marking and its baleful utility in maintaining social orders of privilege. *Errors* contains no characters who are identified as not white, yet, she argues, the bodies of Dromio of Ephesus and Dromio of Syracuse—marked by the bruises of the beatings they both constantly catch from angry masters—provide, for a society in which household servants were routinely beaten, evidence of their own fault. The household management manuals she draws on in this chapter emphasize servants' abject natures and masters' almost forced resort to beatings as a way of controlling them. Servants' bruised bodies manifested a set of beliefs in which domestic workers were always "positioned at the margins of the family and the borders of the household," (93) constantly wrong, constantly in need of correction. Unlike the disciplines a young gentleman might acquire through travel, the beatings a servant might receive were not aimed at improving his or her nature. The manuals emphasize that beatings were about masters' obligations to maintain an orderly household and not about servants' capacity to learn from being beaten; in that way, beatings were much more about the expression of mastery than the hope of reformation. The Dromios' battered appearance, Akhimie argues, offers a constant kind of physical evidence of the state of error in which they live; it marks them as permanently exiled from the polite, self-controlled society of masters, and as permanently relegated to an irrational, debased substrate of the human race. This debased status and "the prejudicial treatment" it elicits from their social betters, she argues, "is best described as racism," (89) given that it cannot be changed, that it is regarded as natural, and that the bruises that mark them as unruly and stupid point to their shared possession of certain "limitations, and moral qualities" that have nothing to do with their religion, place of origin (they come from different places, after all), or skin color. The self-evident need to segregate the Dromios from normal, orderly people and their lack of meaningful recourse for their abuse provide a clear illustration of how marked Shakespearean bodies can determine their own social places regardless of phenotype, and of how the use the plays make of marked bodies can be understood as instances of racism.

The third chapter, on *A Midsummer Night's Dream,* continues chapter 2's interest in class and status with its focus on the "hard-handed men" Peter Quince recruits into his acting company, but does not make as bold a claim about racism and racialization in the play. Quince's actors' bodies bear the immutable marks of the work they do, with their rough hands and generally rustic demeanors. Akhimie suggests that their hands' hardness is the physical token of a kind of intellectual impermeability to the powers of imagination or cultivation that successful art requires, so that once again their bodies point the way to a kind of exclusionary racialization that relegates them to the station they currently occupy, no matter what steps they take to try to raise themselves above it. The sound of Theseus and Hippolyta's hunting horns the morning after the young lovers' night in the woods marks a clear border between who the rude mechanicals hope to become and who the older generation of royals are and will always be, the author argues, because hunting was so strictly reserved for the aristocracy. No matter how confused things get during the long night in the forest, those sudden horns remind us that normal order has never truly been superseded. One night of playful freedom over, normal roles will be resumed, with Peter Quince's amateur actors retaking their proper places as suppliants for aristocratic favor, which may or may not be granted. The wood that hosts the actors' rehearsals as well as the lovers' confusion appears to be a "medial zone" (119) beyond the reach of the court, but in reality is merely another staging area for the demonstration of the degree to which both young lovers and aspiring actors exist under others' watchful eyes. After the final performance of "Pyramus and Thisbe" mutates Ovidian tragedy into slapstick—as though Peter Quince's company would be capable of anything higher—Theseus ends by reminding Hippolyta of his own "capacity" and "might" in condescending to accept the actors' offering at all. Especially useful here is Akhimie's use of recent scholarship on country house entertainments, which supports her argument that *Dream*'s interest in the contrast between aristocratic leisure and aristocratic power provides a place where we can see working men's relegation to their foreordained role of kissing the hand that minimizes their efforts. "This," Akhimie remarks trenchantly, "is the cultivation of difference; the ideology of cultivation distinguishes between people by evaluating the quality of their conduct even as it endorses insurmountable barriers for some groups to the very practices that might earn them higher esteem" (144). The actors' hard hands mark their bodies as incapable of executing the kind of performance that could raise their status, because their bodies' markings tell us that they cannot be raised or changed. Once again, race inheres in the body, but not always in the manner modern sensibilities assume it will.

Race resides in the range of bodily markings that Akhimie notes, although other kinds of markings than the modern emphasis on skin color matter as crucially to the ways in which bodies can be racialized. In her final chapter, on *The Tempest,* which is also indispensable to a discussion of early modern formations of race, she returns to a full focus on cultivation with a discussion of how the play is compelled to contain two "competing theories" (152) of its efficacy. On one hand, Ferdinand, Miranda, and Prospero all exemplify cultivation's success, as they benefit from education and lessons in conduct. On the other, of course, Caliban cannot be raised above his identity as mere laborer, just as Stephano and Trinculo are born to serve. Akhimie suggests that the fact that Prospero pinches and punishes Caliban works both to punish him for bad deeds or poor performance in the domestic circle and to mark him physically as someone who has been punished. Like the Dromios, his battered and bruised body announces his inferiority. If an early modern understanding of "cultivation" includes the physical labor that created landlords' profit from the land as well as the ability (or inability) to improve one's conduct and behavior, then the question of Caliban's relation to cultivation foregrounds the role of labor—husbandry—in the colonial enterprises that *The Tempest* is so often understood as rehearsing. Akhimie is correct when she notes that the play "revises" (155) usual representations of colonial labor. Drayton's "Ode: To the Virginian Voyage," for example, celebrates the new land's bounty that "Without . . . toil" will generate three generous harvests instead of the single one normal agriculture would expect to raise. By emphasizing that Caliban sweats to cultivate Prospero's estate, the play admits that the work "hard-handed men" contribute is what produces landlords' wealth and comfort. But by the play's end, while Ferdinand's cultivation through labor on the island is what makes him a suitable husband for Miranda, Caliban's labor and its central role in the island's cultivation is "effaced" (159). His "pinched" body ineradicably identifies him as someone suited only to a lifetime of servitude—a fate he freely embraces in his last words. It points as well to the limits of cultivation, of which certain bodies are simply not capable. The "natural" limits of racially marked bodies that the chapter describes would eventually be marshaled to justify slavery in the New World.

Two of Akhimie's chapters address plays which are absolutely canonical in early modern race studies. Two of her chapters take up plays which do not often figure in such critical discussions, which is why her discussions of *A Midsummer Night's Dream* and especially *The Comedy of Errors* feel so fresh and innovative to me. Even when the book approaches *Othello* and *The Tempest,* it does so in ways that do not replicate more common kinds of critical concerns with these plays. Akhimie gives us a *Tempest* discussion that is not particularly concerned with postcolonialism, for example; her Othello's experience of race is mediated through acculturation to invisible systems of social control. *Shakespeare and the Cultivation of Difference* combines deft local readings with its larger analytical commitment to unfolding how race manifests in bodies but also across class, and how these two systems of social differentiation work to maintain each other. Akhimie's dedication to tracing how the varied and multiple operations of race become visible in social practice (rather than in literary texts alone) is logically connected to the political work in the present she believes that early modern race studies is capable of accomplishing. She writes that one reason she wants to explore race's appearances in the past and to attend to the pain and oppression it caused "is to make it more recognizable in our contemporary moment" (11). In the midst of a current U.S. politics that often trades in denigrating nonwhite bodies, Akhimie's call for discernment, recognition, and attending to the pain of others that using race as a weapon causes feels refreshing. Regardless of any political insights that might further energize Akhimie's bold, detailed analyses in the minds of her readers, however, *Shakespeare and the Cultivation of Difference* is a significant, thoughtful, and original addition to the growing body of studies that consider how race signified in Renaissance England. I recommend it highly.

Forms of Faith: Literary Form and Religious Conflict in Early Modern England,
Edited by Jonathan Baldo and Isabel Karremann
Manchester: Manchester University Press, 2016

Reviewer: Devin Byker

As a volume dedicated to early modern religion and literature, *Forms of Faith* finds itself in a now well-established area of early modern research and publication. Although such monographs are too numerous to list here, other significant essay collections include Kenneth Graham and Patrick Collinson's *Shakespeare and Religious Change* (New York: Palgrave MacMillan, 2009); Ken Jackson and Arthur F. Marotti's *Shakespeare and Religion: Early Modern and Postmodern Perspectives* (Notre Dame: University of Notre Dame Press, 2011); Graham Hammill and Julia Reinhard Lupton's *Political Theology and Early Modernity* (Chicago: University of Chicago Press, 2012); and, more recently, David Loewenstein and Michael Witmore's *Shakespeare and Early Modern Religion* (New York: Cambridge University Press, 2015). In addition to casting its nets beyond Shakespeare, *Forms of Faith* distinguishes itself from this existing work by exploring the implications of historical formalism for religion and literature. The volume's most fundamental claim, signaled by its title, is that form is an underexamined element of religious and literary discourse in the period: "To study religion in early modern England is to study the forms and reforms of memory, and to study memory is to study forms of faith," and the essays here "aim at exploring the complex interplay between form and faith" (7, 9). Through this claim, this volume situates itself in response to a growing discontent surrounding new historicism's "reduction of religion to ideology" (9).

The second claim the volume pursues is that early modern literature offers tools for diminishing religious conflict, fostering "possible sites of de-escalation" (3). Inherent in this claim is the exploratory conceit that literary forms "allow for a suspension of faith that may not have been possible in theological discourse" (3), a notion that recalls Richard McCoy's distinction between "religious" and "poetic" faith in his monograph *Faith in Shakespeare* (New York: Oxford University Press, 2013). Both argumentative facets here culminate in the volume's assertion that "literary forms served as important tools in an earlier age for challenging a hermeneutics of suspicion that underlies the escalation of conflict" (14).

The two major inflections of this claim are explored, respectively, in the first and second parts of the volume—Part I, "Religious ritual and literary form," and Part II, "Negotiating confessional conflict." Rather than comment on every essay, I will focus on a few examples in the volume that illustrate the most notable contours of its larger argument. The essays in Part I skillfully place diverse religious phenomena in conversation with literary texts, ranging from ancient Easter liturgical vigils and *The Mer-*

chant of Venice (Brooke Conti); early modern Christmas celebrations (Phebe Jensen); "goodnight ballads," or first-person musical renditions of last dying words spoken from the scaffold, and *Eastward Ho* (Jacqueline Wylde); theologies of the Eucharist and the *Arcadia* (Christina Wald); and rituals of mourning and memory in relation to Spenser's *The Ruines of Time* (Isabel Karremann). While these essays further a well-established vein of historicizing religious practices alluded to in early modern literature, they also highlight movements toward détente, disavowal, or deflection in response to religiously incendiary questions. Among these essays, Christina Wald's contribution, "Romancing the Eucharist: confessional conflict and Elizabethan romances," offers a worthwhile illustration of volume's larger contention. In her examination of Sidney's *Arcadia,* Wald explores the pronounced transformations of substance and accident involved in Pyrocles's disguise as Cleophila, a ruse that announces its Eucharistic affinity through statements such as Pyrocles's self-assertion, "Transformed in show, but more transformed in mind" (78). Although there has been no shortage of ink spilled on early modern literary explorations of Eucharistic controversies, Wald's essay nevertheless illustrates new and alluring resonances between the formal structures of transformation offered by theology and mined by romance. Rather than arguing that Sidney's *Arcadia* embraces or rejects, say, traditional Catholic justifications of transubstantiation, Wald insists instead that the *Arcadia* deploys Eucharistic logic for "ambiguous uses" (80), in that it "creatively adapts hotly contested theological and liturgical issues for its thematic concerns and its aesthetic experiment in the form of prose fiction rather than making a religio-political case for one particular form of faith" (84). Such an argument unfolds the refreshing possibilities of answering, "None of the above," to the sometimes tiresome question of which confessional allegiances—Protestant, Catholic, or otherwise—literary texts are assumed to espouse, as if they were themselves living, breathing persons. Wald's argument instead reframes theological materials as resources for formal innovation that also enable distant thematic explorations, here in the context of Pyrocles's cross-dressed disguise and identity.

Nevertheless, even as Wald disavows any confessional overtones to Pyrocles's disguise—arguing instead that authors like Sidney "redeploy the epistemological and emotional thrills of the Eucharist for secular concerns and utilize them for experimenting with

the possibilities of the relatively new mode of vernacular prose fiction" [77–78])—it must be acknowledged that this latter redeploy-
ment of forms also involves itself in ideological purposes.
Although Pyrocles's transfiguration may buttress neither a Protestant nor a Catholic purchase on the Eucharist, it nevertheless enters
other metaphysical debates as Pyrocles voices his own cynicism
toward sartorial or performative transformations of gender: Wald
observes that, "as it turns out, Pyrocles's claim of a gender transformation by love is, above all, a rhetorical strategy which justifies his
disguise" (79). Although the "real" or "true" nature of the Eucharist
may here be immaterial, the structure of the debate has nevertheless mapped these categories instead onto a different region of
contention—in this case, the authenticity or illegitimacy of gendered performance and/or essence. If literary forms do "de-escalate" religious conflict, then, they might only do so by deflecting or
transposing those conflicts into other, homologous—or even struc-
turally linked—ideologically fraught zones and registers.

The essays in Part II, "Negotiating confessional conflict," examine the possibility of de-escalation even more explicitly. These
essays explore topics that include representations of incomplete,
partial, and ever-evolving religious reforms in *When You See Me
You Know Me* (Brian Walsh); the conciliatory possibilities of critique in *The White Devil* (Thomas J. Moretti); the ambiguous agency
of *Macbeth*'s witches (James R. Macdonald); the relationship
between "an interrogative conscience" and *Henry V* (Mary A.
Blackstone); Donne's use of opposing semiotic models in relation
to the sacraments (Alexandra M. Block); and an approach to Donne's idea of confession through the framework of Foucault's late
work (Joel M. Dodson). While the notion of mitigating religious
conflict can sound rather lofty in its aims, as if literary forms inher-
ently transcend bitter sectarian squabbles, these essays also expose
a pragmatic rather than altruistic dimension to such efforts, as
James Macdonald illustrates in his essay, "'A deed without a
name': evading theology in *Macbeth*." Explaining how Calvinist
theologians narrowed previous understandings of a witch's self-
determined agency to a more constrained, instrumental relation to
the devil's will, Macdonald suggests that *Macbeth*'s depiction of its
witches effectively punts on the question of the witches' agency
altogether, "evincing conformity to neither model by refusing to
articulate the degree of supernatural power which the Sisters themselves possess" (147). Arguing that Shakespeare's initial structure

and Middleton's expansion of the occult material together "create a middle ground of deniable ambiguity," Macdonald proposes that the mysteries surrounding the witches' agency allow the play both to avoid theological clarity as well as to enhance the allure of a murkily defined menace (155). When put in these terms, it is no surprise that literary forms might mitigate religious tension when authors may wish to avoid needlessly committing themselves to particular religious positions, but Macdonald's essay pushes us to recognize that such acts of hesitation may not merely help to keep the peace but also can bolster a particular literary or dramatic effect.

Even as the volume compellingly absorbs pragmatic motives into its exploration of literary forms of de-escalation, it also raises doubts about the extent to which different modes, such as critique, can be fairly attributed to this endeavor. Thomas J. Moretti's essay, "Tragic mediation in *The White Devil*," evokes such questions by arguing that "cynicism mediates religious tension" in Webster's play, musing, "Perhaps cynical representations of various Christian professions and practices could offer an ironic service to religion, one neither moral nor denominational but nonetheless inclusive, irenical, or ecumenical" (127). Like Marlowe's iconoclastic drama before him, Webster's equal-opportunity levelling of all religious positions certainly robs any one sectarian from claiming moral authority over another. Yet even as Moretti importantly urges critics to de-couple specific genres from "one particular religious perspective or epistemology," it is nevertheless difficult to see Webster's tragedy as able to foster "Christian inclusivity and religious cohesion" (128, 127). Furthermore, if such community is created, as Moretti acknowledges, at least in partial opposition to stage stereotypes of villainous Jews and Moors, this dramatic arrangement once again only mitigates internecine Christian conflict by translating it into other religious, ethnic, or nationalist registers.

While this volume is largely tacit about explicitly theoretical approaches, its final pages—Joel M. Dodson's essay, "Foucault, confession, and Donne," and Richard Wilson's Afterword—devote significant attention to Foucault. This shift toward Foucault appropriately acknowledges the tensions that have historically existed between his work and an interest in either religion or form. While Dodson reminds his readers that Foucault's early attitudes toward early modern religion as a form of disciplinary biopower has led the "religious turn" away from Foucault, Dodson instead elects to highlight his later work, often neglected in early modern studies, on "the care of the self" described in the 1984 final volume of *The History of Sexuality*. Approaching early modern doctrinal confessions of faith "as a form of care rather than subjection," Dodson turns to Donne's 1619 sermon at The Hague to argue that "Donne can be seen giving theoretical expression to confessional identity as a similar form of care, training, or exercise," for "it is the work, or *askesis*, of defining the demands of the confessional life that renders it a meaningful imperative for early modern English writers" (203, 209, 210). This invocation of Foucault's later work contributes a welcome, if not belated, re-visitation of our field's often narrow and incomplete representation of his thought. In so doing, it opens up new opportunities for involving Foucault in returns not only to religion but also to questions of form.

Despite these rosy assertions, Wilson's Afterword ultimately casts doubt on the optimistic, conciliatory portrait offered by the larger volume, insisting on "the risk in reducing faith to its forms" and the trouble with a superficially irenic literary spirit that ultimately effaces the religious violence underwriting its legitimacy (230). While the volume's introduction hopes that it will have an "effect on promoting understanding across religious divides," Wilson questions the "liberal concept [. . .] of culture as a happy medium between Church and state" and notes instead that "[t]he shadow of such divine violence falls [. . .] across [. . .] every communal rite described in *Forms of Faith*" (14, 229, 231). In her recent manifesto on the return to formalism, *Forms: Whole, Rhythm, Hierarchy, Network* (Princeton: Princeton University Press, 2015), Caroline Levine cautions against merely reading "literary forms as epiphenomenal, growing out of specific social conditions that it mimics or opposes," for such approaches fail to take "account one of forms' affordances: the capacity to endure across time and space" (12). In this manner, Wilson illustrates that the temporal and geographic portability of religious forms needs to be more fully acknowledged in this volume's work: he not only reminds us that "more real blood was shed over the Eucharist in Shakespeare's time than was ever drunk symbolically," but he also highlights Foucault's personal fascination and later disillusionment with Ayatollah Khomeini's rise in Iran, as well as "televised images of religious vandalism and beheading" that we face in our contemporary moment (233). This volume's final attention to religious violence ultimately qualifies its claims about the peaceable nature of literary forms, presenting a more complex portrait of early modern religion and literature and a sturdier representation of the stakes of a historical-formalist approach. Taken together, this particular confection of argument and counter-argument valuably illuminates how literature might not only de-escalate post-Reformation theological conflict but also transpose this conflict in slippery and sometimes ethically dubious ways into other ideologically charged registers. At the same time, this volume makes apparent that, without attending to the trans-historical circulation of religious and literary forms, such work risks producing reductive accounts of their relationship. Because it unfolds many possibilities for literary forms to negotiate religious conflict, while also probing the limits of this endeavor, *Forms of Faith* offers both a nuanced conversation and a promising instruction manual for future considerations of form, literature, and religion in early modern studies.

Stage Directions and Shakespearean Theatre
Edited by Sarah Dustagheer and Gillian Woods
London: Bloomsbury Arden Shakespeare, 2018

Reviewer: Evelyn Tribble

Stage Directions and Shakespearean Theatre is a well-conceived and timely book. The collection takes a fresh approach to a complex and contested area. Stage directions are important to editors, to directors, to actors, to theater historians, to readers, to audiences. Yet despite their ubiquity, they are seldom given sustained critical scrutiny. Sarah Dustagheer and Gillian Woods seek to fill this gap. In their introduction, Dustagheer and Woods call attention to the multiple agencies and temporalities that comprise stage directions, which are "fundamentally, mutable, enigmatic, and various" (2). Perhaps as a consequence, editors assume the license to alter, omit, and expand stage directions, in a way that they would hesitate to do with the dialogue.

In their introduction, Dustagheer and Woods introduce a motif that will be repeated, with variations, across the volume: "stage directions highlight the ways that a play is stretched between text and performance" (5). The ambiguities and problems that such liminalty creates are seen by the editors as an opportunity rather than a problem: "these complications of provenance and purpose are provocative starting points for investigation" (6). The shadows of Alan Dessen and Leslie Thomson, authors of the indispensable *Dictionary of Stage Directions: 1580–1642* (Cambridge, 1999), loom large over the collection, as well they should. Dustagheer and Woods point out that Dessen and Thomson were well aware of the provisional nature of their work, and many of the essays expand upon, challenge, or contest this fundamental work of scholarship.

The book is organized very effectively, moving from general principles to specific applications, and examining the topic from a range of perspectives. Part I, "Taxonomy," engages first principles: what is a stage direction, anyway? Are stage directions natural kinds, or are they simply fabrications designed to paper over our sparse knowledge of what happens on stage? Are they text or paratext? What authority do they have? The collection opens with a characteristically acute chapter by Tiffany Stern: "Inventing Stage Directions; Demoting Dumb Shows." Stern notes that the term "stage direction" itself was coined by Lewis Theobald, and it was not meant as a compliment. In Theobald's view, stage directions were intrusions upon the authorial domain, produced either by "player-editors" for the reader or by prompters for the actor. Indeed, as Stern deftly shows, the term has always obscured the variety of labor and agencies lying behind the play: "It has hidden the varied people for whom these paratexts were intended— scribes, stage keepers, prompters (and perhaps, though that is less certain, actors); and hidden, too, the varied people by whom they may have been written" (41). This vivid and provocative opening chapter is followed hard upon by another methodological gem: Laurie Maguire's "The Boundaries of Stage Directions." Stage directions are always liminal, as befits the dramatic text itself, which is "about the mediation of boundaries" (46). Stage directions mediate between theater and fictional location, between reader and viewer, between actor and director. They police the edges of the play, juggling in and out, place and stage, actor and character, comedy and tragedy.

The final chapter in this section takes a surprising turn: Paul Menzer and Jess Hamlet examine "nonce" stage directions, often bizarre one-offs that resist categorization and systemization. Do such oddities as "Peter falls into the hole" challenge the idea of recovering a "common theatrical vocabulary," as Dessen describes it? What does attention to the idiosyncratic and the quirky tell us about the stage that dwelling only upon the typical does not? Written with wit and verve, this essay—and the other two in the introductory section—present a "taxonomy" that unsettles as much as it systematizes. And this is a good thing.

Part II takes up "Text," with two closely linked essays written by Emma Smith and Douglas Bruster, both of which take issue with the distinction between theatrical and literary (or fictional) directions. In "Reading Shakespeare's Stage Directions," Smith argues that the Quarto *Othello* shifts from the speech prefix of "*Oth*" to "*Moore*" at three junctures at which the play seems to "reinscribe [Othello] as the sexual or violent early modern racial generalization, 'Moor'" (95). Stage directions are not, as commonly thought, ways of invoking performance; instead, they are "the property of readers . . . instances of a different mode of narration in printed playbooks" (97). Smith uses narratological theory to approach stage directions, arguing that they function as different types of narrative, marked off by variant typeface, just as black letter passages, indented texts, section headings, and the like signal different modes of reading in the prose fiction of the period. Compellingly, she suggests that we might think of stage directions as forms of "free indirect discourse," a form of focalization that mediates between action and representation. In "Shakespeare's Literary Stage Directions," Bruster also notices homologies between the language of dialogue and the language of stage directions in Shakespeare's plays. He too challenges Greg's distinction between "literary" and "theatrical" stage directions, arguing that they "are literary only to the extent that everything in a play is literary" (137).

Part III on "Editing" features chapters by two editors of Shakespeare's plays who have taken very different approaches to stage directions: Suzanne Gossett and Terri Bourus. Suzanne Gossett's title itself poses her question: "When is a Missing Stage Direction Missing?" From the perspective both of an editor and a general editor of the *Norton Shakespeare,* Gossett notes the difficulties arising from even so seemingly simple a rule of thumb as ensuring that the characters are brought on and off the stage. On this point contemporary documents are often of little help: the extant plots rarely specify exits, surviving dramatic manuscripts are often spotty and inconsistent in the directions, and "massed entries" such as occur in some Folio texts leave much for the editor to supply. So if a stage direction is "missing," "what is it missing from and for whom is it missing?" (146). Gossett uses the helpful phrase "the logic of the action" (147) to describe moments at which an editor may decide to intervene; as she shows, however, often such decisions reflect critical and theoretical judgments that are not always fully disclosed. Terri Bourus, also writing from the perspective of editor and general editor, discusses the constraints of the space of the page, both in the 1623 Folio with its cramped double columns and in modern editions. Bourus reflects upon her own use of the margins of the pages of *The New Oxford Shakespeare,* where the space is deployed to describe performance choices as they have been taken up by past productions. While some may quibble about her individual choices, her invitation to use the marginal space "to ask questions and invite possibilities" (186) raises provocative and interesting questions about the role of the editor.

Part IV takes up "Space," particularly stage space. This section opens with a discussion by Martin White of his practice-led research at the University of Bristol and at the Sam Wanamaker playhouse. White's extensive research into stage lighting shows the importance of understanding how lighting in indoor performances affected all other elements of staging. Stage directions for indoor performances must be read with an awareness of the importance of stage lighting. White concludes this chapter with a deft reading of the little-known Massinger play, *The Guardian,* that elucidates the range of lighting effects the play deploys.

Sarah Dustagheer's chapter is co-authored with Philip Bird, and this dialogic effect aptly fits the collaborative and questioning nature of the essay, and indeed of the volume as a whole. Dustagheer examines moments at which a dead body is "discovered" on stage, and the essay develops as a conversation between her discussion of the trope and Bird's reflections upon the practicalities of staging such moments on reconstructed stages. (I would note here that the bold type used for Bird's comments is not easy to distinguish from the roman font). This chapter is particularly noteworthy for its intertwining of historical, cultural, and theatrical perspectives on the ways that death is "reconceptualized and re-imagined" (236) in stage directions.

Part V, "Plays" concludes with three strong readings of stage directions in individual plays: Andrew Hiscock on *Macbeth;* Sarah

Lewis on *The Duchess of Malfi;* and Gillian Woods on *The White Devil.* Hiscock begins by thinking about directions as a form of institutional memory. The chapter as a whole elucidates the sensory elements of stage directions: acoustic stage directions, for instance, can function as "memorial prompts" (254), creating patterns across the play. He concludes by arguing that scholars and practitioners should be alert not only to the lacunae stage directions represent, but also to their "textual and theatrical potentiality" (260). The middle chapter in this section, Lewis's essay on " '*(From the Dutchesse Grave)*': Echoic Liminalities in *The Duchess of Malfi,*" explores the puzzling echo scene at the conclusion of the play, arguing that the stage direction's ambiguity evokes the "Duchess's contested subjective identity" (284). Gillian Woods rounds off the volume with a thorough discussion of the "contradictory function of dumb shows," an appropriate bookend to Stern's consideration of the subject in the opening chapter. Woods suggests that an apt analogy for the dumb show is "theatrical punctuation" (289), which both situates and discomfits the audience.

The final section left me wanting more, not from the individual essays, but more readings of stage directions responding to the provocations of this volume. This thoughtful and illuminating collection will no doubt inspire further work and spur scholars to integrate the stage direction into their consideration of early modern drama.

Culinary Shakespeare: Staging Food and Drink in Early Modern England
Edited by David B. Goldstein and Amy L. Tigner
Pittsburgh: Duquesne University Press, 2016

Reviewer: Emily Gruber Keck

Early modern food studies has grown exponentially within the last decade and a half. Among literary scholars, several analytical approaches have dominated this critical field: the careful mapping of the social and cultural significance of individual foodstuffs or ingredients; the unpacking of recipes and cooking as forms of intellectual labor and creativity, particularly as engaged in by women; and the reading of banquets as spectacles, both on- and offstage. *Culinary Shakespeare*'s project—"to articulate the centrality of food, eating, and drinking for Shakespeare, and to illustrate the diversity of approaches that have the potential to reshape our understanding of culinary culture"—is recognizably shaped by these preoccupations (3). At the same time, the volume succeeds in re-defining familiar lines of inquiry in ways that break new analytical ground, and, in some instances, reimagine "culinary" reading practices.

As *Culinary Shakespeare* seeks to address how Shakespeare articulated the questions, tensions, and polysemic significance surrounding food and consumption in early modern England, the volume stands out from the critical field in its expansive understanding of what "culinary" can mean. In his book *Eating and Ethics in Shakespeare's England,* Goldstein previously asserted the importance of the communal dimensions of consumption, focusing on commensality: shared eating and drinking. In many ways, this volume valuably develops that approach, understanding the "culinary" as including, even demanding, engagement with commensality. The readings of food and drink in almost every chapter benefit from nuanced understandings of how they were consumed within local, national, and global communities. This attention to how the culinary defines relationships—from the economic and political to the romantic and ecological—may be the most valuable aspect of the collection. Rebecca Lemon and Julian Yates bring intriguing analytical frameworks to bear in chapters that broaden our conception of the range of meanings commensality, or lack thereof, can carry in Shakespeare. The editors also offer a corrective to what they see as a critical imbalance; noting that drinking is underexplored in early modern food scholarship, they examine "eating and drinking as complementary meaning-making phenomena. . . . [and] aspects of the same literary formations" (6). While every section of the collection benefits from considering drinking in tandem with eating, this approach (perhaps inevitably) foregrounds Falstaff, who serves as something of a magnetic pole for the collection—four of ten pieces focus in some detail on his habits of consumption. *Culinary Shakespeare* also stands out among recent scholarship in its commitment to exploring not only theatrical acts of cooking, eating and drinking, but cooking, eating and drinking *as* theater. These concerns are focused in the collection's third section, but scholars throughout the volume focus productively on the specifically theatrical articulations of culinary tensions and transformations. In particular, chapters by Julia Reinhard Lupton and Karen Raber demonstrate the value of tracking food and wine as theatrical phenomena by attending to patterns of eating and drinking across the Shakespearean canon.

The first section of the collection, "Local and Global," seeks to map locations of origin, marketing and consumption as symbolic domains that shape the meanings that attach to food and drink. Reading beer, sack, and Seville oranges as commodities with fraught relationships to English markets and Englishness, the essays in this section explore how these relationships help define Shakespearean expressions of community and commensality. Perhaps the greatest critical payoff of this approach comes with Peter Parolin's " 'The poor creature small beer': Princely Autonomy and Subjection in *2 Henry IV*," which examines Hal's confessed affinity for small beer in light of the drink's history as a "naturalized" English product. Originally an import from the Low Countries, beer gradually overtook ale in popularity, to such an extent that a love of beer became a gastronomic litmus test for Englishness. In the process, increased production of beer contributed to social and economic shifts, driving urban growth, capital investment, and the professionalization and masculinization of brewing. As Parolin explains, shifting tastes were entangled with, and stood in for, these changes, "presiding over new identity formations" including "new models of Englishness" (26, 23). Thus Hal's predilection for small beer—the drink of the poorest Londoners—not only links him with lowness in ways that he cannot completely control, but also marks the networks of relationship in which he is implicated, and to which he is subject, as essentially English. Parolin argues that this predilection also speaks to the tetralogies' concerns about the nature of kingship; over the course of *2 Henry IV*, "the unfeeling model of autonomous rule outlined in *Part 1* gives way . . . to a properly English model . . . in which the king's dominance is achieved through acknowledging shared characteristics with his subjects" (31).

The dramatic weight of Hal's drinking derives partly from its contrast with Falstaff's consumption of foreign wine, which makes

Barbara Sebek's "'Wine and sugar of the best and the fairest': Canary, the Canaries, and the Global in Windsor"—along with Raber's chapter in the second section—useful companions to Parolin's. Sebek seeks to "un-English" *The Merry Wives of Windsor* by mapping the instability that complicates familiar local/global binaries in the history of the Anglo-Spanish wine trade, in part by recognizing London as not only an urban center, but a port, where global trade was a local concern. Tracking how Windsor's wines register concerns about England's role in emerging global economies, and anxieties about domestic trade rivalries, Sebek argues that sacks and canaries dispel the former by offering a global vision of English hospitality that can include foreign goods, while negotiating domestic conflicts of gender, class, and trade.

Closing the "Local and Global" section, Peter Kanelos's "So Many Strange Dishes: Food, Love, and Politics in *Much Ado about Nothing*" begins with the Seville orange, which Kanelos reads as a culinary expression of the play's varied romantic attachments. Associated through the Seville trade with passion, exoticism, delicacy, and rarity, the orange's pocked skin also paradoxically rendered it a common image of corruption, especially prostitution, and deception. Kanelos argues that *Much Ado*'s rhetorical oranges call on both sets of meanings in a discourse that links the play's perspectives on culinary and romantic consumption. Though the international origins of the orange are less central to his analysis, Kanelos maps the complex connections between a single comestible and the text's larger patterns of culinary language, an approach that is richly rewarded. Oranges serve as a metonymic lens that brings the importance of consumption into focus throughout the play. Just as the opening lines linking war and eating emphasize the consequences of treating emotion as a game, Claudio's comparison of Hero to a rotten orange shows the justice, Kanelos argues, in Beatrice's tirade against him: "men are eaters of hearts," whose "radical selfishness, cloaked in codes of honor and allegiance, is bound to a bestial appetite" that treats women as food to be devoured (71). Don John's melancholic refusal to share the festive table links his determination to "feed" on those he manipulates with this selfishness.

The following section on "Body and State" considers the relationship of culinary frameworks to frameworks of power, particularly the body politic. Driven by the insight that how and if one eats is fundamentally shaped by these frameworks, the pieces in this section examine how Shakespeare mobilizes the culinary to draw attention to religious and secular power structures, questioning the limits of the polity and highlighting the corruption of a false sacrament. In "Feeding on the Body Politic: Consumption, Hunger, and Taste in *Coriolanus,*" Ernst Gerhardt contrasts Menenius's vision of the body of Rome with contemporary texts that focused on food production as important to the health of the state, arguing that *Coriolanus* redefines the body politic by rendering that production liminal and unseen. In the context of competing early modern explanations for grain scarcity and high prices, Menenius focuses on the circulation of grain in order to reimagine reliance on an unknowable market as self-sufficiency rather than dependence. As he excludes food production from the body politic, he institutes a metaphoric logic by which Rome distributes political representation—tribunes—in lieu of grain, and citizens exercise political power by "tasting" Martius in the marketplace. This logic shapes the play's preoccupation with food and language; Gerhardt identifies a provocative chain of associations linking political voice with breath and taste. Martius's contempt for the citizens' voices is rooted in what he sees as their inferior political palate, and their tasting shifts quickly to a threatening desire to consume him. These associations frame consumption as "a core signifier of one's membership in the body politic," and they outline a vision of state power that depends, at least in Rome, on the "communal tasting" of the body's members to define its own limits (109, 111).

Gerhardt's chapter is bookended by readings that engage more implicitly with the image of the body politic, examining how wine's capacity to corrupt the individual through drunkenness is articulated dramatically as foreign contamination and domestic treason. Karen Raber's "Fluid Mechanics: Shakespeare's Subversive Liquors" and Rebecca Lemon's "Sacking Falstaff" both offer useful correctives to dietary readings of drunkenness. As Raber argues, focusing solely on wine's effect on the individual body cannot fully comprehend the drink's significance, "since that body is always linked metaphorically and materially to the condition of the nation's political and economic corpus" (96). Raber's analysis resonates with both Parolin's and Sebek's earlier chapters, as she explores how the body's relation to wine became a figure for England's relation to foreign entanglement, particularly as the wars in the Low Countries were blamed for encouraging the growth of English drunkenness. Falstaff's drunkenness and resulting vices metonymize England's dependence on foreign goods and frame that dependence as a source of moral and political corruption. These connections can also be seen in Clarence's death by malmsey, and in *The Tempest*'s wine-fueled treason against Prospero. Drawing on accounts of European exploration that focus on Spanish and Portuguese religious abuses, Raber reads Caliban's susceptibility to wine, introduced to the island by two Catholics, as a false sacrament that converts the unwitting "native," invoking anxieties about England's vulnerability to Catholic Europe in the realm of exploration. Lemon's approach takes a different trajectory to arrive at a parallel conclusion, identifying Falstaff as a figure whose addiction to a foreign substance, sack, supersedes his loyalty to the monarch. Mapping the early modern semantic shift of "addiction" from indicating devotion to marking a loss of control, Lemon argues that the trajectory of Falstaff's relationship with sack presents a paradigmatic evolution from commensality to a compulsion that exploits and damages his relationships with women and companions, as the "tyrant" drink determines his behavior. The contrast between the fat knight's encomium to fraternal drinking practices and his ultimate loyalty to sack alone draws attention to alcohol's power to both create and threaten community, a paradox of commensality registered in early modern discourses. In contrast to Raber, Lemon sees wine less as a foreign threat than as an agent of domestic rebellion, as Falstaff's distance from court culture evolves into opposition to the monarchy—opposition driven by his appetites.

Perhaps because they start from the same character's engagement with the same beverage, however, both analyses draw on similar imaginative and discursive formations surrounding wine, some of which Parolin's and Sebek's earlier pieces also share. This leads to significant sections of parallel analysis that bring into focus exactly how Falstaff-centric this volume is. It is difficult to argue with the editors' claim that Falstaff's "importance to issues of Shakespearean eating and drinking is surely unrivaled," and each piece that includes him has much to recommend it (6). Raber's work is particularly compelling, reading the character as the key to a larger pattern of corrupt commensality across the Shakespearean canon. In a collection of ten chapters, however, it seems problematic to feature four pieces on any single character, including three chapters on the same consumable, sack. Even if, as the editors state, their goal is in part to "give a sense of the ramifying potential that a single facet of such a study can entail," the degree of analytical overlap suggests the limits of that potential, and such focus may compromise their other goal of "provid[ing] a strong foundation for scholars wishing to study Shakespearean eating" (6).

In its final section, "Theater and Community," *Culinary Shakespeare* examines the connections between culinary and theatrical practices and the ways in which both can generate and destroy community. While these chapters speak to many of the foundational questions of Shakespearean food studies—the material and ephemeral aspects of food, the changes effected by food on bodies, the role of banquets as metonymically-rich spectacles—they take radical perspectives that attend to the space of the theater itself, and how the playhouse engages with ontological and epistemological questions raised by food preparation and ingestion. Tobias Döring's chapter, "Feasting and Forgetting: Sir Toby's Pickle Herring and the Lure of Lethe," exemplifies this approach, as it unpacks how the playing space invokes both community and social memory to accomplish specific imaginative work onstage. Seeking to complicate readings of the playhouse as a repository of cultural memories, Döring connects the theater's appeal to the senses with contemporary humoral understandings of food's capacity to prompt forgetting. As Sir Toby's revelry in *Twelfth Night* associates him with older religious and feasting traditions, his excessive consumption also offers a strain of oblivion that the play links with early modern ideas of deposition, or an active "cultural forgetting" of memories, pushing against Olivia's pseudo-Catholic memorializing of her dead. Like the kitchen, Döring argues, the theater facilitates transformations of cultural ingredients, reviving older traditions onstage in order to consume them as spectacles before consigning them to be forgotten. Evoking a community within the walls of the theater, Toby's revelry invites the audience to understand themselves as sharing commensality, transforming spectators into feasting participants and thus enabling them to engage in cultural work central to the project of the Reformation: forgetting's "productive and inventive aspects that are crucial in . . . establishing something new" (173).

In his similarly groundbreaking chapter on "Shakespeare's Messmates," Julian Yates re-examines the culinary from an ecocritical perspective, mobilizing Donna Haraway's analytical framework of "messmates" to move beyond anthropocentric understandings of cuisine, community, and hospitality. Reading the death, decay, and consumption of the body as non-anthropic "cuisine," Yates defines commensality as a moment of asocial, nonintegrative association strictly delimited in time and space. Like *Hamlet*'s politic worms that gather to consume Polonius, any community must be continually assembled by the shared "table," and lasts only as long as the meal. The Ephesus of *The Comedy of Errors,* Yates argues, is a kitchen that, like the theater itself, enables transformations, and presents a vision of hospitality as a time-bound "convoking" that is impossible to extend or to recreate—a temporary commensality similarly instituted by the abortive banquet in *The Tempest* that "kitchens" or transforms Alonso. At the same time, the island stages Prospero's kitchen not as space, but as biopolitical process: "a set of routines that constitutes the differences between humans and other animals, between sovereign and subjects" (197). These invite us, like Caliban, Stephano and Trinculo, to imagine alternative routines that convoke other forms of social constitution.

This final section begins and ends by examining how staged scenes of consumption resonate not only as spectacles, but as spaces for intellectual engagement. In "Cynical Dining in *Timon of Athens,*" Douglas Lanier argues for a widespread disillusionment among humanists surrounding sixteenth- and seventeenth-century court feasts that fell short of banqueting ideology, an ethical and sociopolitical framework that linked the sensual elements of the meal with its moral role of fostering conversation. Reading this disillusionment in dramatizations of banquets that focus on their excesses and moral corruption, Lanier sees *Timon*'s parallel meals as similar "respon[ses] to one of the period's cultural traumas: the perceived failure of the promise of humanism" (155). Where the first, apparently commensal, banquet registers violations of these ideals that echo Jacobean masques and feasts, the second, "anticonvivial," banquet attempts to rehabilitate the gathering's moral value by banishing all patronage and spectacle. Linking the titular character's misanthropy with the "souring" of feeling toward humanist ideals, Lanier attributes Timon's pursuit of roots both to his embrace of Apemantus's Cynicism and to contemporary reassessments of root vegetables' value as staples in conditions of food scarcity, framing their simplicity as redemptive. Julia Reinhard Lupton's "Room for Dessert: Sugared Shakespeare and the Dramaturgy of Dwelling," by contrast, examines the dramatic resonances of the "banquet" of sweets that often ended lavish meals, which was marked as a forum for reflection and renewal by its spatial and temporal separation from the main meal. Paying valuable attention both to the role of performance in creating meaning and to the stage as a constructed space that hosts the audience, Lupton argues that Shakespeare capitalizes on the forms of intellectual work that the space-time of the banquet enables by collating dramatic and domestic architectures. In the banquets orchestrated in *The Taming of the Shrew* and *Romeo and Juliet,* the theater becomes a spatial palimpsest in which culinary labor and theatrical labor are one, as the stagehands set forth the table. As these banquets variously reframe the stage as a humanist symposium and as a space for renewal, they also lead spectators to reflect on the meal as theater, calling attention to their overlapping aesthetic and communal dimensions. As "both dinner and drama manifest themselves as collaborative enterprises," they activate a "phenomenological machine, a frame for the production and disclosure of aesthetic effects achieved through choreographed acts . . . that include the routines of hospitality and conviviality" (214, 218). Lupton concludes by exploring how *The Winter's Tale* and *The Tempest* invoke the banquet's structures of removal and renewal in order to highlight the near-magical healing qualities of commensality, and the absences on which it depends.

Like the banquets Lupton examines, *Culinary Shakespeare* opens a space for reflection on the state of early modern food studies. Above all, the volume reveals the interdependency among different metaphorical and material aspects of food, and the discursive entanglements that challenge straightforward analytical methodologies. Several chapters, particularly those by Kanelos and Gerhardt, benefit from rich analysis of this interdependency. The challenges arising from such entanglements also register across the collection in chapters—among them Raber's, Lemon's, and Yates's contributions—that resonate with more than one approach. While these resonances highlight the range of work still to be done, *Culinary Shakespeare* suggests how such scholarship might proceed. Offering the possibility of what Robert Appelbaum has called a "hermeneutics of everything," the collection's strongest critical moments benefit from the full range of meanings that attach to the culinary.[1]

Note

1. Robert Appelbaum, *Aguecheek's Beef, Belch's Hiccup, and Other Gastronomic Interjections: Literature, Culture, and Food Among the Early Moderns* (Chicago: University of Chicago Press, 2006), 9.

Shakespeare Dwelling: Designs for the Theater of Life
By Julia Reinhard Lupton
Chicago: University of Chicago Press, 2018

Reviewer: Shankar Raman

Julia Lupton's most recent monograph could be said to follow the titular injunction of her own earlier book: to think with Shakespeare. In *Shakespeare Dwelling* she evocatively recreates environments or surrounds that resonate with the plays on the levels of both text and performance. She explores how entanglements of text and performance, the mutual shaping of the labor they express, open onto the "neighborhoods" in which we act, and their ecologies. Each of the main chapters is less an interpretation of the eponymous play around which it circles, than an inhabiting of internal domains called into being when we take the text as inspiration to think with, both backward and forward in time and space. In this spirit, each chapter moves alongside the text as it were, seeing it as a space of more-or-less structured possibilities that can be activated (or not). Suggesting an alternative to either presentism or historicism, Lupton opens the Shakespearean text to historical flows in non-reductive ways, expanding the kinds of histories we see operative in the plays.

The strengths and weaknesses of Lupton's approach are evident in the first of the Shakespeare-directed chapters, on *Romeo and Juliet*. Its opening sections seek to show how the play's theatrical "taskscapes"—a much-used term in this book, borrowed from the social anthropologist Tim Ingold, to denote an active environment consituted by a mutually interlocking ensemble of things to be done—"rehears[e] the continuity between stage management and household management" (58). She creates this continuity out of the double valence of the "two hours' traffic of our stage" (Prologue, 12), reading this stage business simultaneously extra-diegetically as mise-en-scène, and, diegetically, in relation to the reconfiguration or "rezoning" of stage space within the play's narrative. Thus, for example, the short exchange among the servingmen in 1.4 prior to the Capulet party does double duty, clearing the stage in order to "redistrict" the space from city street to domestic interior, as well as arranging for the party where Romeo and Juliet's first encounter will take place, removing a variety of objects in order to make hospitality possible. For Lupton, this represents a quintessential way in which the play opens "service economies and representational economies to each other" (57).

The remainder of the chapter locates a similar "rezoning" in how both poetic language and things in the play re-inscribe and re-describe spaces and bodies, projecting environments that express particular affective states, as for instance in creating "melancholic assemblages" (61, a term owed to Drew Daniel), which connect bodies to the physical spaces they occupy, in order to convey Romeo's solitary mood: "he hath hid himself among these trees / To be consorted with the humorous night" (2.1.31–32). According to Lupton, "the play's actions and images variously stretch and contract the real, symbolic, and psychic space among actors in order to create compelling opportunities for dramatic engagement" (42). A good example of this may be found in how the play recollects architectural spaces in Juliet's first scene to project a dynamic environment "that resonates in the time and space of performance" (73). The Nurse's use of the "ecology of the courtyard" to describe how she weaned Juliet is productively read here as a primal scene of the daughter's emergence into autonomy (her "birth into action out of the recesses of dwelling" (70)) as well as—via the memory of the earthquake that turns the sheltering dovecote into a threat— of the precarity of coming into one's own. Finally, Romeo's things —the torch in 1.4. and crowbar and lantern in 5.3—function as case studies for using tools to extend "bodily architecture" both physically and ideationally. His insistence on being the torchbearer when they crash the Capulet party opens up a spectatorial world of radiant light and its reflection by the ambient environment, even as it evokes a rich array of emblematic associations with love and fidelity. But the torch affords the further possibility of a different sort of clearing, a demarcation of Romeo's own space into which he can subsequently draw Juliet. This space in turn "draws on the affordances of the Catholic multimedia sensorium" (77) to position their relationship on the threshold, as it were, of the sacred and the profane, just as the clearing seems caught between the torch's radiance and the shadows that define the clearing's limits. By contrast, the crowbar marks a different sort of entry into Juliet's cryptic or funereal space, one that both turns the play towards its tragic conclusion and introduces an element of farce. Yet this destabilization, too, is reversed by the lantern, as Romeo reimagines Juliet's face, radiant, as source of light. In all these instances, the goal is to understand the actions, atmospheres and environments solicited through the language of architecture and of things (see 84).

I have purposely offered a rather extended description of this chapter to convey the difficulty of summarizing it, which stems in good measure from Lupton's tendency here and throughout to build up chapters associatively rather than to prioritize the line of argument. While this practice yields local gems—as with the nuanced reading of the scene in which the Nurse recounts the weaning of Juliet—it equally often feels digressive or meandering. There is no doubt something deeply salutary in thinking about the Shakespearean stage as "a theater of affordances," namely, "an environmental and phenomenological theatre, a space in which things, persons, settings, and forms of life are solicited to appear in the intricacy and volatility of their interdependence" (42). But, as even this sentence suggests, the countervailing tendency is aggregation and the associative sliding from topic to topic—leading, in its worst form, to a certain arbitrariness with regard to what finds its way into each chapter.

Unfortunately, this predilection seems especially evident in the book's introduction, "Entries into Dwelling," where Lupton glides from one cluster of ideas to another, without dwelling on their interrelationships. The introduction emphasizes three conceptual sources upon which Lupton relies: Heidegger's later philosophy, which focuses on built spaces and things; Hannah Arendt's philosophy of action in *The Human Condition;* and theories of "affordances," originating in the work of ecological psychologist James J. Gibson and increasingly absorbed into modern design theory. But their development draws in so many other theoretical positions putatively underpinning Lupton's project that I find myself unable to develop an adequate account of how these are meant to relate to one another. Lost in the welter of names and associations are conceptual distinctions. To give just one example: it is certainly true that Arendt sees objects as bearers of durability, lending "the human artifice stability and solidity without which it could not be relied upon to house the unstable and mortal creature which is man" (*The Human Condition,* 137; cited on 175). Arguably, however, Arendt's ethos and in particular her insistence on natality as a uniquely human capacity—does not dwell peacefully alongside the claims of "object-oriented" thinkers, such as Graham Harman or Bruno Latour, who are among those cited as underpinning the postsecular and posthumanist approach Lupton espouses. In a sense, the manner of proceeding in this chapter echoes Lupton's sense that ecological relationships amongst systems, environments, objects, and people ought to be considered as openings, as possibilities for action and reaction, producing syncretic landscapes rather than schismatic ones (as she later argues in her chapters on the romances). But I cannot help feel that there is something a little unconvincing, and occasionally even fallacious, in constructing one's critical discourse in the image of what one hopes to reveal.

I slide over the chapter on *Macbeth,* which is primarily concerned with how the protagonist's murder of sleep "assaults the conditions of dwelling as such, disrupting commensality and assaulting shelter itself" (85). Of importance in Lupton's reading is, I think, her suggestion that the assertions of the world's reality, which flash up in the wake of the murder—e.g., as with "Will all great Neptune's ocean wash this blood / Clean from my hand" (2.2.56–60)—are not so much projections of human actions, choices, or moods as effects occurring in concert with them. What emerges is an idea of "tragic dwelling," wherein the consequences of one's actions are "reencounter[ed] . . . as environmental disturbances that trumpet the reality of the forms of personhood and the varieties of creatureliness disavowed" (109) by those deeds. In short, the play's atmosphere is not a projection by the experiencing subject of its internal states, but a coming face-to-face with the consequences of its actions in features of the setting or location (see 116).

This sense of tragic dwelling sets up the three concluding chapters, each dedicated to one of Shakespeare's romances. These form a relatively coherent unit, and are thematically linked by their exploration of the possibility and limits of reparation after grievous damage to the ties binding individuals to their social environments. If in the tragedies an "accelerated causality" (109) leads to the unravelling of landscape and self, Shakespeare's romances reverse the movement, opening characters to new possibilities in their surroundings. This may seem a familiar claim about the romances, but how one reaches such a conclusion matters. In Lupton's case, the overarching concern is theological, and her individual readings are shaped, to lesser or greater degree, by a desire to identify in these plays a Christian messianism aimed at irenic accommodation rather than forcible takeover. Thus, Shakespeare's deployment of Christianity in these plays does not so much negate or reject either its Judaic heritage or schismatic alternatives within Christianity, as preserve these in a way that promises, opens onto the hope signified by the messiah.

The first of the romance chapters, on grace and place in *Pericles,* pursues the play's engagement with the Judaic and Christian discourses of messianism through the twinned figures of Jonah and Paul, whose spatial and theological itineraries the play echoes. Lupton traces a geographical arc that, beginning with Pericles's flight from Antioch, follows him to his partial redemption in Pentapolis through the graces of Thaisa; continues with his daughter Marina's "leafy bower" in Mytilene; and concludes at Diana's temple in Ephesus, where father and daughter are reunited with the lost Thaisa. This spatial movement embeds in effect a theological one, encapsulating what Lupton calls a "dissolved messianism," indicating by this term "a redemptive or reparative potentiality that resides in human relationships and the promises of locales" (118). Thus, *Pericles* enacts a "phenomenology of spatial experiences" by means of which "transcendence becomes world" (118), the metaphysical yearning for redemption finding its partial realization in the fragile forms of community and action that sustain and shelter the self. The scene of the fishermen mending nets, following Pericles's surviving the shipwreck, becomes an allegory of sorts for the networking, the building of new associations and communities that the play will trace: from the initial liaison with Thaisa that marks Pericles's rebirth into sociality and selfhood; through Marina's creation of a communal space of refuge and solace, her "messianic house of hope" (141); to the re-establishment of the family in multi-ethnic and multi-religious Ephesus. At this final location, Thaisa's labors in Diana's temple evoke the promise of a pluralist, harmonious accommodation that might overcome the schisms of religion, dissolving "tensions between Catholic and Protestant, Jewish and Christian, and Judeo-Christian and Greco-Roman traditions." This conclusion of *Pericles* expresses an impulse that Lupton sees as underlying all the romances, which build on multiple religious traditions but read these "syncretically rather than schismatically" (124), yearning for a world in which "the language of faith . . . unite[s] rather than divide[s] Christians" (126, citing Thomas Betteridge).

While more Christianity-inflected, a similar syncretism, drawing together Judaic, Christian and humanist traditions, is on view in *Cymbeline* as well, where Lupton senses that Hebraic undercurrents have been subsumed into the play's complex engagement with the messianic topos of the Nativity. As others have recognised, *Cymbeline*'s time straddles that of the messiah's birth, and yet the play seems conspicuously to avoid any direct reference to that momentous event. Lupton's ingenious reading locates in the play a "displaced nativity" that indicates both its absence (as an event not bound to single time, place, or theological tradition) and its reimagined presence in the shape of Hannah Arendt's concept of natality, which is to say, the radical contingency and possibility for future action introduced into the world by the birth of any individual. For Arendt as for Lupton here, the Nativity can be understood as a *figura,* in Auerbach's sense, for natality: that is, an event that retains its historical character, even as it receives its true meaning, as it were, in natality, in every new beginning. The proximate figuration for natality in Shakespeare's play is Innogen, whose autopoesis or self-birthing the play follows, beginning with her electing Posthumus as husband, the courageous act through which she separates herself from her household, to suffer exile from where she dwells.

While always rich and suggestive, in this chapter, too, the readings are not always fully convincing. One such instance may be found in the somewhat overwrought parallel, based on the motif of a suspended sacrifice, that Lupton identifies between the action in *Cymbeline*'s 3.4, on the one hand, and the story of the *Akedah,* or the binding, on the other, with Innogen as Isaac, Pisanio in Abraham's place, and the bloody cloth for the ram in the thicket. The homology motivates her interpretation of the spousal restoration of faith at the play's end as a new binding or covenant that brings together Judaic and Christian traditions, honoring "courage as well as suffering, doubt and anger as well as love and trust, and Isaac unbound as well as Christ crucified" (169). Perhaps—but only if one brackets the differences between Pisanio and Abraham, most notably the former's refusal to do his "master's bidding," or the role of contingency in suspending the sacrifice (the doctor having substituted a sleeping draught for the Queen's poison that Pisanio unwittingly gives her to overcome sickness on sea or land).

And indeed the discussion of the *Akedah* does seem a bit of a detour from the remainder of the chapter, which seeks at some length to establish in Innogen's exile from the sheltered dwelling of the court and her subsequent career a courageous re-invention of herself, an act of re-birthing. Lupton relies in these sections on Arendt's idea, cited earlier, that the durability of material objects counters the fragility of human existence, lending it support and stability. The furnishings in Innogen's bedroom are from this point of view "techniques of self-fashioning" (171) that have to be abandoned (along with the self that dwelled amongst them) when Giacomo's ploy forces her "exit from the thickness of things, and . . . into a new kind of environmental education" (182). Abandoning her possessions, but bringing her "routines of living" (193) with her, Innogen proves resilient, re-making herself repeatedly through impromptu forms of dwelling in the Welsh countryside. While interesting in themselves, the extended discussion in these sections of the dynamic role of *furnitura* in Innogen's self-making nonetheless seems rather far removed from the earlier disclosures of the play's Judaic heritage. Concluding the chapter, Lupton asserts that her *Cymbeline* "is messianic (with a small *m*) and catholic (with a small *c*), in the sense that its reach is as vast as its sources and emotional palettes are varied" (194). Even as this sentence forces together Lupton's theological and environmental investments, its final clause betrays, I think, the difficulty the chapter has in holding its diverse material together.

The book's concluding meditation, on *The Winter's Tale,* is both the shortest and least developed. It falls into two halves, whose connection could, I feel, be more firmly established, made more organic. The first half offers an often fascinating discussion of the place and emergence of the dessert in early modern Europe, showing how this final course came into its own, demarcating "a space-time for digestion in its more reflective and ruminative senses" (199). Central here is the deepening association of the dessert course with "acts of retreat" (204) that enable reflection upon as well as rebuild the ethos and the community celebrated upon the occasion of the meal. This overview is followed by a brief foray into Shakespeare's play via the young shepherd's shopping list of ingredients for Perdita's planned desert. Remarkably, Lupton manages to specify this dessert, first identifying it as "whitpot," a fruit and dairy pudding associated with Pentecost, and then re-inscribing this fusion as a "messianic gathering of flavors and faiths": the pudding "melds Jewish, Christian . . . urbanites" (216)." This sense of commensality is then transferred by Lupton into the play's final scene, where, despite its courtly setting, the "emphasis on the rhythm of withdrawal keeps in play the existential function of clearing that gives dessert its dramatic character as well as its intimacy" (217). What justifies such a transference is, of course, Leontes's unforgettable response to touching the statue: "Oh, she's warm! / If this be magic, let it be an art / Lawful as eating" (5.3.109–11). The reconciliation of nature, law and art in these lines stands for Lupton as an emblem of the play as a whole, "which does not typologically replace the Old Testament with the New so much as tap their shared yearning for a messianic art 'lawful as eating' " (218). And, in a final, and somewhat unexpected turn, this desire for reconciliation becomes for Lupton an apt metaphor to defend the humanities in an instrumental world increasingly hostile to its claims: the humanities as dessert, considered not as superfluous luxury but as a mode of clearing that enables reflection and rumination. Her epilogue, "Fight Call," further pursues this possibility of defending the humanities' function in terms not of utility but as the space for self-renewal in the theater of life.

As I hope to have shown, Lupton's is a rich and wide-ranging book, often nuanced in its readings and often insightful in cathecting the Shakespearean text through new environments—as with the unexpected connection between desserts and *The Winter's Tale*'s pastoral scenes. However, it must also be said that far too often the writing makes the going heavier than it needs to be. In part, *Shakepeare Dwelling* seems too much a prisoner of its terminology. Take, for example, Lupton's use of the technical term, affordances. Early on, the word usefully reminds us that the objects on stage and page are not simply there but make available or invite opportunities for action in an environment. However, after a while repetition turns the word into stylistic tic, and encountering it simply slows the reader's passage through a sentence. Or, to pick another bone, assertions perfectly clear on their own are shuttled through terminological by-lanes in a manner that ends up making them feel less convincing. Thus, for example, Juliet's first scene is described as one that "concerns the origins, limits and spatial disposition of intimacy" (65), a plausible abstraction that needs only a little concreteness from the scene to be established firmly. And this Lupton indeed provides, but only after a page-long detour which first recalls Edward T. Hall's *The Hidden Dimension* to rename this spatial disposition "proxemics"; and then to suggest that proxemics itself is a concept cousin to the much used "affordances"; in order to give us a brief account of how proxemics has entered into the conceptual arsenal of architects, interior designers and theatre studies. What such a digression sacrifices—with very little illumination in return—is precisely the readerly intimacy with the text, which Lupton then strives to re-discover. In instances like these, excision or a judicious relegation to footnotes would have helped the book substantially. And neither is clarity helped by the preference for rarely used words—such as "intrication" (119, 144)—or obscure ones—e.g., "sexuation"on 123, which I suspect to be the translation of a Lacanian neologism that has not as yet left a trace in English dictionaries—when more everyday alternatives would in my estimation do just as well. This is unfortunate, since, for this reader at least, the stylistic exposition too frequently mitigates the impact of this intelligent and thought-provoking book.

Believing in Shakespeare: Studies in Longing
By Claire McEachern
Cambridge: Cambridge University Press, 2018

Reviewer: Heather Hirschfeld

It may be counter-intuitive to begin at the end of a book that proposes to substitute a hermeneutics of suspense for a hermeneutics of suspicion. But the Epilogue of *Believing in Shakespeare: Studies in Longing* offers such a precise articulation of Claire McEachern's project and its stakes that it deserves the lede. The book, as she explains, charts the "mechanics and affects and origins of Reformation believing"—particularly Protestant doctrines of predestination—as constitutive of Shakespeare's formal techniques and thus his "manufacturing of illusion[s]." And his believable, cherished illusions sustain audiences today because they elicit a kind of care, both personal and political, that is "not a simulacrum of the connections we form with 'real' people; it is their original" (297).

The historical and analytical scaffolding for this claim, with its earnest appeal in a time of increased challenges to the relevance of the humanities, represents a persuasive, original contribution to contemporary discussions about Shakespeare and religion. McEachern herself provides a comprehensive review of earlier as well as more recent scholarship (14–18) before turning to her own account, a sustained argument that the doctrinal changes of the Reformation influenced the production and consumption of age-old dramaturgic principles. Her proposal is an elegant instance of contextualized formalism: Protestant soteriology, however variegated, instructed its followers in forms of belief and practices of piety that incorporated feelings of doubt as potentially positive signs of salvation, and these forms and practices are developed and deployed in Shakespeare's treatment of characters, plot design, dramatic irony and *anagnorisis.* These treatments, in turn, invite the audience to believe in and long for them.

In its discussion of Shakespeare's absorption of distinctly Calvinist theological premises into his plays, the proposal is also daring. The trend in much recent scholarship on Shakespeare and religion has been either to emphasize the playwright's lingering attachments to Catholic theology and the pietistic or festive medieval practices associated with it, or to analyze his challenges to the spiritual losses or anxieties that follow on Reformed positions on predestination, the Eucharist, or confession. Such work is consistent with other historical or literary studies that focus on the continuities in both doctrine and practice across a Reformation divide. But McEachern grounds her argument on the differences, rather than the continuities, between Reformed theologies of salvation and those of medieval or post-Tridentine Catholicism. She is careful, of course, to admit the persistence of "confessional commonalities," but her interest is "less [in] doctrinal overlap than the way in which a shared awareness of the political and personal stakes of the changes underway in the Reformation conditioned all species of contemporary Christianity" (19). And those changes were nowhere as salient as in doctrines of salvation. Calvinist predestination, then, and the ways in which it motivated spiritual thought and practices designed to gauge the status of one's soul, are thus at the core of the book. These in turn, she argues, influenced the "dramaturgical technologies" of Shakespeare's plays in ways that condition our relationships to them today (20).

The connection hinges on the experience of believing: believing in election, and believing in plays. And this kind of belief includes doubt. The book's first two deeply researched chapters establish the grounds of this premise, with a thorough discussion of the "English absorption of the Calvinist imperative to self-knowledge" prompted by the conviction that one's salvific status is always already determined and known by God (7). While earlier scholars such as John Stachniewski understood this theory as a source first of doubt and then of anxiety and desperation ("the doctrine of reprobation made for despair"), McEachern offers a more optimistic interpretation, one that makes doubt—and all the emotions and sensations attendant upon it—proof or assurance of one's redemption.[1] English Calvinism, especially in the experimental forms promulgated by theologians such as William Perkins and Henry Smith, "imagined for itself" a "new and better believing . . . in which doubt did not erode belief but worked to thicken and substantiate it in ways that were both affectively positive and empirically positive" (23). Invoking Francis Bacon, whose empiricism did not evacuate the role in the world of the divine, she suggests that the inclusion of skepticism in the pursuit of knowledge about the predetermined fate of the soul generates an "intense imaginative commitment" to the self and to others, including staged others (36). As McEachern explains, experimentalism and Shakespeare's plays were "fellow responses to the disconcerting prospect posed by predestination, namely that God knows something about us that we may hope to discover." Even more crucial, the plays "curate our knowledge" to "engage our emotional involvement: how we feel implicated in, touched, or moved by the plights of characters" (82). One of McEachern's most compelling, as well as salutary, claims here is that this engagement does not come in the form of identification, the customary model for our attachment to the plays. Rather, as the rest of the book elaborates, it comes in the form of charity or *caritas,* a feeling *for* or *toward* the character that is "not the experience of recognizing ourselves in a character but the longing to be recognized by one" (90).

From this foundation McEachern launches two robust chapters that explore Reformation effects on dramatic recognition and irony. Chapter 3 suggests that in a world shaped by Calvinist predestination, dramatic irony does not distance the audience, secure in its superior knowledge, from the characters but makes them feel for or involved with them in acute ways. The same kind of feeling informs scenes of recognition, in which the characters' knowledge meets up with ours so that it "feels to us *like we have been recognized. In a word, elect*" (100). Prior to this moment, we have been kept in a position of uncertainty, a distinctly Protestant "literary suspense" which, McEachern claims, "Calvin and Shakespeare, between them, invented . . . from our wanting to be known" (105). Here McEachern makes her confessional distinctions clear, recruiting Shakespeare to the Protestant side: "Catholic salvation is thus what we might call the more cliffhangerish" while "the suspense of Protestantism resides instead in the work of discovery, which is a kind of hide-and-seek between divine knowledge and human inquiry" (106, 107). Her test cases for these models are four *Oedipus* plays, since "resemblances between Oedipus's fate and Christian predestination were certainly not lost on Reformation writers" (118). She compares the dramas of Sophocles and Seneca, against which she then contrasts two Tudor versions, Alexander Neville's translation (1563) and a manuscript from a grammar school production thought to date from the 1580s (121). The Tudor plays, she suggests, are more Sophoclean than Senecan, distancing us from the protagonist and his plight at the famous moment of recognition. They thus offer a kind of anti-example for a range of Shakespearean characters. None of them are Oedipus himself, but they grapple with the question of their salvation in ways that, McEachern argues, solicit our charity in accordance with the "sense the drama conjures of events hanging in the balance" (124).

Chapter 4 picks up these questions of asymmetrical knowledge between audience and characters in terms of two generically opposed cuckold plays, *Much Ado About Nothing* and *Othello.* As McEachern notes, scholars have long recognized that for Shakespeare's male characters the threat of female infidelity is linked to cosmic crises of faith in the self and the universe. She even sketches a religious allegory of this dilemma, according to which Shakespeare's concerns, and Elizabethan "horn humor" more generally, "could be said to express the unnerving soteriological condition of being at a disadvantage concerning knowledge. . . . What better expression of this unruly and alienated inwardness—of not possessing what most ought to be one's own—might there be than an otherwise self-possessed man undone by the question of whether an enigmatic subaltern loves him" (139). But McEachern's interest is less in the male characters' inward suffering from disbelief in their beloved than in the audience's suffering from an imbalance of knowledge, the fact that we know the beloved is faithful. "Our stake in the play lies not in doubting female fidelity along with the hero but in wondering whether, how, and when our hero will come to know what we do: that he has erred" (142). Her argument includes an exciting account of the iconography of the cuckold's horn (with reference to both Acteon and Moses) and the kinds of confession-driven humor it invited, as well as a reflection on the generic instability of the two plays, so that the ending of *Othello* can feel "triumphant" while a significant portion of *Much Ado* can "hover near tragedy" (156).

But the heart of the chapter is its discussion of the select moment from each of the plays that invites our movement toward the stage in a surge of pity or charity. For *Much Ado,* that moment is Beatrice's demand of Benedick that he "kill Claudio," since we feel with her the pressure of the knowledge, rendered inefficacious, of Hero's chastity. Perhaps more surprisingly, for *Othello* McEachern locates that moment in Emilia's revelation that she gave Iago the handkerchief. Throughout the play, she explains, we have been dogged by our sense of "the limited nature of our witnessing power" (169) and burdened by the knowledge not only that Desdemona is chaste but that "Othello is bent on murder" (172). So, whether or not we are already familiar with the play or its Italian source, we remain invested in its outcome—not the narrative inevitability of Desdemona's death but rather "in seeing Othello disabused. . . . we want him to see how wrong he was, which is only possible if he kills her" (179). Thus our point of maximum entry to the play is Emilia in her final protestations, when she speaks to and against both Iago and Othello in ways that "make our version of the story stick" (180).

The final three chapters of the book tackle the categories of character, plot, and place, and the ways in which Shakespeare orients them based on doubt-produced believing. The excellent premise of chapter 5, on character, is to "nudge discussion of belief in Shakespeare away from verisimilitude," focusing instead on his characters' strangeness or incongruities in order to discover "what it is about character that *requires caritas* of us" (189). The test case for McEachern is *Richard II,* although she approaches the play only after an extended consideration of the ways in which both tetralogies cultivate the audience's knowledge. The *Henry VI* plays and *Richard III,* she explains, "are formally designed to produce the pleasure of recognition," while the second tetralogy "assumes, cultivates, compounds, and prolongs our ignorance" (195, 202). Her discussion of the rhythms of *Richard II* is bracing: in the opening act, the King is mysterious, opaque, beyond our ken; by act 3, he has to catch up to what we already know, Bolingbroke's return. We are repelled, she suggests, by his initial arbitrariness and then by his histrionic self-pity. But by act 4 Shakespeare has fashioned, on the model of Christ on the cross, "a king whose loss we mourn" (213). His exclamation in the deposition scene of 4.1, that "Fiend, thou torments me ere I come to hell," is the moment of contact, as "we watch a monarch that we seem to accompany in real time, as if we were moving into an unknown future with him, whom we know not less than, or more than, but with" (221). And this tense experience, she emphasizes, is the result of Protestant experimentalism: "Much as a soul might keep the possibility of salvation in play by means of self-inflicted doubts, the uncertainty surrounding the moment of deposition is what makes us feel something is at stake in this play, every time as if for the first time" (221).

The two chapters on plot and place are less effective than the one on character. Chapter 6 surveys critical suspicion of seemingly artificial plots, concluding that in fact such doubt, in a predestinarian epistemology, contributes to, rather than distracts from, a play's believability. It is an auspicious opening. But it is difficult to separate these concerns from those of character, so when McEachern turns to a reading of *King Lear,* her focus is inevitably on the protagonist, on Lear as the cause of the destruction he wished to avoid. The plot's terrifying ending comes to seem not "impersonal, bespeaking a random or even cosmic indifference to the person it befalls," but rather the consequence of the protagonist himself (236). This is a classic definition of tragedy and the tragic hero, and it seems impervious to the soteriological influence that McEachern elsewhere tracks with such acumen. Indeed, this chapter, like the following one, loses its moorings in Calvinist belief, so that McEachern is thrown back onto arguments from performance rather than audience experience. She admits rather startlingly that her "reflections may be of no use to even a seasoned observer of *King Lear* while the scene is in train. However. they are the kinds of things actors must ponder in order to find a place from which to inflect Shakespeare's language" (251). This is not to discount the actor's concerns; it is to notice that something has gone awry when the author herself, who has not considered the player's perspective for some 250 pages, suddenly invokes it to make sense of her account of the first scene and Lear's various possible motives for the division of the kingdom. Her answer to this perennial question, designed to establish the protagonist as a "particular and exceptional creature in whose loss the world loses something rare and irreplaceable," is the counter-intuitive proposition that Lear might actually understand himself, his family, and the demands of sovereignty all too well rather than, as his daughters say, "slenderly" (269). McEachern thus suggests that the curses Lear gives his daughter or his declamations on the heath reflect not the see-saw ravings and epiphanies of a shocked, aging man but the insights of a wise, able king who "speaks with the fury of one wishing others could just *see* what he has always seen" (271). Such a reading involves some interpretive gymnastics, but the analysis of Cordelia's death it yields is deeply moving: McEachern treats it as "the unbelievable but wholly believable thing, the event [Lear] cannot credit has come to pass even though he always knew it was not just possible but maybe even an inevitable outcome of his very own actions" (273).

The final, brief chapter is about place, or, more accurately, place as the setting for the carefully timed encounters of the characters we care about. Protestant soteriology here is less a structuring influence than an evidentiary standard that allows for the coincidences of romance—or the programmatic machinations of an autocratic magician. McEachern's reading of the *The Tempest* traces Prospero's efforts to keep characters separated from one another until he orchestrates the ending—the marriage of his daughter, the punishment and forgiveness of his enemies, the drowning of his books—he has promised by the end of day. Prospero has given himself a deadline, McEachern reminds us, in order to create a "sense of occasion," but it is also a dramaturgic ploy that asks us to inhabit Prospero's perspective, "to see as a god might see" (295). And that perspective, like Prospero himself—whether we take him for a benign creator or a malevolent imperialist—is less interesting than the human one. That's why, McEachern says, Prospero breaks his staff, because "the view from ground level—our view—is the sight to which belief belongs" (296).

This is a fitting, moving end to a deeply researched book that folds into its study of Shakespeare and belief a range of concerns central to contemporary scholarship—epistemology, cognition, affect—while attending to principles of dramatic form and their appeal to audiences. Also embedded here is McEachern's engagement with questions of secularization, and she earns her conviction that the perceived modernity or secularity of Shakespeare's plays is the result of their commitment to Reformed principles of belief.

But there are some weaknesses—unavoidable in a book that runs to nearly 300 pages. Indeed, the length itself is a dilemma, one that McEachern refers to explicitly, and one that could have been solved, at least partially, with more scrupulous editing. There was no need, for instance, to query all of Lear's possible reasons for dividing his kingdom, just as there was no need to query all of Prospero's reasons for imposing upon himself a deadline: "Is it because he needs to keep his own desire to punish his enemies within a self-ordained limit? Will a brisk pace help with bewildering them into a state of tractability? Is he attempting to distract himself from the pain of and resistance to losing his own child or to disguise the true nature of his project from himself—or her? Is it so as not to procrastinate the imminent abdication of his powers? Are short good-byes easier than long ones? Is he tired? Are his elves restless?" (295).

The tone at the end of this list, a kind of glib good humor, is also a problem. It can make McEachern's summaries of contemporary criticism seem dismissive (as when she explains that "much of the scholarship of recent generations has in fact sought to determine what we can assume about what sorts of cultural literacy Tudor-Stuart audiences implicitly brought to their viewing experience," and then shrugs it off with the observation that it endows "Joe Elizabethan with an encyclopedic command of reference and resonance" [194]). It also seems incongruous as well as unnecessary during discussions of theology (as when she explains that Protestant experimentalism was "extremely practical, anchoring the evidence for salvation in physiological signs . . . . These are considered to be involuntary and hence presumably (in advance of method acting) incapable of fabrication" [50]).

But of greater concern is the assumption of the uniformity and transhistoricity of the "we" and "our" that dominate the book's discussions of audience response. McEachern's first premise is that Shakespeare's plays participated in the structures of belief presented by Reformed doctrines of predestination, and that their use of standard dramaturgic principles such as irony or recognition both rehearsed these structures and exploited their capacity to make audiences believe and care for the characters and situations they saw. Her second premise—which suffuses the book in its sustained discussions of how Shakespeare directs "our experience" or determines what "we know" in relation to the characters—is that the plays operate in the same way today, for contemporary audiences. Shakespeare's dramaturgic techniques, she maintains, precisely because of their theological attachments, continue to provoke belief, even for audiences which are, at least in considerable part, far removed from the injunctions of Calvinist experimentalism. I am not unsympathetic to claims on behalf of the power of Shakespearean dramaturgy and language, or to the possibility that plays rooted in a particular context can have maximal impact in a later one. Shakespeare's plays, that is, are both for an age and for all time. But it is difficult to avoid the feeling that the "believing in Shakespeare" that McEachern imagines for "us" unavoidably depends upon our becoming experimentalist Protestants in the process, whether Shakespeare intended to indoctrinate us or not. McEachern has taken too little care of this in what is otherwise a learned, methodologically expansive, and acutely observed book.

Note

1. John Stachniewski, *The Persecutory Imagination: English Puritanism and the Literature of Religious Despair* (Oxford: Clarendon Press, 1991), 25.

Antipodal Shakespeare: Remembering and Forgetting in Britain, Australia and New Zealand, 1916–2016
By Gordon McMullan and Philip Mead, with Ailsa Grant Ferguson, Kate Flaherty, and Mark Houlahan
London and New York: Bloomsbury Arden Shakespeare, 2018

Reviewer: Laurie Johnson

Timeliness is a difficult goal to achieve in academic publishing, although it is one that would seem to rarely apply in Shakespeare studies, where the mantra of our subject's timelessness usually inures scholars against some of the harsh realities of the publishing marketplace. An obvious exception to this is publishing books that may be made marketable on the basis of their ability to capitalize on one of the occasional milestones in commemoration of the life and death of Shakespeare. *Antipodal Shakespeare* appears to set itself up as a book that will consider not just one, but two, such milestones, as it announces its interest in commemoration across the century spanning from the tercentenary celebrations of 1916 to the quatercentenary or worldwide "Shakespeare 400" celebrations of 2016. Yet readers expecting that the book is banking on its timeliness in relation to the Shakespeare 400 milestone will be disappointed. The introduction does include some discussion of 2016, but the editors Gordon McMullan and Philip Mead answer the question of how the Quatercentenary remembrance compared with the events of a century earlier by conceding: "It is, in many ways, too soon to say" (17). With the book being finished in February 2017, the editors claim the events of 2016 are still "too close . . . for any adequate perspective" (17). The book had, of course, been some time in the making: it had its origins in an Australia Research Council Discovery project "Monumental Shakespeares: a transcultural investigation of commemoration in twentieth-century England and Australia" (2010 to 2012). It is thus hard to imagine why, when the book was conceived, or when the publishing contract for a 2018 release was secured, or during 2016 as the book was in preparation, neither editors nor publisher recognized that a contributor might be tasked with offering the adequate perspective on 2016 that the book's title would seem to demand.

Despite being curiously untimely, *Antipodal Shakespeare* does reward the reader prepared to join with the contributors in forgetting 2016 in order to better remember a more distant past. The book posits an "antipodal" framework to focus on the interdependent relationship of local interests in British and Australasian societies, reminding us that there would have been no imperial project constituting Britain's place in the world without its antipodean outposts. This antipodal framework is well fitted to the study of the Tercentenary commemorations of 1916, coinciding as they did with the Great War in which the ANZAC legend was formed.

McMullan and Mead begin their introduction by reminding readers that in the Tercentenary year, Australian and New Zealand soldiers serving in the European circuit marked April 25 as the first

ANZAC day in memory of the beginning of the ill-fated Gallipoli campaign on that date a year earlier. The editors compare two very different crowds that poured into London's Waterloo Station on that day, "each of which had that afternoon attended commemorative events of national and cultural significance, one responding to the death of a playwright three hundred years earlier, the other to a military debacle that had taken place only twelve months previously" (2). While the two crowds they describe might seem to be only coincidentally in the same location, their presence becomes emblematic of numerous points of convergence that the following chapters are intended to trace. *Antipodal Shakespeare* is thus "a relatively brief and focused book, deliberately so" (9), built around "presenting a specific case study, one that connects Shakespeare, war, commemoration, monumentalization, myth-making and nationhood at a precise historical moment, and that follows some of the outworkings of that moment across the past century" (8).

For the most part, the book succeeds in this ambition, as the chronological reach of the five chapters differs only by virtue of what each contributor considers to be the "outworkings" of that precise historical moment. McMullan's opening chapter may not be so evidently invested in the "antipodal" framework of the collection, but it provides a very clear statement of how the Tercentenary "moment" serves to highlight the themes of Shakespeare commemoration, war, and nationhood. He studies the forgotten role played by Israel Gollancz in Tercentenary planning, including the plan to relocate the epicenter of Shakespeare commemoration from Stratford-upon-Avon to London. As back story, McMullan notes the "ongoing, unresolved struggle" between these two locations "for ownership of the Shakespeare industry" (32) had been waged ever since Stratford's two-week festival dominated the 1864 Tercentenary of Shakespeare's birth. Gollancz's role in the events of 1916 is shown to have played a major part also in shaping the future of the institutions of Shakespeare commemoration—without Gollancz, he argues, "the histories of the National Theatre, the Royal Shakespeare Company, and even Shakespeare's Globe would have been very different" (32). McMullan argues that the histories of such institutions tend to forget Gollancz in particular and the 1916 events in general because of the intervention of the war, which forestalled Gollancz's plans to build a Shakespeare Memorial National Theatre. Lacking the funds and resources for such a grand venture during wartime, Gollancz instead threw his support behind the construction of the Shakespeare Hut, erected to provide some comfort and a little culture for the soldiers so far away from their homes throughout the Empire. In the grandiose scheme from which the RSC and other such institutions are usually seen to have sprung, the "Hut" would never normally rate a mention.

Only at the end of McMullan's chapter does the antipodal framework make an appearance, in what is perhaps an unnecessary afterthought attempting to position his argument as a natural fit with the broader theme of the collection. At this moment, the singular personal pronoun that had accompanied McMullan's claims throughout is replaced in the final instance by the plural, when he concludes that Gollancz's project "may have been a national one, yet it was always already, we suggest, antipodal—that is, by 1916 Shakespeare had long been the poet not only of nation but also of empire" (60). Such retrofitting of chapter content to book theme seems a little too arbitrary, and in this instance I suggest the chapter had already done a fine job at setting the scene for what follows in the collection. In describing the background to the Shakespeare Hut, McMullan provides valuable context on which the chapters by Ailsa Grant Ferguson and Mark Houlahan build explicitly, and in elaborating in detail on some of the key local ambitions, plans, and disputes behind the Tercentenary commemorations in Britain, the chapter establishes the personal and institutional politics defining one pole of the antipodal relationship, to which the chapters by Kate Flaherty and Philip Mead provide the necessary counterpoint.

The chapters by Ferguson and Houlahan represent, to my mind at least, the highlights of the collection, with their work (and McMullan's) on the Shakespeare Hut arguably providing enough data on which to build an entire book. This alone would have been a commendable project of recovery given that these chapters demonstrate the value of remembering the site. Contrary to the speed with which it was erased from the institutional memory of ANZAC experience and of Shakespeare commemoration, Ferguson provides the broader background story of the creation of the Shakespeare Hut and explains the way it operated as recreation house and performance space that managed to align Shakespeare "for both the wider British public and for its Anzac users, much more with the 'fighting man', its user (son), and the 'caring woman', its volunteer (mother and sister), than with the government or commanding officer (father)" (102). The site represented a strong link to homeland for soldiers serving on foreign soil rather than a site that only encapsulated either imperial or military authority. Houlahan's chapter offers a fascinating insight into the recollections of the Shakespeare Hut by New Zealand servicemen who had been in London during their tours of duty from 1916 to 1919, strengthened in no small part by his opening account of his maternal grandfather's own experiences of service in the war. This account helps to reinforce the tyranny of distance that the European conflict presented to soldiers from the southern hemisphere.

Houlahan's chapter offers a brief "Coda" to bring readers back to the Shakespeare 400 year by discussing the Pop-up Globe that was erected in Auckland from February to May 2016 (140–43). In terms of the antipodal framework of the book, the "Coda" is a valuable addition but must have been a very late one, so late that the index fails to include it in the references to "antipodal" even though it explicitly offers an analysis of the New Zealand productions using the Pop-up Globe as "antipodal Shakespeares" (142) that continue to exist ephemerally and then be forgotten just as quickly. Yet as a coda to Houlahan's fascinating reading of soldiers' experiences and memories of the Shakespeare Hut, I fear the late intrusion of the discussion of the Pop-up Globe risks repeating the problem he had already diagnosed, moving our eyes away from the past just as the project of recovery appeared to have our gaze transfixed on its rich but fading textures. It is a tension felt throughout the collection, and not one I suspect that could or should be easily overcome.

Apart from the shift in that "Coda" to a temporary structure in New Zealand, Mead's and Flaherty's chapters perform the bulk of the work in shifting the geographical focus to acts of commemoration in the southern hemisphere. Mead's chapter deals with the Shakespeare monument first touted by the President of the New South Wales Shakespeare Society, Henry Gullett, in 1909 but not unveiled until 1926. As with the British Tercentenary plans, the war was a significant obstacle to the monument's being finished earlier. This chapter provides a neat counterpoint to McMullan's analysis of those British plans, since the same debate about whether to focus commemorations on a theater or a monument was played out on both sides of the planet. While London had opted to build a national theater instead of erecting a statue for the Tercentenary of 1916, Sydney would opt for a monument, although, as Mead argues, the city settled on this option once the war prevented many other plans from being realized. A highlight of this chapter, for me, is the realization that the story of the monument and of its relocation to Shakespeare Place provide the back story to one of the more intriguing elements of Jeffrey Smart's famous painting of the Cahill Expressway, 1962: the built environment in this image seems all but deserted save for the menacing presence of one of the "fat men" of Australian social history, but the monument haunts the background of the image, turned away from the viewer as a stark parable "of the ruins of memory and the renovation of monumental history" (83).

Flaherty's chapter looks at how Australians have repeatedly reworked that most militaristic of Shakespeare's plays, *Henry V*, to renegotiate their antipodal relationship with Britain and its cultural heritage. The chapter provides a dizzying local performance history of the play from the Sydney Shakespeare Festival of 1916 to the program of the Bell Shakespeare Company in the twenty-first century. It is thus also—Houlahan's "Coda" on 2016 notwithstanding—the most far reaching of the chapters in terms of how it traces the "outworkings" of the historical moment of 1916; yet I suggest its focus on a single play makes this chapter the least able to maintain its connection to that precise historical moment on which the collection purports to fix its gaze. Flaherty devotes the opening section to describing the work of Gullett ahead of the Tercentenary, thereby situating the Sydney Shakespeare Festival performance of *Henry V* within that moment, but the effect within this collection is to merely revisit material Mead had already covered, and Flaherty certainly acknowledges her debt to Mead's work in this book and elsewhere in setting this scene. The chapter becomes stronger, though, once it sets its sights on what comes after that moment. As always, Flaherty's scholarship is impeccable and the history of how Shakespeare's play has been reimagined for an Australian context makes an impressive statement about the "antipodal" nature of Shakespeare performance in this country.

Just as McMullan's and Mead's chapters present contrasting perspectives on Tercentenary plans on either side of the antipodal divide, and then as Ferguson's and Houlahan's chapters present detailed studies of the Shakespeare Hut, it might have served the tail end of the book well to have a sixth chapter that provides a neat pairing with Flaherty's performance history. Catherine Moriarty's "Afterword"—which at fifteen pages seems more substantial than this epithet suggests and yet which the editors have decided is not sufficient to warrant including her name on the cover as one of the book's "authors"—does not quite fit the bill for such a pairing. Instead, the "Afterword" engages at length with the arguments made in the other chapters about the Tercentenary and monumental commemoration, with only a brief nod toward Flaherty's chapter on the penultimate page. To the question of whether the book succeeds, in the end, in delivering the focus promised in the introduction, the answer in my mind is: no, or at least, not quite. A number of decisions made late in the book's preparation seem to undermine that focus. To the more pressing question of whether the contributors to this collection offer valuable insights into the commemoration of Shakespeare across British and Australasian contexts, the answer is a firm "yes" albeit with the caveat that the reader should not be expecting these insights to encompass Shakespeare 400 in any detailed or cohesive way.

Elizabethan Publishing and the Makings of Literary Culture
By Kirk Melnikoff
Toronto, Buffalo, London: University of Toronto Press, 2018

Reviewer: Tara L. Lyons

In *Elizabethan Publishing and the Makings of Literary Culture,* Kirk Melnikoff argues that we have been overlooking a critical agent and stakeholder in the formation of English vernacular literature in the mid-to-late sixteenth century: bookselling publishers. This six-chapter monograph contends that publishers engaged in a range of practices that went well beyond the tasks of acquiring texts and financing their material production. Bookselling publishers wrote, translated, and edited; they commissioned, compiled, and arranged; they reissued titles and invented generic categories; they responded to literary discourses and shaped them. With case studies exploring travel narratives, sonnet sequences, epyllia, and sententious drama, Melnikoff's monograph leaves little doubt that

publishers from approximately 1550 to 1600 were making books
and, in the process, participating in the "makings" of a rich literary
tradition in England.

Melnikoff's work fits neatly into the growing field of "critical bibliography" in early modern literary studies. As Marta Straznicky
explains in the introduction to *Shakespeare and the Stationers*
(2013), critical bibliography highlights the agency of members of
the book trade, recognizing that while they were often profit-
driven, they were engaged in the cultural and political debates of
the time.[1] Zachary Lesser introduced this methodological approach
in his monograph *Renaissance Drama and the Politics of Publication* (2004), which foregrounded English book publishers as dis-
cerning readers who assessed contemporary politics and trends
and whose speculative investments in dramatic texts recorded
their critical judgments.[2]

Melnikoff's methodology owes much to previous scholarship in
this field (an earlier version of his fourth chapter, for instance,
appears in Staznicky's 2013 collection), and yet his monograph
also charts its own path. First, Melnikoff's chapters address English
literary texts and culture, including but certainly not limited to
professional plays by Marlowe and Shakespeare. Second, Melnikoff extends his analysis beyond the interventions of individual
publishers, as he traces the rich networks that were forged by men
and women in the trade at the time. What Melnikoff newly emphasizes is the collaborative nature of publishing: he notes partner-
ships among Stationers, Drapers, and Grocers, as well as with
printers, booksellers, bookbinders, authors, translators, and editors. Consistent with this approach is Melnikoff's careful choice of
terminology throughout the book. Namely, he describes those in the
trade by their activities, differentiating the "printer publisher" from
the "bookselling publisher"; or the "trade printer" from the "publishing printer"; or the "draper bookbinder" from the "bookselling
stationer." The dual-term phrasing is stylistically clunky and somewhat pedantic, but it successfully underscores Melnikoff's commitment to descriptive accuracy, an invaluable feature of the book as
a whole. Moreover, the terminology is vital to the book's central
arguments, as Melnikoff depicts publishing as a series of activities
that were taken on by a range of figures in the book trade. That said,
his study primarily attends to "bookseller publishers," men and
women who knew which titles and genres were selling and were
thus best able to gauge how to select and market new literary texts.

Melnikoff identifies the "bookseller publishers" as key players in the emergence of English vernacular literature and its conceptualizations.

After an introductory chapter that articulates the book's major claims, chapter 1 sets the groundwork by presenting an "*unprecedented* overview of various practices that constituted book-trade publishing" (24, my emphasis). This is not an overstatement. This chapter is currently the most thorough survey of the endeavors of late-Elizabethan English literary publishing, exploring six activities of English publishers: acquiring, compiling, reissuing, altering, translating, and specializing. Melnikoff infers some of these tasks from bibliographical and company records; others are explicitly documented in the publishers' own printed statements, including dedications, commendatory poems, and notes to readers. Melnikoff turns to these accounts as historical evidence of the conditions of literary publishing. In this way, his work departs from scholarly accounts that tend to dismiss publishers' testimonials as disingenuous or mercenary. While Melnikoff certainly acknowledges that publishers used paratexts to hawk their wares, his chapters demonstrate the value of carefully reading and interpreting these devices as publishers' self-representations of their labors and trends in the trade. Alone, this clear and well-written chapter would be useful to scholars or students seeking to learn about English literary publishing in the period, although the examples are all culled from latter half of the sixteenth century and hence should be understood within this temporal context.

Chapter 2, the first extended case study in the book, focuses on the bookselling publisher Thomas Hacket who was procuring and publishing travel narratives in the 1560s and 1570s. Melnikoff reveals that books on travel made up more than 33 percent of the edition sheets that Hacket published during his career, and Hacket himself provided translations of three travel accounts and part of a fourth. By fashioning travel narratives such as *The Whole and True Discovery of Terra Florida* (1563) and *The New Found World of Antarctic* (1568) for a wide English audience, Hacket departed notably from previously printed ones in the vernacular, which had targeted specialist readers, those planning to set sail or finance an expedition to the New World. Through close analysis of prefatory addresses and title page blurbs, Melnikoff asserts that Hacket was the first publisher to fashion travel narratives into pleasure reading, paying careful attention to aesthetics of language in translations and stimulating delight and "wonder" at the novelty of new worlds and peoples. Melnikoff also asserts that Hacket's own Protestant leanings informed his framing of travel narratives as texts that could encourage moral reform, and in this sense, satisfy the Horation injunction to both delight and instruct.

The third chapter, the longest in the monograph and the most ambitious in scope, considers the understudied career of the bookselling draper, Thomas Smith, who was responsible for publishing George Gascoigne's *Hundreth Sundry Flowers* (1573), Aesop's fables rendered into English by Smith himself (1577), and Henry Constable's sonnet sequence *Diana* (1592, 1594?). Melnikoff argues that Smith prioritized multivocality and heterogeneity in his publications, rather than unity or coherence, and did so at a time when many poetry collections were trending towards the centralized and author centered. Through dedicatory and prefatory poems, Smith advertises his books as browsable, and he arranged and rearranged the contents in subsequent editions, inserting partitions to appeal to readers who wished to drop in and out of a given volume. Melnikoff finds that the heterogeneous design of *Hundreth Sundry Flowers,* although often attributed solely to Gascoigne, was influenced by Smith's marketing approach. Moreover, in both his translation of Aesop's fables and in the second and third editions of *Diana,* Smith rejects the stabilizing single-author model and instead offers his readers books from which they can pick and choose among various compiled options. The chapter's success is its demonstration of concurrent impulses. It shows both publishers following trends in shaping literary collections around authorial figures such as Sir Philip Sidney, and a publisher like Smith diversifying the contents of books to satisfy readers' tastes for literary variety under the title page.

In the fourth and fifth chapters, Melnikoff turns to specific editions of two works of professional drama, Christopher Marlowe's *The Tragedie of Dido, Queen of Carthage* (1594) and Shakespeare's *Hamlet* (1603), respectively. Readers will notice that both chapters follow a similar structure, beginning with an introduction to the practices of booksellers who developed publishing specialties in the book trade, followed by an argument situating each play within those publishers' specialties and, finally, new literary readings of the plays based on this bibliographical context. Although other chapters in the book also offered analysis of the literary works, these two final chapters are more deeply invested in producing new literary readings than others in the monograph. In chapter 4, Melnikoff takes on Marlowe's *Dido* (1594), arguing that after its initial publication, it was reissued by the bookbinder bookseller John Flacket and bookseller Paul Linley alongside Paul Dickenson's Arcadian prose narrative, *Arisbas, Euphues Amidst His Slumbers, Or Cupid's Journey to Hell* (1594). Melnikoff documents a record from 1600 in the Stationers' Register that suggests the titles were issued together. That, combined with Flacket's and Linley's habits of reissuing previously printed independent titles in nonce collections, allows Melnikoff to explore how *Dido* may have been read alongside *Arisbas* as Ovidian epyllion. In chapter 5, Melnikoff turns to the first quarto of Shakespeare's *Hamlet* (1603), published by Nicholas Ling, a bookselling publisher who specialized in both sententious texts marked for commonplacing and those with a republican political ethos. The chapter proposes that *Hamlet Q1* reflects Ling's speculative reading of the play as a republican text, featuring carefully marked pithy phrases that reinforced the necessity of wise counsel and the limits of monarchial governance. Especially astute is this chapter's analysis of how "treason" is levelled against the king in Shakespeare's play, which Melnikoff claims may have appealed to Ling's interest in texts that explored the justifications for lawful resistance.

While both chapters 4 and 5 provide thought-provoking literary analysis of their chosen plays, they are more speculative in their assertions about how publishers approached the dramatic texts at hand. In chapter 4, for instance, Melnikoff's argument largely rests on his interpretation of a record from June 26, 1600 in the Stationers' Register that, he argues, conveys that the titles had been treated by the publishers as parts of one book—"Cupydes Journey to hell with the tragedie of Dido." Melnikoff offers other examples of multi-title books recorded in a similar way; however, with no extant copy of a bundled *Dido* and *Arisbas,* the foundation from which Melnikoff derives his literary readings somewhat falters, leading one to question whether the literary analysis has any historic basis. Similarly, Melnikoff's fifth chapter on *Hamlet* cannot produce statements written by Ling about *Hamlet's* republican themes or notes to the reader emphasizing how the stationer conceived of the play's political relevance in 1603. This lack of direct evidence might be seen as a weakness of the monograph, and yet, these final two chapters do make significant contributions to both Marlowe and Shakespeare studies, respectively, with their provocative new literary readings; neither chapter strains the limits of possibility in their textual interpretations of the chosen plays, and as chapters focused on individual plays, they demonstrate the rich cultural contexts in which plays as books might have been read. Furthermore, Melnikoff's speculative arguments on the bibliographical record serve as a necessary reminder that the archives of the early modern book trade were not constructed to provide contemporary scholars with neat answers to questions about literary texts by Marlowe and Shakespeare. To some extent then, making sense of publisher's intentions is always an interpretive act, a reading of available evidence. Melnikoff's monograph artfully demonstrates methods for facing those glaring gaps and offering well-reasoned, tentative answers.

The book lacks a concluding chapter or afterword, which could have synthesized Melnikoff's fresh and innovative findings across the book's chapters or offered a preview of literary developments in the next half-century. Such a chapter could have helped reinforce the larger implications of Melnikoff's research on why and how literary culture developed in the way that it did, which can often get lost within his tightly woven case studies. For instance, this book seems well positioned to define the "literary" in the late-Elizabeth period based not on the criticism of Sir Philip Sidney or George Puttenham, but on the activities of the bookselling publishers. Melnikoff certainly leans in this direction, identifying publishers who attended to the aesthetics of language, foregrounded texts that would teach and delight, prioritized pleasure over utility, or engaged in political or historical discourses; however, his chapters veer away from sweeping claims. As his introduction makes clear, this study "eschews a teleological account of the literary" (24). Melnikoff is comfortable interpreting the rumblings of an emerging literary culture, an archive that may simply refuse to conform to delineations about the "literary."

Indeed, one of the monograph's most notable accomplishments is bringing these many important but idiosyncratic moments of literary "making" into contact with each other and thus into the scholarly purview. Without a doubt, Melnikoff's archive testifies to the wealth of opportunities for further research on the intersections between multi-tasking publishers and the English literary tradition. This, combined with Melnikoff's impeccable research on the men and women of the booktrade, positions this book as essential reading for both literary critics and book historians for a long time to come.

Notes

1. Marta Straznicky, ed., *Shakespeare's Stationers: Studies in Critical Bibliography* (Philadelphia: University of Pennsylvania Press, 2013).
2. Zachary Lesser, *Renaissance Drama and the Politics of Publication: Readings in the English Book Trade* (Cambridge: Cambridge University Press, 2004).

Shakespeare and Posthumanist Theory
By Karen Raber
London: Bloomsbury, 2018

Reviewer: Jean E. Feerick

"The human is already inhuman" (145), quips Karen Raber, echoing the rhythms of Bruno Latour's famous title that delivered actor network theory to the world amid a call to rethink the division of culture and nature as instead an assemblage.[1] In her new book for the Arden Shakespeare and Theory series, Raber takes up the dynamic and expansive field of posthumanism and the cluster of theories that subtend its philosophical position and demonstrates their relevance for and intersections with Renaissance culture, as embodied not only by Shakespeare but by a range of art practitioners, philosophers, rhetoricians, and scientists. Flouting the unity that posthumanist theorists tend to assign Renaissance humanism, which Raber sardonically mocks as a view of the era as a "premodern bondage machine" (4), she builds her claims out from an assertion she shares with a recent volume edited by Scott Maisano and Joseph Campana that Renaissance humanism was a set of practices that yielded less a stable notion of the human, than a compellingly self-divided way of reading that makes it a compelling contributor to posthumanist practice.[2]

Of course, this can be confusing if we construe the "post" in posthumanism as denoting temporal sequence—seeming to call up the paradox of turning the "preface" of early modernity into the "prologue" to our now. But Raber urges us to bracket linear models of thinking—which are themselves symptoms of the "exceptionalist" paradigm posthumanism assaults—and associate the prefix instead with an inclination to scatter the category of the human, construing it as an ontology that is ongoing, mediated, extended, unstable, and always in progress as it seeks to define itself in opposition to a moving assemblage of "others." In exposing and exploring the breadth of human embeddedness in and attachment to various objects, environments, and creatures in the work of Shakespeare and others, Raber reads Renaissance materials as providing important access to a moment that was open to the paradoxes of human identity, one not yet seeking cover in Cartesian dualism and the myth of a transcendent reasoning faculty it helped to fuel. As she argues, "Renaissance humanism did not (always) seek to extract humanity from the mesh of beings in the world" (21). Rather, in her account, it understood and at times even celebrated an awareness that the human has never been fully human, although it is also true that Enlightenment humanism has sometimes obscured our access to this point.

Raber's book is lively, informative, theoretical, and expressive of sharp close readings. I see it as a treasure trove for critics and students alike. One of the things I found particularly exciting about her account of posthumanism is how she treats this capacious theory as a kind of switchboard that opens pathways to and from a range of philosophical and political projects, including ecocriticism, new materialism, animal studies, phenomenology, extended and distributed cognition, embodied identity, disability theory, and cyborg studies, among others. Raber has distilled the wisdom of an impressive range of theorists—from Hayles and Braidotti to Derrida, Delueze, Haraway, Bennett, and Latour—presenting each in digestible chunks for her readers, while also placing them in relation to one another. This is one of her particular skills—identifying and clarifying the salient points of complex theoretical arguments and then putting them in dialogue with one another. Toward this end, she animates Haraway's critique of Deleuze and her embrace of Latour. And she narrates Derrida and Agamben as they respond to Descartes. She is on very sound footing philosophically, although she occasionally apologizes for condensing whole traditions into a few paragraphs. Since that is precisely what the volume calls for, she meets the challenge with aplomb. She also tracks the development and significance of whole fields in Renaissance studies such as humoralism, phenomenology and animal studies, showing how they contribute to and echo the foundational claims of posthumanism. Reading her book as I was designing a graduate course on Ecocriticism and Renaissance Literature, I came to see it as a terrific resource for students who might need a crisp account of Latour, Bogost, or Agamben to allow them to join the critical conversation.

Her chapters, too, had a design that emblematized the feel of networks and assemblages in action, as opposed to taut, linear arguments set up to overturn earlier readings or critical models. Raber has opted to creatively cluster her chapters around a theoretical approach, such as animal studies or cyborg theory; a defining trope, such as the face as interchange between body and mind or the centaur as emblem of the human/animal dyad; and a set of texts, including Shakespeare's plays but also a range of other cultural artifacts. At times, she dives deeply into readings of the plays, as she does in her first chapter in grappling with *King Lear*'s "queer cosmos," a phrase she borrows from Laurie Shannon.[3] Elsewhere, her method shifts, as when she turns to well-charted areas such as animal studies or theories of embodiment, which have been deeply mined by recent criticism and have yielded multiple rich, capacious studies in article and monograph form. In chapter 3, for instance, she spends less time in providing a new reading of a play than in threading connections between the work of posthumanist theorists like N. Katherine Hayles and Stacy Alaimo and that of early modernists like Gail Paster, Bruce Smith, and Holly Dugan in areas like humoral embodiment, phenomenology, or disability theory. As she demonstrates in accounting for scholarship that spans roughly two decades, early modern critics have been uncovering in Renaissance texts a conception of the human that is dispersed, extended, and embedded, one that bears uncanny resemblance to posthumanism and supports her thesis that returning to this era can creatively inflect and enrichen the posthumanist project, as well as revitalize study of Shakespeare by posing new questions and making us alert to new archives and angles.

In the second half of the book, she explores the animal and cyborg dimensions of human identity for Renaissance writers. Chapter 4 charts the ubiquity and conceptual centrality of animals—or creaturely life—in Shakespeare's plays, concluding with a discussion of *Titus Andronicus.* Notable in this chapter is her discussion of the name that Shakespeare's character Chiron shares with the eldest centaur of Greek mythology, etymologically linked to the word for "hand," which identifies and explains the figure's longstanding association with skill in the use of tools, instruments, and other objects to denote his human-like mastery over nature. Compellingly, Shakespeare's character inverts all such associations when he unleashes bestial violence on Rome, beginning with his ravagement of Lavinia, thereby dismantling the category of the human and exposing violence as the foundation upon which civilization rests. Raber's last full chapter tacks toward the inhuman, exploring imaginative engagements with the shaping powers of technology in a Renaissance era defined by a "seismic shift in the speed and nature of knowledge transmission" (130). Discussions of Giovanni Bracelli's and Albrecht Dürer's geometric renderings of the human body as an assemblage of object-like parts—a kind of robot—dovetails into a discussion of the cyborgian armored warrior of Shakespeare's history plays, which stage a relentless twinning of men and metal on the battlefield. In donning armor, wielding weapons, and commanding men, Shakespeare's warriors operate as "extended, fortified beings . . . made up of other human and non-human stuff" (152–53). They morph, that is, into iron men.

And yet, it was in the sustained close reading that comprises her first chapter on *Lear* that I found Raber to be at her best in enacting the value that posthumanist theories and reading practices have for canonical plays. Itself a play that has been at the center of important articles from the perspective of animal studies (Shannon) and eco-critical approaches (Egan and Mentz), *Lear* here is yet made to articulate a new kind of posthumanist perspective, as Raber weighs the shifting representations of the natural world that express the characters' disparate moral and political sensibilities, from the self-interested cunning of an Edmund to the ethical certainty of an Edgar or Kent. Positioning herself against theories of orderly and hierarchical life made famous by Tillyard and aligning her reading instead with theories of tumult and disharmony implicitly advanced long ago by Arthur Lovejoy and, more recently, by Steve Mentz, Raber argues that the play stages the strategies of control that humans use to counter the overwhelming experience of being confronted by "hyperobjects," the term Timothy Morton has assigned to material forces so large and powerful that they confound human conceptualization.[4] In the case of *Lear,* the dance between assertions of an ordered and providential universe and the abiding sense of nature as an unwieldy, entropic force that haunts the play serves as a tacit acknowledgment by the dramatist that powerful cosmic activities leave us bewildered, grasping at organizing patterns to hold chaos at bay. For Raber, the play reduces its characters to the "humility of unknowing" (52), a posture that she sees as powerfully emblematized by the stumbling, foolish figure of Gloucester, who smells and feels his way to Dover, a mere groveling creature unable to distinguish life from death. Notably, Raber returns to the figure of Gloucester in her brief final chapter, identifying the unknowing man-animal as a fitting emblem of posthumanism, one who disperses the comforting fictions of "life, love, and family" (161) that gather around the "plays' charismatic megafauna like Cordelia, Edgar, Kent, or Lear himself" (161).

In threading the theory of hyperobjects into this play, Raber echoes a question once raised by A. C. Bradley who asked, in effect, why must Gloucester head all the way to Dover to die? Raber follows this lead in speculating that part of Dover's appeal lies in its recent devastation at the hands of a massive earthquake in 1580 that tumbled houses and spawned tsunamis, seeming to strike at the very symbols of human civilization. Shakespeare's characters evoke this place repeatedly in the play, Raber proposes, as a sort of return to and evocation of a moment of collective trauma. I confess, I was intrigued by these details, not knowing of these associations or events. But I also found the shift to topicality as a guiding heuristic at a key moment in the chapter to sit in uneasy relation with Raber's dexterous use of more agile theoretical models elsewhere. Topicality has, it should be said, become a preferred analytical mode for some, if not all eco-critics, who seem to gravitate toward and privilege empirical facts—pollution, deforestation, fossil fuels—to bridge early modernity to the "now" of ecological devastation. But Raber understands that even as eco-criticism and posthumanism overlap, they are not contiguous and may even occasionally be in tension. I see such a tension in her turn to the topical as a kind of key that grants privileged access to the text, precisely because it seems to underscore a way of thinking that privileges "turning points or historical pivots" (159) and thereby betrays a bid for epistemological mastery that is at odds with posthumanism. I applaud instead the skeptical posture Raber elsewhere applies to "stabilizing" readings that concede a privileged view to the modern critic, preferring to guard against totalizing critical moves in order to underscore the presence of a range of actants historically, whether ontologically or epistemologically. Her final brief chapter, in fact, is an eloquent call for such a practice, which she describes as a "slow, disabled, but environmentally aware posthumanism," which "arises out of millions of cellular pulses across the strands of culture, the academy and individuals over a longer temporal arc" (160–61). It is a posthumanism not limited to Shakespeareans, nor to practitioners of the humanities, nor even to humankind. She may be appealing to a scholarly version of the Parliament of Things famously evoked by Latour as a working model for a more equitable political practice in which the voice and interests of all actants—human and nonhuman—affected by a given policy gain representation in the political process. Raber's book helpfully points us in a similar direction for our scholarly practice, urging us to be on the lookout for those moments when "human subjectivity is king and the earth [or the past] merely an object to know" (49). She concludes by puzzling over the potentially crippling paradox for the kind of posthumanism she advocates, which is a deeply ethical and political practice as well as a theoretical model. If there is no human subject to stand as the "origin of decision-making" and the engine of ethical practice, how do posthumanists purport "to transform and improve human beings—if not the beings themselves, then their effects on their fellow creatures and on the places we have to live" (25), the goal that inspires much of this work? In response, Raber fittingly provides another question: "Might we need both a strategic subjectivity and a strategic exceptionalism to put ethics into practice as politics or law?" (162). Open-ended, qualified, dialogical, and performative—this and the other questions with which she concludes her study invite us to add our voices and our studies to the network of "millions of cellular pulses" (160) which she identifies with the slow work of undoing human exceptionalism.

Notes

1. Bruno Latour, *We Have Never Been Modern,* trans. Catherine Porter (Cambridge, MA: Harvard University Press, 1993).

2. See the Introduction to Joseph Campana and Scott Maisano, eds., *Renaissance Posthumanism* (New York: Fordham University Press, 2016).

3. Laurie Shannon, "Lear's Queer Cosmos" in Madhavi Menon, ed., *Shakesqueer: A Queer Companion to the Complete Works of Shakespeare* (Durham, NC: Duke University Press, 2011): 171–78.

4. Timothy Morton, *Hyperobjects: Philosophy and Ecology after the End of the World* (Minneapolis: University of Minnesota Press, 2013).

Temporality, Genre, and Experience in the Age of Shakespeare: Forms of Time
Edited by Lauren Shohet
London: Bloomsbury Arden Shakespeare, 2018

Reviewer: Edward Gieskes

Lauren Shohet's volume in Bloomsbury's Shakespeare criticism series opens with an introduction that considers ways that theater affords opportunities to think about time (and about the difficulties in thinking about time). Shohet writes that "this volume asks how temporality looks different when we emphasize form, and how forms look different when we emphasize time" (7). The volume suggests that "old-fashioned-sounding genre criticism can be usefully integrated into historicist, politico-theological and polychronous approaches" (11). This is a timely and productive suggestion, and the essays, in their different ways, demonstrate that genre criticism complements other approaches to the drama of the period. The thirteen essays that make up the book are divided into five sections. The essays in each section discuss in turn how form "illuminates, synthesizes, misaligns, multiplies, or pleats time" (21). These section headings are both abstract enough to indicate how diverse the arguments in each essay are and specific enough to make meaningful distinctions between the sets of essays. As a whole, the essays are more focused on time and temporality than genre, but as Shohet states in the introduction their discussions of time are framed and structured by considerations about form.

The first section, "Illuminating," has essays by Kent Cartwright, Raphael Falco, and Philip Lorenz. Cartwright's essay on comic time details various ways that comedy "represents time as variable and contradictory, plastic, both objective and subjective—rather like Shakespeare's comic world itself" (27). Comedy, in Cartwright's view, engages audiences more directly, perhaps, than other genres in the experience of time because many comic effects depend on "right timing" (42). As he concludes, right timing becomes "an ideal of comic action itself" (42). Falco's essay on suspense addresses the way that dramatic suspense "requires a shared and simultaneous experience of dramatic time" (44) that is at odds with the way that "conventional time-markers estrange the audience from any genuine feeling of, or identification with, temporality in the course of the dénouement" (43–44). Dramatic suspense "both suspends the viewers in a privileged temporal space and . . . implicates them in the anticipated action" (50). Suspense (tragic or comic) alleviates the estrangement from time Falco describes as an effect of dramatic time-markers. Lorenz's essay on *Henry VIII* opens by arguing that reading *Henry VIII* as what Walter Benjamin calls a "mourning play," allows the play to be seen as being "about the modern problem of entrapment in fallen time" (58). Lorenz offers a compelling and detailed reading of the play that shows how *Henry VIII*'s "representation of time exemplifies the convergence and crisis of sovereignty, representation and time that Benjamin identifies as emblematic of the baroque period" (62). Thinking about the play in terms of its affinity to the genre of the mourning play makes the play's experiments with "different conceptions of time in relation to power" visible (76).

Part Two, "Synthesizing," contains two essays, the first, by Andrew Griffin, on *Henry V* and the second, by Lauren Shohet, on *Troilus and Cressida* and *Pericles*. Both essays focus on how drama produces "usable" presents or pasts. After an opening that points to some of the difficulties in thinking about the "history play" as a genre, Griffin's essay moves on to discuss how, in a carefully constructed phrase, "a sense of 'intelligibility' is created in the plays identified as history plays" (83). *Henry V,* in Griffin's account, assiduously stages a kind of historical inquiry that establishes an intelligible past through "acts of narrativization" (94), and Griffin argues that the past becomes unintelligible not because of distance, but when narratives fall apart (94). Shohet's essay on *Troilus and Cressida* and *Pericles* shows how these two plays "illuminate relations of form and temporality" (97) by attending to similar questions about literary history but in different genres. In *Pericles,* Shohet argues, "more versions are better, and recapitulation is delightful," but in *Troilus and Cressida,* "evoking multiple versions . . . more often diminishes the present" (105). In romance, repetition and recapitulation of the past in renewal allows for dramatic closure. In the satire-inflected *Troilus and Cressida,* reiteration and repetition deny closure, leaving the audience haunted, rather than renewed (114). The effect of stories about the past, Shohet argues, differs starkly between romance and satire. In romance, stories "heal and renew," but in satire "stories . . . injure and debase" (120).

Part Three, "Misaligning," has essays by Matthew Harrison on *Love's Labour's Lost,* Lucy Munro on *The Knight of the Burning Pestle,* and Rebecca Bushnell on *Antony and Cleopatra.* Harrison discusses what his title calls the "layered temporality of poetic reception" (123). He situates the play in three literary contexts that map onto temporal contexts. First, the sonnet sequence's interest in poetic failure, which connects to *Love's Labor's Lost*'s original performance in 1595–96, second, the emergence of verse satire which coincides with the play's first printing in 1598, and third, the "consolidation of the stage poet into a social type" (126) which can be mapped onto the play's court revival in 1604/5. Harrison argues that "as poets revisit and reconfigure past representations of poetic failure, the poetics of *Love's Labour's Lost* shift even as the text itself remains stable" (127). This shift helps Harrison discuss how "we revise the past" (127). Munro's essay on *Knight of the Burning Pestle* shows how the play is "consumed" with questions of time and "both inhabits and resists its own cultural moment" (143). Walter Burre's letter that prefaces the play calls attention to the untimeliness of the play's first performance, and Munro convincingly argues that the play's structure, its generic mixings, its attention to recent drama all work to, "meddle productively with our own sense of its timing" (155). That meddling is a feature of the play's reception from its first production to the present. Bushnell's essay on time and the text of *Antony and Cleopatra* shows how the editorial tradition has "attempted to control the play's temporality" (157) through choices about spelling and about act and scene divisions. She shows that this is a response to the play's representation of struggles over time and temporality that attending to the text in the Folio complicates rather than resolves. She makes a persuasive case that editors, in Romanizing names of characters and imposing a classicizing set of act and scene divisions inherited from the nineteenth century, have classicized the text and put time under control where the Folio "exposes the dynamics of the control of tragic time" (170). She makes the salient point that such editorial practices have stakes that are worth remembering.

Part Four, "Proliferating," centers on tragedy and temporality with essays by William Carroll, Lara Dodds, and Meredith Beales. Carroll's essay on succession and time shows how *Hamlet, Macbeth,* and *King Lear* share a vision of succession that produces a secular sense of time structured by generational change, always moving forward in a linear fashion because it is "a product of biological reproduction" (187) that subordinates the protagonists to time envisioned as a line heading to an always-known end in death. Dodds' essay on *The Tragedy of Mariam* shows how Cary's play interrogates its final Chorus's sense of "the relationship between time and tragedy" (191). The play's narrative counterfactuals, linked to passionate counterfactuals (the false news of Herod's death and Herod's desire for and immediate regret for Mariam's death), produce a series of imagined pasts and futures that complicates any simple sense of the relationship between time and tragedy. Beales's essay on future histories in *King Lear* points to how the play imagines futures that the play's action forecloses, the "anticipated future can never quite come to pass" (207). The future that produces Shakespeare's England, Beales argues, is foreclosed by the deaths of "characters who can envision a future for England" (217) and this foreclosure denies "any suggestion that this history should provide any kind of foundation for the future" (218).

Part Five, "Pleating," with its two essays by Robin Stewart and Valerie Wayne, discusses how form can bring different times together. Stewart's essay on the "semiotics of collective temporality" (223) moves from a discussion of images of the Last Judgment, which show time ending, to a reading of the frontispiece of Hobbes' *Leviathan,* which shows Leviathan as enabling time to continue by delaying the advent of the Last Judgment. This shift lines up with a movement from Christian eschatology to a modern, secular sense of time. Wayne's essay on *Cymbeline* attends to the way the play shifts back and forth between first century Britain and Renaissance Rome. The play yokes these times together and "collapses time in on itself" (259) in a way that "reveals its affinity both with everyday experience and with the political cross-currents of its own Jacobean moment" (259), pleating past and present together.

Taken together, the essays in this volume suggest rich possibilities for thinking about time and temporality afforded by the lens of genre. Form, as Shohet argues in the introduction, has a great deal to say about time, and this collection shows the range and complexity of form's mediations when it comes to time and temporality.

Index